McGraw-Hill's
SSAT/ISEE
HIGH SCHOOL ENTRANCE EXAMS

McGraw-Hill's
SSAT/ISEE
HIGH SCHOOL ENTRANCE EXAMS

Nicholas Falletta

Foreword by Gregg W. M. Maloberti,
Dean of Admission, The Lawrenceville School

New York   Chicago   San Francisco   Lisbon   London   Madrid
Mexico City   Milan   New Delhi   San Juan   Seoul   Singapore
Sydney   Toronto

3 4 5 6 7 8 9 10 11 12 13 14 15 16   QPD/QPD   0 9 8 7

Contributor
Dr. Janet E. Wall contributed the mathematics review chapters and mathematics portions of the Practice Tests in this book.

McGraw-Hill's SSAT/ISEE

ISBN 0-07-145397-0

McGraw-Hill books are available at special quantity discounts to use as premiums and sales promotions or for use in corporate training programs. For more information, please write to the Director of Special Sales, Professional Publishing, McGraw-Hill. Two Penn Plaza, New York, NY 10121-2298. Or contact your local bookstore.

*SSAT is a registered trademark of the Secondary School Admission Test Board, which was not involved in the production of, and does not endorse, this product. ISEE is a registered trademark of Educational Records Bureau, which was not involved in the production of, and does not endorse, this product.

Product or brand names used in this book may be trade names or trademarks. Where we believe that there may be proprietary claims to such trade names or trademarks, the name has been used with an initial capital or it has been capitalized in the style used by the name claimant. Regardless of the capitalization used, all such names have been used in an editorial manner without any intent to convey endorsement of or other affiliation with the name claimant. Neither the author nor the publisher intends to express any judgment as to the validity or legal status of any such proprietary claims.

Library of Congress Cataloging-in-Publication Data
Falletta, Nicholas.
McGraw-Hill's SSAT/ISEE high school entrance exams/by Nicholas
Falletta.– 1st ed.
p. cm.
ISBN 0-07-145397-0 (alk. paper)
1. Secondary School Admission Test--Study guides. 2. Independent School Entrance Examination–Study guides. 3. High schools–United States–Entrance examinations–Study guides. I. Title: SSAT/ISEE high school entrance exams. II. McGraw-Hill Companies. III. Title.
LB3060.33.S42F34 2006
373.126'2–dc22
2005024867

CONTENTS

Foreword: What to Expect at an Independent School

Gregg W. M. Maloberti
Dean of Admission

The Lawrenceville School

If you or your parents have purchased this book, then you are most likely hoping to be admitted to an independent school. This short introduction will tell you more about independent schools. You'll learn about some of the benefits and advantages that an independent school can offer you, and you'll find out some important facts about the admissions process.

The Benefits of Attending an Independent School

When asked why they wish to attend an independent school, many students say they want to get a "better" education or to attend a "good" college. Parents often say they are looking for a school of the "highest" quality to give their children the "best" opportunity for success. Statements like these help explain how much students and parents value education, but they offer little insight into the advantages that independent schools offer their students.

By definition, independent schools exist as an alternative to public schools as well as to one another. Independent schools come in all shapes and sizes, coeducational and single sex, and day and boarding. They are free to specialize in anything and everything from academic rigor, to performing or fine arts, to character and leadership development, to helping students with learning disabilities. For you as a student, that means that you can choose an independent school that shares your values and allows you to focus on what is important to you. By choosing a school that has a mission and purpose closely aligned with your own principles, you can move closer to achieving your own goals.

Faculty Above all, independent schools pride themselves on the quality of their faculty. Independent school teachers often boast degrees from top-flight academic institutions, years of classroom experience, and a commitment to educational research and curricular development. They have been involved with many cutting-edge programs that are reshaping American education. For example, it was at independent schools that the Harkness method of teaching, sometimes called the Conference Plan, was originally introduced in the 1930s. Prior to this innovation, nearly all instruction took place in the form of a lecture. Now it is commonplace to see students seated around oval or round tables actively discussing the day's lesson. The Advanced Placement Program, known better as the APs, was originally initiated in the 1950s through collaboration between three independent schools and three leading universities. Many programs and schools that include outdoor leadership training and experiential learning can trace their roots back to faculty who were given support, resources, and encouragement by independent schools.

Small Classes One of the greatest benefits that you're likely to find in an independent school is the small class size. Independent schools create student-to-teacher ratios that enable small classes and greater personal interaction. In these classes, teachers are able to give students the kind of individual attention that promotes student achievement. When the classroom experience includes discussion, active participation, and debate, students are much more likely to be actively engaged in the learning process. Just imagine yourself in this kind of classroom: If you and your classmates know you will be called upon in class, you will be far more likely to arrive in class better prepared and more willing to engage in the lesson. Many independent school faculty value student participation so much that it becomes a factor in assessing performance and assigning grades.

Class size becomes even more important when you consider the total number of students each teacher meets with daily. If a teacher meets 5 classes of 30 students each day, there are 150 papers to mark every time a writing assignment is given. Independent schools typically keep class sizes small enough and teaching loads reasonable enough to accommodate regular review of student work. The National Association of Independent Schools (NAIS) reported that the average class size in their member schools was 15 and the average faculty-to-student ratio was 8.8:1. Teaching takes time and energy, and with fewer students and fewer sections, teachers not only perform better in their classrooms but also are able to meet with their students on an individual basis. Many schools reserve time during the school day when teachers are available to meet with their students in small groups or one-on-one. The chance to work individually with a teacher is just as important to a student who is in need of remedial attention as it is to a student who needs mentoring or enrichment.

Student-Teacher Interaction Independent school teachers often play a multitude of roles over the course of a school day. They may serve as teachers, coaches, academic advisers, or club sponsors, and in boarding schools they may be dormitory parents as well. While it sounds exhausting for the teachers, you as a student can benefit through interacting with teachers in a variety of places and situations. At nine o'clock in the morning, your teacher may be helping you as you struggle with a geometry proof, but at four in the afternoon, that same teacher may be coaching you in soccer as you score the winning goal. Situations like these that allow you to see and work with your teachers in a variety of situations help develop real relationships that can increase trust and communication. Few students can ever explain why, but they all know that they perform better for teachers that they like, and they like teachers who show an interest in them.

Some independent schools organize their dining halls to facilitate interactions between students and their teachers by offering family-style meals with a faculty member at the head of each table. Others create a casual environment where students and faculty can intermingle naturally. Regardless of the method, creating social situations outside the classroom helps students develop more natural and meaningful relationships with their teachers.

Environmental Awareness Increasingly, independent schools are taking an interest in the environment. Many independent schools are large land holders, and simply holding onto their land, which can be thousands of acres in some cases, helps stem the tide of urban and suburban sprawl. Schools that preserve open space are contributing to wildlife preservation, green space, and clean water supplies. Many independent schools are developing aggressive recycling and smart purchasing programs to curb the flow of packaging and containers into the waste stream. For instance, many independent schools now lease computers, a practice which frees them from the expense of their disposal at the end of their use cycle. Leased computers are then returned to the manufacturer for recycling, reselling, or proper disposal. Faculty and students take an active role in developing and implementing environmentally sound practices at their schools. By involving the students directly in issues related to the environment, independent schools are developing the awareness and skills that will help their students become more environmentally responsible as adults.

Sports Athletics play a major role in many independent schools. Competitive, intramural, and recreational sports are often offered as an alternative to traditional physical education. Great emphasis is placed on sportsmanship and fair play. Some independent school athletic leagues have rivalries that date back over a hundred years. Independent schools offer a uniquely wide range of sports options. In addition to American favorites such as football, basketball, baseball, and soccer, sports such as crew, squash, fencing, field hockey, and lacrosse are widely available.

Student Diversity Independent schools have embraced diversity as a way of preparing their students for leadership roles in a rapidly changing global society. Initially, financial aid helped break through the economic barriers of affording tuition. Through concerted efforts at recruiting minority students, independent schools offer an experience in racial diversity that is approaching the current composition of American society. Since independent schools can freely cross municipal boundaries to draw students, they are able to overcome the obstacles of real estate prices and taxes that have kept public schools from becoming less homogeneous. Indeed, boarding schools can draw from any neighborhood in the country or the world.

Through affiliations with outreach programs such as the Albert G. Oliver Program, Prep for Prep, the White Foundation, NJ Seeds, the Boys and Girls Clubs of New York City, A Better Chance, and the Black Student Fund, independent day and boarding schools have been able to identify talented and motivated students from even the most impoverished schools in urban cities and rural America. Increasingly, independent schools are becoming attractive to the growing population of affluent minority families who wish to provide their children with the best educational opportunities.

According to the U.S. Department of Education, National Center for Educational Statistics, Private School Universe Survey, 1999–2000 and 2002–2002, there were 1,207,182 minority students included in the total population of 5,341,513 private school students. This figure represents a 3.46 percent increase over the previous year. The trend is expected to continue as the population of the United States continues to change.

Independent schools are taking a leadership role in developing a multicultural approach to education. By recognizing and celebrating the racial, ethnic, religious, and cultural differences between their students, independent schools are building stronger communities by debunking stereotypes and building trust where there was once only fear and suspicion. Some independent schools are modifying their curricula to include perspectives that have not always been well represented, such as African-American literature and Asian history.

Preparing for College In standardized testing, students at NAIS schools demonstrate consistently high results. According to data from the College Board for the 2003–2004 academic year, SAT scores of independent school students exceeded the national average by more than 150 points, continuing the trend since the NAIS began keeping records in 1975–1976. Independent school students achieved an average verbal score of 593 and a math score of 600, compared to the national average of 508 for verbal and 518 in math. In the SAT II subject tests, independent school students outscored the national mean in 16 of the 23 subject areas.

As college attendance dominates the list of reasons why most families choose independent schools, it is reassuring to report that NAIS data reports that 98.9 percent of their member schools' students graduated from high school in the academic year 2000–2001. In the same year, 94.3 percent of NAIS graduating seniors attended four-year colleges.

Applying to an Independent School

When you apply for admission to an independent school, you are typically asked to visit the school, have some type of interview, take a standardized test, write an application, and submit supporting documents including a current transcript and teacher recommendations. The admission office at any school should be able to tell you exactly what is required and give you a schedule that includes any deadlines for testing or the submission of application materials, as well as the date by which you will be notified of whether or not you are accepted. Most schools follow a traditional cycle of inviting visits and interviews in the fall, collecting application materials in midwinter, and mailing decision letters in the early spring. Some schools have open admission year-round, while others may follow a rolling admission program throughout the year. Even the most selective schools sometimes have last-minute openings in the summer months.

School Visits On a school visit, you may do nothing more than take a brief tour and have an interview with an admissions officer or a faculty member. On the other hand, the visit may be a full day program during which you may be given a test and produce a writing sample. School visits may take many forms including open houses, opportunities to visit classes, and individual tours. Most independent schools have fairly firm ideas about how they conduct their visits. Some schools are quite open to guests, encouraging you to pay a lengthy visit and participate fully in school activities. Keep in mind, though, that some schools receive hundreds or even thousands of visitors a year, and these schools must structure their tours in such a way that they do not interfere with the current students' normal school day. If there is a new visitor in a classroom every day, the dynamic between the teacher and the students is likely to be altered in some meaningful way. In almost all cases, once a school has accepted you, you will be invited to pay an extensive visit that will include time in the classroom.

Before you come for a visit, make sure you inquire about dress code. You'll feel more comfortable if you can present yourself in a manner similar to that of students enrolled at the school. Schools typically run on rather tight schedules with only 5 or 10 minutes between class periods, and guides, who may be students or faculty, typically give tours during a free class period or break in their schedule.

Try to be punctual so that your visit gets off to a good start and concludes without anyone feeling rushed or inconvenienced. If you have any special requests to meet with program directors, coaches, teachers, administrators, or other school personnel, make them in advance of your visit. Schools can be very accommodating, but the more notice they have of your expectations, the more likely they will be able to arrange an interesting visit. The most important thing to remember about visits to schools is that first impressions are lasting.

Testing Like any examination at school, preparing for an entrance test such as the SSAT or the ISEE is an important activity. Even though there is no way to know exactly what will be on the test, understanding the kinds of questions that will be on the test and being familiar with the directions for each section will help you be more relaxed and confident on the day of the test.

Good testers come to the exam with an understanding of how the test is scored and have a strategy in mind for guessing. For instance the SSAT gives one point for each correct answer and only takes away one-quarter point for each wrong answer. Given that information, making educated guesses between two answer choices after eliminating the others will likely help you increase your test score. This does not mean that guesses should be made in every instance, as those quarter-point penalties do add up. The message here is that guessing is part of the test-taking strategy and should be formulated well in advance of the test date.

Many students think that taking the test multiple times will increase their scores dramatically. Although students who take the test without adequate preparation, when in poor health, or under emotional duress may benefit from a second try, on average only about 10 percent of testers who use test preparation guides or attend a test preparation course in advance of taking the test improve their scores by 10 percent in subsequent test administrations. In most cases, improving your test scores by 10 percent will not likely significantly alter your admission decision for a given candidate.

Each school has it own philosophy about the importance of test scores and their use in the admission process. It is important to remember that even when a school provides the range or the average of the test scores of the admitted candidates, these ranges or averages should not be viewed as either minimum requirements or guarantees of admission. Admission committees typically consider more than just a candidate's test scores when making an admission decision.

The Application Completing an application for admission should not become an onerous task or require substantial parental involvement. Many applications specifically request that the application be completed in the student's own handwriting. The application affords little opportunity for gamesmanship, and the goal should not be to win an essay contest for originality but instead to present a clear and accurate representation of your interests, talents, activities, and abilities. Experienced admission committees can quickly spot the contrived essay or the heavy hand of the parent as editor.

Both the SSAT and ISEE include a timed writing sample that will be collected during the test. That sample will be compared to other writing samples in your application, and while many students write better with more time or the use of a word processing computer program, wild discrepancies between the writing on the application and that in the writing sample rarely work to the advantage of the candidate.

Some candidates have been known to go to great lengths to create portfolios of their accomplishments, recordings of their musical performances, and even videos showcasing talents and experiences. Not all schools are interested in receiving such materials, and it is worthwhile to inquire as to how such materials may be viewed by the admission committee. On the other hand, schools that are interested in learning more about a candidate's abilities may have specific guidelines for submitting audition tapes, athletic highlight films, or artistic portfolios. You should inquire whether such materials may or may not be returned prior to submitting them. It is not advisable to submit anything that cannot be replaced if lost or damaged. Whenever possible, it is best to limit yourself to answering all the applicable questions and satisfying all the necessary requirements of an application. Exceeding these expectations may not always have the desired effect.

Candidates should be mindful of the fact that their current schools may have many documents to prepare for other students as well. Requests for transcripts and teacher recommendations should be made well in advance of the deadlines for submission. It is a generous courtesy to provide an envelope with postage addressed to the school. In most cases, the current school will send the materials directly to the admissions office. These materials are generally regarded as confidential, and you and your parents should not expect to see or review them once they have been completed.

The admission office will notify candidates when all the materials have arrived and the application is complete. Given the amount of paperwork involved in the process, many parents become quite anxious and make frequent and regular calls to both the school sending the documents and the admissions office receiving them. Until a reasonable amount of time has passed, these calls are not terribly welcome. Looking into these matters takes time away from the actual process of completing the forms or sorting and filing the documents once they arrive. Most schools will notify you of any missing credentials in a timely manner.

To ease the process of applying to multiple schools, many independent schools now receive some version of a common application or recommendation forms. It is wise to consult each school about their policies and preferences regarding the use of such applications. While a growing number of schools accept common recommendations, they may not also accept the candidate statement portion of the common applications. An increasing number of schools are accepting online versions of applications through either their own or the SSAT Web site. These online applications often have Web-based tracking systems that help candidates manage the application process.

Any candidate who is applying to multiple schools should consider using at least common recommendation forms as they are quite convenient for teachers who otherwise have to complete redundant paperwork. If you use a common application or any portion of a common application, be aware that additional forms or materials may be required. Schools that accept these common forms agree not to penalize candidates for availing themselves of these resources that help them complete the application process in a timely and efficient manner. Ultimately, admission committees are more concerned with the content of an application than with how it was completed or delivered.

Affording an Independent School

Applying for financial aid adds another dimension to the application process, but it should not be viewed as a barrier to admission. Nearly all independent schools provide assistance for families who cannot afford the full tuition. While a few schools offer merit awards and loans, in most cases financial aid is awarded on the basis of need as determined by the School and Student Service for Financial Aid, a service of the National Association of Independent Schools (NAIS). Some schools will complete their own evaluations or may use the services of a similar organization.

Application forms for financial aid are available at most admissions offices and through the School and Student Service (SSS) Web site at sss.ets.org. According to the NAIS Web site, in the academic year 2004–2005, a total of $815.7 million in financial aid was awarded by the 956 member schools. At these same schools, an average of 18 percent of the student population received some financial aid in the form of grants with an average award of $14,430 for boarding schools and $8,499 for day schools. While the vast majority of financial aid comes in the form of need-based awards, 317 NAIS member schools reported in 2004–2005 $24.8 million in merit awards, averaging $3,225 per award.

Since fewer than 5 percent of enrolled students receive merit awards, it is worthwhile to inquire about the particulars of a merit program before moving forward with the application process. Most schools either offer their own loan programs or have relationships with lending institutions that offer loans specifically designed to help parents finance the cost of an independent school tuition. Information about these programs is available from most admissions offices or the SSS Web site.

Choosing an Independent School

Identifying and selecting a list of schools to consider may seem a daunting task. Your selection of day schools may be limited by distance or the realities of commuter traffic in your neighborhood, but the possibilities for boarding schools are virtually unlimited. There are many printed directories available in bookstores and libraries that will help both expand and later narrow your search.

School and Other Web Sites The Internet is a wonderful source of information as well. Most schools have invested in rather sophisticated Web sites that reveal as much if not more than traditional printed materials. In addition to describing the academic curriculum, the faculty and students, the athletic programs, the fine and performing arts programs, and the physical plant, many Web sites offer detailed information about the activities and events that shape the culture of the school. Most Web sites are brimming with pictures of events and performances as well as candid shots revealing the character of daily life.

The school's Web site is an excellent place to begin to gather information that will inform your visit to campus. It will give you an idea of questions to ask and some notions about what you might like to see on your tour or even people you would like to meet.

The National Association of Independent Schools collects data on nearly one thousand member schools each year. Most of their data are accessible to the general public at no cost through their Web site, http://www.NAIS.org. You can find statistical data on variety of subjects, ranging from tuition, to class size, to SAT scores. These data represent the schools broadly, and while some reports designate both boarding and day schools, information on individual schools is not offered.

Two other associations do offer information about individual schools. The Secondary School Admission Test Board (SSATB) manages a database of nearly six hundred of their member schools. At http://www.SSAT.org, you can find detailed information about individual schools as well as contact information and a direct link to individual schools' Web sites. The Association of Boarding Schools (TABS) manages a database of over three hundred boarding schools, which includes a host of data that will help you differentiate one school from another. Also, BoardingSchools.org offers a click-through service that connects you directly to individual school's Web sites.

It is worth noting that NAIS, SSAT, and TABS are credible sources that are managed by professional organizations to which independent schools belong and support. Each of these associations is a not-for-profit organization governed by a board made up of independent school educators and dedicates its mission to the promotion of independent schools.

Directories Additionally, there are several printed directories that have long served the promotion of independent schools. These include *Bunting and Lyon Private Independent Schools, Porter Sargent Handbook of Private Schools, Vincent Curtis Educational Register*, and *Peterson's Guide*. Most are available at libraries and bookstores. Some of these publications have accompanying Web sites, and none of them ranks schools.

As is often true on the Internet, there are less credible sources of information. Some of these sources even rank schools. This is a practice that is frowned upon by most schools and all the aforementioned professional associations. In today's consumer-minded society, too much emphasis is placed on ranking, and most educators do not believe that ranking schools helps students make a wise choice between schools.

Furthermore, it may be of interest to know that some of the Web sites that do rank schools accept payment for advertising those same schools. Their fee structures vary according to the amount of exposure a school wishes to receive, and the data on these Web sites are self-reported by the same fee-paying schools. You may notice that some schools are missing from these rankings because they have chosen to not support the practice of ranking and have not posted their information on these Web sites. As with all decisions, consider information from a wide range of sources and then make informed choices.

School Accreditation One way to judge the quality of an independent school is to identify its accrediting body. Independent schools have the option of seeking accreditation from regional, national, and international accrediting organizations. The regional accrediting bodies include: Middle States Association of Colleges and Schools (MSACS), New England Association of Colleges and Schools (NEACS), North Central Association of Colleges and Schools (NCACS), Northwest Association of Schools and Colleges (NASC), Southern Association of Colleges and Schools (SACS), and Western Association of Schools and Colleges (WASC). These are some of the same accrediting bodies that serve colleges and universities throughout the country. In order to receive accreditation, independent schools must complete an evaluation that is supervised by an accrediting organization. The process is designed to ensure that the independent schools hold themselves publicly accountable and operate in a manner that demonstrates that they meet acceptable standards of educational quality, professional competence, and fiscal responsibility. It is important to note that some schools that are not accredited may be in the process of becoming so. Independent schools complete the accreditation process on a schedule dictated by their accrediting body.

McGraw-Hill's
SSAT/ISEE
HIGH SCHOOL ENTRANCE EXAMS

PART I

GETTING STARTED

How to Use This Book

Both the SSAT and ISEE include many different types of questions, and your preparation time may be short. That is why it is important to use your study time wisely. This book provides strategies and practice for all test question types, and it has been organized to make your study program practical and efficient. It will help you:

- Familiarize yourself with the format and question types of the test you'll be taking.
- Review all the verbal and math skills you need for the test.
- Check your progress with Practice Sets at the end of each review chapter.
- Practice your test-taking skills using Practice Tests.

The following five-step study program has been designed to help you make the best use of this book.

Step 1. Learn the Format of the Test You'll Be Taking

Read Chapter 2 of this book, titled "SSAT and ISEE: An Overview." In that chapter you will find charts illustrating the latest format of the test you will be taking. Note that the ISEE has different formats depending on which level of the test you take. You'll also find important information about how each test is scored.

Once you know the format of your test, you'll know what kinds of questions to expect. Then look at the Contents in this book. You'll see that Part II includes separate chapters for each of the verbal, reading, and writing question types on the two tests. You'll also see that one of these chapters is marked "SSAT Only" and another is marked "ISEE Only." The chapters that are not marked with these labels apply to both tests. Next, in Part III of this book you'll see that there are chapters reviewing math skills in four areas: arithmetic, algebra, geometry, and word problems. These chapters will help you prepare for the math sections of both tests. There is also a chapter on a particular math question type that appears only on the upper-level version of the ISEE: Quantitative Comparisons. By knowing the format of the test you'll be taking, you can pick which of all these chapters you need to study. That way, you can focus your time and efforts on what you really need to know for your test.

Also make sure to read Chapter 3, "Strategies for Top Scores." This chapter provides valuable suggestions to help you study smart, solve test problems, and get your best score on test day.

Step 2. Make a Study Schedule

If you have the time, plan to spend at least two weeks or so working your way through Parts II and III of this book, which offer review and practice for the verbal and math question types. Then be sure to set aside enough time at the end of your schedule to take at least one or two of the Practice Tests at the end of the book. However, if you do not have much time before the test, you may want to shorten your review time and focus instead entirely on the Practice Tests.

Step 3. Study the Chapters on the Verbal, Reading, and Writing Question Types

Part II of this book provides detailed explanations and samples for all of the verbal, reading, and writing question types on the two tests. They will also give you strategies for answering the different question types. If you are taking the SSAT, you'll want to study these chapters:

SSAT

- Chapter 4. Strategies for Synonym Questions
- Chapter 5. Strategies for Verbal Analogy Questions
- Chapter 7. Strategies for Reading Comprehension Questions
- Chapter 8. Strategies for the Writing Section

If you are taking the ISEE, you'll want to study these chapters:

ISEE

- Chapter 4. Strategies for Synonym Questions
- Chapter 6. Strategies for Sentence Completion Questions
- Chapter 7. Strategies for Reading Comprehension Questions
- Chapter 8. Strategies for the Writing Section

You do not need to work through these chapters in the order in which they appear. Skip around if you like, but make sure you read all the chapters covering the question types on the test you'll be taking. Each review chapter ends with a set of practice questions that you can use to see how well you have mastered the material. If you get a question wrong, go back and reread the chapter.

Step 4. Study the Math Review Chapters

Part III of this book provides chapters reviewing all the math topics you'll need to know for either test: arithmetic, algebra, geometry, and word problems. No matter which test you're taking, you'll want to study all of these chapters very carefully. Each topic covered in these chapters is followed by an "On Your Own" set of practice questions. Use these questions to check how well you have mastered the material. If you get a question wrong, go back and reread the section covering that topic.

Chapter 13 in Part III covers a math question type called Quantitative Comparisons that appears only on the upper-level version of the ISEE. If you are taking that test, you'll want to study this chapter carefully. If you are not taking the upper-level ISEE, you can skip this chapter.

Step 5. Take Practice Tests

Once you have completed your study and review for all of the question types on the test you'll be taking, get ready for the real exam by taking the Practice Test in either Part IV or Part V that corresponds to the real test you'll be taking. If you are taking the lower-level or upper-level SSAT, you can practice with all three of the SSAT Practice Tests. If you are taking the ISEE, take the Practice Test that corresponds to the level of the real test you'll be taking. You might also want to take the other ISEE Practice Tests for additional practice with the test question types.

When you take each test, try to simulate actual test conditions. Sit in a quiet room, time yourself, and work through as much of the test as time allows. The tests are ideal for practice because they have been constructed to be as much like the real test as possible. The directions and practice questions are very much like those on the real test. You'll gain experience with the test format, and you'll learn to pace yourself so that you can earn the maximum number of points in the time allowed.

Follow the scoring instructions to rate your test performance. Each test will also serve as a review of the topics tested because complete explanations are provided for every question. The explanations can be found at the end of each test. If you get a question wrong, you'll want to review the explanation carefully. You may also want to go back to the chapter in this book that covers the question topic.

SSAT and ISEE: An Overview

The SSAT (Secondary School Admission Test) and the ISEE (Independent School Entrance Examination) are the two most widely used admission tests at private schools in the United States. These tests help school administrators compare the academic abilities of students from a variety of elementary and presecondary schools.

The schools to which you are applying will tell you which test is required, but it is up to you to make your own arrangements for taking the exam and submitting your scores in a timely fashion. Both the SSAT and the ISEE test the same basic verbal, reading, and quantitative skills. This book examines both of these important private school admission tests in depth. It offers valuable tips and strategies for answering each question type and provides full-length sample exams to help you simulate actual test conditions at home. As any good test-taker will tell you, knowing what to expect is half the battle when it comes to earning top scores!

What Is the SSAT?

The SSAT is a standardized test developed and administered by the Secondary School Admission Test Board. Approximately 700 independent schools require SSAT scores as part of their admission process. The test is designed to measure verbal, math, and reading skills.

The SSAT is offered seven times a year—in November, December, January, February, March, April, and June. Complete information about the test and registration forms are available

- online at www.ssat.org.
- by phone at 609-683-4440.
- by mail at SSAT, CN 5339, Princeton, NJ 08543.

The SSAT is offered in two levels:

- Lower level for students in grades 5–7
- Upper level for students in grades 8–11

What Is the Format of the SSAT?

The format of the test is the same for both the upper and lower levels.

Format of the SSAT

Section	Questions	Time
Verbal • Synonyms • Verbal Analogies	60	30 minutes
Quantitative I • Arithmetic • Elementary Algebra • Geometry	25	30 minutes
Reading Comprehension • Humanities • Social Studies • Science	40	40 minutes
Quantitative II • Arithmetic • Elementary Algebra • Geometry	25	30 minutes
Essay	1	25 minutes

*All multiple-choice questions have five answer choices.
*The multiple-choice sections may be administered in any order.
*The essay may be administered either before or after the multiple-choice portion of the test. It is not scored, but a copy is sent to each school to which your SSAT scores are sent.

How Is the SSAT Scored?

SSAT scores are computed by awarding 1 point for each correct answer and subtracting 1/4 point for each incorrect answer. This calculation produces a Raw Score, which is then converted to a Scaled Score by the use of tables constructed specifically for each test.

On the lower-level test, verbal, quantitative, and reading scores are reported on a scale of 230–320. Total scores are also reported on a scale of 690–960.

On the upper-level test, verbal, quantitative, and reading scores are reported on a scale of 250–348. Total scores are also reported on a scale of 750–1050.

On a recent test, median 50th percentile scores for reading, verbal, and quantitative sections were as shown below.

Lower-Level Median 50th Percentile Scores

Grade	Reading	Verbal	Quantitative
5	273	278	271
6	281	288	281
7	287	296	288

Upper-Level Median 50th Percentile Scores

Grade	Reading	Verbal	Quantitative
8	293	304	299
9	298	311	306
10	299	307	314
11	292	301	313

Two to three weeks after you take the test, a score report, along with a copy of your essay, will be sent to each school, educational consultant, and educational organization that you indicated on your registration form. Scores remain active for one academic year.

What Is the ISEE?

Like the SSAT, the ISEE is a test of verbal, reading, quantitative and writing skills designed for students seeking admission to private schools. The ISEE is administered by the Educational Records Bureau (ERB) and developed in conjunction with the Educational Testing Service (ETS) in Princeton, New Jersey.

The ISEE is offered on a variety of dates and in a variety of locations. For a complete listing of test dates and locations, check the *ISEE Student Guide*, which is available through the school to which you are applying or online at www.erbtest.org. The *Student Guide* also contains the registration materials you will need to sign up for the ISEE. You may register by mail, phone, fax, or online, but there is an additional charge for registering by phone or fax.

The ISEE has three levels

- Lower level for students in grades 4 or 5 applying for grades 5 or 6.
- Middle level for students in grades 6 or 7 applying for grades 7 or 8.
- Upper level for students in grades 8 or above applying for grades 9–12.

Each level has the same five sections, but the levels vary slightly in format.

You may take the ISEE only once within a six-month period. It's important to note that you cannot take the ISEE for practice. It may be taken only for the purpose of submitting scores to a participating school as part of the admission process.

What Is the Format of the ISEE?

The charts below show the format of the ISEE at the lower, middle, and upper levels.

Lower Level for Candidates for Grades 5 and 6

Test	Questions	Time
Verbal Reasoning • Synonyms • Sentence Completions	40	25 minutes
Quantitative Reasoning • Comprehension • Interpretation/Application • Higher-Order Thinking	35	35 minutes
Reading Comprehension • Humanities • Science • Social Studies	36	40 minutes
Mathematics Achievement • Knowledge and Skills • Computation/Comprehension • Applications	35	40 minutes
Essay	1	30 minutes

Middle Level for Candidates for Grades 7 and 8

Test	Questions	Time
Verbal Reasoning • Synonyms • Sentence Completions	40	20 minutes
Quantitative Reasoning • Comprehension • Interpretation/Application • Higher-Order Thinking • Quantitative Comparison	35	35 minutes
Reading Comprehension • Humanities • Science • Social Studies	40	40 minutes
Mathematics Achievement • Knowledge and Skills • Computation/Comprehension • Applications	45	45 minutes
Essay	1	30 minutes

Upper Level for Candidates for Grades 9 to 12

Test	Questions	Time
Verbal Reasoning	40	20 minutes
• Synonyms		
• Sentence Completions		
Quantitative Reasoning	35	35 minutes
• Arithmetic/Algebra/Geometry		
• Concepts/Understanding		
• Applications/Higher-Order Thinking		
• Quantitative Comparison		
Reading Comprehension	40	40 minutes
• Humanities		
• Science		
• Social Studies		
Mathematics Achievement	45	40 minutes
• Arithmetic/Algebra/Geometry		
• Knowledge and Skills		
• Computation/Comprehension		
• Applications		
Essay	1	30 minutes

*All multiple-choice questions have four answer choices.

*The multiple-choice sections may be administered in any order.

*The essay is always last. Like the SSAT essay, the ISEE essay is not scored, but a copy is sent to each school to which your ISEE scores are sent.

*Because each level is given to students at more than one grade, you may find some questions are too difficult for you. Don't be concerned. Your score is compared only to the scores of other students in the same grade.

How Is the ISEE Scored?

ISEE scores are computed by awarding 1 point for each correct answer. There is no deduction for incorrect answers, so the number of questions you answered correctly becomes your Raw Score. This Raw Score is then converted to a Scaled Score by the use of tables specifically constructed for each test.

On the middle-level test, verbal reasoning scores are reported on a scale of 763–922, quantitative reasoning scores are reported on a scale of 779–926, reading comprehension scores are reported on a scale of 759–929, and mathematics achievement scores are reported on a scale of 765–932.

In the upper-level test, verbal reasoning scores are reported on a scale of 790–940, quantitative reasoning scores are reported on a scale of 797–940, reading comprehension scores are reported on a scale of 777–940, and math achievement scores on a scale of 800–940.

On a recent test, median 50th percentile scores for verbal reasoning, quantitative reasoning, reading comprehension, and mathematics ability were as shown below:

Middle-Level Median 50th Percentile Scores

Grade	Verbal Reasoning	Quantitative Reasoning	Reading Comprehension	Mathematics Achievement
6	858	866	866	870
7	867	872	873	876

Upper Level Median 50th Percentile Scores

Grade	Verbal Reasoning	Quantitative Reasoning	Reading Comprehension	Mathematics Achievement
8	875	875	883	876
9	880	878	886	884
10	886	884	892	889

ISEE score reports include test scores and diagnostic information. They are sent out to schools and parents approximately 7 to 10 business days after testing. A copy of your essay is sent, along with your score report, to each school you indicated on your registration form.

Strategies for Top Scores

When you take the SSAT or ISEE, you'll want to do everything you can to make sure you get your best possible score. That means studying right, building good problem-solving skills, and learning proven test-taking strategies. Here are some tips to help you do your best.

Study Strategies

- **Get to know the format of the exam.** Use the Practice Tests in this book to familiarize yourself with the test format, which does not change from year to year. That way, you'll know exactly what to expect when you see the real thing on test day.

- **Get to know the test directions.** If you are familiar with the directions ahead of time, you won't have to waste valuable test time reading them and trying to understand them. The format and directions used in the practice exams in this book are modeled on the ones you'll see on the actual SSAT or ISEE.

- **Get to know what topics are covered.** Get to know what specific topics are covered on the exam. You'll find all of them in the strategy sections and practice exams in this book.

- **Study hard.** If possible, plan to study for at least an hour a day for two weeks before the test. You should be able to read all the strategy chapters in this book, work your way through the Practice Sets at the end of each chapter, and complete one or more Practice Tests during that time period. If you are pressed for time, focus on taking at least one Practice Test, reading the explanations, and then reviewing the question types that give you the most trouble.

Math Problem-Solving Strategies

- **Solve math problems in whatever way is easiest for you.** There are usually several ways to solve a math problem and arrive at the correct answer. Do what is easiest for you. Remember that the SSAT and ISEE math questions are all multiple choice. That means that no one is going to be checking your work and judging you by which solution method you chose, so solve the problem any way you like.

- **Build good math problem-solving skills.** When you tackle SSAT or ISEE math questions, try to follow this three-step process:

    1. When you first read a question, make a list of the given values and variables and the units for the variables.

    2. Ask yourself, "What do I know and what do I need to find out?" The answers to those questions will help you figure out how to solve the problem.

    3. Solve the problem and see if the answer makes sense. For example, if you know that one variable should be much larger than another, make sure your answer reflects that relationship. You'll see how this works with many of the problems in this book.

- **Make sure you know what the question is asking.** The questions on the SSAT or ISEE are not deliberately designed to trick you, but it is still important that you look closely at each one to make sure you know what it is asking. Pay special attention to questions that include the word NOT. You may want to circle that word to make sure you take it into account as you choose your answer.

General Test-Taking Strategies

- **Answer all the easy problems first, then tackle the harder ones.** Keep in mind that the longest sections on the SSAT and ISEE are only 40 minutes long. There isn't much time to spend trying to figure out the answers to harder questions, so skip them and come back to them later. There are two reasons why you should do this. The first reason is that every question counts the same in the scoring of the exam. That means that you are better off spending time answering the easier questions, where you are sure to pick up points. The second reason is that by answering the easier questions, you'll build your confidence and get into a helpful test-taking rhythm. Then when you go back to a question you skipped, you may find that it isn't as hard as you first thought.

- **Use the process of elimination**. Keep in mind that on the SSAT and ISEE, like any other multiple-choice test, the answer is right in front of you. Try eliminating answer choices that you know are incorrect. Often this can help you select the correct answer.

- **On the ISEE, guess if you have to.** On the ISEE there is no penalty for wrong answers, so you have nothing to lose by guessing. If time is running out and there are questions you have not answered, you might pick up extra points by guessing answers to those questions.

- **On the SSAT, if you must guess, make an educated guess.** The SSAT has a one-quarter-point penalty for wrong answers to discourage random guessing. So if you have absolutely no idea how to answer a question, you are better off skipping it entirely. However, you may be able to eliminate one or more answer choices. If you can do that, you can increase your odds of guessing the correct answer. If you can make this kind of educated guess, go ahead. If you guess correctly, you'll earn another point.

Tips for Test Day

- **Don't panic!** Once test day comes, you're as prepared as you're ever going to be, so there is no point in panicking. Use your energy to make sure that you are extra careful in answering questions and marking the answer sheet.

- **Be careful when marking your answer sheet.** Remember that the answer sheet is scored by a machine, so mark it carefully. Fill in answer ovals completely, erase thoroughly if you change your mind, and do not make any stray marks anywhere on the sheet. Also, make sure that the answer space you are marking matches the number of the question you are answering. If you skip a question, make sure that you skip the corresponding space on the answer sheet. Every 5 or 10 questions, check the question numbers and make sure that you are marking in the right spot. You may want to mark your answers in groups of 5 or 10 to make sure that you are marking the answer sheet correctly.

- **Watch the time.** Keep track of the time as you work your way through the test. Try to pace yourself so that you can tackle as many of the questions as possible within the time limit. Check yourself at 10 or 15-minute intervals using your watch or a timer.

- **Don't panic if time runs out.** If you've paced yourself carefully, you should have time to tackle all or most of the questions. If you do run out of time, however, don't panic. Make sure that you have marked your answer sheet for all the questions you have answered so far. **If you are taking the ISEE,** guess answers to any remaining questions. You have nothing to lose since there is no penalty on the ISEE for wrong answers. **If you are taking the SSAT**, however, do NOT mark answers to random guesses. Since there is a one-quarter-point penalty on the SSAT for wrong answers, you don't want to lose any credit!

- **Use extra time to check your work.** If you have time left over at the end of the test, go back and check your work. Make sure that you have marked the answer sheet correctly. Check any calculations you may have made to make sure that they are correct. Take another look at any questions you may have skipped. Resist the urge to second-guess your answers, however, as this may lead you to change an already correct answer to a wrong one.

PART II

STRATEGIES FOR THE VERBAL, READING, AND WRITING SECTIONS

Strategies for Synonym Questions

Synonym questions make up one-half of the Verbal Reasoning section on both the SSAT and the ISEE. On the SSAT, synonyms account for 30 of the 60 verbal questions. On the ISEE, synonyms account for 20 of the 40 verbal questions. On both tests, synonym questions are designed to test your knowledge of word meanings.

Format of Synonym Questions

Each synonym question consists of a word in capital letters followed by four (ISEE) or five (SSAT) words or phrases. Your task is to select the one word or phrase whose meaning is closest to the meaning of the word in capital letters.

Sample Synonym Question Explained

Let's look at a sample question to see what's involved.

CANDOR:
(A) charm
(B) patience
(C) honesty
(D) consent
(E) caution

If you know the meaning of the word *candor*, just pick the answer choice that is closest to the word you thought of and move on to the next question. If you don't know the meaning of *candor*, think about the word itself. Have you ever heard it used? Does it look like some other word you know? Perhaps you recognize that *candor* looks a lot like *candid*. A candid photo is one that is unposed or natural. Now look at the answer choices to find one that means something like unposed or natural.

(A) *Charm* means "attractiveness" or "appeal." This is a possibility, but there is probably a better choice.

(B) *Patience* means "tolerance" or "restraint." This is not even close, so you can eliminate it.

(C) *Honesty* means "truthfulness" or "openness." This choice is closer to the idea of natural or unposed than choice A.

(D) *Consent* means "approval" or "agreement." This choice can be eliminated because it has nothing to do with candor.

(E) *Caution* means "carefulness," which has nothing to do with candor.

The answer choice that comes closest to the idea of being unposed or natural is choice C. *Candor* means "frankness," "openness," or "honesty."

Strategies for Answering Synonym Questions

Here is a six-step strategic plan that you can use to answer synonym questions.

1. Look carefully at the capitalized word.
2. If you know what it means, think of another word that means the same and look for that word among the answer choices.
3. If you don't know the word, try to put it in context. If you remember hearing or reading the word, try to remember how it was used.
4. If context doesn't help, look at the word for clues. See if it contains a word or word part that is familiar to you.
5. Read the answer choices and select the one that comes closest to the meaning you thought of.
6. If you have no idea what the word means, eliminate any answer choices you know are not correct and then guess from among the remaining choices.

Try the six-step strategy to help you answer the synonym questions that follow, then compare your answer to the explanation that follows each question.

Sample Synonym Question Set Explained

Directions: Each of the following questions consists of a word in capital letters followed by four (ISEE) or five (SSAT) words or phrases. Your task is to select the one word or phrase whose meaning is closest to the meaning of the word in capital letters.

SSAT/ISEE Coach Says . . .

The correct answer may not be a perfect synonym for the capitalized word, but it will be the one that is closest in meaning to the given word.

---

1. APATHY
   (A) sorrow
   (B) ability
   (C) sickness
   (D) inconvenience
   (E) indifference

1. **E is correct.** *Apathy* is a lack of interest or concern about something, and *indifference*, choice E, is a good synonym. Word parts can help define this word. The word part — *pathy* means "feelings" or "emotions," and the prefix a- means "without." Thus *apathy* can be defined as "without feelings," which is nearly the same as indifference.

SSAT/ISEE Coach Says...
Often you can get a good idea of what a new word means by taking it apart and defining each separate piece.

---

2. REVISE
   (A) relapse
   (B) consider
   (C) prevail
   (D) amend
   (E) reiterate

2. **D is correct.** The prefix *re-* means "again" or "back." To *revise* means to "reconsider (to consider again) and change or modify." *Amend*, which means "to make better or improve" is the best synonym.

   Don't be fooled by the fact that choices A and E both include the prefix *re-*. *Relapse* means "to fall back to a previous condition" and *reiterate* means "to repeat" or "to say again."

3. ABATE
   (A) pretend
   (B) decrease
   (C) finalize
   (D) endanger
   (E) oppose

3. **B is correct.** *Abate* means "to reduce in amount or degree," "to lessen," or "to decrease." Perhaps you remember hearing *abate* mentioned during a weather report: "The storm is expected to abate before nightfall."

SSAT/ISEE Coach Says...
Try to remember where you may have heard a new word used. Just knowing the context in which the word was used can help you define it.

---

4. DECEIVE

    (A) betray

    (B) protect

    (C) deduce

    (D) verify

    (E) disparage

4. **A is correct.** To *deceive* is to mislead, delude, or betray. If you do not know the word *deceive*, perhaps you recognize that it is a word that is used in a negative way. This fact will allow you to eliminate choices B and D since *protect* and *verify* are both positive words. *Deduce* (choice C), which means "to infer by reasoning," is neither positive nor negative. That leaves only choices A and E from which to choose. *Betray* (choice A) means "to break faith with" or "to mislead," and *disparage* (choice D) means to "discredit" or "belittle." Clearly, choice A is the best answer.

SSAT/ISEE Coach Says . . .

Many words convey either a positive or a negative feeling. You may be able to choose the right synonym simply by asking, "Is this word negative or positive?"

---

5. OBSCURE

    (A) obtain

    (B) replace

    (C) ignore

    (D) conceal

    (E) observe

5. **D is correct.** *Obscure* can be an adjective meaning "vague" or "dark." Or it can be a verb meaning to "obliterate" or "hide." All you have to do is look at the answer choices to know which meaning you are looking for. In this case, all the answer choices are verbs. That means you are looking for a word that means the same as hide. Choice D is the best answer.

SSAT/ISEE Coach Says . . .

Many words have different meanings, depending upon whether they are used as nouns or verbs or adjectives. If you can't tell which meaning of a word you are looking for, just look at the answer choices. They will always be the same part of speech as the capitalized word.

On Your Own

Now take the time to apply what you have just learned about synonym questions to see how well you can do on Practice Set A. When you are finished, use the answer key to score your work.

- You may find that some words are easier to deal with than others. Remember that synonym questions get harder as you work through the test. On the ISEE, answer every question, even if you have to take a wild guess. On the SSAT, answer every question for which you know, or think you know, the answer. Whenever you can eliminate at least two of the answer choices as definitely incorrect, make a guess.

- Review the strategies and tips discussed above and then try Practice Set B. Remember that the more you practice with these items, the easier they will become for you to answer correctly.

Practice Set A

Directions: Each of the following questions consists of a word in capital letters followed by five words or phrases labeled (A), (B), (C), (D), and (E). Your task is to select the one word or phrase whose meaning is closest to the meaning of the word in capital letters.

Example:
CANDOR:
(A) charm
(B) patience
(C) honesty
(D) consent
(E) caution

Correct Answer: C

1. PROFOUND:
    (A) deep
    (B) complex
    (C) captivating
    (D) discouraging
    (E) miraculous

2. INADEQUATE:
    (A) diminutive
    (B) subsequent
    (C) deficient
    (D) interminable
    (E) tangible

3. ADVERSARY:
    (A) proverb
    (B) opening
    (C) atrocity
    (D) opponent
    (E) desolation

4. PRESERVE:
   (A) commemorate
   (B) revere
   (C) protect
   (D) warrant
   (E) confine

5. TENTATIVE:
   (A) indefinite
   (B) hidden
   (C) sociable
   (D) critical
   (E) charming

6. CLAMOR:
   (A) mistake
   (B) mixture
   (C) package
   (D) commotion
   (E) recollection

7. CONTEMPORARY:
   (A) appropriated
   (B) current
   (C) momentary
   (D) transient
   (E) convenient

8. CAJOLE:
   (A) sneer
   (B) ridicule
   (C) peek
   (D) persuade
   (E) target

9. PRIMITIVE:
   (A) functional
   (B) wooden
   (C) basic
   (D) fragile
   (E) lowly

10. MUNDANE:
    (A) ordinary
    (B) vigorous
    (C) swollen
    (D) restful
    (E) cautious

Answers and Explanations

1. **A is correct.** *Profound* means "thoroughgoing," "far-reaching," or "deep."
2. **C is correct.** *Inadequate* means "not adequate to fulfill a need" or "deficient."
3. **D is correct.** An *adversary* is an "enemy" or an "opponent."
4. **C is correct.** To *preserve* is to "keep from damage or harm" or to "protect."
5. **A is correct.** *Tentative* means "not fully worked out or agreed upon." To say that you have tentative plans is to say that your plans are "indefinite."
6. **D is correct.** A *clamor* is an uproar or a racket—in other words, a "commotion."
7. **B is correct.** *Contemporary* means "of or in the style of the present," "modern," or "current."
8. **D is correct.** To *cajole* is to "coax with flattery or to persuade with gentle and repeated appeals."
9. **C is correct.** *Primitive* means "not derived from something else," "primary," or "basic."
10. **A is correct.** *Mundane* means "commonplace" or "ordinary."

Practice Set B

Directions: Each of the following questions consists of a word in capital letters followed by five words or phrases labeled (A), (B), (C), (D), and (E). Your task is to select the one word or phrase whose meaning is closest to the meaning of the word in capital letters.

Example:
ALLEVIATE:
(A) sickness
(B) fever
(C) pain
(D) help
(E) result

Correct Answer: D

1. ROBUST:
   (A) mechanical
   (B) fresh
   (C) hearty
   (D) elaborate
   (E) mindful

2. ALLOT
   (A) research
   (B) distribute
   (C) apply
   (D) inform
   (E) ingest

3. BREVITY:
   (A) shortness
   (B) sadness
   (C) determination
   (D) insignificance
   (E) guilt

4. CHRONIC:
   (A) troublesome
   (B) secure
   (C) unknown
   (D) persistent
   (E) difficult

5. PRAISE:
   (A) ascend
   (B) abhor
   (C) aspire
   (D) bolster
   (E) commend

6. APTITUDE:
   (A) height
   (B) ability
   (C) attitude
   (D) retraction
   (E) contrast

7. WINSOME:
   (A) small
   (B) limber
   (C) quiet
   (D) charming
   (E) restless

8. APPREHENSION:
   - (A) consequence
   - (B) beginning
   - (C) dread
   - (D) dismissal
   - (E) imperfection

9. ACCLAIM:
   - (A) prospect
   - (B) aversion
   - (C) delight
   - (D) approval
   - (E) accessory

10. PREVAIL:
   - (A) triumph
   - (B) strain
   - (C) assume
   - (D) precede

Answers and Explanations

1. **C is correct.** *Robust* means "full of health and strength," "vigorous," or "hearty."
2. **B is correct.** To *allot* is to "parcel out" or to "distribute."
3. **A is correct.** *Brevity* is the quality or state of being brief in duration—in other words, shortness.
4. **D is correct.** *Chronic* means "of long duration," "continuing," or "persistent."
5. **E is correct.** To *praise* is to express approval or admiration of, to extol, or to "commend."
6. **B is correct.** *Aptitude* is a talent or natural ability.
7. **D is correct.** *Winsome* means "attractive in an engaging way," or "charming."
8. **C is correct.** *Apprehension* is an anxious feeling or foreboding or "dread."
9. **D is correct.** *Acclaim* is loud or enthusiastic praise, applause, or "approval."
10. **A is correct.** To *prevail* is to be greater in strength or influence—in other words, to "triumph."

Strategies for Verbal Analogy Questions (SSAT only)

Verbal analogy questions account for 30 of the 60 questions in the Verbal Reasoning section of the SSAT. There are no verbal analogy questions on the ISEE, so you can skip this chapter if you are preparing to take the ISEE.

Verbal analogy questions are designed to test your knowledge of word meanings along with your ability to understand how words relate to each other. On the ISEE, verbal analogy questions are arranged in order of difficulty from easiest to hardest.

Format of Verbal Analogy Questions

Analogy questions come in two different formats.

- In one format the question contains three words and each answer choice contains one word. Your task is to find the single word that is related to the third word in the question in the same way that the first two words are related.
- In the other format, each question contains one pair of words and each answer choice contains another pair of words. You are to find the pair of words among the answer choices that is related in the same way as the pair of words in the question.

Sample Analogy Questions Explained

Here are samples of each analogy format to give you an idea of what's involved.

1. **Maintain is to preserve as magnify is to**
   (A) protect
   (B) exert
   (C) amplify
   (D) rectify
   (E) restrain

1. **C is correct**. *Maintain* and *preserve* are synonyms. Therefore the correct answer will be the word that means most nearly the same as *magnify*.

Amplify, which means "to make larger or stronger," is a good synonym for *magnify*. Choice A is wrong because *protect* is a synonym for *maintain* and *preserve*, not for *magnify*. Choice B is wrong because *exert* means "to put forth or use energetically," which has nothing to do with *magnify*. Choice D is wrong because *rectify* means "to correct or improve," which is not related to *magnify*. Choice E is wrong because *restrain* means "to hold back," which is opposite in meaning to *magnify*.

2. **Page is to book as**
   (A) drama is to play
   (B) note is to letter
   (C) pen is to paper
   (D) letter is to word
   (E) arm is to hand

2. **D is correct.** This is a part-to-whole analogy. A *book* is made up of *pages* in the same way that a *word* is made up of *letters*. Choice A is wrong because a *drama* is one type of *play*. Choice B is wrong because a *note* is a type of *letter*. Choice C is wrong because a *pen* is used to write on *paper*. Choice E is wrong because an *arm* is not part of a *hand*.

Common Relationships Found in Analogy Questions

The majority of SSAT analogy questions fall into one of the following categories:

- Contrasts
  Negligent is to careful
  Bravery is to cowardice
- Part to whole
  Keyboard is to computer
  Trunk is to car
- Part to part
  Keyboard is to mouse (parts of a computer)
  Trunk is to hood (parts of a car)
- Activity to result
  Heat is to warmth
  Rain is to flooding
- Use
  Pencil is to write
  Scissors is to cut
- Individual to object
  Doctor is to stethoscope
  Painter is to brush

- Measurement
  Clock is to time
  Decibel is to sound
- Degree of difference or similarity
  Cool is to frozen
  Breeze is to gale

How to Answer Analogy Questions

Here is a helpful five-step strategy for answering verbal analogy questions.

1. Figure out how the first two words are related.
2. Make up a sentence that expresses the relationship between the first pair of words.
3. Try out your sentence on the second pair of words and eliminate the ones that don't work.
4. If you find that your sentence works on more than one answer pair (or on none of the answer pairs), revise your sentence to make it more precise.
5. Choose the answer that works best.

Use the five-step strategy and what you have learned about analogy relationships to answer the practice verbal analogy questions that follow. As you complete each question, compare your answer to the explanation given.

Sample Verbal Analogy Question Set Explained

Directions: The questions that follow ask you to find relationships between words. For each question, select the answer choice that best completes the meaning of the sentence.

SSAT Coach Says . . .
The key to answering an analogy question is being able to express the relationship between the words in a pair.

---

1. **Reap is to sow as**
   (A) suggest is to order
   (B) send is to remit
   (C) assemble is to disband
   (D) furnish is to provide
   (E) plant is to seed

1. **C is correct.** *Reap* and *sow* are related as opposites. To *reap* is to "gather" or to "harvest," and to *sow* is to "scatter seed."
Choice A: Is *suggest* the opposite of *order*? No. *Suggest* and *order* are different degrees of the same concept.
Choice B: Is *send* the opposite of *remit*? No. *Send* and *remit* are synonyms.
Choice C: Is *assemble* the opposite of *disband*? Yes. *Assemble* means "gather together," and *disband* means "separate." This appears to be the correct answer, but let's check the remaining choices to be sure.
Choice D: Is *furnish* the opposite of *provide*? No. *Furnish* and *provide* are synonyms.
Choice E: Is *plant* the opposite of *seed*? No. *Plant* and *seed* are synonyms. The best answer is definitely choice C.

2. **Sprint is to runner as**
   (A) slither is to snake
   (B) gallop is to horse
   (C) hop is to rabbit
   (D) glide is to skater
   (E) race is to track

2. **B is correct.** A *sprint* is an action taken by a *runner*. This sentence eliminates choice E, but it works for choices A, B, C, and D. To arrive at one correct answer, you must go back and revise the initial sentence to make it more precise. *Sprint* is a fast action of a *runner*. This sentence eliminates choices A, C, and D, leaving choice B as the correct answer.

SSAT Coach Says . . .
If your first sentence does not work, revise it to make it more precise.

---

3. **Shovel is to excavate as scissors is to**
   (A) dig
   (B) expose
   (C) scoop
   (D) snip
   (E) tear

3. **D is correct.** The relationship in this analogy is one of an object to its use. A *shovel* is used to *excavate* just as a *scissors* is used to *snip*. Don't be misled by the fact that choices A, B, and C are all synonyms for the word *excavate*. The word you are looking for is a use for a *scissors*, not a synonym for *excavate*.

4. **Tree is to forest as ship is to**
   - (A) vessel
   - (B) fleet
   - (C) captain
   - (D) cargo
   - (E) shore

4. **B is correct.** This is a part-to-whole analogy. A *tree* is part of a *forest* just as a *ship* is part of a *fleet*.

5. **Toe is to heel as**
   - (A) arm is to wing
   - (B) roof is to house
   - (C) chair is to table
   - (D) fruit is to flower
   - (E) wheel is to brake

5. **E is correct.** This is a part-to-part analogy. *Toe* and *heel* are both parts of the *foot*. In the same way, *wheel* and *brake* are both parts of a *bicycle*. No other answer pair has the same part-to-part relationship.

6. **Slip is to fall as drop is to**
   - (A) break
   - (B) flood
   - (C) liquid
   - (D) tempt
   - (E) raise

6. **A is correct.** This is an activity-to-result analogy. A *slip* may result in a *fall*. Similarly *dropping* something may result in *breaking* it.

On Your Own

Now take the time to apply what you have just learned about verbal analogies to see how well you can do on your own. When you are finished, use the answer key to score your work.

You may find that certain types of analogies are easier for you to deal with than others. Remember that analogy questions appear in order of their difficulty, so the last few questions are likely to be tougher than the first ones. Use Practice Set A to determine which types of analogies are most difficult for you.

Review the strategies and tips discussed above and then try Practice Set B. The more you practice answering analogy questions, the easier they will become for you to answer correctly.

Practice Set A

Directions: The questions that follow ask you to find relationships between words. For each question, select the answer choice that best completes the meaning of the sentence.

Example:
Chapter is to book as
(A) note is to letter
(B) scene is to play
(C) story is to novel
(D) writer is to director
(E) reader is to audience

Correct Answer: B
A *chapter* is a division of a *book* and a *scene* is a division of a *play*.

1. **File is to smooth as tape is to**
   (A) gouge
   (B) record
   (C) taper
   (D) roll
   (E) peel

2. **Novel is to entertain as**
   (A) paper is to write
   (B) author is to persuade
   (C) jury is to justify
   (D) newspaper is to inform
   (E) editorial is to read

3. **Donkey is to bray as duck is to**
   (A) waddle
   (B) bill
   (C) quack
   (D) fly
   (E) goose

4. **Core is to center as**
   (A) angle is to acute
   (B) cliff is to steep
   (C) edge is to border
   (D) circumference is to circle
   (E) sharp is to dull

5. **Engine is to jet as paddle is to**
   (A) swim
   (B) reprimand
   (C) ball
   (D) boat
   (E) otter

6. **Pound is to weight as**
   (A) radius is to point
   (B) diameter is to across
   (C) height is to inch
   (D) mile is to measure
   (E) ounce is to volume

7. **Portray is to depict as**
   (A) swindle is to cheat
   (B) influence is to bribe
   (C) behave is to decide
   (D) affirm is to deny
   (E) determine is to subvert

8. **Claw is to lobster as**
   (A) callous is to hand
   (B) paw is to bear
   (C) tail is to monkey
   (D) ink is to octopus
   (E) elephant is to trunk

9. **Inquire is to ask as acquire is to**
   (A) obtain
   (B) take
   (C) agree
   (D) concede
   (E) leave

10. **Wool is to sweater as**
    (A) cotton is to soft
    (B) denim is to jeans
    (C) house is to wood
    (D) container is to store
    (E) leather is to rugged

Answers and Explanations

1. **B is correct**. The relationship presented in this sequence is one of object to use. A *file* is used to *smooth* a rough surface, just as *tape* is used to *record* audio or video signals.

2. **D is correct**. This analogy is one of usage. People read a *novel*, and other works of fiction, to be *entertained*. Similarly, people read a *newspaper* in order to be *informed* about issues and events of importance.

3. **C is correct**. Initially, the relationship in this sequence may strike you as one of part to whole. However, you will need to take the analogy one step further in order to arrive at the correct answer. *Bray* is the name given to the sound a *donkey* makes just as *quack* is the name given to the sound a *duck* makes.

4. **C is correct**. This sequence tests your knowledge of synonyms. *Core* means the same as *center* in the same way that *edge* means the same as *border*.

5. **D is correct**. This is a part-to-whole analogy. An *engine* propels a *jet* just as a *paddle* propels a *boat*. An *otter* may also use its tail as a *paddle* to navigate; however, both a jet and a boat are vehicles while an otter is an animal. This distinction makes *boat* a better answer than *otter*.

6. **E is correct**. This analogy tests your knowledge of measurement units. *Weight* is measured in *pounds* and *volume* is measured in *ounces*. Choice C is incorrect because the order is reversed.

7. **A is correct.** The analogy presented in this sequence is one of synonyms. When you *portray* someone you are *depicting* that person. Similarly, when you *swindle* someone you are *cheating* that person.

8. **B is correct**. This is a part-to-whole analogy. However, in order to arrive at the correct answer, you will have to take the comparison to a second step. A *lobster* has a *claw* for a hand just as a *bear* has a *paw* for a hand. No other choice provides a similar comparison.

9. **A is correct**. This sequence tests your knowledge of synonyms. When you *inquire* about something, you *ask* about it. Similarly, when you *acquire* an item you *obtain* it. None of the other options is a synonym for *acquire*.

10. **B is correct**. In order to arrive at the correct answer for this analogy, you will have to conclude that the relationship between the first two

words is that *sweaters* are often made out of *wool*. Similarly, you will have to recognize that *jeans* are most often made from *denim*. Choice C cannot be correct because the relationship between the two words is reversed.

Practice Set B

Directions: The questions that follow ask you to find relationships between words. For each question, select the answer choice that best completes the meaning of the sentence.

Example:
Chapter is to book as
(A) note is to letter
(B) scene is to play
(C) story is to novel
(D) writer is to director
(E) reader is to audience
Correct Answer: B

A *chapter* is a division of a *book* and a *scene* is a division of a *play*.

1. **Card is to deck as**
    (A) note is to symphony
    (B) garden is to flower
    (C) sun is to shine
    (D) box is to handle
    (E) cupboard is to dish

2. **Flicker is to blaze**
    (A) pace is to walk
    (B) gasp is to frighten
    (C) toss is to lob
    (D) trickle is to flow
    (E) crease is to fold

3. **Disinfectant is to cut as detergent is to**
    (A) teeth
    (B) hands
    (C) sink
    (D) dry
    (E) laundry

4. **Clock is to time as**
   (A) height is to inch
   (B) thermometer is to temperature
   (C) weight is to mass
   (D) length is to width
   (E) second is to minute

5. **Cap is to bottle as**
   (A) lid is to pot
   (B) house is to roof
   (C) handle is to pitcher
   (D) heat is to steam
   (E) head is to hat

6. **Tomato is to vine as**
   (A) apple is to stem
   (B) grape is to seed
   (C) stalk is to corn
   (D) vanilla is to bean
   (E) coconut is to tree

7. **Salve is to balm as**
   (A) snake is to bite
   (B) sentry is to guard
   (C) choke is to suffocate
   (D) thorn is to prickly
   (E) oil is to filter

8. **Storm is to flood as fire is to**
   (A) water
   (B) food
   (C) heat
   (D) weapon
   (E) attack

9. **Pedestrian is to original as**
   (A) bright is to brilliant
   (B) stable is to variable
   (C) insolent is to rude
   (D) foolish is to absurd
   (E) critical is to wise

10. **Golfer is to club as**
   (A) dentist is to teeth
   (B) boxer is to ring
   (C) teacher is to student
   (D) carpenter is to wood
   (E) surgeon is to scalpel

Answers and Explanations

1. **A is correct.** The relationship provided in this sequence is one of part to whole. A *card* is part of a *deck* just as a *note* is part of a *symphony*. Choices B and D are incorrect because the relationship in each choice is inverted—that is, the whole comes before the part.

2. **D is correct.** The comparison in this sequence is one of degrees of contrast. To *flicker* is to "burn unsteadily or fitfully," while to *blaze* is to "shine brightly." Similarly, to *trickle* is to "run slowly and unsteadily," while to *flow* is to "pour forth in a steady stream."

3. **E is correct.** The analogy presented in this question is one of object to use. *Disinfectant* is used to clean a *cut* or wound, just as *detergent* is used to clean *laundry*.

4. **B is correct.** This analogy asks you to identify a measurement and the object used to register the measurement. A *clock* measures *time* just as a *thermometer* measures *temperature*. Choice A is incorrect because the order of the comparison is reversed.

5. **A is correct.** In order to arrive at the correct answer for this part-to-whole analogy, you will have to take the comparison a step further. Several of the answer choices offer sequences that are part to whole, however, only choice A is correct. A *cap* is placed on top of a *bottle* just as a *lid* is placed on top of a *pot*. Choices B and E are incorrect because they invert the order, and choice C is incorrect because a *handle* is located on the side (rather than the top) of a pitcher.

6. **E is correct.** To answer this analogy correctly, you will need to know that a *tomato* grows on a *vine*. Of the answer choices available, only choice E is correct; a *coconut* grows on a *tree*.

7. **B is correct.** This sequence tests your knowledge of synonyms. Both *salve* and *balm* are oils or resins that are rubbed onto the skin to soothe, heal, or comfort. Likewise, both a *sentry* and a *guard* are people who are posted at a given spot to monitor activity and prevent the passage of unauthorized persons.

8. **C is correct.** The relationship in the question is one of cause and effect. A *storm* is the cause and a *flood* the effect. Similarly, *fire* is the cause and *heat* the effect.

9. **B is correct.** The relationship in this analogy is one of contrast. *Pedestrian*, which means "commonplace" or "ordinary" is the opposite

of *original*, which means "fresh and new." In the same way, *stable*, which means "static" or "unchangeable," is the opposite of *variable*, which means "inconstant" or "changeable."

10. **E is correct.** This analogy is one of individual to object. The tool used by a *golfer* is a *club* just as the tool used by a *surgeon* is a *scalpel*. No other choice reflects this relationship.

CHAPTER 6

Strategies for Sentence Completion Questions (ISEE Only)

Sentence completion questions account for 20 of the 40 questions in the Verbal Reasoning section of the ISEE. There are no sentence completion questions on the SSAT, so you can skip this chapter if you are preparing to take the SSAT.

Sentence completion questions are designed to test your knowledge of word meanings along with your ability to understand the logical structure of a sentence. On the ISEE, sentence completion questions are arranged in order of difficulty from easiest to hardest.

Format of Sentence Completion Questions

Each sentence completion question consists of a statement with one or two blanks. Each blank indicates a missing word. Following each sentence are four words or sets of words labeled (A), (B), (C), and (D). You are to select the word or set of words that, when inserted in the sentence, best fits the meaning of the sentence as a whole.

Often more than one pair of words among the answer choices will fit the structure of the sentence that appears in the question stem. However, in order to answer sentence completion questions correctly, you must determine which pair of words *best* completes the meaning of the sentence. To do this, you must consider both word meaning and logic.

ISEE Coach Says . . .

Sentence completion questions come after synonyms in the ISEE Verbal Reasoning section, but you can choose to do these questions first if you find them easier to answer.

Sample Sentence Completion Question Explained

Let's look at a sample question to see what's involved.

Although she was habitually _____, Jenna was first in line when the concert tickets went on sale.
(A) aloof
(B) impatient
(C) tardy
(D) realistic

The word *although* provides an important clue that this sentence involves a contrast. The sentence says that Jenna did something different from her usual habit. That means you are looking for a word that is the opposite of being "first in line" for tickets. Now look at each of the answer choices to find the one that best reflects this relationship.

(A) *Aloof* means "distant" or "reserved." It could be correct, but *aloof* is not really the opposite of being "first in line," so keep looking for a better answer.

(B) *Impatient* means "eager" or "excitable," which is similar to the idea of wanting to be "first in line," so you can eliminate this choice.

(C) *Tardy* means "late." Someone who is always late is not likely to be "first in line." That makes *tardy* a better choice than *aloof*, and (C) is the best answer.

(D) *Realistic* means "practical," which has nothing to do with being "first in line."

Strategies for Answering Sentence Completion Questions

Here is a six-step strategic plan that you can use to answer sentence completion questions.

1. Read the sentence to get the overall meaning.
2. Look for clue words that show how sentence parts are related.
3. Use the clue words to anticipate the answer based on the relationship indicated.
4. Read the answer choices and select the one that is best.
5. Check your answer by reading the sentence with your answer choice in place.
6. If you still cannot determine the correct answer, eliminate answer choices that do not make sense. Then, guess from among the remaining answer choices.

> **ISEE Coach Says . . .**
> Circle clue words in your test book that show relationships.

Using Clue Words

Use this chart to help you determine how sentence parts are frequently related in sentence completion questions.

Logical Relationship	Clues
Contrasting ideas *Even though the plane was late taking off, we arrived at our destination right on time.*	although, but, despite, even though, however, instead of, nonetheless, not, on the contrary, rather, yet
Complementary ideas *The hurricane destroyed homes all along the coastline; furthermore, it knocked down power lines, leaving millions without electricity.*	additionally, also, and, because, besides, consequently, for, furthermore, likewise, moreover, similarly
Cause and effect *Because they were so hot and thirsty after the ballgame, they could hardly wait to get a cold drink from the picnic cooler.*	accordingly, because, consequently, for, hence, in order to, since, so, therefore, thus
Definition or explanation *Maria was extremely unselfish, willing to share even her most prized possessions with her friends.*	comma, semicolon, colon

Use the six-step strategy and what you have learned about sentence logic to answer the practice sentence completion questions that follow. Then compare your answer to the explanation given.

Sample Sentence Completion Question Set Explained

Directions: Each sentence below has one or two blanks. Each blank indicates that something is missing. Following each sentence are four words or sets of words labeled (A), (B), (C), and (D). You are to select the word or set of words that, when inserted in the sentence, best fits the meaning of the sentence as a whole.

ISEE Coach Says . . .
In choosing your answer, consider both word meaning and logic.

---

1. Carl had a reputation for being a _____ because he fearlessly skied down the steepest trails.
   (A) leader
   (B) dreamer
   (C) clown
   (D) daredevil

1. **D is correct.** The word *because* is a clue that the sentence shows a cause-and-effect relationship. Skiing fearlessly down the steepest trails is likely to earn someone the reputation for being a *daredevil*. No other answer choice makes sense in this context.

ISEE Coach Says...
Remember that words such as *because, for,* and *since* often signal that a sentence completion question has a structure based on cause and effect, so look for words that express an expected causal relationship.

---

2. The model of _____, he displayed impeccable manners and excellent taste.
   (A) duplicity
   (B) decorum
   (C) depravity
   (D) versatility

2. **B is correct.** The comma in this sentence completion question is a clue that the missing word means the same as "impeccable manners and excellent taste." *Decorum*, which means "propriety and good taste in behavior, speech, or dress," is the best choice. Choices A, C, and D are all wrong because they have nothing to do with good manners or taste. *Duplicity* (choice A) means "cunning or deception." *Depravity* (choice C) means "corruption or wickedness." *Versatility* (choice D) means "ability to do many things."

ISEE Coach Says...
Remember that the use of a comma may signal that a sentence completion question has a structure based on definition.

---

3. The directions to the airport were _____; consequently we missed our flight and had to stay an extra day.
   (A) clear
   (B) convenient
   (C) confusing
   (D) expert

3. **C is correct.** This question asks you to find complementary, rather than contrasting, statements. Directions that are *confusing* are most likely to result in a missed flight.

ISEE Coach Says...
Remember that words such as *additionally, consequently, besides, so,* and *also* often signal that a sentence completion question has a structure based on complementary ideas. With these questions, look for words among the answer choices that best complete the meaning of the sentence.

---

4. Easy-to-reach by car, the house was also _____ by public transportation.
   - (A) accessible
   - (B) isolated
   - (C) enhanced
   - (D) hindered

4. **A is correct.** This question asks you to find complementary, rather than contrasting, ideas. The word *also* is a clue that the word you are looking for is a word that is similar to or supports *easy-to-reach*. The best choice is *accessible*, which means "approachable" or "capable of being reached."

5. The detectives believed that the fingerprint on the glass was _____ evidence; it definitely placed the defendant at the scene of the crime.
   - (A) negligible
   - (B) incorrigible
   - (C) incriminating
   - (D) inevitable

5. **C is correct.** The semicolon is a clue that the second part of the sentence describes or explains the first part of the sentence. Evidence that places someone at the scene of a crime is *incriminating*; it involves the person and makes that person look guilty.

   (A) is wrong because *negligible* means "trifling or unimportant." Choice B is wrong because *incorrigible* means "incapable of being corrected or improved." Choice D is wrong because *inevitable* means "unavoidable."

ISEE Coach Says . . .
Remember that sentence completion questions arc generally arranged in order of difficulty, from easiest to hardest. Pace yourself accordingly.

---

6. Despite our best efforts to protect the environment and keep it safe, until the problems of pollution are _____, the future of our environment seems, at best, _____.
   - (A) created . . . gloomy
   - (B) revoked . . . secure
   - (C) solved . . . uncertain
   - (D) replaced . . . revered

6. **C is correct.** *Despite* is a clue that the sentence sets up a contrast. We want to keep the environment safe, but there are problems with pollution. The first blank requires a word that tells what we want to do about the problems of pollution. The best choice is to end them or solve them as in choice C. Until those problems can be *solved*, the future of the environment is not safe, but rather it is *uncertain*.

   Choice A can be eliminated because the first word makes no sense in the first blank. Choices B and D can be eliminated because the second word does not work in the second blank.

7. Knowledgeable dog owners recommend obtaining a purebred dog from a _____ breeder, one who is _____ and respected by customers and breeders alike.

(A) humble . . . feared
(B) demanding . . . flexible
(C) churlish . . . charming
(D) reputable . . . admired

7. **D is correct.** The comma following the word *breeder* is a clue that the words that follow will define or explain what kind of breeder is recommended. Only choice D provides two words that can define or explain each other. A *reputable* breeder is one who is *admired* and respected.

Choice A is wrong because a *humble* breeder is not likely to be *feared*. Choice B is wrong because a *demanding* breeder is not likely to be *flexible*. Choice C is wrong because a *churlish* (rude or boorish) breeder is not likely to be *charming*.

On Your Own

Now take the time to apply what you have just learned about the structure and types of sentence completion questions to see how well you can use the strategies. When you are finished, use the answer key to score your work.

You may find that certain types of structure are easier for you to deal with than others. Remember that sentence completion questions appear in order of their difficulty. Use Practice Set A to determine which types of questions give you the most difficulty.

Review the strategies and clues discussed above and then try Practice Set B, focusing on the kinds of items that you found difficult. Remember that the more you practice with these items, the easier they will become for you to answer correctly.

Practice Set A

1. Knowing that her dental appointment might run late, Donelle made _____ plans to get together with Irene afterward.
(A) absurd
(B) tentative
(C) authoritative
(D) cantankerous

2. The critic dismissed the movie as _____ because of its unlikely plot and improbable dialogue.
(A) banal
(B) articulate
(C) boisterous
(D) hallowed

3. Both _____ and _____, Mrs. Dowd is typically full of enthusiasm and enjoys being around people.
(A) fervent . . . effervescent
(B) outgoing . . . flippant
(C) impervious . . . cordial
(D) cheerful . . . extroverted

4. As a way to _____ the undefeated season, the booster club presented the coach with a plaque engraved with all of the team's winning scores.
(A) convene
(B) contend
(C) ascertain
(D) commemorate

5. The concert featured a number of _____ jazz compositions, and for fans of the music, the evening was an example of harmonic _____.
    (A) spirited . . . bile
    (B) vivacious . . . impasse
    (C) vibrant . . . bliss
    (D) choleric . . . euphoria

6. Many historians of the nineteenth century believe that the railroad was the _____ of the future, the first sign of the coming of the Industrial Revolution.
    (A) bravado
    (B) harbinger
    (C) debt
    (D) entourage

7. Despite being in training, Elise knew she would soon _____ to the temptation of her mother's freshly baked cookies.
    (A) reckon
    (B) yield
    (C) obstruct
    (D) suppress

8. Unable to _____ the jury to believe his sketchy alibi, the defendant finally acknowledged committing the crimes he stood accused of.
    (A) induce
    (B) imply
    (C) deplore
    (D) raze

9. Having achieved enormous success with his books, J. D. Salinger quit publishing his work, hid from public view, and became literature's most famous _____.
    (A) reminiscence
    (B) shanty
    (C) surrogate
    (D) recluse

10. Although at first the senator had been one of the candidate's most _____ supporters, her support waned as the candidate's _____ voting record came to light.
    (A) ardent . . . dubious
    (B) facetious . . . undependable
    (C) impassioned . . . indisputable
    (D) bereft . . . suspect

Answers and Explanations

1. **B is correct.** *Tentative*, meaning "not fully worked out, concluded, or agreed on," is the only choice that supports the information in the sentence that the girls' plans had not been finalized.

2. **A is correct.** Because the movie features "an unlikely plot and improbable dialogue," you should be able to conclude that the critic did not like it very much. Of the four choices, *banal* (choice A), meaning "drearily commonplace and often predictable," has the strongest negative connotation.

3. **D is correct.** This type of question is known as a vocabulary-in-context question. The key to solving this type of question is to recognize that the meanings of the words you are looking for are located in the sentence. Because Mrs. Dowd is described as "typically full of enthusiasm and enjoys being around people," you should look for words that have meanings that reflect these characteristics. *Cheerful*, meaning "happy," and *extroverted*, meaning "outgoing and interested in others," is the only word pair that works in both blanks.

4. **D is correct.** Sometimes it is helpful to come up with an answer to a sentence completion question on your own, without even looking at the answer choices. For this sentence, you might come up with *mark* or *celebrate*. Now, look at the answer choices and choose the one that is closest in meaning to the words you thought of. *Commemorate*, meaning "to serve as a memorial to," is correct.

5. **C is correct.** It is often easier to solve two-blank sentence completion questions by focusing on one of the blanks and eliminating any obviously wrong answers. Looking at the first blank, you should be able to eliminate *choleric* (choice D), meaning "easily angered or bad tempered." Choices A, B, and C all offer positive words to describe the jazz compositions. Thus the sense of the sentence requires a positive word for the second blank as well. Only choice C provides two positive words and it is the best choice.

6. **B is correct.** The comma is a clue that the words that follow will define or explain the missing word. The word that means the same as "a sign of something to come" is *harbinger*. As used in the context of this sentence, many historians believe that the railroad was the true indication of the coming Industrial Revolution. None of the other answer choices makes sense.

7. **B is correct.** The logic of the sentence indicates that despite the fact that Elise was in training, she knew that she would soon give in to the temptation of her mother's cookies. *Yield* (choice B) meaning "to give up," "to surrender" or "to submit," is the correct answer.

8. **A is correct.** The logic of this question indicates that the defendant was unable to influence the jury or convince them to accept his weak alibi. Since neither *influence* nor *convince* is among the answer

choices, you want to try to select the word you believe comes closest in meaning. *Induce* (choice A) meaning "to lead or move, as to a course of action, by influence or persuasion," is correct.

9. **D is correct.** Knowing the definitions of the words you have to choose from will help you select the correct answer to this question. Someone who withdraws from the world to live in seclusion is a recluse. Thus, choice D is the only possible answer.

10. **A is correct.** Be on the lookout for sentences that feature words and phrases such as "although," "despite," "even though," and "in spite of." Typically, these words are a sign that the sentence contains two contrasting ideas. Starting with the first blank, you can immediately eliminate choices B and D since neither *facetious*, which means "humorous," nor *bereft*, which means "deprived" or "sorrowful," makes sense as a description of a supporter. What kind of voting record is more likely to make an ardent or an impassioned supporter withdraw that support? A *dubious* record, meaning "one that is open to doubt or suspicion," or an *indisputable* record, meaning "one that is impossible to doubt"? Clearly, *dubious* is the best answer and choice A is correct.

Practice Set B

Directions: Each sentence below has one or two blanks. Each blank indicates that something is missing. Following each sentence are four words or sets of words labeled (A), (B), (C), (D), and (E). You are to select the word or set of words that, when inserted in the sentence, best fits the meaning of the sentence as a whole.

Example:
1. Despite our best efforts to protect the environment and keep it safe, until the problems of pollution are _____, the future of our environment seems, at best, _____.
    (A) created...gloomy
    (B) revoked . . . secure
    (C) solved . . . uncertain
    (D) replaced . . . revered

Correct Answer: C

1. Before she opened her boutique, Jocelyn used to _____ the jewelry she made at flea markets and bazaars.
    (A) inhibit
    (B) entice
    (C) peddle
    (D) emulate

2. The _____ of traveling to see the Aurora Borealis is that while the spectacular display is well worth the trip, it is impossible to predict whether the event will take place during your travels.
   (A) configuration
   (B) prestige
   (C) ingenuity
   (D) paradox

3. Although the manager's relationship with her assistant had never turned intolerable it had always been _____ at best.
   (A) cordial
   (B) staunch
   (C) tempestuous
   (D) tenacious

4. Before the book was _____, references to several living people were

   _____.
   (A) banned . . . deleted
   (B) published . . . expunged
   (C) printed . . . informed
   (D) reviewed . . . added

5. One of the most _____ songwriters of her generation, Joni Mitchell has written and recorded over 300 songs since 1968.
   (A) regal
   (B) independent
   (C) prolific
   (D) pretentious

6. The teacher had refused to disclose what would be on the test, but as far as the students could _____, it would cover everything since the midterm.
   (A) propose
   (B) deject
   (C) grovel
   (D) surmise

7. In his prime, Muhammad Ali was a _____ boxer whose ability to land a knockout punch inspired fear and commanded respect among his opponents.
   (A) scathing
   (B) ostentatious
   (C) obtuse
   (D) formidable

8. After the spelling bee's nerve-wracking final round, Sheila could only _____ at her competitor's composure.
   (A) lunge
   (B) stipulate
   (C) marvel
   (D) wander

9. The scholarly and thoughtful mayor was well known for her _____ disposition.
   (A) insurgent
   (B) judicious
   (C) lenient
   (D) kinetic

10. Although the scientist's _____ was that the results could be duplicated, the review board did not find her theory _____.
    (A) assertion . . . celestial
    (B) contention . . . plausible
    (C) enigma . . . credible
    (D) avowal . . . eminent

Answers and Explanations

1. **C is correct.** The message that this sentence conveys is that before Jocelyn opened her boutique, she used to travel from place to place to sell her jewelry. *Peddle* (choice C), meaning "to travel about selling wares," is correct.

2. **D is correct.** The logic of this sentence is based on the problem that it is worth traveling to see the Aurora Borealis, but you cannot predict if the spectacular display will take place during your travels. A *paradox* (choice D) is "a seemingly contradictory statement that may nonetheless be true." Therefore, choice D is correct.

3. **C is correct.** The key to this question are the phrases "had never turned intolerable" and "at best." With these clues, you should be able to conclude that the word you are looking for is not as extreme as "intolerable." Tempestuous (choice C), meaning "tumultuous or stormy," is the correct answer.

4. **B is correct.** The key word in this sentence is "before," which sets up a logical structure for the sentence and tells you that before *this* can occur, *that* must occur. Choice A can be discounted almost immediately because names do not have to be deleted before a book is banned. Choice D is incorrect because by the time a book is reviewed, it is too late to add any material to the manuscript. Choice C is wrong because a reference is an inanimate object, and therefore cannot be informed of anything. Choice B is correct.

5. **C is correct.** The word you are looking for should reflect the information the sentence provides—that Joni Mitchell has written over 300 songs since 1968. *Prolific* (choice C), meaning "producing abundant works or results," is the choice that best fits the sentence's context.

6. **D is correct.** Sometimes supplying your own answer before looking at the options can help you determine the right choice. Perhaps you came up with the word "guess" or "infer." Even if you don't know the correct answer, you should be able to eliminate some choices that are clearly wrong. *Surmise* (choice D), meaning "to infer (something) without sufficiently conclusive evidence," is correct.

7. **D is correct.** The word you are looking for is one that means "inspired fear and commanded respect." *Formidable* (choice D), meaning "arousing fear, dread, or alarm," is the correct choice.

8. **C is correct.** *Wander* (choice D) is an attractive distracter, but don't mistake it for "wonder." *Wonder* means "to be filled with curiosity or doubt," but *wander* means "to move about without a definite destination or purpose." *Marvel* (choice C), meaning "to become filled with wonder or astonishment," is the correct answer.

9. **B is correct.** The clue to this sentence is the phrase "scholarly and thoughtful," because the correct answer will likely have a definition that supports this description of the mayor. *Judicious* (choice B), meaning "sensible," "prudent," or "wise," is correct.

10. **B is correct.** Try focusing on the second blank and eliminating any obviously wrong answers. Neither *celestial* (choice A), meaning "of or relating to the sky or the heavens," nor *eminent* (choice D), meaning "prominent" or "towering above others," seem to fit the context of the sentence, and both can be discounted. Turning your attention to the first blank, you should be able to conclude that *contention* (choice B), meaning "an assertion put forward in an argument," is a better choice than *enigma* (choice C), meaning "one that is puzzling, ambiguous, or inexplicable."

Strategies for Reading Comprehension Questions

Reading comprehension is tested on both the SSAT and the ISEE. Each exam includes one Reading Comprehension section consisting of 40 questions based on six to eight reading passages. The passages can be as short as 100 words or as long as 500 words. They cover a variety of categories from the fields of the humanities (literature, art biography, poetry), social studies (history, economics, sociology), and science (medicine, meteorology, zoology). Each passage is followed by four to seven questions based on its content.

Types of Reading Comprehension Questions

Whatever the subject matter of the reading passages on your test, the questions you will have to answer will fall into one of the following major categories:

- *Main Idea Questions*—test your ability to select the main idea in the passage, to determine the purpose of the passage, or to select the best title for a passage.
- *Detail Questions*—test your ability to understand specific references or to identify specific things about a passage.
- *Inference Questions*—test your ability to see relationships between ideas or to make assumptions based on information provided by the passage.
- *Tone or Mood Questions*—test your ability to determine the tone or mood of the passage, to tell whether it is serious or humorous, formal or informal, personal or impersonal for example.
- *Vocabulary Questions*—test your ability to determine the meaning of words based on their use in the passage.
- *Organization or Logic Questions*—test your ability to recognize how a passage is organized or to follow an author's logic.

Each question is followed by four answer choices (on the ISEE) or five answer choices (on the SSAT). Your job is to identify the best answer from among the choices presented.

How to Answer Reading Comprehension Questions

Here's a helpful four-step plan that you can use for answering reading comprehension questions.

1. Skim the questions to focus on the information you will need. Ignore the answer choices for now.
2. Read the passage to get the big picture.
   - Ask yourself: What's this passage all about? Why did the author write it?
   - Mark up the passage or make notes in the margin as you read.
3. Read the questions with the answer choices.
   - Choose the answer if you know it.
   - If not, go back to the passage to find it.
   - Use line references to help locate information.
   - Cross out answer choices you can definitely eliminate.
4. Answer every question on the ISEE, even if you have to guess. On the SSAT, guess if you can eliminate even one or two of the answer choices.
   - Try to answer all the questions based on a reading passage the first time around.
   - If you have to go back to an unanswered question, you'll have to reread the passage, which takes valuable time.

Remember:

- Long passages tend to be harder than short ones, so start with the shortest passage and leave the longest one for last.
- The answer to a reading question can be found in or inferred from the passage.
- An answer choice that is true is not necessarily the correct answer. The correct choice must be both a true statement and the one that best answers the question.
- When a question refers to a numbered line go back to the passage and read the information around the line reference. It will clarify the question and help you choose the best answer.
- Read the passage. Don't try to memorize it.

Sample Reading Comprehension Question Set Explained

Here is a sample reading passage with questions illustrating each of the six most common types of reading questions. Read the passage first. Then answer the questions based on what is stated or implied in the passage.

Can you imagine shoppers lining up just to buy ballpoint pens? It happened at Gimbel's Department Store in New York City in October 1945. Gimbel's sold out its entire stock of 10,000 pens on the very first day ballpoint pens were sold commercially anywhere in the United States.

Before 1945, most people wrote with fountain pens. The biggest problem with a fountain pen is that it has to be filled, sometimes more than once a day. The ballpoint pen solved this problem. However, it took nearly 60 years for inventors to get it to work properly.

In a ballpoint pen, the writing tip is a tiny ball that rolls as you write. Part of the ball is inside the pen and picks up ink from the ink supply. As the ball rolls, the ink-covered part rolls outside. The ink then flows from the ball to the paper you are writing on.

Inventors had been working on ballpoint pens since 1888 when John Loud, an American leather tanner, patented a marking pen with a roller ball tip. Loud's rolling ball pen was never produced, nor were any of the other 350 patents for ball-type pens issued over the next 50 years. The major problem with all these pens was the ink. If the ink was too watery, the pens would leak. If the ink was too thick, it would harden inside the pen. Depending on the temperature, the ink would sometimes do both. Ballpoint pens had another problem, too. Because they depended on gravity to carry the ink down to the rolling ball at the bottom of the pen, ballpoints had to be held straight up, but most people tilt a pen when they write.

Two Hungarian brothers, Georg and Ladislas Biro, found the solution to both problems. Working as a journalist, Georg Biro noticed that newspaper ink dried quickly, leaving the paper smudge-free. This gave him the idea to use this syrupy ink for pens. However, the thicker ink would not flow from a regular metal tip, so he fitted his pen with a ball bearing that acted like a sponge. The roller ball soaked up ink from the tube inside the pen. Now the pen could be held at an angle.

The Biro brothers filed a patent for their ballpoint pen in Paris in 1938, just after they escaped the Nazi regime in Hungary. They emigrated to Argentina and established a successful business selling pens that could "write for a year without refilling." In 1945, Milton Reynolds, a Chicago businessman, discovered the Biro brothers' invention while vacationing in Argentina. Ignoring patent rights, Reynolds copied the Biro design and in less than four months the Reynolds Pen Company was manufacturing millions of ballpoint pens. Reynolds signed a deal with Gimbel's, making it the first retail store in America to sell his pens. Gimbel's took out a full-page ad in *The New York Times* to advertise the "fantastic . . . miraculous . . . guaranteed" new pens for $12.50. Five thousand people crowded the sidewalk before the store opened the next day, and Gimbel's sold all 10,000 pens before the end of the day. Within a few years, the pen that took over 50 years to reach the market would become the most used pen in the world.

SSAT/ISEE Coach Says . . .
Feel free to mark up the passage as you read. Highlight main ideas, important supporting details, and words that indicate special relationships.

1. Which of the following is the best title for this selection?
   (A) A Short History of the Ballpoint Pen
   (B) The Biro Brothers: Millions of Dollars from Millions of Pens
   (C) Ballpoint Pens Change Writing Habits around the World
   (D) Miraculous Writing Tool Sweeps the Nation
   (E) How Gimbel's Sold Thousands of Ballpoint Pens

This is a **main idea question**. A good title suggests both the topic and the purpose of a selection. In this case the topic is the ballpoint pen and the purpose is to provide a brief history of its development from the marking pen invented by John Loud in 1888 to the Brio pen patented in 1938 to the Reynolds pen sold at Gimbel's in 1945. Choice A is the best title for this selection.

Choice B is wrong because it concerns only the Biro brothers, and the one who seemed to make millions of pens was Milton Reynolds.

Choice C is wrong because the article never explains how ballpoint pens changed writing habits around the world.

Choice D is wrong because the passage does not focus on how a miraculous writing tool swept the nation.

Choice E is wrong because Gimbel's is the focus of only the first and last paragraphs, not of the passage as a whole.

SSAT/ISEE Coach Says . . .
Remember that virtually every sentence in a well-written passage relates to the main idea.

---

2. From the passage you can infer that after 1945
   (A) fountain pens became cheaper and more reliable
   (B) people spent more time writing, since they didn't have to refill their pens
   (C) people used fewer fountain pens
   (D) people got used to holding pens straight up when they wrote
   (E) expensive ballpoint pens became a status symbol

This **inference question** asks you to draw a conclusion based on the information that is given in the passage. According to the passage, before 1945 "most people wrote with fountain pens." Now, however, the ballpoint pen has become "the most used pen in the world." From this information, you can reasonably conclude that with the growing popularity of the ballpoint pen fewer and fewer fountain pens were used in the years after 1945.

Choice C is the correct answer.

Choices A, B, and E are not supported by information in the passage.

Choice D is mentioned as one of the problems of ballpoint pens that was resolved by the Biro brothers.

3. According to the article, which is true about the ink used in newspaper printing compared to the ink used in fountain pens?
   (A) It is cheaper.
   (B) It is thinner.
   (C) It hardens inside the pen.
   (D) It dries mores quickly.
   (E) It smudges more easily.

This **detail question** asks you to locate a particular piece of information in the passage. Newspaper ink is mentioned in the fifth paragraph. "Working as a journalist, Georg Biro noticed that newspaper ink dried quickly, leaving the paper smudge-free." Thus choice D is the best answer.

Choice A is incorrect because the passage never mentions the cost of the ink.

Choice B is incorrect because the passage mentions that the "syrupy" newspaper ink was thicker than fountain pen ink.

Choice C is incorrect because the passage mentions that one of the problems Biro solved by using newspaper ink was the problem of the ink hardening inside the pen.

Choice E is incorrect because the passage states that the newspaper ink "dried quickly, leaving the paper smudge-free."

SSAT/ISEE Coach Says . . .
Locate the key words "newspaper ink" and then read the surrounding sentences to find your answer.

4. The tone of the passage indicates that the author considers the invention of the ballpoint pen to be
   (A) insignificant
   (B) impressive
   (C) unfortunate
   (D) miraculous
   (E) disappointing

This is a **tone question**. It asks you to determine the author's attitude or point of view toward the topic. Tone is revealed by the author's choice of words and details. In this passage, phrases such as "Gimbel's sold out its entire stock of 10,000 pens on the very first day," "it took nearly 60 years for inventors to get it to work properly," "five thousand people crowded the sidewalk," and "within a few years, the pen that took over 50 years to reach the market would become the most used pen in the world" suggest that the author thought the invention of the ballpoint pen was a notable or impressive achievement. Choice B is correct.

Choices A, C, and E are incorrect because they are negative words, and the author obviously has a positive attitude toward the invention of the ball-point pen.

Choice D reflects a positive attitude, but it is too extreme to describe this account of the history of the ballpoint pen.

SSAT/ISEE Coach Says . . .

Look carefully at the way the author uses words.

---

5. In this passage, the term "patent" refers to
    (A) a ballpoint pen
    (B) a fountain pen
    (C) John Loud's marking pen
    (D) a license or exclusive right for an invention
    (E) a pen that could write for a year without refilling

This is a **vocabulary question**. The word "patent" appears several times in this passage: John Loud "patented a marking pen," the Biro brothers "filed a patent for their ballpoint pen," Milton Reynolds ignored "patent rights." From these uses you should be able to conclude that a patent is a license or an exclusive right for a new product or process. Choice D is correct.

SSAT/ISEE Coach Says . . .

Substituting each answer choice in the original sentences is helpful in eliminating some obviously wrong answers.

---

6. Which of the following best describes the relationship of the first paragraph to the passage as a whole?
    (A) The first paragraph presents an interesting anecdote that introduces the topic of the selection.
    (B) The first paragraph begins a chronological look at the development of the ballpoint pen.
    (C) The first paragraph identifies key developments that are explained in the rest of the selection.
    (D) The first paragraph presents a theory about ballpoint pens that is proved by the rest of the selection.
    (E) The first paragraph criticizes early attempts at the development of the ballpoint pen.

This **organization question** tests your ability to recognize how the author has organized a passage. In this case, the first paragraph tells what happened when ballpoint pens were first offered for sale in the United States. This anecdote is intended to catch the reader's interest, which it does by creating the image of thousands of people waiting in line to buy ballpoint pens, and to introduce the topic of the selection, which is the development of these pens. Choice A is correct.

Choice B is wrong because the passage begins with the successful introduction of the ballpoint pen and then goes back in time to show how the pen was developed.

Choices C and D are wrong because the paragraph is not a presentation of key development nor of a theory.

Choice E is wrong because the paragraph is not critical of early attempts to develop the ballpoint pen.

SSAT/ISEE Coach Says . . .

Go back and reread the lines referenced in the question.

Vocabulary-in-Context Questions

Some reading comprehension questions ask you to define the meaning of a word as it is used in the context of the passage that you have read. Such vocabulary-in-context questions will always give you a line indicator or a paragraph reference so that you can easily find the word in the passage.

Some vocabulary-in-context questions deal with difficult words that you likely do not know. In other cases, a vocabulary-in-context question will be about an unusual meaning of an easier, familiar word. Regardless of which type of vocabulary-in-context question that you are dealing with, your goal is always the same: find the meaning of the word as it is used within the context of the passage.

Strategies for Vocabulary-in-Context Questions

Below you will find four simple strategies that will help you to answer vocabulary-in-context questions correctly.

1. Use the line reference to locate the word.
2. Read the entire sentence.
3. Try to come up with a synonym on your own, and then look for your word among the answer choices.
4. If you can't come up with a synonym, try substituting each answer choice in the original sentence to see which one makes the most sense.

Sample Vocabulary-in-Context Questions Explained

Use the vocabulary strategies you studied earlier to answer the sample questions that follow the passage.

Directions: The passage below is followed by questions based on its content. Answer each question on the basis of what is stated or implied in the passage and the introductory material.

Questions 1–3 are based on the following passage.

Participation in regular physical activity—at least 30 minutes of moderate activity on at least five days per week, or 20 minutes of vigorous physical activity at least three times per week—is critical to sustaining good health. Youth should strive for at least one hour of exercise a day. Regular physical
5　activity has beneficial effects on most (if not all) organ systems, and consequently it helps prevent a broad range of health problems and diseases. People of all ages, both male and female, derive substantial health benefits from physical activity.

Regular physical activity can help improve the lives of young people
10　beyond its effects on physical health. Although research has not been conducted to conclusively demonstrate a direct link between physical activity and improved academic performance, such a link might be expected. Studies have found participation in physical activity increases adolescents' self-esteem and reduces anxiety and stress. Through its effects on mental health,
15　physical activity may help increase students' capacity for learning. One study found that spending more time in physical education did not have harmful effects on the standardized academic achievement test scores of elementary school students; in fact, there was some evidence that participation in a two-year health-related physical education program had several significant
20　favorable effects on academic achievement.

In line 13, "critical" most nearly means
(A) decisive
(B) demeaning
(C) dangerous
(D) cynical
(E) risky

1. **A is correct.** "Critical" is a multiple-meaning word that can have any of the meanings offered. To determine which meaning is correct, locate the sentence in which critical is used: "Participation in regular physical activity . . . is critical to sustaining good health." Try substituting each answer choice in the original sentence and you will see that in this context only "decisive" makes sense.

In line 14, "stress" most nearly means
(A) force
(B) emphasis
(C) importance
(D) tension
(E) significance

2. **D is correct.** "Stress" can mean any of the words offered as answer choices, depending upon the context in which it is used. In this case, the word *stress* occurs in the following sentence: "Studies have found participation in physical activity increases adolescents' self-esteem and reduces anxiety and stress." If you substitute each answer choice in the sentence, you will see that the only one that makes sense is "tension."

In line 15, "capacity" most nearly means
(A) commitment
(B) content
(C) aptitude
(D) magnitude
(E) creativity

3. **C is correct.** The word "capacity" is used in this sentence: "Through its effects on mental health, physical activity may help increase students' capacity for learning." The only answer choice that makes sense in this context is aptitude.

On Your Own

Below you will find a variety of types of passages and questions that you encounter on the SSAT and ISEE reading tests.

- Review the strategies discussed above before you try Practice Set A. You may find that certain types of questions are easier for you to deal with than others. For example, vocabulary-in-context questions are likely to be easier to answer than inference questions.
- Focus on the kinds of items that you found difficult as you worked through the samples. Use the practice set to determine which types of questions continue to give you difficulty. Then, complete Practice Set B. Remember that the more you practice with these items, the less trouble-some you are likely to find them.

Practice Set A

Directions: Each reading passage is followed by questions about it. Answer the questions that follow a passage on the basis of what is stated or implied in that passage. For each question, circle the letter of the answer you think is best.

Nature
As a fond mother, when the day is o'er,
Leads by the hand her little child to bed,
Half willing, half reluctant to be led,
And leave his broken playthings on the floor,
5 Still gazing at them through the open door,

Nor wholly reassured and comforted
By promises of others in their stead,
Which, though more splendid, may not please him more;
So Nature deals with us, and takes away
10 Our playthings one by one, and by the hand
Leads us to rest so gently, that we go
Scarce knowing if we wish to go or stay,
Being too full of sleep to understand
How far the unknown transcends the what we know.

Henry Wadsworth Longfellow

1. In this poem, the author compares
   (A) a mother to a child
   (B) childhood to adulthood
   (C) life to sleep
   (D) death to sleep
   (E) a mother to Mother Nature

2. Which best describes the author's attitude toward death?
   (A) Children are not afraid of death.
   (B) Death is not to be feared.
   (C) The death of a child is a terrible thing.
   (D) A sudden death is better than a long and lingering one.
   (E) Death brings an end to illness and pain.

3. What are the "playthings" mentioned in line 10?
   (A) a child's toys
   (B) adult status symbols
   (C) the people and things that fill our lives
   (D) irritating things that happen in life
   (E) favorite activities

4. The tone of this poem is best described as
   (A) calm and reassuring
   (B) hostile and angry
   (C) troubled and sad
   (D) full of fear
   (E) troubled and uncertain

5. In which line does the speaker switch points of view?
   (A) 2
   (B) 5
   (C) 9
   (D) 12
   (E) 14

One of the most impressive feats in nature is the ability of birds to travel hundreds or even thousands of miles to distant lands where they breed and spend the winter. Migration is not just the seasonal movement of birds each fall and spring. In every month, some percentage of the Western Hemisphere's five billion birds are in the midst of migration. Their journeys can take weeks or months to complete, depending on the species and difficulties encountered along the way.

Impending cold weather is one of a number of factors that encourage birds to migrate. The main trigger is depletion of the food supply, as when insects go into hibernation or when snow cover makes seeds inaccessible. Diminishing daylight means that there is less time to feed, and birds begin to have difficulty maintaining sufficient energy stores to cope with lower temperatures. This cause-and-effect relationship creates another signal that it is time to head south. Once the instinct to migrate is triggered, activities such as feeding, resting, and aggression are often suppressed, allowing birds to focus on little else but reaching their destination.

Most large-scale migration occurs at night when the air is cool and calm and there are few predators. Warblers, vireos, thrushes, and tanagers are all nighttime flyers, as are shorebirds. Daylight migrants include ducks, geese, cranes, loons, swallows, and swifts. Soaring birds, such as hawks and vultures, migrate during the day to take advantage of the warm updrafts created by heat from the sun.

Migrating birds use mountain ranges, narrow peninsulas, and coastlines as landmarks to help them navigate. They are also known to use the setting sun and star patterns for migration, and some bird species appear to rely on the magnetic field of the Earth. Overcast or foggy nights can hamper the progress of birds that rely on the stars for navigational cues. Birds have help, however, from seasonal wind patterns that blow in the general direction they need to travel. Whatever the means of navigation, it is extraordinary that many species are capable of returning not only to their home ranges, but to their exact nesting or winter feeding sites.

6. This passage is primarily about
   (A) how and why birds migrate
   (B) using landmarks to navigate
   (C) reasons why birds fly at night
   (D) locating the right nesting and feeding sites
   (E) preparations for a long flight

7. All of the following prefer to migrate at night EXCEPT
   (A) thrushes
   (B) warblers
   (C) hawks
   (D) shorebirds
   (E) tanagers

8. Which of the following best describes the author's attitude toward migration?
    (A) hostile
    (B) admiring
    (C) amused
    (D) skeptical
    (E) concerned

9. The author suggests that most large-scale migration occurs at night primarily because
    (A) there are few predators at night
    (B) birds can fly faster at night
    (C) birds are better able to take advantage of seasonal wind patterns at night
    (D) birds have good night vision
    (E) the stars make it easier for birds to navigate

10. The instinct to migrate is triggered primarily by
    (A) longer days
    (B) warmer temperatures
    (C) increased activity of predators
    (D) insufficient food supplies
    (E) the need to hibernate

11. According to the passage, which of the following is NOT true?
    (A) Migrations can take months to complete.
    (B) Spring and fall are the times when birds migrate.
    (C) Many species return to their exact nesting sites.
    (D) During migration instincts such as feeding and resting may be suppressed.
    (E) Seasonal wind patterns blow in the direction birds need to travel.

There was at this time among the Onondagas a chief of high rank whose name, variously written—Hiawatha, Hayonwatha, Ayongwhata, Taoungwatha—is rendered, "he who seeks the wampum belt." He had made himself greatly esteemed by his wisdom and his benevolence. He was now past middle age.
5 Though many of his friends and relatives had perished by the machinations of Atotarho, he himself had been spared. The qualities which gained him general respect had, perhaps, not been without influence even on that redoubtable chief. Hiawatha had long beheld with grief the evils which afflicted not only his own nation, but all the other tribes about them, through
10 the continual wars in which they were engaged, and the misgovernment and miseries at home which these wars produced. With much meditation he had elaborated in his mind the scheme of a vast confederation which would ensure universal peace. In the mere plan of a confederation there was nothing new. There are probably few, if any, Indian tribes which have not, at one time
15 or another, been members of a league or confederacy. It may almost be said

to be their normal condition. But the plan which Hiawatha had evolved differed from all others in two particulars. The system which he devised was to be not a loose and transitory league, but a permanent government. While each nation was to retain its own council and its management of local affairs, the general control was to be lodged in a federal senate, composed of representatives elected by each nation, holding office during good behavior, and acknowledged as ruling chiefs throughout the whole confederacy. Still further, and more remarkably, the confederation was not to be a limited one. It was to be indefinitely expansible. The avowed design of its proposer was to abolish war altogether. He wished the federation to extend until all the tribes of men should be included in it, and peace should everywhere reign. Such is the positive testimony of the Iroquois themselves; and their statement, as will be seen, is supported by historical evidence

Horatio Hale from *The Iroquois Confederation*

12. Which of the following best describes the author's attitude toward Hiawatha?
 (A) amused
 (B) dubious
 (C) hostile
 (D) respectful
 (E) unimpressed

13. It can be inferred from the passage that the Onondagas looked upon Hiawatha as
 (A) fierce and warlike
 (B) ruthless and unsparing
 (C) caring and wise
 (D) old and frail
 (E) cautious and indecisive

14. As used in line 3, the word "rendered" most nearly means
 (A) provided
 (B) translated
 (C) surrendered
 (D) handed down
 (E) caused to become

15. According to the passage, Hiawatha's plan for a confederation of Indian nations contained all of the following provisions EXCEPT:
 (A) It was to be a permanent government.
 (B) Each nation was to retain its own council and manage its local affairs.
 (C) Control was to be in the hands of a federal senate composed of elected representatives.
 (D) Membership in the confederation was open to all nations.
 (E) Only the head chief could declare war.

16. The author's main purpose for writing this passage is to
   (A) describe the conditions under which native peoples lived at the time
   (B) inform readers about Hiawatha's plan for a confederacy of Indian nations
   (C) compare Hiawatha to other chiefs of the time
   (D) dispel myths about Hiawatha
   (E) describe the derivation of the name Hiawatha

17. The style of the passage is most like that found in a
   (A) personal letter
   (B) novel about native peoples
   (C) history textbook
   (D) explorer's diary
   (E) autobiography

   Today, the U.S. Environmental Protection Agency announced the availability of an additional $10 million in grants to eligible states, territories, and tribes to monitor beach water quality. This brings the five-year total to nearly $42 million. As a critical part of the Administration's Clean Beaches
5 Plan, this is the fifth year that grants are being made available since the Beaches Environmental Assessment and Coastal Health (BEACH) Act passed in October 2000.
   "Americans want clean and healthy beaches," said EPA's Assistant Administrator for Water Ben Grumbles. "These funds will help improve
10 water monitoring and public information programs to alert beachgoers about the health of their beaches."
   The grants are designed to support water monitoring, which helps to ensure that the public receives information on how to protect their health when visiting beaches. Beach water monitoring results are used to issue
15 warnings and closures if bacteria levels are at unsafe levels and to help identify actions needed to reduce pollution.
   In addition, as part of the Clean Beaches Plan, EPA is developing new technology that will provide faster test results, which will enable local health agencies to more quickly determine if a beach should be open for swimming.

18. This passage is mainly about
   (A) the Environmental Protection Agency
   (B) how to get an EPA grant
   (C) monitoring the quality of beach water
   (D) developing better ways to test water
   (E) what the public can do to ensure beach safety

19. This passage can best be described as a
    (A) news item
    (B) textbook excerpt
    (C) biography
    (D) short story
    (E) research report

20. Beach water monitoring results are used primarily to
    (A) direct swimmers to the nearest public beaches
    (B) close beaches that do not test water
    (C) alert swimmers to rough surf conditions
    (D) issue warnings when bacteria levels are too high
    (E) make the public aware of what they can do to keep beaches clean

21. Which of the following questions is answered by information in the passage?
    (A) What is the Environmental Protection Agency?
    (B) When was the Beaches Environmental Assessment and Coastal Health Act passed?
    (C) How much grant money is available to a particular state, territory, or tribe?
    (D) When should grants be submitted?
    (E) How many individual grants have been awarded over the past five years?

22. The tone of the passage is best described as
    (A) humorous
    (B) cautious
    (C) impersonal
    (D) argumentative
    (E) enthusiastic

End of Practice Set A

Answers and Explanations

1. **D is correct**. The poet compares a mother leading her child to sleep in lines 1–8 to Nature leading a person to his or her final sleep (or death) in lines 9–14.

2. **B is correct**. By comparing death to a "fond mother" (line 1) leading her child to sleep the author paints a soft image of death as a gentle rest (line 11), not something to be feared.

3. **C is correct**. The author mentions "playthings" twice in this poem. In lines 3–4, he says that the child is reluctant to "leave his broken playthings on the floor." In lines 9–10, the author says that Nature "takes away our playthings, one by one" and leads us gently to rest. The first mention of playthings refers to a child's toys. The second mention of playthings refers to all the people and things that fill an adult's life and that are taken away by death.

4. **A is correct**. Tone is the author's attitude or point of view toward a topic. It is conveyed through the author's word choice. Here, the tone is calm and reassuring as evidenced by the mother and child image and the use of words such as "fond mother" and "leads us to rest so gently." The last line "How far the unknown transcends the what we know" indicates the author's belief that the afterlife will be better than the life we know.

5. **C is correct**. Lines 1–8 describe a mother leading her child to bed at the end of the day. Lines 9–14 describe Nature leading a man or woman to the final sleep at the end of life. The change is signaled by line 9 ("So nature deals with us, and takes away").

6. **A is correct**. The entire passage concerns how and why birds migrate. In contrast, choices B and D are mentioned only in paragraph 4 and choice C is mentioned only in paragraph 3. Choice E is not covered by this passage.

7. **C is correct**. The answer to this question can be found in the third paragraph: "Warblers, vireos, thrushes, and tanagers are all nighttime flyers, as are shorebirds. . . . Soaring birds, such as hawks and vultures, migrate during the day to take advantage of the warm updrafts created by heat from the sun."

8. **B is correct**. Attitude is revealed through the author's word choice. In this case, the author refers to migration as "one of the most impressive feats in nature" and later calls it "extraordinary" that many species are able to return to their exact nesting or feeding sites. This highly positive language makes it apparent that the author is admiring of the act of nature known as migration.

9. **A is correct**. The first sentence of the third paragraph lists two reasons why most large-scale migration occurs at night: "the air is cool and calm and there are few predators." Choice B is incorrect because the passage never mentions whether birds fly faster by day or by night. Choice C is incorrect because the passage states just the opposite. Choices D and E may be correct, but neither one is

specifically cited in the passage as being a reason for migration to take place at night.

10. **D is correct**. This detail is found in paragraph 2, which states that the main trigger for migration "is depletion of the food supply, as when insets go into hibernation or when snow cover makes seeds inaccessible." Choice A is incorrect because migration is triggered by "diminishing daylight," not longer days. Choice B is incorrect because "impending cold weather," not warmer weather, is a factor that encourages migration. Choice C is incorrect because it is not supported by information in the passage. Choice E is incorrect because it is the insects, not the birds, that hibernate in winter.

11. **B is correct**. As stated in the first paragraph, "Migration is *not* just the seasonal movement of birds each fall and spring. In every month, some percentage of the Western Hemisphere's five billion birds are in the midst of migration." Choice A is stated in the last sentence of paragraph 1. Choice C is stated in the last sentence of the passage. Choice D is stated in the last sentence of paragraph 2. Choice E is stated in the next-to-last sentence of the passage.

12. **D is correct**. The author uses highly positive words to describe Hiawatha: "esteemed by his wisdom and benevolence," possessed of "qualities which gained him general respect," and capable of devising a system of government "which would ensure universal peace." Such language indicates that the author is respectful of Hiawatha.

13. **C is correct**. The first sentence describes Hiawatha as an Onondaga chief "of high rank." The next sentence goes on to say, "He had made himself greatly esteemed by his wisdom and his benevolence."

14. **B is correct**. The word "rendered" can have any of the meanings offered as choices. However, in this context the one that fits best is "translated." In other words, the name Hiawatha means "he who seeks the wampum belt."

15. **E is correct**. The aim of the confederation was "to abolish war altogether." Nowhere in the passage is there any mention of declaring war, by the head chief or by anyone else. Choice A is specifically mentioned in lines 17–18: 'The system which he devised was to be not a loose and transitory league, but a permanent government." Choice B is specifically noted in line 19: "each nation was to retain its own council and its management of local affairs." Choice C is mentioned in lines 20–21: "the general control was to be lodged in a federal senate, composed of representatives elected by each

nation." Choice D is mentioned in lines 23–26: "the confederation was not to be a limited one. . . He wished the federation to extend until all the tribes of men should be included in it."

16. **B is correct**. The author's main purpose is to provide information about Hiawatha's plan for a confederacy of Indian nations and to show how this plan differed from other similar plans. Choices A and C are wrong because the passage does not describe living conditions or compare Hiawatha to other chiefs. Choice D is wrong because there is no mention of myths about Hiawatha. Choice E is wrong because the translation of the name Hiawatha is the focus of only one sentence in the passage.

17. **C is correct**. The language in this selection may seem old-fashioned, but it is actually representative of the language used in 1881 when this passage was written. Choice A is incorrect because the passage is too formal in tone for a personal letter. Choice B is wrong because the passage is fact, not fiction. Choice D and E are wrong because the passage is written in the third person (using pronouns such as *he* and *him*), not the first person (using pronouns such as *I* and *me*). The style of the passage most closely resembles that of a history textbook or historical research published in the nineteenth century.

18. **C is correct**. The entire passage concerns monitoring the quality of beach water. The aspects of the topic covered include: a source of funds for testing beach water, benefits of water monitoring, new technology for faster results, where to find more information about the program and the grants.

19. **A is correct**. The word "today" at the start of the passage is a clue that this is a timely announcement typical of a news item The first paragraph also follows the classic news article structure by answering these questions: Who?(U.S. Environmental Protection Agency) What? (announced availability of $10 million in grants) When? (today) Why? (to monitor beach water quality as part of the Clean Beaches Plan).

20. **D is correct**. As stated in paragraph 3, "Beach water monitoring results are used to issue warnings and closures if bacteria levels are at unsafe levels and to help identify actions needed to reduce pollution." Choice A is wrong because water monitoring has nothing to do with directing swimmers to a public beach. Choice B is wrong because water monitoring results can be used to close beaches that have unsafe bacterial levels, not those that do not test their waters. Choice C is wrong because water monitoring tests for bacteria in the water,

not for surf conditions. Choice E is wrong because the water monitoring results do not tell people what they can do to keep beaches clean.

21. **B is correct**. As stated in the first paragraph, the Beaches Environmental Assessment and Coastal Health Act was passed in October 2000. The passage does not provide answers for choices A, C, D, or E.

22. **C is correct**. The passage merely states the facts in a straightforward and impersonal way. Choice A is wrong because the author makes no attempt to be humorous about the topic. Choice B is wrong because the passage contains no words of caution. Choices D and E are wrong because nothing in the passage could be considered either argumentative or enthusiastic.

Practice Set B

Directions: Each reading passage is followed by questions about it. Answer the questions that follow a passage on the basis of what is stated or implied in that passage. For each question, circle the letter of the answer you think is best.

When the door below was opened, a thick stream of men forced a way down the stairs, which were of an extraordinary narrowness and seemed only wide enough for one at a time. Yet they somehow went down almost three abreast. It was a difficult and painful operation.

5   The crowd was like a turbulent water forcing itself through one tiny outlet. The men in the rear, excited by the success of the others, made frantic exertions, for it seemed that this large band would more than fill the quarters and that many would be left upon the pavements. It would be disastrous to be of the last, and accordingly men, with the snow biting their faces, writhed 10 and twisted with their might. One expected that from the tremendous pressure, the narrow passage to the basement door would be so choked and clogged with human limbs and bodies that movement would be impossible. Once indeed the crowd was forced to stop, and a cry went along that a man had been injured at the foot of the stairs. But presently the slow movement 15 began again, and the policeman fought at the top of the flight to ease the pressure on those who were going down.

   A reddish light from a window fell upon the faces of the men when they, in turn, arrived at the last three steps and were about to enter. One could then note a change of expression that had come over their features. As they 20 thus stood upon the threshold of their hopes, they looked suddenly content and complacent. The fire had passed from their eyes and the snarl had vanished from their lips. The very force of the crowd in the rear, which had previously vexed them, was regarded from another point of view, for it now made it inevitable that they should go through the little doors into the 25 place that was cheery and warm with light.

The tossing crowd on the sidewalk grew smaller and smaller. The snow beat with merciless persistence upon the bowed heads of those who waited. The wind drove it up from the pavements in frantic forms of winding white, and it seethed in circles about the huddled forms, passing in, one by one, three by three, out of the storm.

Stephen Crane from *"The Men in the Storm"*

1. According to the author, the men forcing their way down the stairs most closely resembled which of the following?
   (A) a swirling blizzard
   (B) a raging stream
   (C) a marching band
   (D) a roaring fire
   (E) a strong wind

2. The men are pushing their way down the stairs primarily because they want to
   (A) escape from the police
   (B) get medical help
   (C) find shelter from the storm
   (D) go home
   (E) avoid being crushed by the crowd

3. Based on the passage each of the following words may be used to describe the men waiting at the top of the stairs EXCEPT:
   (A) frozen
   (B) snarling
   (C) frantic
   (D) vexed
   (E) complacent

4. Which of the following caused the change of expression to come over the faces of the men when they reached the last three steps?
   (A) They knew that the snowstorm was over.
   (B) They knew that they would make it into the shelter.
   (C) They found other family members inside.
   (D) They watched in dismay as a fire broke out.
   (E) Their faces were illuminated by a red light.

5. The passage suggests that the men in the story regard the room at the foot of the stairs as a
   (A) place to be feared
   (B) place to be avoided
   (C) welcoming place
   (D) prison
   (E) place for sick people

6. This passage can best be described as an excerpt from
   (A) a news article
   (B) a research study
   (C) an epic poem
   (D) a short story
   (E) an autobiography

   The results of a four-year study of the Arctic conducted by an international team of 300 scientists show that the region is warming much more rapidly than previously known. Some areas in the Arctic have warmed 10 times as fast as the world as a whole, which has warmed an average of 1 degree
5 Fahrenheit ($5/9$°C) over the past century. Increasing greenhouse gases from human activities are projected to make the Arctic warmer still.
   At least half of the summer sea ice in the Arctic is projected to melt by the end of this century, along with a significant portion of the Greenland Ice Sheet because the region is expected to warm an additional 7 to 13°F
10 (4–7°C) by 2100. These changes will have major global impacts. They will contribute to global sea-level rise and intensify global warming. In addition, the disappearance of summer sea ice is likely to have devastating consequences for some arctic animal species such as ice-living seals and for local people for whom these animals are a primary food source, according to the
15 final report of the Arctic Climate Impact Assessment (ACIA).
   The assessment was commissioned by the Arctic Council (a ministerial intergovernmental forum comprised of the eight Arctic countries, and six Indigenous Peoples organizations) and the International Arctic Science Committee (an international scientific organization appointed by 18 national
20 academies of science). The assessment's projections are based on a moderate estimate of future emissions of carbon dioxide and other greenhouse gases. They incorporate results from five major global climate models used by the Intergovernmental Panel on Climate Change.
   "The impacts of global warming are affecting people **now** in the Arctic,"
25 says Robert Corell, chair of the ACIA. "The Arctic is experiencing some of the most rapid and severe climate change on earth. The impacts of climate change on the region and the globe are projected to increase substantially in the years to come."

7. The primary purpose of this passage is to
   (A) argue the need for immediate action to halt Arctic warming
   (B) record the impact of Arctic warming on the Greenland Ice Sheet
   (C) illustrate the impact of global warming on the world as a whole
   (D) relate the results of a research study of the Arctic
   (E) compare Arctic warming with warming in the world as a whole

8. In line 6, "projected" most nearly means
   (A) promoted
   (B) predicted
   (C) designed
   (D) delegated
   (E) prepared

9. Which of the following best describes the Arctic Council?
   (A) an international scientific organization
   (B) an intergovernmental forum
   (C) an organization commissioned to study global warming
   (D) an organization that governs Arctic nations
   (E) an organization of Indigenous Peoples

10. According to the passage, all of the following are true about Arctic warming EXCEPT:
    (A) The Arctic is warming more rapidly than the world as a whole.
    (B) Melting summer sea ice will have major global impacts.
    (C) The world as a whole has warmed an average of 1 degree F ($5/9$ degree C) over the past century.
    (D) The impacts of global warming are already affecting people in the Arctic.
    (E) Climate change in the Arctic is less pronounced than it is in other parts of the world.

11. Melting sea ice will result in
    I. a rise in global sea level
    II. more greenhouse gases
    III. intensified global warming
    (A) II only
    (B) III only
    (C) I and III only
    (D) I, II, and III
    (E) Neither I, II, or III

12. According to the passage it is reasonable to assume that
    (A) Arctic warming is affected by greenhouse gases
    (B) the Greenland Ice Sheet will disappear by 2100
    (C) Arctic temperatures will return to normal by the end of this century
    (D) the impact of climate change on the Arctic will decrease over time
    (E) increasing arctic temperatures primarily affect arctic wildlife

As president of the United States, Thomas Jefferson was responsible for one of the largest and most peaceful land transactions this country has ever known. In 1803, Jefferson purchased 828,000 square miles, an area known then as the Louisiana Territory, from France in exchange for $15 million.
5   At the time this acquisition was met with both joy and opposition. Those who

praised Jefferson saw the Louisiana Territory as a vast region with unlimited natural resources and economic opportunities. Those who opposed the purchase saw the territory as nothing but a burden and a waste of money. To Jefferson, this purchase was a chance of a lifetime for both him and the country. Practically overnight, the country doubled in size adding new resources to its already impressive supply. Jefferson believed that out west there was "Land enough for our descendants to the thousandth and thousandth generation." There was a potential for endless economic opportunities and new trade routes. Overall, the Louisiana Purchase provided Jefferson with an opportunity to build a strong independent nation that is founded upon democracy and freedom.

Thomas Jefferson looked at the West the way people look at outer space today. For him, the West evoked the same excitement and wonder that many people feel today as they gaze at the stars and dream of traveling to other galaxies. Jefferson believed that in the West anything could exist. However, the purchase of the Louisiana Territory raised many questions. At that time the Louisiana Territory extended from the Mississippi River all the way to the Rocky Mountains. Even as late as 1803 much of this territory had yet to be explored. Jefferson had heard many stories about the West from explorers and trappers. There were stories about wooly mammoths and giant seven-foot beavers, about active volcanoes and huge pillars of salt. Perhaps the most intriguing story of all concerned a Northwest Passage, a body of water that extended from the Mississippi River to the Pacific Ocean. If such a passage did exist, it could speed up the country's ability to export goods. To unlock the mysteries of the West, Jefferson decided to send an expedition into this region to determine just what was out there.

13. Which of the following is the best title for this selection?
    (A) Thomas Jefferson: Third President of the United States
    (B) The Legacy of Thomas Jefferson
    (C) Double or Nothing
    (D) Thomas Jefferson and the Louisiana Purchase
    (E) Reach for the Stars

14. Which of the following best describes the author's opinion of Thomas Jefferson?
    (A) a visionary leader
    (B) a spendthrift
    (C) an impractical dreamer
    (D) unscrupulous
    (E) confused

15. All of the following were true of the Louisiana Territory at the time of its purchase EXCEPT
    (A) It encompassed an area of 828,000 square miles.
    (B) It extended from the Mississippi River to the Pacific Ocean.
    (C) It was purchased from France.
    (D) Its purchase doubled the size of the United States.
    (E) It was largely unexplored.

16. In line 19, "gaze" most nearly means
    (A) aim
    (B) laugh
    (C) lunge
    (D) stare
    (E) exclaim

17. Which of the following can be inferred about Jefferson's attitude toward the Louisiana Territory?
    (A) He looked upon it as more exciting than space travel.
    (B) He saw it as a land of limitless opportunity.
    (C) He expected to meet great resistance from the French.
    (D) He believed the West had little of value to offer the new country.
    (E) He feared it would be too great a drain on the treasury of the new nation.

18. Which of the following questions is NOT answered by the passage?
    (A) How much land was included in the Louisiana Purchase?
    (B) What was the cost of the Louisiana Purchase?
    (C) What was the new territory actually like?
    (D) What was the reaction of the U.S. public to the purchase?
    (E) Why did Jefferson want to purchase the Louisiana Territory?

19. The style of this passage is most like that found in
    (A) a news article
    (B) a personal letter
    (C) an historical novel
    (D) an autobiography
    (E) a history textbook

End of Practice Set B

Answers and Explanations

1. **B is correct.** In the first sentence of the second paragraph, the author says the crowd forced its way down the narrow stairs "like a turbulent water forcing itself through one tiny outlet." The motion of the crowd is compared to a raging stream of water attempting to force itself through a tiny opening. A swirling blizzard (choice A) and a strong

wind (choice E) are what the men are trying to escape from, but neither one describes how the men looked as they tried to force their way to shelter. Although the passage refers to the crowd as a "large band," this means only that they were a large group of men; it has nothing to do with a marching band (choice C). There is nothing to support the comparison of the crowd of men to a roaring fire (choice D).

2. **C is correct.** The aim of the men is to escape the snow that was "biting their faces" and beating "with merciless persistence" upon their heads. Their hope was to "go through the little doors into the place that was cheery and warm with light." Choice A is wrong because the only mention of the police is the policeman who fought at the top of the stairs "to ease the pressure on those who were going down." Choice B is wrong because "the difficult and painful operation" to which the author refers means only getting into the shelter, not getting medical aid. Choice D is wrong because the men in this passage are seeking refuge from the cold and snow in a shelter, which implies that they do not have a home to go to. Choice E is wrong because, although it is possible that pushing one's way down the stairs can result in being hurt, this is certainly not the reason for the pushing.

3. **E is correct.** The passage describes the men standing at the top of the stairs with "snow biting their faces" and beating "with merciless persistence upon the bowed heads of those who waited." Thus it is reasonable to describe the men as *frozen*, or *cold*, as in choice A. When the men finally reach the last three stairs, "the snarl had vanished from their lips"; therefore, it is reasonable to assume that the men waiting to get in out of the cold are *hostile* or *snarling* with anger as in choice B. The men at the rear "made frantic exertions" to avoid being left out in the cold, so they can be described as *frantic* as in choice C. When the men reached the bottom steps the force of the crowd "which had previously vexed them" was now regarded from a different point of view. Thus, the men at the top could be described as *worried* or *vexed*, as in choice D. Only once they reached the bottom step and it became inevitable that they would get inside, did the men look "content and complacent."

4. **B is correct.** As stated in the third paragraph, a change of expression came over the features of the men once they reached the last three steps. "As they thus stood upon the threshold of their hopes, they looked suddenly content and complacent. The fire had passed from their eyes and the snarl had vanished from their lips. The very force of the crowd in the rear, which had previously vexed them, was regarded from another point of view, for it now made it inevitable that they should go through the little doors into the place that was cheery and warm with light."

5. **C is correct.** The men in the story are pushing and shoving to get to the bottom of the stairs from which point they were assured of going

through the little doors "into the place that was cheery and warm with light." Everything in the passage makes it clear that the men desperately want to get into this place. Therefore, it is not a place to be feared (choice A) or avoided (choice B). Nor is it a prison (choice D) or a hospital for treating the sick (choice E).

6. **D is correct**. The passage describes an event as seen through the eyes of the author. The vivid imagery and literary language make it more likely to be an excerpt from a short story than a news article (choice A) or a research study (choice B). The prose passage has no similarity to an epic poem (choice C) and, since it is written in the third person, rather than the first person, it is not typical of an autobiography (choice E).

7. **D is correct**. The first sentence announces that the passage will present the "results of a four-year study of the Arctic conducted by an international team of 300 scientists." The remainder of the passage covers the findings of the study and who commissioned it. Choice A is wrong because the passage merely presents the findings without suggesting action to be taken. Choice B is wrong because the melting of the Greenland Ice Sheet is only one of the findings of the study, not its entire purpose. Choice C is wrong because the study focused on the Arctic, not the world as a whole. Choice E is wrong for the same reason as choice B; it concerns only one part of the study.

8. **B is correct**. The word "projected" is used several times in the passage: "increasing greenhouse gases from human activities are projected to make the Arctic warmer still"; "At least half of the summer sea ice in the Arctic is projected to melt by the end of this century"; "The impacts of climate change on the region and the globe are projected to increase substantially in the years to come." In each case, "projected" means "forecasted" or "predicted."

9. **B is correct**. The words in parentheses following the mention of Arctic Council define the council as "a ministerial intergovernmental forum comprised of the eight Arctic countries, and six Indigenous Peoples organizations." Choice A refers to the International Arctic Science Committee. Choice C refers to the Arctic Climate Impact Assessment. There is no mention of a single organization that governs the Arctic nations as in choice D, and choice E names only part of the makeup of the Arctic Council.

10. **E is correct**. The study shows that "the Arctic . . . is warming much more rapidly than previously known." In fact, some areas in the Arctic "have warmed 10 times as fast as the world as a whole." Thus climate change in the Arctic is more, not less, pronounced than it is in other parts of the world and choice E is false. Choice A is mentioned in the first paragraph. Choices B and C are mentioned in the first and second paragraphs. Choice D is mentioned in the last paragraph.

11. **C is correct**. The effects of melting sea ice "will contribute to global sea-level rise and intensify global warming." As noted in the first paragraph, the increase in greenhouse gases comes from human activities, not from melting sea ice.

12. **A is correct**. As stated in the first paragraph, "Increasing greenhouse gases from human activities are projected to make the Arctic warmer still." Thus, it may be assumed that greenhouse gases have an effect on Arctic warming. Choice B is incorrect because the passage says only that "a significant portion of the Greenland Ice Sheet" is projected to melt by the end of this century. Choices C and D run counter to everything in the passage, which points toward ever-increasing arctic temperatures. Choice E is incorrect because the passage specifically mentions the effect of increasing temperatures upon both "arctic animal species such as ice-living seals" and "local people for whom these animals are a primary food source."

13. **D is correct**. A good title indicates both the topic and the purpose of the selection. In this case, the selection is a straightforward expository passage about Thomas Jefferson's purchase of the Louisiana Territory. That makes choice D the best answer. Choices A and B are too broad for this passage, which is limited to Jefferson's part in the Louisiana Purchase. Choices C and E may be catchy phrases, but they fail to name the topic of the selection and they are too informal for this textbook-type passage.

14. **A is correct**. The author's positive opinion of Jefferson is revealed in statements such as these: "Thomas Jefferson was responsible for one of the largest and most peaceful land transactions this country has ever known." "Practically overnight, the country doubled in size adding new resources to its already impressive supply." "Overall, the Louisiana Purchase provided Jefferson with an opportunity to build a strong independent nation that is founded upon democracy and freedom." Choice C is wrong because, although the author may have thought of Jefferson as a dreamer, there is no indication that the author thought him to be impractical. There is no support in the passage for choices B, D, or E.

15. **B is correct**. The passage states that the Louisiana Territory "extended from the Mississippi River all the way to the Rocky Mountains." It did not extend to the Pacific Ocean. Choices A and C are mentioned in lines 3–5: "Jefferson purchased 828,000 square miles, an area known then as the Louisiana Territory, from France." Choice D is mentioned in line 10: "Practically overnight, the country doubled in size." Choice E is mentioned in lines 23–24: "as late as 1803 much of this territory had yet to be explored."

16. **D is correct**. Gaze appears in the following sentence: "For him, the west evoked the same excitement and wonder that many people feel today as they gaze at the stars and dream of traveling to other galaxies."

Try substituting each answer choice in the original sentence and you will see that choice D fits best. To "gaze" is to "look intently" or to "stare."

17. **B is correct.** The passage says the following about Jefferson's attitude toward the Louisiana Purchase: "To Jefferson, this purchase was a chance of a lifetime for both him and the country." "There was a potential for endless economic opportunities and new trade routes." From these statements it is reasonable to infer that Jefferson saw the Louisiana Territory as a land of great opportunity, as stated in choice B. There is no support in the passage for any other answer choice.

18. **C is correct.** The only thing the passage says about what the territory was actually like is that "Jefferson decided to send an expedition into this region to determine just what was out there." Thus the passage does not say what the new territory was actually like.

    Choice A is answered in line 3: "Jefferson purchased 828,000 square miles." Choice B is answered in line 4: "in exchange for $15 million." Choice D is answered in line 5: "At the time this acquisition was met with both joy and opposition." Choice E is answered in lines 9–16: "To Jefferson, this purchase was a chance of a lifetime for both him and the country . . . There was a potential for endless economic opportunities and new trade routes. Overall, the Louisiana Purchase provided Jefferson with an opportunity to build a strong independent nation that is founded upon democracy and freedom."

19. **E is correct.** The passage is written in the straightforward expository style most likely to be used in a history textbook. Choice A is wrong because the passage has none of the timely references common to a news article. Choice B is wrong because the passage lacks the informal, chatty style of most personal letters. Choice C is wrong because the passage is fact, not fiction. Choice D is wrong because the passage is not Jefferson's own account of his life.

CHAPTER 8

Strategies for the Writing Section

Both the SSAT and the ISEE include a writing section that requires you to respond to an assigned topic. Your essay is not scored. Instead, a copy is sent to each of the schools that receive your score report. Schools may use your writing sample as an indication of how well you can write under controlled conditions.

The SSAT writing section may be administered either before or after the multiple-choice sections of the test. You will have 25 minutes to plan and write your essay. Each essay question consists of a topic and an assignment. Basically, the topic is a short phrase or proverb and the assignment is to agree or disagree with the position taken by the topic. There are no right or wrong answers to an essay question. Just be sure to take a clear position and to support your position with specific examples from your own experience, the experience of others, current events, history, or literature.

Sample SSAT Writing Section Topic

Topic: Experience is the best teacher.

Assignment: Do you agree or disagree with the topic statement? Support your position with one or two specific examples from your own experience, the experience of others, current events, history, or literature.

The ISEE writing section is always administered after the multiple-choice sections of the test. You will have 30 minutes for your ISEE essay. A typical ISEE essay topic will ask a question which you are expected to answer with details and examples. As with the SSAT questions, there are no right or wrong answers. Just be sure to write on the assigned topic. An essay on any other topic is unacceptable.

Sample ISEE Writing Section Topic

If you were given the power to change one thing about the way in which we choose a president of the United States, what would you change and why?

Essay-Writing Strategies

Here's a simple four-step strategy for writing a well-organized SSAT or ISEE essay.

1. Brainstorm
   - Quickly jot down words or phrases about the topic
2. Outline
   - Organize your thoughts by numbering points or drawing lines to connect related ideas.
   - Make sure your essay has an introduction, body, and conclusion (in other words, a beginning, middle, and end)
3. Write
   - Take a position and have a clear point of view.
   - Start each paragraph with a topic sentence.
   - Provide at least two supporting details or examples for each main point.
4. Proofread
   - Correct mistakes by crossing out neatly and adding new words legibly above the crossed out material.

A Sample SSAT Essay

Topic: The grass is always greener on the other side of the fence.

Assignment: Do you agree or disagree with the topic statement? Support your position with examples from your own experience, the experience of others, current events, history, or literature.

Essay:

Introduction:	Interpret topic and take a stand.
	Include a thesis sentence.

There is a well-known proverb that says, "The grass is always greener on the other side of the fence." This common saying means that most people are not satisfied with what they have, always thinking that what someone else has is better. In general, this statement is true. My little brother Matt's ideas about pets are a perfect example of what it means to want something just because someone else has it.

Body Paragraph 1:	Point A—Our pet vs. pet Matt wants
	Supporting details or examples

We have a wonderful dog named Max. Max is everyone's best friend. He greets us everyday when we get home from school with his tail wagging and a toy in his mouth ready to play. If you sit down on the sofa, Max will curl up on your lap, and if you lie down on the floor, he will stretch out right next to you. Is this enough for Matt? No. He wants a different kind of pet, a pet like his friends have.

Body Paragraph 2:	Point B—One pet Matt wants—fish
	Supporting details or examples

First, Matt wanted a big aquarium full of exotic fish, just like the one he saw at his friend Eric's house. Mom said he could start with a fishbowl and a couple of goldfish. If that went well, she would consider a small aquarium and a few tropical fish. For a while, Matt was intrigued by the fish, and he would feed them and care for them without being told to do so. Soon, however, the novelty wore off and Matt forgot all about his desire for an aquarium.

Body Paragraph 3:	Point C—Other pets Matt wants—hermit crabs, frog
	Supporting details or examples

Next, Matt had to have hermit crabs after he saw the ones his friend Ty had. This interest lasted for a month or two. Then one day Matt visited Mike and saw Mike's pet frog. Now Matt wanted a frog too.

Conclusion:	Our own pet is best.
	Connect to thesis sentence.

This time Mom put her foot down. No more exotic pets for Matt. He would have to make do with our own pet Max. As for Max, he was happy to have Matt for a playmate again.

Hints for Writing Excellent Essays

1. Read the question carefully.
   - Rephrase the question in your own words to make sure you understand it.
2. Answer the question.
   - Follow all directions and do exactly what you are asked to do. You can be creative in your approach to the subject, but you *must* write on the topic you are assigned.

3. Have a plan.
    - Allow at least 2–3 minutes to plan your essay. Jot down your main points and at least two examples or details for each one. A good plan will make the writing go more smoothly.
4. Start to write.
    - For the SSAT, allow about 15–20 minutes to write and revise your essay. For the ISEE, allow about 20–25 minutes for the writing and revising process.
    - Write as neatly and legibly as you can. You must write in ink on the lined pages provided. If you change your mind, you may strike through a word or phrase and change it, but remember that someone has to be able to read what you have written.
5. Stick to your plan.
    - Stay focused on your topic and follow your plan.
6. Proofread.
    - Allow at least 3–5 minutes to read over your essay and make any necessary corrections and changes. Check for careless errors in spelling and grammar. Make sure that your essay says what you intended to say.

Now try an essay on your own. Use the strategies and hints you have just learned to write an essay on one of the sample topics below. Set a timer for 25 minutes (for the SSAT), or 30 minutes (for the ISEE) to get a feel for how much time you will have to plan and write your essay on the actual test.

On Your Own

Essay Practice A

Directions: You will have 25 minutes to plan and write an essay on the topic below. Read the topic carefully. Jot down some brief notes on scratch paper and organize your thoughts before you begin to write. Write your final essay on the ruled lines below.

Topic: Beauty is in the eye of the beholder.

Assignment: Do you agree or disagree with the topic statement? Support your position with examples from your own experience, the experience of others, current events, history, or literature.

Essay Practice B

Directions: You will have 30 minutes to plan and write an essay on the topic given below. You must write on the assigned topic only. An essay on another topic will not be acceptable. You may make notes in the space provided for that purpose. Write your final essay on the two lined pages that follow. Write or print legibly in blue or black ink.

> How would you define courage? Give an example of a courageous man or woman and explain why you have chosen this person.

PART III

REVIEW FOR THE MATH SECTIONS

The Arithmetic You Need to Know

Arithmetic on the SSAT and ISEE

Whether you are taking the SSAT or the ISEE, you will need to be familiar with the following topics in arithmetic:

Topics

Place Value	Adding and Subtracting Mixed Numbers
Addition	Decimals
Subtraction	Multiplying and Dividing Decimals
Multiplication	Changing Decimals to Fractions
Division	Changing Fractions to Decimals
Order of Operations	Percents
Positive and Negative Numbers	Finding a Percent of a Number
Multiplying and Dividing by Zero	Finding the Percent of Increase or Decrease
Factors	Mean (Average), Median, and Mode
Multiples	Graphs
Least Common Multiple	Units of Measure
Proper and Improper Fractions	
Reducing Fractions to Lowest Terms	

If you are taking the upper level version of the SSAT or ISEE, you should also be familiar with the following:

- Exponents
- Roots

This chapter will give you a complete review of all of these arithmetic topics. After you study each topic, check your progress by working through the practice sets called "On Your Own." Answers for these practice sets appear at the end of the chapter.

Arithmetic Review

Place Value

In numbers, the *place* is the position held by a digit. *Place value* is the product of the digit multiplied by its place. Here are some examples.

42, 657, 203.123

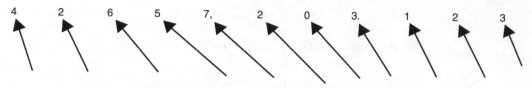

23,456,789.247
2 (the first 2) is in the ten millions place
3 is in the millions place
4 (the first 4) is in the hundred thousands place
5 is in the 10 thousands place
6 is in the thousands place
7 (the first 7) is in the hundreds place
8 is in the tens place
9 is in the ones place
2 is in the tenths place
4 is in the hundredths place
7 is in the thousandth place

On Your Own—Place Value

1. For the number 98,345.47, which number is in the ones place?
2. For the number 77,456,782.09, which number is in the tenths place?
3. For the number 45,234.006, which number is in the thousandths place?

Addition

There are two ways to show addition:

$$\begin{array}{r} 234 \\ +\,123 \\ \hline \end{array} \qquad \text{or} \qquad 234 + 123 =$$

In either case you need to add the two numbers to get the sum. Many SSAT or ISEE problems will require you to add numbers. Practicing the skill will allow you to perform the tasks accurately and quickly.

On Your Own — Addition
Find the answers to the following addition questions.

1. 731
    + 14

2. 16,790
    + 4670

3.   1,677
    + 23,999

4.   18,998
    + 78,988

5. 98,068,459
    + 673,899

6. 3,450,989
    + 9,999

7. 670,369
    + 135

8.   1,700,009,856
    + 2,853,990,975

9.   1,434,209
    + 5,478,999

10.   169,801
    + 34,788,976

Subtraction

There are also two ways to show subtraction:

  234   or   234 – 123 =
– 123

Some SSAT or ISEE problems will ask to you subtract numbers in order to calculate the correct answer. Practicing subtraction will help you get the correct answer in a short period of time.

Subtraction of Whole Numbers with Renaming Sometimes you have to "rename" numbers in order to complete subtraction.

  731
– 465

To subtract the 5 from the 1 in the ones place, "rename" the "31" in the top number as "2 tens and 11 ones." Write "2" above the 3 in the tens place and "11" above the 1 in the ones place. Subtract 5 from 11 to get 6.

  2 11
  731
– 465
    6

Next, you need to subtract the 6 from the (new) 2 in the tens place, so rename "72" as "6 hundreds and 12 tens." Write "6" above the 7 in the hundreds place and "12" above the 3 in the tens place. Subtract 6 from 12 to get 6. Then subtract 4 from 6 in the hundreds place to get 2, completing the subtraction.

$$
\begin{array}{r}
{\scriptstyle 6\ 12\ 11} \\
731 \\
-\ 465 \\
\hline
266
\end{array}
$$

On Your Own—Subtraction
Find the answers to the following subtraction questions.

1. $\begin{array}{r} 890 \\ -\ 78 \\ \hline \end{array}$

2. $\begin{array}{r} 3{,}456 \\ -\ 961 \\ \hline \end{array}$

3. $\begin{array}{r} 87{,}589 \\ -\ 65{,}178 \\ \hline \end{array}$

4. $\begin{array}{r} 89{,}923 \\ -\ 34{,}478 \\ \hline \end{array}$

5. $\begin{array}{r} 34{,}789{,}909 \\ -\ 23{,}784{,}498 \\ \hline \end{array}$

6. $\begin{array}{r} 674{,}329 \\ -\ 84{,}498 \\ \hline \end{array}$

7. $\begin{array}{r} 88{,}320{,}087 \\ -\ 3{,}497{,}698 \\ \hline \end{array}$

8. $\begin{array}{r} 1{,}000{,}997 \\ -\ 9{,}809 \\ \hline \end{array}$

9. $\begin{array}{r} 145{,}000{,}045 \\ -\ 14{,}409 \\ \hline \end{array}$

10. $\begin{array}{r} 1{,}798 \\ -\ 1{,}699 \\ \hline \end{array}$

Multiplication
Multiplication is a bit more complicated in that it can be shown in various ways.

$10 \times 3 = 30$
$10\,(3) = 30$
$(10)\,3 = 30$
$10 \cdot 3 = 30$
$(10)(3) = 30$

$$
\begin{array}{r}
10 \\
\times\ 3 \\
\hline
30
\end{array}
$$

Be sure to know your multiplication tables. You should know the answers already to any numbers multiplied up to 12, but the table below is a refresher.

Knowing the multiplication tables without any hesitation will help you answer many of the math items quickly and accurately. To know this table by heart will give you a bit of extra time to answer the tougher items.

x	0	1	2	3	4	5	6	7	8	9	10	11	12
0	0	0	0	0	0	0	0	0	0	0	0	0	0
1	0	1	2	3	4	5	6	7	8	9	10	11	12
2	0	2	4	6	8	10	12	14	16	18	20	22	24
3	0	3	6	9	12	15	18	21	24	27	30	33	36
4	0	4	8	12	16	20	24	28	32	36	40	44	48
5	0	5	10	15	20	25	30	35	40	45	50	55	60
6	0	6	12	18	24	30	36	42	48	54	60	66	72
7	0	7	14	21	28	35	42	49	56	63	70	77	84
8	0	8	16	24	32	40	48	56	64	72	80	88	96
9	0	9	18	27	36	45	54	63	72	81	90	99	108
10	0	10	20	30	40	50	60	70	80	90	100	110	120
11	0	11	22	33	44	55	66	77	88	99	110	121	132
12	0	12	24	36	48	60	72	84	96	108	120	132	144

On Your Own—Multiplication

Calculate the following multiplication items.

1. $(4)(5) =$

2. $(5)(4) =$

3. $9 \times 7 =$

4. $27 \times 65 =$

5. $67 \times 98 =$

6. $899 \times 457 =$

7. $\begin{array}{r} 1,649 \\ \times\, 8,942 \end{array}$

8. $\begin{array}{r} 76,834 \\ \times\, 78,459 \end{array}$

9. $\begin{array}{r} 275,849 \\ \times\, 769,422 \end{array}$

10. $\begin{array}{r} 9,750,439 \\ \times\, 56,893,478 \end{array}$

Division

Division can also be shown in more than one way.

$12 \div 3 = 4$

$12/3 = 4$

$\dfrac{12}{3} = 4$

Many SSAT or ISEE problems will require you to solve division problems. Division also relates to the use of fractions and the calculation of percentages.

On Your Own—Division

Calculate the following division items.

1. $16 \div 4 =$

2. $48 \div 4 =$

3. $90 \div 45 =$

4. $25,536 \div 56 =$

5. $121,401 \div 123 =$

6. $254,646 \div 987 =$

7. $41,536 \div 1298 =$

8. $18,895,065 \div 899,765 =$

9. $144 \div 12 =$

10. $1,655 \div 5 =$

Symbols

$=$ is equal to

$\neq$ is not equal to

$<$ is less than

$\leq$ is less than or equal to

$>$ is greater than

$\geq$ is greater than or equal to

$\parallel$ is parallel to

$\cong$ is approximately equal to

$\approx$ is approximately

$\perp$ is perpendicular to

$| \, |$ absolute value

$\pm$ plus or minus

$\%$ percent

$a{:}b$ ratio of a to b or $\dfrac{a}{b}$

On Your Own—Symbols

True or False? Write "T" or "F" in the blank to indicate whether each statement below is true of false.

1. _____ $9 > 7$

2. _____ $6.99 \cong 7$

3. _____ $47 \geq 47$

4. _____ $89 < 64$

5. _____ 99% is 99 percent

6. _____ $7 \neq 7$

7. _____ 2:4 = $\frac{2}{4}$

8. _____ | −7 | = 7

9. _____ 8 = −8

10. _____ 49 ≤ 34

Order of Operations

If addition, subtraction, multiplication, and division are all in the same mathematical statement, the order of operations (what you do first, second, third, etc.) is

1. Perform operations shown within **P**arentheses.
2. Attend to **E**xponents and square roots.
3. Perform **M**ultiplication or **D**ivision, whichever comes first left to right.
4. Perform **A**ddition or **S**ubtraction, whichever comes first left to right.

Order Is Important! You almost certainly will get an SSAT or ISEE math item that will require you to know order of operations rules. You can use the sentence "**P**lease **E**xcuse **M**y **D**ear **A**unt **S**ally" to help you remember the order of operations.

Examples

$2 + 3 \times 4 =$
$2 + 12 = 14$

$3^2 + 4 (5 − 2) =$
$9 + 4 (5 − 2) =$
$9 + 4 (3) =$
$9 + 12 = 21$

$5(10 + 2) + 2 + 3 =$
$5(12) + 2 + 3 =$
$60 + 5 = 65$

$3^3(8 + 3) \times (15 \sqrt 5) + (9 \times 2) − (298 + 300) =$
$3^3 (11) \times (3) + (18) − (598) =$
$27(11) \times (3) + (18) − (598) =$
$297 \times 3 + 18 − 598 =$
$891 + 18 − 598 =$
$908 − 598 = 310$

ORDER OF OPERATIONS
1. Simplify groupings inside parentheses, brackets and braces first. Work with the innermost pair, moving outward.
2. Simplify the exponents.
3. Do the multiplication and division in order from left to right.
4. Do the addition and subtraction in order from left to right.

On Your Own—Order of Operations
Calculate the answers to the following.

1. $(17 + 3) + 20 =$

2. $(45 - 43) + (16 + 32) =$

3. $(12 + 3)(2 \times 3) =$

4. $14 \div 2 + 14 =$

5. $6^2 + 3 + 2 =$

6. $12 \times 12 + 2^3 =$

7. $3^2 + 4(5 - 2) =$

8. $(4+2)^3 + (3 \times 2) - 2^2 =$

Positive and Negative Numbers

Positive numbers are numbers that are greater than 0, such as +6. Negative numbers are numbers that are less than 0, such as –4. Positive and negative whole numbers are called *integers*.

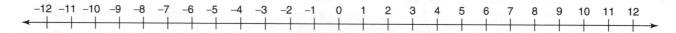

The *absolute value* of a number is the distance of the number from 0 on a number line. For example, the absolute value of +6 is 6. The absolute value of –4 is 4.

Adding Positive and Negative Numbers *To add numbers with the same sign*, add their absolute values. The sum will have the same sign as the numbers you added.

Examples

Add: $\begin{array}{r} -4 \\ \underline{-3} \\ -7 \end{array}$

To add numbers with different signs, first find their absolute values. Subtract the lesser absolute value from the greater absolute value. Give the sum the same sign as the number with the greater absolute value.

> **SSAT/ISEE Coach Says . . .**
> **Know Negative Numbers!** Be sure to practice adding, subtracting, multiplying, and dividing using negative numbers.

Examples

Add: $\begin{array}{r} +4 \\ \underline{-3} \\ +1 \end{array}$

Add: $\begin{array}{r} +4 \\ \underline{-6} \\ -2 \end{array}$

On Your Own—Adding Positive and Negative Numbers
Add the following numbers.

1. $4 + (-3) =$

2. $-10 + 3 =$

3. $75 + (-34 -32) =$

4. $80 + (75 - 25) =$

5. $-64 + 18 - 12 =$

6. $1,000 - (800) =$

7. $1,000 - (800 - 120) =$

8. $200 - 325 =$

Subtracting Positive and Negative Numbers Look again at the number line.

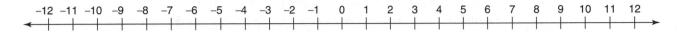

- When you subtract a positive number, you move *left* on the number line the distance equal to the absolute value of the number being subtracted.
- When you subtract a negative number, you move *right* on the number line the distance equal to the absolute value of the number being subtracted.

Examples
Subtract positive numbers (move *left* on the number line):

$$\begin{array}{r} +7 \\ - (+12) \\ \hline -5 \end{array}$$

$$\begin{array}{r} -7 \\ - (+12) \\ \hline -19 \end{array}$$

Subtract negative numbers (move *right* on the number line):

$$\begin{array}{r} 7 \\ - (-12) \\ \hline +19 \end{array}$$

$$\begin{array}{r} -7 \\ - (-12) \\ \hline +5 \end{array}$$

Note: A simple rule is that when you subtract negative numbers, all you really need to do is change the sign of the number being subtracted from negative to positive, and then add.

On Your Own—Subtracting Positive and Negative Numbers
Subtract the following numbers.

1. $12 - (4) =$

2. $12 - (-4) =$

3. $12 - (-8) =$

4. $45 - (12) =$

5. $125 - (-3)^2 =$

6. $500 - (5)^2 =$

7. $1,500 - (-10)^2 =$

8. $1,500 - (10)^2 =$

9. $42 - (45-5) - (-60) =$

Absolute Value
A number regardless of its sign (+ or −) is called the *absolute value*. The absolute value of a number is shown as the number placed between two vertical parallel lines; for example: $|-4|$ or $|4|$. In each of these cases, the absolute value of the number is 4. When using absolute values, just ignore the sign.

Examples
$|-x| = x$

$|-5-6| = |-11| = 11$

$8 + |-9| = 17$

Multiplying and Dividing Negative Numbers
These operations are easy if you use just one trick. To multiply or divide negative numbers, first treat all the numbers as positive and perform the operation as normal.

- If there are an *odd number of negative signs*, the answer will be a negative.
- If there is an *even number of negative signs*, the number will be positive.

Examples

$(-5)(+6)(+2) = -60$ This expression has 1 negative sign. Since 1 is an odd number, the result is negative.

$(-5)(-6)(+2) = +60$ This expression has 2 negative signs. Since 2 is an even number, the result is positive.

$\dfrac{-88}{+11} = +8$ This expression has 2 negative signs. Since 2 is an even number, the result is positive.

$\dfrac{-88}{+11} = -8$ This expression has 1 negative sign. Since 1 is an odd number, the result is negative.

On Your Own—Multiplying and Dividing Negative and Positive Numbers
Evaluate the following expressions.

1. $(-2)(-2)(-2) =$

2. $(-2)(-2)(2) =$

3. $(5)(-2)(-4) =$

4. $\dfrac{90}{-45} =$

5. $\dfrac{-90}{-45} =$

7. $(-4)(-5)(-2)(-8) =$

6. $\dfrac{-90}{45} =$

8. $(5)\ (-5)\ (2) =$

Subtracting Numbers within Parentheses
If there is a minus sign in front of numbers in parentheses, change the sign of all the numbers within the parentheses and then add.

Examples
$11 - (+3 - 5 + 2 - 8)$
changes to
$11 + (-3 + 5 - 2 + 8) =$
$11 + (-5 + 13) =$
$11 + (+8) = 19$

$20 - (-3 + 5 - 2 + 8) =$
$20 + (+3 - 5 + 2 - 8) =$
$20 + (+5 - 13) =$
$20 + -8 = 12$

On Your Own—Subtracting Numbers within Parentheses
Evaluate the following expressions.

1. $200 - (90 - 10) =$

5. $1,000 - (750) =$

2. $50 - (45) =$

6. $22 - (-12 + 15) =$

3. $125 - (45 - 55) =$

7. $95 + (34 - (-22)) =$

4. $575 - (400 - 300) =$

Multiplying and Dividing by Zero
Any number multiplied by zero = zero.
Zero divided by any number = zero.
Dividing by zero is considered to be "undefined."

Examples
$45 \times 0 = 0$
$1,232, 456 \times 0 = 0$
$10.45399 \times 0 = 0$
$0 \div 5 = 0$
$0 \div 500 = 0$
$7 \div 0$ is undefined
$\dfrac{32}{0}$ is undefined

$\dfrac{89}{0}$ is undefined

On Your Own—Multiplying and Dividing by Zero
Evaluate the following expressions.

1. $02316 \times 0 =$

2. $1,457,956,002.234 \times 0 =$

3. $4.78 \times 0 =$

4. $0 \div 6,000 =$

5. $6,000 \div 0 =$

Factors
Factors are numbers that are multiplied together to create another number.

Examples
$2 \times 4 = 8$ (2 and 4 are factors of 8.)
$1 \times 8 = 8$ (1 and 8 are factors of 8.)
So 1, 2, 4, and 8 are all factors of 8.

$1 \times 32 = 32$ (1 and 32 are factors of 32.)
$2 \times 16 = 32$ (2 and 16 are factors of 32.)
$8 \times 4 = 32$ (8 and 4 are factors of 32.)
So 1, 2, 4, 8, 16, 32 are all factors of 32.

Knowing about factors will be very useful when solving equations.

Common Factors Common factors are factors that are shared by two or more numbers. As shown above, 8 and 32 share the common factors 1, 2, 3, and 8.

Multiples
Multiples of a number are found by multiplying the number by 1, 2, 3, 4, 5, 6, 7, 8, etc. So multiples of 5 are 10, 15, 20, 25, 30, 35, 40, etc.

Common Multiples Common multiples are multiples that are shared by two or more numbers.
Example

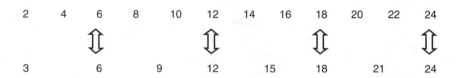

In the example above, 3 and 2 share the common multiples 6, 12, 18, and 24.

1. $1\frac{3}{4} + 3\frac{3}{4} =$

2. $6\frac{5}{6} + 9\frac{1}{3} =$

3. $12\frac{1}{3} + \frac{4}{5} =$

4. $8\frac{7}{8} - 4\frac{1}{4} =$

5. $10\frac{2}{3} - 3\frac{1}{9} =$

Multiplying Fractions To multiply fractions, just multiply the numerators and multiply the denominators. Reduce the resulting fraction to lowest terms.

Examples

$\frac{5}{12} \times \frac{2}{3} =$

Multiply the numerators: $5 \times 2 = 10$
Multiply the denominators: $12 \times 3 = 36$

Result: $\frac{10}{36} = \frac{5}{18}$

$\frac{4}{5} \times \frac{7}{8} =$

Multiply the numerators: $4 \times 7 = 28$
Multiply the denominators: $5 \times 8 = 40$

Result: $\frac{28}{40} = \frac{7}{10}$

SSAT/ISEE Coach Says . . .

Simplify, Simplify. Sometimes it is possible to simplify terms before performing any math operation. Take the same example we have already completed:

$\frac{4}{5} \times \frac{7}{8}$

Find a number (or greatest common factor) that divides into one of the numerators and one of the denominators. In this example the number 4 divides into 4 and into 8.

$\frac{^1 4}{5} \times \frac{7}{8_2}$

To finish the problem, multiply 1×7 and 5×2, making the final answer

$\frac{7}{10}$

On Your Own—Multiplying Fractions

1. $\dfrac{3}{4} \times \dfrac{7}{10} =$

2. $\dfrac{12}{15} \times \dfrac{1}{5} =$

3. $\dfrac{2}{7} \times \dfrac{2}{5} =$

Dividing Fractions To divide fractions, invert the second fraction and multiply. Reduce the result to lowest terms.

Examples

$= \dfrac{1}{2} \div \dfrac{1}{3}$

$= \dfrac{1}{2} \times \dfrac{3}{1}$

$= \dfrac{3}{2} = 1\dfrac{1}{2}$

$\dfrac{3}{4} \div -\left(\dfrac{1}{2}\right)$

$= \dfrac{3}{4} \times -\left(\dfrac{2}{1}\right)$

$= -\left(\dfrac{6}{4}\right) = -1\dfrac{2}{4} = -1\dfrac{1}{2}$

SSAT/ISEE Coach Says . . .
Dividing Fractions. Always remember that when you are dividing fractions, just invert and multiply.

---

1. $\dfrac{1}{2} \div \dfrac{2}{4} =$

2. $\dfrac{4}{5} \div \dfrac{1}{3} =$

3. $\dfrac{8}{9} \div \dfrac{1}{3} =$

On Your Own—Dividing Fractions

Multiplying Mixed Numbers To multiply mixed numbers, change each mixed number to a fraction and then multiply as usual. Reduce to lowest terms.

Examples

$1\dfrac{1}{4} \times 2\dfrac{1}{2} =$

$= \dfrac{5}{4} \times \dfrac{5}{2} =$

$$\frac{25}{8} = 3\frac{1}{8}$$

$$3\frac{2}{3} \times 9\frac{1}{2} =$$

$$\frac{11}{3} \times \frac{19}{2} =$$

$$\frac{209}{6} = 34\frac{2}{6}$$

Simplify the fraction.

$$34\frac{1}{3}$$

SSAT/ISEE Coach Says . . .
Dividing Fractions. Sometimes you might see division of fractions in this format.

$$\frac{1}{2}$$
$$\frac{1}{3}$$

Treat it the same as

$$\frac{1}{2} \div \frac{1}{3}$$

SSAT/ISEE Coach Says . . .
Watch the Signs! To multiply or divide negative numbers, first treat the numbers and perform the operation as normal. Then if there is an odd number of negative signs, the answer will be a negative. If there is an even number of negative signs, the number will be positive.

On Your Own—Multiplying Mixed Numbers

1. $2\frac{2}{3} \times 7\frac{2}{5} =$

2. $5\frac{1}{5} \times 4\frac{1}{2} =$

3. $12\frac{2}{3} + 2\frac{1}{3} =$

Dividing Mixed Numbers To divide mixed numbers, rename the mixed numbers as fractions and then follow the rule for dividing fractions: invert the second fraction and multiply.

Example

$$3\frac{1}{2} \div 1\frac{1}{4} =$$

$$\frac{7}{2} \div \frac{5}{4} =$$

$$\frac{7}{2} \times \frac{4}{5} =$$

$$\frac{28}{10} =$$

$$2\frac{8}{10} =$$

Simplify the fraction

$$2\frac{4}{5}$$

SSAT/ISEE Coach Says . . .

Fractions and Decimals. All proper fractions are less than one, so the corresponding decimals will be to the right of the decimal point. Numbers to the left of the decimal point will be whole numbers.

On Your Own—Dividing Mixed Numbers

1. $12\frac{2}{3} \div 2\frac{1}{3} =$

2. $6\frac{1}{2} \div \frac{1}{2} =$

3. $6\frac{1}{2} \div 2\frac{1}{2} =$

Decimals

A decimal is a number with one or more digits to the right of the decimal point. 0.862 and 3.12 are decimals. (Note that a zero is shown to the left of the decimal point when the decimal is between 0 and 1.)

Operations with Decimals

Adding and Subtracting Decimals To add or subtract decimals, line up the decimal points one above the other. Then add or subtract as you would normally. Place a decimal point in the answer beneath the other decimal points.

Examples (Addition)

```
   14.50
  200.32
 1245.89
 1460.71
```

14.50
200.047
48.0075
10.6

Add zeros in the blank decimal places to make this problem easier to tackle.

14.5000
200.0470
48.0075
10.6000
273.1545

Examples (Subtraction)
475.89
62.45
413.44

475.84   Since 9 is larger than 4, rename 84 as 7 tens and 14 ones.
62.69
413.15

On Your Own—Adding and Subtracting Decimals

1.   325.45
    + 221.12

2.   12,456.213
    + 32,114.788

3.   788.99
    + 102.12

5.   5,612.12
    − 4,599.99

4.   788.99
    − 102.12

6.   45.00
    − 12.89

Multiplying Decimals To multiply decimals, follow the usual multiplication rules. Count the number of places to the right of the decimals in each factor. Add the numbers of places. Put that many decimal places in the answer.

Examples
12.43 (two decimal places)
× 2.4 (one decimal place)
29.832 (total of three decimal places in the answer)

6.624 (three decimal places)
× 1.22 (two decimal places)
8.08128 (total of 5 decimal places)

On Your Own—Multiplying Decimals

1. 12.89
    × 2.04

3. 144.45
    × 16.23

2. 56.12
    × 2.89

Dividing Decimals To divide decimals, follow the usual division rules. If the divisor (the number you are dividing by) has decimals, move the decimal point to the right as many places as necessary to make the divisor a whole number. Then move the decimal point of the dividend (the number you are dividing) that same number of places to the right. (You may have to add some zeros to the dividend to make this work.) Put the decimal point in the answer directly above the decimal point in the dividend.

Examples

$$12.76\overline{)58.696} = 1276\overline{)5869.6}$$ with quotient 4.6 Note that the decimal point is moved two places to the right in each term. The decimal point in the answer is directly above the decimal point in the dividend.

$$1.25\overline{)50} = 125\overline{)5,000}$$ with quotient 40 In this example the decimal point is moved two places to the right in 1.25 to make 125. The dividend 50 can also be expressed as 50.00 (adding zeros), and moving the decimal point the same number of places to the right makes 5,000. No decimal point needs to be shown in the answer because the answer is a whole number.

On Your Own—Dividing Decimals

1. $144.55 \div 12.15 =$

3. $62.12 \div 2.2 =$

2. $8.88 \div 12.4 =$

Changing Decimals to Fractions Read the decimal and then write the fraction. Reduce the fraction to its lowest terms.

Examples

$0.5 =$ five tenths or 5 over 10: $\dfrac{5}{10} = \dfrac{1}{2}$

$0.66 = 66$ hundredths or 66 over 100: $\dfrac{66}{100} = \dfrac{33}{50}$

$0.75 = 75$ hundredths or 75 over 100: $\dfrac{75}{100} = \dfrac{3}{4}$

$0.006 = 6$ thousandths or 6 over 1,000: $\dfrac{6}{1,000} = \dfrac{3}{500}$

$0.0006 = 6$ ten thousandths or 6 over 10,000: $\dfrac{6}{10,000} = \dfrac{3}{5,000}$

On Your Own—Changing Decimals to Fractions

1. $0.80 =$

2. $0.33 =$

3. $0.05 =$

Changing Fractions to Decimals To change a fraction to a decimal, divide the numerator by the denominator.

Examples

$\dfrac{1}{2} = 1 \div 2 = 0.5$

$\dfrac{3}{4} = 3 \div 4 = 0.75$

$\dfrac{6}{1,000} = 6 \div 1,000 = 0.006$

$^2/_3 = 2 \div 3 = 0.6\overline{6}$ (The bar over the final 6 indicates that this is a *repeating decimal*. That means that you could keep on dividing forever and always have the same remainder.)

On Your Own—Changing Fractions to Decimals

1. $\dfrac{1}{8} =$

2. $\dfrac{12}{36} =$

3. $\dfrac{5}{6} =$

Percent

Percent means "out of 100" or "per hundred." For example, "70%" is read as "70 percent," meaning 70 out of 100 equal parts. Percents are useful ways to show parts of a whole. They can also be easily changed into decimals or fractions.

Changing Percents to Decimals Percent means "per 100." So 70% means "70 per 100," which is 70/100 or 70 ÷ 100, which is 0.70. So to change percents to decimals, delete the percent sign and place the decimal point two places to the left. You may need to add zeros.

Examples

67% = 0.67
6% = 0.06 (A zero was added to the left of the 6.)
187% = 1.87
0.14% = 0.0014 (Two zeros were added to the left of the 14.)

On Your Own—Changing Percents to Decimals

1. 78% =   3. 443% =

2. 12% =

Changing Decimals to Percents To change decimals to percents, merely move the decimal point two places to the right and add a percent sign. (You may need to add a zero on the right.)

Examples

0.67 = 67%
0.4 = 40% (A zero was added to the right of the 4.)
1.87 = 187%
28.886 = 2888.6%
0.0014 = 0.14%

On Your Own—Changing Decimals to Percents

1. 0.75 =   3. 0.4 =

2. 0.225 =

Changing Percents to Fractions A percent is some number over (divided by) 100. So every percent is also a fraction with a denominator of 100. For example, 45% = 45/100. To change percents to fractions, remove the percent sign and write the number over 100. Reduce the fraction to lowest terms.

Examples

$$50\% = \frac{50}{100} = \frac{5}{10} = \frac{1}{2}$$

$$25\% = \frac{25}{100} = \frac{1}{4}$$

$$30\% = \frac{30}{100} = \frac{3}{10}$$

On Your Own—Changing Percents to Fractions

1. 34% =   3. 99% =

2. 57% =

Changing Fractions to Percents

To change fractions to percents, change the fraction to a decimal and then change the decimal to a percent.

Examples

$$\frac{1}{2} = 0.5 = 50\%$$

$$\frac{1}{4} = 0.25 = 25\%$$

$$\frac{1}{10} = 0.10 = 10\%$$

$$\frac{6}{20} = \frac{3}{10} = 0.3 = 30\%$$

$$\frac{1}{3} = 0.33 = 33\%$$

On Your Own—Changing Fractions to Percents

1. $\frac{1}{5}$ =

2. $\frac{2}{5}$ =

3. $\frac{3}{8}$ =

Time Savers: Fractions, Decimals, and Percents

Memorizing some of these relationships might save you some calculation time.

Fraction(s)		= Decimal	= Percent (%)
$\frac{1}{100}$		0.01	1%
$\frac{1}{10}$		0.1	10%
$\frac{1}{5} = \frac{2}{10}$		0.2	20%
$\frac{3}{10}$		0.3	30%
$\frac{2}{5} = \frac{4}{10}$		0.4	40%
$\frac{1}{2} = \frac{5}{10}$		0.5	50%

Memorizing some of these relationships might save you some calculation time.

Fraction(s)	= Decimal	= Percent (%)
$\dfrac{3}{5} = \dfrac{6}{10}$	0.6	60%
$\dfrac{4}{5} = \dfrac{8}{10}$	0.8	80%
$\dfrac{1}{4} = \dfrac{2}{8} = \dfrac{25}{100}$	0.25	25%
$\dfrac{3}{4} = \dfrac{75}{100}$	0.74	75%
$\dfrac{1}{3} = \dfrac{2}{6}$	$0.33\dfrac{1}{3}$	$33\dfrac{1}{3}\%$
$\dfrac{2}{3}$	$0.66\dfrac{2}{3}$	$66\dfrac{2}{3}\%$
$\dfrac{1}{8}$	0.125	12.5%
$\dfrac{3}{8}$	0.375	37.5%
$\dfrac{5}{8}$	0.625	62.5%
$\dfrac{1}{6}$	$0.16\dfrac{2}{3}$	$16\dfrac{2}{3}\%$
1	1.00	100%
1.5	1.50	150%

Finding a Percent of a Number

The SSAT and ISEE may include problems that ask you to find a percent of a number. Problems are often worded like this: "What is 25% of 1,000?" There are two ways you can solve this kind of problem. You can start by changing the percent into a fraction, or you can change it into a decimal.

If you change 25% into a fraction, solve the problem like this:

$$\frac{25}{100} \times 1,000 = \frac{25,000}{100} = 250$$

If you change 25% into a decimal, solve the problem like this: $0.25 \times 1,000 = 250$. You should use the approach that is easiest and best for you.

Percent problems are sometimes stated in another way. For example, a problem may ask, "25 is what percent of 200?" When you see a problem like this, make it into an equation:

$25 = x(200)$ where x is the percent.

$$x = \frac{25}{200} = \frac{1}{8} = 0.125 = 12.5\%$$

Example
30 is what percent of 90?
$30 = x(90)$

$$\frac{30}{90} = \frac{1}{3} = 0.33 = 33\%$$

There is a third way in which percent problems are sometimes stated. Here is an example: "20 is what percent of 25?"

When you see this kind of question, start by setting up a proportion:

Some unknown percent $(x\%) = \dfrac{20}{25}$

$x\%$ is really $\dfrac{x}{100}$ So the equation becomes $\dfrac{x}{100} = \dfrac{20}{25}$.

Reduce the fraction and solve:

$$\frac{x}{100} = \frac{4}{5}$$
$5x = 400$
$x = 80$. So 20 is 80 percent of 25.

Example
30 is what percent of 120?

$$\frac{x}{100} = \frac{30}{120}$$

$$\frac{x}{100} = \frac{3}{12}$$

$12x = 300$

$$x = \frac{300}{12} = 25$$

$x = 25\%$

On Your Own—Finding a Percent of a Number

1. 25% of 125 =

2. 50% of 250 =

3. 80% of 200 =

Finding the Percent of Increase or Decreae

You might also encounter these types of percent problems on the SSAT or ISEE. Here is an example: "What is the percent increase in Kim's salary if she gets a raise from $12,000 to $15,000 per year?" Set this up as an equation with the following structure

$$\frac{\text{Amount of change}}{\text{Original number}} = \text{Percent of change}$$

Example: Increase

For the problem above about Kim's salary, the amount of change is 3,000 because Kim's salary increased by that amount. The original number is 12,000. Plug those numbers into the formula:

$\frac{3,000}{12,000} = \frac{3}{12} = 0.25 = 25\%$. Kim's salary increased by 25%.

Example: Decrease

A CD player has its price reduced from $250 to $200. What is the percent decrease? Use the same process as with the previous problem.

$$\frac{\text{Amount of change}}{\text{Original number}} = \text{Percent of change}$$

The amount of change (decrease) is 50 (250 minus 200). The original number (original price) is $250. Plug these numbers into the formula:

$\frac{50}{250} = \frac{5}{25} = \frac{1}{5} = 0.20$. The CD price decreased by 20%.

On Your Own—Finding the Percent of Increase or Decrease

1. An iPOD went on sale from $500 to $350. What is the percent decrease?
2. A house was purchased at $200,000 and sold for $350,000. What is the percent increase?
3. A car that cost $24,000 went on sale for $21,000. What is the percent decrease?

Exponents

An *exponent* is a number that tells how many times another number is multiplied by itself. In the expression 4^3, the 3 is an exponent. It means that 4 is multiplied it by itself three times or $4 \times 4 \times 4$. So $4^3 = 64$. The expression 4^2 is read "4 to the second power" or "4 squared." The expression 4^3 is read "4 to the third power" or "4 cubed." The expression 4^4 is read "4 to the fourth power." In each of these cases, the exponent is called a "power" of 4. In the expression 5^2 ("5 to the second power" or "5 squared"), the exponent is a "power" of 5.

Examples

$3^5 = 3 \times 3 \times 3 \times 3 \times 3 = 243$

$6^2 = 6 \times 6 = 36$

Negative Exponents Exponents can also be negative. To interpret negative exponents, follow this pattern:

$$2^{-3} = \frac{1}{2^3} = \frac{1}{8}$$

Examples

$$3^{-2} = \frac{1}{3^2} = \frac{1}{9}$$

$$4^{-3} = \frac{1}{4^3} \text{ or } \frac{1}{64}$$

Multiplying Numbers with Exponents To multiply numbers with exponents, multiply out each number and then perform the operation.

Examples

$3^4 \times 2^3 = (3 \times 3 \times 3 \times 3) \times (2 \times 2 \times 2)$
$= 81 \times 8 = 648$
$2^9 \times 12^2 = (2 \times 2 \times 2 \times 2 \times 2 \times 2 \times 2 \times 2 \times 2) \times (12 \times 12)$
$= 512 \times 144 = 73,728$

On Your Own—Multiplying Numbers with Exponents

1. $3^3 \times 6^2 =$ 3. $8^1 \times 6^3 =$

2. $6^2 \times 12^2 =$

Square Roots

The *square* of a number is the number times the number. The square of 2 is $2 \times 2 = 4$. The *square root* of a number is the number whose square equals the original number. One square root of 4 (written $\sqrt{4}$) is 2, since $2 \times 2 = 4$. -2 is also a square root of 4 since $-2 \times -2 = 4$.

SSAT/ISEE Coach Says . . .
Watch the Signs! Remember that a negative number multiplied by itself results in a positive number.

Some Examples

$\sqrt{1} = $ 1 or -1

$\sqrt{4} = 2$ or -2

$\sqrt{9} = 3$ or -3

$\sqrt{16} = 4$ or -4

$\sqrt{25}$ = 5 or –5

$\sqrt{36}$ = 6 or –6

$\sqrt{49}$ = 7 or –7

$\sqrt{64}$ = 8 or –8

$\sqrt{81}$ = 9 or –9

$\sqrt{100}$ = 10 or –10

$\sqrt{121}$ = 11 or –11

$\sqrt{144}$ = 12 or –12

$\sqrt{169}$ = 13 or –13

$\sqrt{196}$ = 14 or –14

$\sqrt{225}$ = 15 or –15

On Your Own—Square Root

1. $\sqrt{256}$ =

2. $\sqrt{400}$ =

3. $\sqrt{441}$ =

Mean (Average)

The *mean* of a set of numbers is the average. Add the numbers and divide by the number of numbers.

Examples

What is the mean of the numbers 2, 4, 7, 4, and 5?
The sum is 22. Since there are 5 numbers, divide 22 by 5 to get a mean or average of 4.4.
What is the mean of the numbers 3, 4, 2, 6, 7, 12, 56, and 104?
The sum is 194. There are 8 numbers, so divide 194 by 8 to get 24.25.

On Your Own—Calculating the Mean

Calculate the mean of the following numbers.

1. 2, 4, 5, 6, 7, 12, 43, 55, 78, 4, 27 =

2. 44, 67, 80, 10, 23, 23, 23, 77, 88, 100 =

3. 125, 334, 522, 16, 822 =

Median

Order a set of numbers from least to greatest. If there is an odd number of numbers, the *median* is the number in the middle of that sequence of numbers. If there is an even number of numbers, the median is the mean or average of the two middle numbers.

Examples

What is the median of the following numbers?

14, 999, 75, 102, 456, 19

Reorder the numbers from least to greatest: 14, 19, 75, 102, 456, 999
The middle number is 75, so that is the median.

What is the median of the following numbers?

15, 765, 65, 890, 12, 1

Reorder the numbers from least to greatest: 1, 12, 15, 65, 765, 890
Since there is an even number of numbers, find the average of the middle two numbers.

15 + 65 = 80
80 ÷ 2 = 40
40 is the median

Mode

The *mode* of a set of numbers is the number that appears most frequently in that set.

Example

What is the mode of the following set of numbers?

12, 14, 15, 15, 15, 17, 18

The number 15 appears most often in this set, so it is the mode of the set.

Graphs

Often it is helpful to represent numbers in a visual form called a *graph*. The most common graphs are circle graphs, bar graphs, and line graphs. You won't be asked to construct such graphs on your test, but you may have to interpret one or more of them.

Circle or Pie Graph This kind of graph uses a circle divided into parts to show fractional or percentage relationships.

Example

In a survey at a local high school, students were asked to name their favorite lunch food. The results of that survey are shown in the circle graph below.

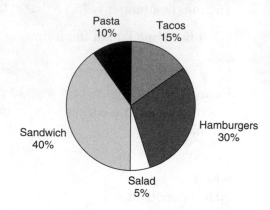

Favorite Lunch Food of High School Students

Questions such as the following are typical.

- Which food was most (or least) popular with the students? (most: sandwich; least: salad)
- Which two food selections of the students make up 50% of the total? (sandwich and pasta: 40% and 10% = 50%)
- What is the ratio of the students who selected sandwiches to students who selected hamburgers? (4:3)
- If the total number of students surveyed was 2,500, how many chose salad as their favorite lunch? (125; 2,500 × 0.05 = 125)

On Your Own—Pie Graph

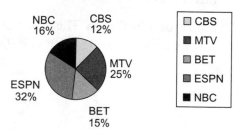

Percent Watching Various TV Stations on Monday Night

1. Which station was the most watched?
2. What is the ratio of NBC watchers to ESPN watchers?
3. Which was the least-watched station?

Bar Graph This kind of graph uses bars to provide a visual comparison of different quantities.

Example

The following bar graph compares the number of different types of sandwiches sold on Tuesday at a certain sandwich shop.

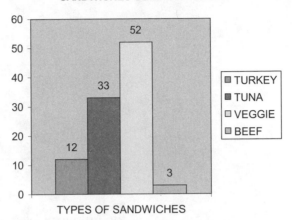

Questions such as the following are typical.

- Which kind of sandwich did the store sell the most of on Tuesday? (veggie)
- How many more tuna sandwiches than turkey sandwiches were sold on Tuesday? (21)
- How many tuna sandwiches and beef sandwiches were sold on Tuesday? (36)

On Your Own—Bar Graph

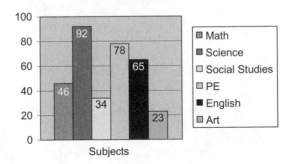

1. According to the bar graph, which subject is the most favorite of the most students?
2. Which subject is the favorite of the fewest students?

3. What is the total number of students who picked their favorite subject?

4. What is the ratio of students who picked art as their favorite subject to students who picked math?

Line Graph This kind of graph is generally used to show change over time.

Example

The following line graph shows the change in attendance at this year's football games.

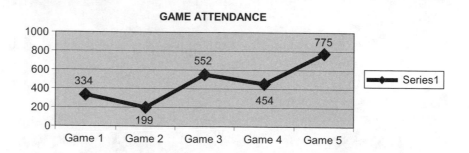

Questions such as the following are typical.

- How many more people attended game 3 than game 2? (353)
- Which game had the highest attendance? (Game 5)
- How many people attended the first game of the year? (334)

On Your Own—Line Graph

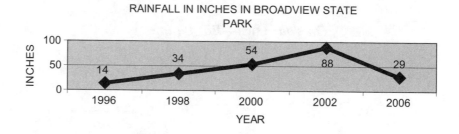

1. Which year had the greatest rainfall?

2. Which year had the least rainfall?

3. What was the average yearly rainfall in the park during this time period?

4. How many more inches of rain fell in 2000 than in 1996?

Units of Measure

If you don't know the following units of measure, you just need to memorize them.

UNITS OF MEASURE

Customary System

Length

12 inches (in) = 1 foot (ft)

3 feet = 1 yard (yd)

36 inches = 1 yard

5,280 feet = 1 mile (mi)

Area

1 square foot (ft^2) = 144 square inches (in^2)

9 square feet = 1 square yard (yd^2)

Weight

16 ounces (oz) = 1 pound (lb)

2,000 pounds = 1 ton (t)

Liquid Volume

2 cups (c) = 1 pint (pt)

2 pints = 1 quart (qt)

4 quarts = 1 gallon (gal)

Time

7 days = 1 week

4 weeks = 1 month

12 months = 1 year

52 weeks = 1 year

10 years = 1 decade

Metric System

Length

100 centimeters (cm) = 1 meter (m)

1,000 meters = 1 kilometer (km)

Volume

10,000 milliliters (mL) = 1 liter (L)

Mass

1,000 grams (g) = 1 kilogram (kg)

1,000 kilograms = 1 metric ton

Converting Between Systems

1 meter ≈ 39.37 inches

1 kilometer ≈ 0.62 miles

1 centimeter ≈ 0.39 inches

1 kilogram ≈ 2.2 pounds

1 liter ≈ 1.057 quarts

1 gram ≈ 0.035 ounce

Answers to "On Your Own" Practice Sets

On Your Own—Addition

1. 745

2. 17,250

3. 25,676

4. 97,986

5. 98,742,358

6. 3,460,988

7. 670,504

8. 45,540,007

9. 6,913,208

10. 34,958,777

On Your Own—Subtraction

1. 812

2. 2,495

3. 22,411

4. 55,445

5. 11,005,411

6. 589,831

7. 84,822,389

8. 991,188

9. 14,485,595

10. 99

On Your Own—Multiplication

1. 20

2. 20

3. 63

4. 1,755

5. 6,566

6. 410,843

7. 14,745,358

8. 6,028,318,806

9. 212,244,289,278

10. 1,257,806,631

On Your Own—Division

1. 4

2. 12

3. 2

4. 456

5. 987

6. 258

7. 32

8. 21

9. 12

10. 331

On Your Own—Symbols

1. T	6. F
2. T	7. T
3. T	8. T
4. F	9. F
5. T	10. F

On Your Own—Order of Operations

1. 40	5. 41
2. 50	6. 152
3. 90	7. 21
4. 21	8. 218

On Your Own—Adding Positive and Negative Numbers

1. 1	5. −58
2. −7	6. 200
3. 9	7. 320
4. 130	8. −125

On Your Own—Subtracting Positive and Negative Numbers

1. 8	6. 475
2. 16	7. 1400
3. 20	8. 1400
4. 33	9. 62
5. 116	

On Your Own—Multiplying and Dividing Positive and Negative Numbers

1. −8	5. +2
2. +8	6. −2
3. +40	7. 320
4. −2	8. −50

On Your Own—Subtracting Numbers within Parentheses

1. 120

2. 5

3. 135

4. 475

5. 250

6. 19

7. 151

On Your Own—Multiplying and Dividing by Zero

1. 0

2. 0

3. 0

4. 0

5. undefined

On Your Own—Least Common Multiples

1. 2

2. 3

3. 3

4. 2

On Your Own—Changing Improper Fractions into Mixed Numbers

1. $12\frac{1}{2}$

2. $2\frac{1}{3}$

3. $11\frac{1}{4}$

4. $39\frac{1}{2}$

5. $16\frac{4}{5}$

6. $7\frac{7}{10}$

On Your Own—Renaming a Mixed Number as a Fraction

1. $\frac{10}{3}$

2. $\frac{25}{4}$

3. $\frac{71}{12}$

4. $\frac{15}{4}$

5. $\frac{37}{5}$

On Your Own—Finding Equivalent Fractions

1. $\dfrac{2}{6}$; $\dfrac{3}{9}$; $\dfrac{4}{12}$

2. $\dfrac{4}{6}$; $\dfrac{6}{9}$; $\dfrac{8}{12}$

3. $\dfrac{1}{2}$; $\dfrac{4}{8}$; $\dfrac{6}{12}$

On Your Own—Reducing Fractions to Lowest Terms

1. $\dfrac{1}{3}$

2. $\dfrac{1}{2}$

3. $\dfrac{1}{4}$

4. $\dfrac{1}{2}$

5. $\dfrac{1}{8}$

6. $\dfrac{1}{13}$

On Your Own—Adding and Subtracting Fractions

1. $\dfrac{5}{6}$

2. $1\dfrac{13}{24}$

3. $1\dfrac{5}{8}$

4. $\dfrac{2}{3}$

5. $\dfrac{7}{15}$

On Your Own—Adding and Subtracting Mixed Numbers

1. $5\dfrac{1}{2}$

2. $16\dfrac{1}{6}$

3. $13\dfrac{2}{15}$

4. $4\dfrac{5}{8}$

5. $7\dfrac{5}{9}$

On Your Own—Multiplying Fractions

1. $\dfrac{21}{40}$

2. $\dfrac{12}{75}$

3. $\dfrac{4}{35}$

On Your Own—Dividing Fractions

1. 1

2. $2\frac{2}{5}$

3. $2\frac{2}{3}$

On Your Own—Multiplying Mixed Numbers

1. $19\frac{11}{15}$

5. $23\frac{2}{5}$

3. $86\frac{1}{3}$

On Your Own—Dividing Mixed Numbers

1. $5\frac{3}{7}$

3. $2\frac{3}{5}$

2. 13

On Your Own—Adding and Subtracting Decimals

1. 546.57

4. 686.87

2. 44,571.001

5. 10,12.13

3. 891.11

6. 32.11

On Your Own—Multiplying Decimals

1. 26.2956

3. 2,199.9735

2. 162.1868

On Your Own—Dividing Decimals

1. 11.8911

3. 28.236

2. 3.942

On Your Own—Changing Decimals to Fractions

1. $\frac{4}{5}$

3. $\frac{1}{20}$

2. $\frac{1}{3}$

On Your Own—Changing Fractions to Decimals

1. 0.125

2. 0.33

3. 0.83

On Your Own—Changing Percents to Decimals

1. 0.78

2. 0.12

3. 4.43

On Your Own—Changing Decimals to Percents

1. 75%

2. 22.5%

3. 40%

On Your Own—Changing Percents to Fractions

1. $\dfrac{17}{50}$

2. $\dfrac{57}{100}$

3. $\dfrac{99}{100}$

On Your Own—Changing Fractions to Percents

1. 20%

2. 40%

3. 37.5%

On Your Own—Finding a Percent of a Number

1. 31.25

2. 125

3. 160

On Your Own—Finding the Percent of Increase or Decrease

1. 30%

2. 75%

3. 12.5%

On Your Own—Multiplying Numbers with Exponents

1. 1,764

2. 5,184

3. 1,728

On Your Own—Square Root

1. 16

2. 20

3. 21

On Your Own—Calculating the Mean

1. 21.45

2. 53.5

3. 363.8

On Your Own—Pie Graph

1. ESPN

2. 1:2

3. CBS

On Your Own—Bar Graph

1. SCIENCE

2. ART

3. 338

4. 2:1

On Your Own—Line Graph

1. 202

2. 1,996

3. 43.8

4. 40 inches

The Algebra You Need to Know

Algebra on the SSAT and ISEE

If you are taking the lower level version of the SSAT or the ISEE, you will need to know some very simple concepts in algebra. If you are taking the upper level version of either test, you may need to be familiar with some more advanced algebra concepts and with probability. This chapter will review the following topics:

Topics

Evaluating Expressions	Operations with Algebraic Expressions
Solving Simple Equations	Probability
Ratios and Proportions	

This chapter will give you a complete review of all these algebra topics. After you study each topic, check your progress by working through the practice sets called "On Your Own." Answers for these practice sets appear at the end of the chapter.

Algebra and Probability Review

The Language of Algebra

Algebra uses arithmetic functions and processes, but some of the numbers are replaced by letters. The letters merely represent numbers that are currently unknown or that can change in value according to circumstances. In algebra, a letter representing a number that can change in value is called a *variable*.

- An expression such as $6x$ means "6 times x or x times 6."
- An expression such as $x + 7$ means "some number, currently unknown, plus 7."
- An expression such as $x - 12$ means "some number, currently unknown, less 12."
- An expression such as $\frac{x}{5}$ means "some number, currently unknown, divided by 5, or the ratio of some number and 5."

Very often verbal expressions in word problems need to be translated into algebraic expressions before they can be solved. Below are some examples of verbal expressions and their algebraic counterparts.

Verbal Expression	Algebraic Expression
Some number plus 7	$x + 7$
Some number subtracted from 8	$8 - x$
8 subtracted from some number	$x - 8$
The product of some number and 12	$12x$
The product of 5 and the sum of x and y	$5(x + y)$
Some number divided by 4	$\dfrac{x}{4}$
The ratio of 6 and some number	$\dfrac{6}{x}$
9 times some number plus the sum of 5 and y	$9x + (5 + y)$
12 less the sum of 3 and some number	$12 - (3 + x)$

On Your Own—Algebra Language
Write the following using algebraic expressions.

1. Six times some number plus four squared
2. Twelve times the sum of six plus some number
3. The product of x and y times the product of 11 plus the product of x and y.
4. Some number divided by 40 and the product of x and y.
5. Some number squared plus that number times 14 equals minus 21.

Evaluating Expressions
To evaluate an algebraic expression, substitute a given value for the unknown and then perform the arithmetic as indicated.

Examples

Evaluate $a + b + c$ if $a = 2$, $b = 4$, and $c = 3$
Substitute each value for the corresponding letter and then do the addition as indicated.

$2 + 4 + 3 = 9$

Evaluate $2x^2 + 4y + 5$ if $x = 2$ and $y = 3$
$2(2)^2 + 4(3) + 5$
$= 2(4) + 12 + 5$
$= 8 + 12 + 5 = 25$

Evaluate $\dfrac{a+b}{4} + \dfrac{a}{b+c}$ if $a = 2$, $b = 6$, and $c = 10$

$$\dfrac{2+6}{4} + \dfrac{2}{6+10}$$

$$= \dfrac{8}{4} + \dfrac{2}{16}$$

$$= 2 + \dfrac{2}{16}$$

$$= 2\dfrac{1}{8}$$

SSAT/ISEE Coach Says . . .

Don't Forget: Order of operations is critical!
- Simplify anything within the parentheses.
- Apply the powers or exponents.
- Multiply and divide in order from left to right.
- Add and subtract in order from left to right.

On Your Own—Evaluating Expressions
Evaluate the following:

1. $x + y + z$ if $x = 2$, $y = 6$, $z = 10$
2. $(x + y)^2 + (y - 1)$ if $x = 8$, $y = 4$
3. $6x + (y + z)^2$ if $x = 5$, $y = 2$, $z = 3$

Solving Simple Equations

An *equation* is a mathematical statement having an equals (=) sign. When an equation contains a letter standing for an unknown number, you can use the equation to find the value of that unknown. This is called *solving the equation for the unknown.*

Think of an equation as a balanced scale. Everything to the right of the = sign has to balance with everything on the left side of the = sign.

Because an equation is balanced, it will stay in balance if you do the same thing to the numbers on both sides of the = sign. For example, the equation $10 = 10$ will stay balanced if you add 3 to both sides. The new equation will be $13 = 13$. Similarly, the equation $x + y = x + y$ will stay balanced if you subtract 10 from both sides. The new equation will be $x + y - 10 = x + y - 10$.

Similarly, the equation $x + y = a + b$ will stay balanced if you subtract 8 from both sides. The new equation will be $x + y - 8 = a + b - 8$.

To solve an equation and find the value of an unknown, you need to get the *unknown on one side of the equation* and all the other terms on the other side of the equation. Consider this example.

Solve: $y - 4 = 20$

Add 4 to both sides:

$y - 4 + 4 = 20 + 4$
$y = 20 + 4$
$y = 24$

SSAT/ISEE Coach Says . . .

Another Way to Think about It. Here is a simple way to think about using addition or subtraction to solve an equation: Just move the number you are adding or subtracting from one side of the = sign to the other and change its sign (either − to + or + to −). So in the equation shown, move the − 4 to the other side of the = sign and make it + 4. This makes the equation $y = 20 + 4$ or 24.

An equation will also stay balanced if you multiply or divide both sides by the same number. You can also use these operations to solve equations.

Example (Division)

Solve: $3x = 18$

You want to get x all alone on the left side of the equation, so divide $3x$ by 3. Since $\frac{3}{3} = 1$, $\frac{3x}{3} = x$. To maintain the balance, divide the right side of the equation by 3 as well:

$\frac{18}{3} = 6.$ So $x = 6$

SSAT/ISEE Coach Says . . .

Another Way to Think about It. Here is another way to think about using division to solve an equation: in a problem such as $3x = 18$, instead of trying to divide both sides by 3, simply move the 3 across the = sign and make it the denominator of the other side of the equation:

$3x = 18$

$x = \frac{18}{3}$

$x = 6$

Example (Multiplication)

$$\frac{x}{3} = 12.$$

Multiply both sides by 3:

$$3\,\frac{x}{3} = 3(12)$$

$$x = 3(12)$$
$$x = 36$$

SSAT/ISEE Coach Says . . .

Another Way to Think about It. Here is another way to think about using multiplication to solve an equation: In a problem such as $x/2 = 20$, move the denominator 2 across the $=$ sign and make it the multiplier on the other side.

$$\frac{x}{2} = 20$$

$$x = 2(20)$$

$$x = 40$$

Examples

Solve for z:

$$16 + z = 24$$

Subtract 16 from both sides.

$$z = 24 - 16 = 8$$

Solve for x:

$$\frac{x}{5} - 4 = 2$$

Add 4 to both sides.

$$\frac{x}{5} = 2 + 4$$

$$\frac{x}{5} = 6$$

Multiply each side by 5 to isolate x on the left side.

$$x = 5(6) = 30$$

Solve for a:

$$\frac{2}{3}a - 5 = 9$$

Add 5 to both sides.

$$\frac{2}{3}a = 9 + 5$$

$$\frac{2}{3}a = 14$$

Multiply each side by $\frac{3}{2}$.

$$a = 14\left(\frac{3}{2}\right)$$

$$a = \frac{42}{2} = 21$$

SSAT/ISEE Coach Says . . .
Divide Out Common Factors. Another way to do this final step is to divide out common factors.

$$\frac{^{7}\cancel{14}}{1} \times \frac{3}{\cancel{2}_{1}} = 21$$

Solve for y:

$$7y = 3y - 12$$

$$7y - 3y = -12$$

$$4y = -12$$

$$y = -\frac{12}{4}$$

$$y = -3$$

On Your Own—Solving Simple Equations
Solve for the unknown in each equation.

1. $20 + z = 32$

2. $\frac{x}{10} - 5 = 25$

3. $\frac{x}{3} = -15$

4. $y - 12 = -20$

Ratios and Proportions
A *ratio* is a comparison of one number to another. A ratio can be represented by a fraction.

Example
On a certain road, there are 6 cars for every 4 trucks. The ratio is $\frac{6}{4}$ or $\frac{3}{2}$.

A *proportion* is an equation stating that two ratios are equivalent. Ratios are equivalent if they can be represented by equivalent fractions. A proportion may be written

$$\frac{a}{b} = \frac{c}{d}$$

where a/b and c/d are equivalent fractions. This proportion can be read "a is to b as c is to d."

Like any other equation, a proportion can be solved for an unknown by isolating that unknown on one side of the equation. In this case, to solve for a, multiply both sides by b:

$$\frac{ba}{b} = \frac{bc}{d}$$

$$a = \frac{bc}{d}$$

Examples

Solve for p:

$$\frac{c}{p} = \frac{h}{j}$$

Multiply both sides by p.

$$(p)\frac{c}{p} = (p)\frac{h}{j}$$

$$c = \frac{ph}{j}$$

Solve for a:

$$\frac{a}{4} = \frac{3}{6}$$

$$(4)\frac{a}{4} = (4)\frac{3}{6}$$

$$a = \frac{12}{6}$$

$$a = 2$$

Another Way to Solve It. Another way to solve proportion problems is to find the cross products.

Solve for a:

$$\frac{a}{4} = \frac{3}{6}$$

Cross-multiply:

$a \times 6 = 4 \times 3$
$6a = 12$
$a = 2$

Solve for k:

$$\frac{2}{5} = \frac{8}{k}$$

$2k = 40$

$k = 20$

On Your Own—Ratios and Proportions

1. Solve for m. $\quad \dfrac{2}{5} = \dfrac{16}{m}$

2. Solve for q. $\quad \dfrac{2}{5} = \dfrac{m}{16}$

3. Solve for d. $\quad \dfrac{a}{b} = \dfrac{c}{d}$

Operations with Algebraic Expressions

Study the following examples to learn how to add, subtract, multiply, and divide simple algebraic expressions.

Adding and Subtracting Algebraic Expressions As long as the variables are the same, just add or subtract the numbers.

Examples

Add:
$\quad 9y$
$\underline{\ 11y}$
$\quad 20y$

Subtract:
$\quad 30b$
$\underline{-15b}$
$\quad 15b$

Add:

$$12 \ a^2bc$$
$$\underline{\ 4 \ a^2bc}$$
$$16 \ a^2bc$$

Subtract:

$$12 \ a^2bc$$
$$\underline{-4 \ a^2bc}$$
$$8 \ a^2bc$$

Multiplying Algebraic Expressions When multiplying simple algebraic expressions, multiply any numbers, then multiply unknowns. Add any exponents. Keep in mind that in a term like x or $2x$, the x is understood to have the exponent 1 even though the 1 is not shown.

Examples

$$(2k)(k) = 2k^2$$

$$(3x)(2y) = 6xy$$

$$(k^2)(k^3) = k^5$$

$$(j^3k)(j^2k^3) = j^5k^4$$

$$-5(b^4c)(-3b^3c^5) = 15b^7c^6$$

Dividing Algebraic Expressions To divide simple algebraic expressions, divide the numbers and subtract any exponents (the exponent of the divisor from the exponent of the number being divided).

Examples

$$\frac{2g^5}{6g^3} = \frac{1}{3}g^2$$

$$3\frac{g^5}{g^3} = 3g^2$$

$$\frac{12a^6b^2}{3a^3b} = 4 \ a^3b$$

$$\frac{m^5}{m^8} = m^{-3} = \frac{1}{m^3}$$

$$\frac{-5 \ (ab) \ (ab^2)}{ab} =$$

This example can be handled in two ways. One way is to simplify the numerator:

$$\frac{-5a^2b^3}{ab} = -5 \ ab^2$$

Another way is to divide out similar terms:

$$\frac{-5\ (ab)\ (ab^2)}{ab} = -5\ ab^2$$

Either way works just fine and will give you the correct answer.

On Your Own—Operations with Algebraic Expressions

1. Add:
   $6\ a^2bc$
   $\underline{3\ a^2bc}$

2. Subtract:
   $12\ a^2bc$
   $\underline{-16\ a^2bc}$

3. Multiply:
   $5(g^4c)\ (-3g^3c^5)$

4. Divide:
   $$\frac{3\ x^3y^5}{xy^2}$$

Probability

When every event in a set of possible events has an equal chance of occurring, probability is the chance that a particular event (or "outcome") will occur. Probability is represented by the formula

$$\text{Probability} = \frac{\text{Number of positive outcomes}}{\text{Number of possible outcomes}}$$

Let's say you have a spinner with an arrow that spins around a circle that is divided into six equal parts. The parts are labeled from 1 to 6. When you spin the arrow, what is the probability that it will land on the part labeled 4? Following the formula:

$$\text{Probability} = \frac{\text{Number of positive outcomes}}{\text{Number of possible outcomes}}$$

$$\text{Probability} = \frac{1}{6} \text{ or 1 in 6}$$

Let's take that same spinner. What is the probability that the arrow will land on the number 2 or the number 3 when spun? Using the formula:

$$\text{Probability} = \frac{\text{Number of positive outcomes}}{\text{Number of possible outcomes}}$$

$$\text{Probability} = \frac{2}{6} = \frac{1}{3} \text{ or 1 in 3}$$

Examples

Solve: The National Fruit Growers' Association is conducting a random survey asking people to tell their favorite fruit. The chart shows the results so far.

Favorite Fruit	Number of People
Apples	236
Peaches	389
Oranges	250
Pears	125

What is the probability that the next randomly selected person will say that pears are his or her favorite fruit?

To solve probability problems, follow this word problem solution procedure.

Procedure

What must you find? Probability that a certain event will occur.
What are the units? Fraction or decimal or percent.
What do you know? The number of people selecting each fruit as their favorite.
Create an equation and solve.

$$\text{Probability} = \frac{\text{Number of positive outcomes}}{\text{Number of possible outcomes}}$$

Substitute values and solve.
Number of positive outcomes = 125 people who named pears as their favorite fruit
Number of possible outcomes = all people surveyed = 236 + 389 + 250 + 125 = 1,000

$$\text{Probability} = \frac{125}{1,000} = \frac{1}{8} = 1:8 = 0.125 = 12.5\%$$

Solve: A box is filled with 25 black balls, 50 white balls, and 75 red balls. If Wendell reaches into the box and picks a ball without looking, what is the probability that he will pick a black or a white ball?

Procedure

What must you find? Probability that either of two events will occur.
What are the units? Fraction, decimal, or percent.
What do you know? How many of each kind of ball are in the box.
Create an equation and solve.

$$\text{Probability} = \frac{\text{Number of positive outcomes}}{\text{Number of possible outcomes}}$$

Substitute values and solve.

Number of positive outcomes = number of black balls + number of white balls = 25 + 50 = 75

Number of possible outcomes = 25 + 50 + 75 = 150

Probability = $\dfrac{75}{150}$ = $\dfrac{1}{2}$ 1:2 = 0.5 = 50%

On Your Own—Probability

1. The local travel bureau is conducting a random survey asking people to indicate how they will spend their next vacation. The chart shows the results so far.

Type of Vacation	Number of People
Spending time at the beach	56
Cruising the islands	89
Hiking in the mountains	50
Scuba diving	40
Visiting museums	67
Reading and relaxing	98
Total number of people surveyed	400

What is the probability that the next randomly selected person will say that hiking in the mountains will be how he or she will spend his or her vacation?

2. A box is filled with 50 black balls, 75 white balls, and 25 red balls. If Marty reaches into the box and picks a ball without looking, what is the probability that he will pick a black or a red ball?

Answers to "On Your Own" Practice Sets

On Your Own—Algebra Language

1. $6 \times (4)^2$

2. $12(6 + x)$

3. $(xy)(11 + xy)$

4. $\dfrac{g}{40 + xy}$

5. $x^2 + 14x = -21$

On Your Own—Evaluating Expressions

1. 18

3. 45

2. 147

On Your Own—Solving Simple Equations

1. $z = 12$

3. $x = -45$

2. $x = 300$

4. $y = -8$

On Your Own—Ratios and Proportions

1. $m = 40$

3. $ad = cb$

2. $q = 6\dfrac{2}{5}$

On Your Own—Operations with Algebraic Expressions

1. $9a^2bc$

3. $-15g^7c^6$

2. $28a^2bc$

4. $3x^2y^3$

On Your Own—Probability

1. $\dfrac{1}{8}$

2. $\dfrac{1}{2}$

The Geometry You Need to Know

Geometry on the SSAT and ISEE

If you are taking the lower level version of the SSAT or the ISEE, you will need to know some very simple concepts in geometry. If you are taking the upper level version of either test, you may need to be familiar with some more advanced geometry concepts. This chapter will review the following topics:

Topics

Points, Lines, and Angles	Types of Quadrilaterals
Identifying Congruent Angles	Circles
Solving Angle Problems	Perimeter and Area
Types of Triangles	Types of 3-Dimensional (Solid)
Base and Height of a Triangle	Figures
Median of a Triangle	Finding the Volume of Solid Figures

This chapter will give you a complete review of all these geometry topics. After you study each topic, check your progress by working through the practice sets called "On Your Own." Answers for these practice sets appear at the end of the chapter.

Geometry Review

Points, Lines, and Angles
To work with geometry, you need to understand points, lines, and angles.

- A *point* is an exact location in space. It is represented by a dot and a capital letter.
- A *line* is a set of points that form a straight path extending in either direction without end. A line that includes points B and D is represented as follows: BD.
- A *ray* is a part of a line that has one end point and continues without end in the opposite direction. A ray that ends at point A and includes point B is represented as follows: AB.

- A *line segment* is a part of a ray or a line that connects two points. A line connecting points A and B is represented as follows: AB.

An *angle* is a figure formed by two rays that have the same end point. That end point is called the *vertex* (plural: *vertices*) of the angle. An example is shown below.

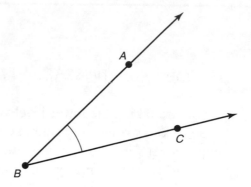

In this example, rays BA and BC have the same end point, which is point B. So point B is the vertex of the angle. The two line segments BA and BC are called the sides of the angle. The symbol $\angle$ is used to indicate an angle.

An angle is labeled or identified in several different ways:

- By the vertex: $\angle B$
- By the letters of the three points that form it: $\angle ABC$ or $\angle CBA$. (The vertex is always the middle of the three letters.)

The measure of the size of an angle is expressed in *degrees* (°).

SSAT/ISEE Coach Says . . .
Bisect. You will see the word *bisect* used in some geometry problems. To *bisect* merely means to split into two equal parts.

Classifying Angles
There are three types of angles that you should know for the SSAT or ISEE. They are right angles, acute angles, and obtuse angles.

Right Angles. A right angle measures exactly 90°. Right angles are found in squares, rectangles and certain triangles. $\angle ABC$ is a right angle.

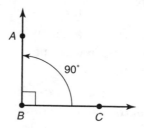

Examples

Both angles below are right angles.

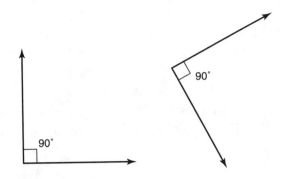

Acute Angles. An angle that measures less than 90° is called an acute angle. $\angle ABC$ is an acute angle.

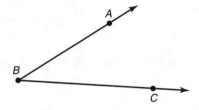

Examples

The angles below are all acute angles.

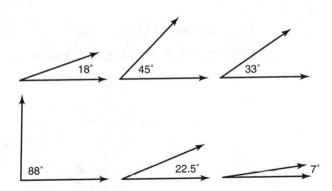

Obtuse Angles. An angle with a measure that is greater than 90° but less than 180° is called an obtuse angle. ∠DEF is an obtuse angle.

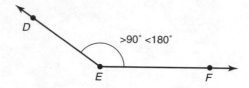

Examples

The angles below are all obtuse angles.

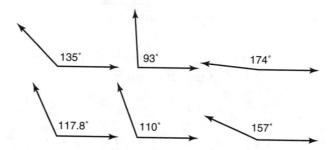

Straight Angles. A straight angle is one that measures exactly 180°. This kind of angle forms a straight line. ∠ABC is a straight angle.

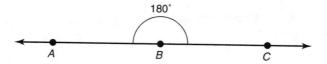

Classifying Pairs of Lines

Intersecting Lines. Intersecting lines are lines that meet or cross each other.

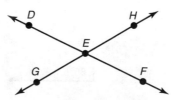

Line *DF* intersects line *GH* at point *E*.

Parallel Lines. Parallel lines are lines in a plane that never intersect.

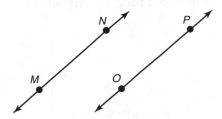

Line *MN* is parallel to line *OP*. In symbols, *MN* ∥ *OP*.

Perpendicular Lines. Perpendicular lines intersect to form right angles.

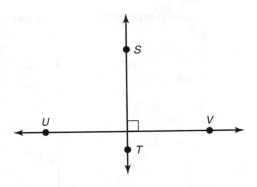

Line *ST* is perpendicular to line *UV*. In symbols, *ST* ⊥ *UV*.

Classifying Pairs of Angles

Adjacent Angles. Adjacent angles have the same vertex and share one side. ∠ABC and ∠CBD are adjacent angles.

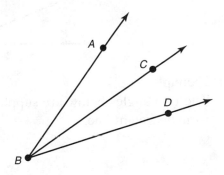

Complementary Angles. Two adjacent angles whose measures total 90° are called complementary angles. ∠*MNO* and ∠*ONP* are complementary. Their measures total exactly 90°.

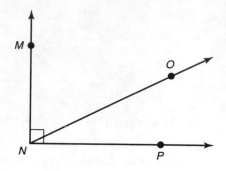

Example
These two angles are complementary. Together they measure 90°.

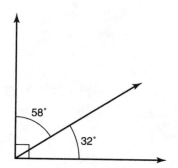

Supplementary Angles. Two adjacent angles whose measures total 180° are called supplementary angles. Together they make a straight line. ∠*KHG* and ∠*GHJ* are supplementary because together they add to 180° or a straight line.

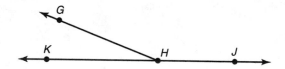

Example
The two angles below are supplementary. Together they measure 180° and form a straight line.

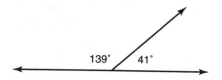

Vertical Angles. Two angles formed by intersecting lines are called vertical angles if they are not adjacent. In the figure below, ∠AED and ∠BEC are vertical angles. ∠AEB and ∠DEC are also vertical angles. Vertical angles are often said to be "opposite" to each other as shown in the figure.

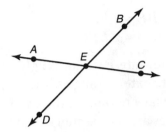

Vertical angles are *congruent*. That is, their measures are the same. ∠AED = ∠BEC and ∠AEB = ∠DEC.

Example

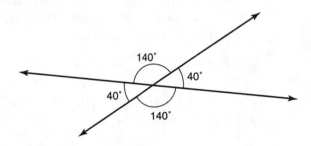

Identifying Congruent (Equal) Angles

In the figure below, lines *AC* and *DF* are parallel. They are intersected by a third line *GH*. This third line is called a *transversal*.

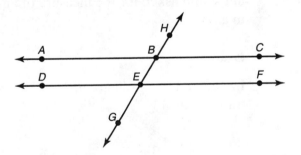

This intersection creates eight angles. There are four pairs of vertical congruent angles:

∠ABH = ∠EBC
∠ABE = ∠HBC
∠DEB = ∠GEF
∠DEG = ∠BEF

Alternate Interior Angles. In addition, four of these angles make two pairs of alternate interior angles. These are angles that are on opposite sides of the transversal, are between the two parallel lines, and are not adjacent. When parallel lines are intersected by a transversal, alternate interior angles are congruent. The two pairs are:

$\angle ABE = \angle BEF$
$\angle DEB = \angle EBC$

Alternate Exterior Angles. Four of the angles also make two pairs of alternate exterior angles. These are angles that are on opposite sides of the transversal, are outside the two parallel lines, and are not adjacent. When parallel lines are intersected by a transversal, alternate exterior angles are congruent. The two pairs are:

$\angle ABH = \angle GEF$
$\angle HBC = \angle DEG$

Corresponding Angles. Eight of the angles also make four pairs of corresponding angles. These are angles that are in corresponding positions. When parallel lines are intersected by a transversal, corresponding angles are congruent. The four pairs are:

$\angle ABH = \angle DEB$
$\angle HBC = \angle BEF$
$\angle ABE = \angle DEG$
$\angle EBC = \angle GEF$

Solving Angle Problems

On the SSAT or ISEE, you may be asked to use what you know about angles and angle relationships to solve problems. You may be asked to tell which angles in a figure are congruent. Or you may be given the measure of one angle and asked for the measure of an adjacent angle or some related angle in a figure.

Examples

In the following diagram, parallel lines *MO* and *RT* are intersected by transversal *WV*.

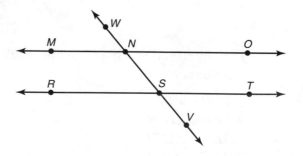

Which angle is congruent to ∠MNW?
A ∠MNS
B ∠WNO
C ∠RSV
D ∠VST

Of the choices, the only one that is congruent to ∠MNW is ∠VST because they are alternate exterior angles.

Which angle is congruent to ∠MNS?
A ∠RSV
B ∠SNO
C ∠VST
D ∠MNW

Of the choices, the only one that is congruent to ∠MNS is ∠RSV because they are corresponding angles.

If ∠RSN measures 50°, what is the measure of ∠RSV?
A 90°
B 110°
C 130°
D 150°

∠RSN and ∠RSV are supplementary angles. That is, together they form a straight line and their measures add up to 180°. So if ∠RSN measures 50°, then ∠RSV measures 180 − 50 = 130°.

On Your Own—Angles

1. Which of the following is an obtuse angle?

2. A straight angle has how many degrees?
3. What is the measure of ∠A in the figure below?

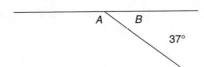

4. If ∠ABC is a right angle, what is the measure of ∠ABD?

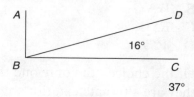

16°

37°

5. In the figure below, if ∠AEB measures 24°, what is the measure of ∠CED?

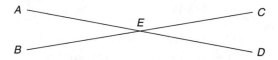

6. In the figure above, if ∠AEB measures 24°, what is the measure of ∠AEC?

7. In the figure below, if ∠IHK measures 43°, what is the measure of ∠JBA?

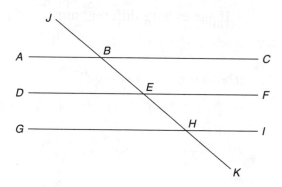

8. In the figure above, if ∠FEH measures 40°, what is the measure of ∠ABE?

9. In the figure above, if ∠FEH measures 30°, what is the measure of ∠JBC?

10. In the figure above, if ∠JBC measures 110°, what is the measure of ∠DEH?

Triangles

A *polygon* is a closed figure that can be drawn without lifting the pencil, It is made up of line segments (sides) that do not cross. A triangle is a polygon with three sides. Every triangle has three angles that total 180°.

SSAT/ISEE Coach Says . . .

Look for Tick Marks and Arcs. When sides of a polygon are congruent (equal), they may be marked with an equal number of tick marks. When angles are congruent, they may be marked with an equal number of arcs.

Example

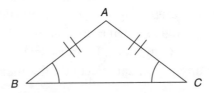

The tick marks indicate that sides *AB* and *AC* have the same length. The arcs indicate that ∠*ABC* has the same measure as ∠*ACB*.

If sides have different numbers of tick marks, they are not congruent. If angles have different numbers of arcs, they are not congruent.

SSAT/ISEE Coach Says . . .

All triangles have three angles that total 180°.

Identifying the Longest Side of a Triangle. The longest side of a triangle is always opposite the largest angle. So, if a triangle has angles of 45°, 55°, and 80°, the side opposite the 80° angle is the longest.

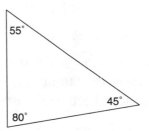

There are four main types of triangles. They are equilateral, isosceles, scalene, and right. Each has special characteristics that you should know.

Equilateral Triangle. This kind of triangle has three congruent (equal) sides and three congruent (equal) angles. In an equilateral triangle, each angle measures 60°.

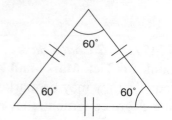

Isosceles Triangle. This type of triangle has at least two congruent sides, and the angles opposite the congruent sides are also congruent. In the isosceles triangle shown below, sides AB and BC are congruent. ∠BAC and ∠BCA are also congruent. In an isosceles triangle, if you know the measure of any one angle, you can calculate the measures of the other two.

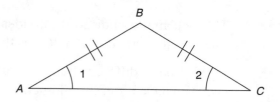

Examples

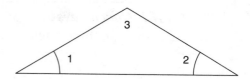

In this isosceles triangle, if ∠1 measures 30°, what is the measure of ∠3?

Since ∠1 and ∠2 are congruent, ∠2 must also measure 30°. Together, ∠1 and ∠2 add up to 60°. Since the sum of all three angles in any triangle is 180°, ∠3 must be 180 − 60 = 120°.

If ∠3 measures 100°, what are the measures of ∠1 and ∠2?

Since the sum of all three angles in any triangle is 180°, the sum of the measures of ∠1 and ∠2 must be 180 − 100 = 80°. Since angles 1 and 2 are congruent, each one must measure 80° ÷ 2 = 40°.

Scalene Triangle. This kind of triangle has no equal sides or angles.

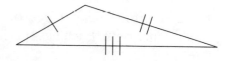

Right Triangle. This kind of triangle has one angle that measures 90°. This angle is the *right angle*. It is identified in the figure by the little "box." Since the sum of all three angles in any triangle is 180°, the sum of the two remaining angles in a right triangle is 180 − 90 = 90°.

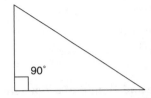

In a right triangle, there is a special relationship among the lengths of the three sides. This relationship is described by the *Pythagorean theorem*.

In the right triangle below, $\angle C$ is the right angle. The side opposite the right angle is called the *hypotenuse* (c). It is always the longest side. The other two sides (a and b) are called *legs*.

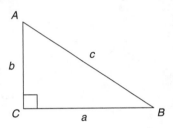

According to the Pythagorean theorem, in any right triangle, the sum of the squares of the legs equals the square of the hypotenuse. In symbols:

$a^2 + b^2 = c^2$

So if you know the lengths of any two sides of a right triangle, you can calculate the length of the third side.

Examples

If $a = 2$ and $b = 3$, what is c?

Following the Pythagorean theorem,

$2^2 + 3^2 = c^2$
$4 + 9 = c^2$
$13 = c^2$
$\sqrt{13} = c$

If $a = 3$ and $b = 4$, what is c?
$3^2 + 4^2 = c^2$
$9 + 16 = c^2$
$25 = c^2$
$5 = c$

If $a = 6$ and $c = 10$, what is b?

$6^2 + b^2 = 10^2$

$36 + b^2 = 100$

$b^2 = 100 - 36$

$b^2 = 64$

$b = \sqrt{64}$

$b = 8$

Base and Height of a Triangle

Any side of a triangle can be called the *base*. The *height* is the length of a line segment that connects a base to the vertex opposite that base and is perpendicular to it.

Look at the triangle below. Dashed line CD is the height. Line CD is perpendicular to the base AB. Where line CD meets base AB, it creates two right angles, $\angle CDA$ and $\angle CDB$.

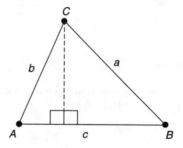

SSAT/ISEE Coach Says . . .
Sometimes you will see the word *perpendicular* represented by the symbol $\perp$. So in the triangle shown, $\overline{CD} \perp \overline{AB}$.

Median of a Triangle

A *median* of a triangle is a line drawn from any vertex to the middle of the opposite side. This line splits the opposite side into two equal lengths.

Example

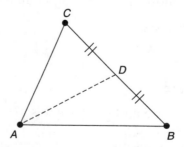

Dashed line AD is a median of triangle ABC. It splits side BC into two equal lengths, $\overline{CD}$ and $\overline{BC}$.

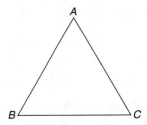

1. The triangle above is an equilateral triangle. What is the measure of ∠*ACB*?

2. In the triangle above, if line *AC* measures 4 inches, what is the length of line *BC*?

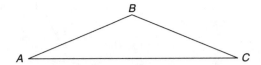

3. If the triangle above is an isosceles triangle and ∠*ABC* measures 100°, what is the measure of ∠*BAC*?

4. In the triangle above, if line *AB* measures 15 cm, what is the length of line *BC*?

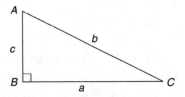

5. In the triangle above, if ∠*ACB* measures 30°, what is the measure of ∠*CAB*?

6. In the triangle above, which side is the longest?

7. In the triangle above, if side *c* measures 5 cm, what are the lengths of sides *a* and *b*?

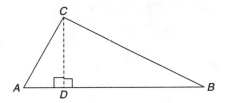

8. In the figure above, if ∠*CBD* measures 25°, what is the measure of ∠*CAD*?

Quadrilaterals

A *quadrilateral* is a polygon with four sides and four angles. The sum of the four angles is always 360°.

There are several different kinds of quadrilaterals. Each type is classified according to relationships among its sides and angles. The square, rectangle, parallelogram, and rhombus are all types of quadrilaterals.

Parallelogram. A parallelogram is a quadrilateral with both pairs of opposite sides parallel and congruent. The opposite angles are also congruent. Around the edge of the parallelogram, the pair of consecutive angles are supplementary; that is, their sum is 180°. Diagonal lines drawn from opposite vertices *bisect* each other (divide each other exactly in half), but the diagonals themselves are not equal in length.

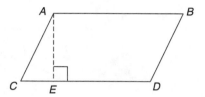

$\angle A = \angle D$
$\angle C = \angle B$

$\angle A + \angle B = 180°$
$\angle B + \angle D = 180°$
$\angle D + \angle C = 180°$
$\angle C + \angle A = 180°$

SSAT/ISEE Coach Says . . .
Consecutive angles are angles that are next to each other. *Supplementary* means that the angles add to 180°.

Like triangles, quadrilaterals have bases and height. Any side of this parallelogram can be a base. Dashed line is a height of this parallelogram. The *height* is a line originating at a vertex and drawn perpendicular to the opposite base. The height forms two right angles where it meets the base.

Rhombus. A rhombus is a parallelogram with four congruent sides. Opposite angles are also congruent.

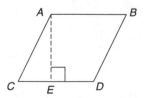

Rectangle. A rectangle is a parallelogram with four right angles. Diagonal lines drawn from opposite vertices of a rectangle bisect each other (divide each other exactly in half) and are equal in length.

Square. A square is a rectangle with four congruent sides. Diagonal lines drawn from opposite vertices of a rectangle bisect each other (divide each other exactly in half) and are equal in length.

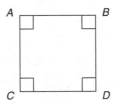

Trapezoid. A trapezoid is a quadrilateral with only one pair of parallel sides. Like other quadrilaterals it has bases and height. In the example below, dashed line CE is the height. Sides AB and CD are parallel, but sides AC and BD are not parallel.

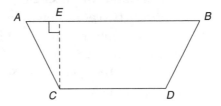

On Your Own—Quadrilaterals

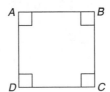

1. In the square above, what is the sum of all four angles?
2. In the square above, if side *AD* measures 16 inches, what is the length of side *DC*?

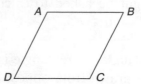

3. In the rhombus above, what is the sum of all four angles?
4. In the rhombus above, if ∠*ADC* measures 60°, what is the measure of ∠*ABC*?

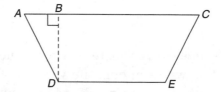

5. In the trapezoid above, what is the measure of ∠*CBD*?

Circles

A circle is a closed figure having all points the same distance from a *center*. A circle with its center at point *A* is called circle *A*.

Parts of a Circle. A *chord* is a line segment that has end points on a circle. A *diameter* is a chord that passes through the center of a circle. A *radius* is a line segment that connects the center of a circle and a point on the circle. Its length equals half the length of the diameter. In the figure below, *A* is the center of the circle. *EF* is a chord. *BC* is a diameter of the circle. *AC* and *AB* are each a radius of the circle.

   An *arc* is two points on a circle and the part of the circle between the two points. In the figure below, *CD* is an arc of the circle. A *central angle* is an angle whose vertex is the center of a circle. In the figure below, ∠*CAD* is a central angle. Its measure is 50°. The sum of the measures of the central angles in a circle is 360°.

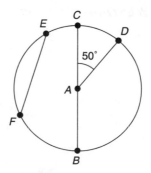

Perimeter and Area

The *perimeter* is the distance around a closed two-dimensional figure. The *area* is the amount of surface a two-dimensional figure covers. Area is measured in square units such as square inches (in²) or square centimeters (cm²). A square inch is the area of a square with sides 1 inch long.

Finding the Perimeter of a Polygon

To find the perimeter of a polygon, just add the length of each side to find the total.

Example

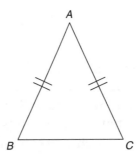

$\triangle ABC$ is an isosceles triangle. If side AB has a length of 25 cm and side BC has a length of 15 cm, what is the perimeter?

Since $\triangle ABC$ is an isosceles triangle, side AB = side AC. So if side AB has a length of 25 cm, side AC also has a length of 25 cm. Thus the perimeter is 25 + 25 + 15 = 65 cm.

Finding the Area of a Polygon

There are special formulas you can use to calculate the areas of various types of polygons. You will want to memorize these as you may be asked a question about area on the SSAT or ISEE.

Area of a Triangle The area (A) of a triangle is one-half the base (b) multiplied by the height (h) or

$$A = \frac{1}{2}bh$$

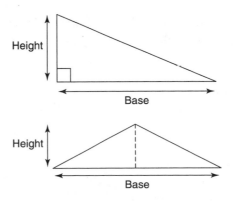

Example

If a triangle has a height that measures 30 cm and a base that measures 50 cm, what is its area?

$b = 50$ cm
$h = 30$ cm

$$A = \frac{1}{2} bh$$

$$A = \frac{1}{2} (50)(30)$$

$$A = \frac{1}{2} 1{,}500$$

$A = 750$ cm^2

SSAT/ISEE Coach Says . . .
Any time you see units squared, you are dealing with area. Examples: sq inches (in^2), sq centimeters (cm^2), sq yards (yd^2), etc.

Area of a Square or Rectangle. The area (A) of a square or rectangle is its length (l) multiplied by its width (w) or $A = lw$

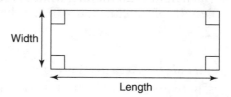

Example

If this rectangle is 10 miles long and 6 miles wide, what is its area?

$A = lw$
$A = (10)(6)$
$A = 60$ square miles (60 mi^2)

Area of a Parallelogram (Including the Rhombus): The area (A) of a parallelogram is its base (b) multiplied by its height (h) or $A = bh$.

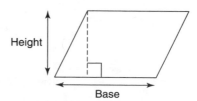

Example

If a parallelogram has a base of 6 meters and a height of 4 meters, what is the area?

$A = bh$
$A = (6)(4)$
$A = 24$ square meters (24 m^2)

Area of a Trapezoid. The area (A) of a trapezoid is one-half the height (h) multiplied by the sum of the two bases (b_1 and b_2), or $A = \dfrac{1}{2}(b_1 + b_2)h$

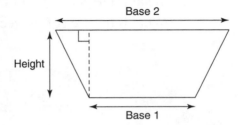

Example

If a trapezoid has one base of 30 meters and another base of 60 meters and its height is 20 meters, what is the area?

$A = \dfrac{1}{2}(b_1 + b_2)\, h$

$A = \dfrac{1}{2}(30 + 60)\, 20$

$A = \dfrac{1}{2}(90)\, 20$

$A = \dfrac{1}{2}(1{,}800)$

$A = 900$ square meters (900 m^2)

On Your Own—Perimeter and Area

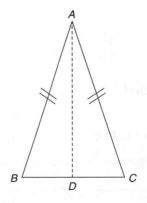

1. In the triangle above, if side *AB* measures 3 inches and side *BC* measures 2 inches, what is the perimeter of the triangle?

2. In the triangle above, if line *AD* measures 6 inches and side *BC* measures 2 inches, what is the area of the triangle?

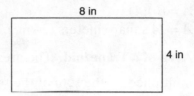

3. What is the perimeter of the rectangle above?

4. What is the area of the rectangle above?

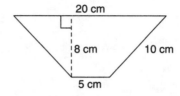

5. What is the perimeter of the trapezoid above?

6. What is the area of the trapezoid above?

Finding the Circumference and Area of a Circle

The *circumference* of a circle is the distance around the circle. The circumference (*C*) divided by the diameter (*d*) always equals the number π (pi). Pi is an infinite decimal, meaning that its decimal digits go on forever. When you use it to solve problems, you can approximate π as 3.14 or $^{22}/_7$.

To find the circumference of a circle, use the formula $C = \pi d$.

Example

If a circle has a radius of 3 inches, what is the circumference?

Since the diameter is twice the radius (2*r*), the diameter is 6 inches.

$C = \pi d$
$C = 3.14(d)$
$C = 3.14\ (6)$
$C = 18.84$ in

To find the area of a circle, multiply π times the square of the radius: $\pi = \dfrac{22}{7}$

SSAT/ISEE Coach Says . . .

If you prefer working with fractions, then $\pi = \dfrac{22}{7}$

Example

If a circle has a radius of 4 centimeters, what is its area?

$A = \pi r^2$
$A = 3.14 \, (4)^2$
$A = 3.14 \, (16)$
$A = 50.24 \text{ cm}^2$

On Your Own—Circles: Circumference and Area

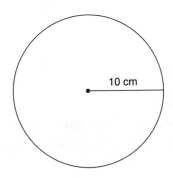

1. What is the circumference of the circle above?
2. What is the area of the circle above?

Three-Dimensional (Solid) Figures

A figure is *two-dimensional* if all the points on the figure are in the same plane. A square and a triangle are 2-dimensional figures. A figure is *three-dimensional* (solid) if some points of the figure are in a different plane from other points in the figure.

On solid figures, the flat surfaces are called *faces*. *Edges* are line segments where two faces meet. A point where three or more edges intersect is called a *vertex*.

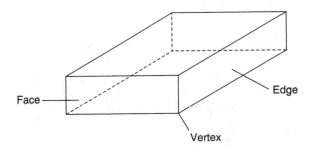

On the SSAT or ISEE, you may see problems related to these solid figures: rectangular solid (prism), cube, cylinder, and sphere.

Rectangular Solid (Prism). On a rectangular solid (also called a prism), all the faces are rectangular. The top and bottom faces are called bases. All opposite faces on a rectangular solid are parallel and congruent.

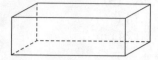

Cube. A cube is a rectangular solid on which every face is a square.

Cylinder. A cylinder is a solid figure with two parallel congruent circular bases and a curved surface connecting the boundaries of the two faces.

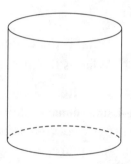

Sphere. A sphere is a solid figure that is the set of all points that are the same distance from a given point, called the center. The distance from the center is the radius (r) of the sphere.

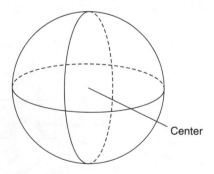

Center

Finding the Volume of Solid Figures

Volume is the amount of space within a three-dimensional figure. Volume is measured in cubic units such as cubic inches (in^3) or cubic centimeters (cm^3). A cubic inch is the volume of a cube with edges 1 inch long.

Volume of a Rectangular Solid. To find the volume (V) of a rectangular solid, multiply the length (l) times the width (w) times the height (h). The formula is $V = lwh$.

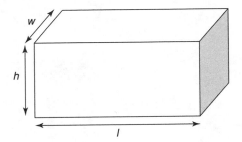

Example

If a rectangular solid has a length of 3 yards, a height of 1.5 yards, and a width of 1.5 yards, what is its volume?

$V = lwh$
$V = (3)(1.5)(1.5)$
$V = 6.75$ cubic yards (6.75 yd^3)

Volume of a Cube. On a cube, the length, width, and height are all the same: each one equals 1 side (s). To find the volume (V) of a cube, multiply the length $\times$ width $\times$ height. This is the same as multiplying side $\times$ side $\times$ side. The formula is $V = s \times s \times s = s^3$.

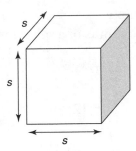

Example

If each side of a cube measures 9 feet, what is its volume?

$V = s^3$
$V = (9)^3$
$V = 729$ cubic feet (729 ft^3)

Volume of a Cylinder. To find the volume (V) of a cylinder, first find the area of the circular base by using the formula $A = \pi r^2$. Then multiply the result times the height (h) of the cylinder. The formula is $V = (\pi r^2)h$.

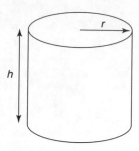

Example

If a cylinder has a height of 7 meters and a radius of 2 meters, what is its volume?

$V = (\pi r^2)h$
$V = 3.14 \, (2)^2 \, (7)$
$V = 3.14 \, (4) \, (7)$
$V = 87.92$ cubic meters (or 87.92 m³)

Volume of a Sphere. To find the volume of a sphere, multiply ⁴/₃ times π times the radius cubed. The formula is $V = \dfrac{4}{3} \pi r^3$

Example
If the radius of a sphere measures 12 inches, what is its volume?

$V = \dfrac{4}{3} \pi r^3$

$V = \dfrac{4}{3} \pi (12)^3$

$V = \dfrac{4}{3} (3.14)(1728)$

$V = \dfrac{4}{3} (5,425.92)$

$V = 7,234.56$ cubic inches (7,234.56 in³)

On Your Own—Volume

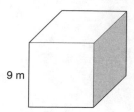

9 m

1. What is the volume of the cube above?

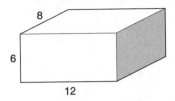

8

6

12

2. What is the volume of the rectangular solid above?

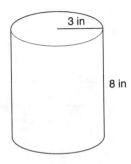

3 in

8 in

3. What is the volume of the cylinder above?

5 cm

4. What is the volume of the sphere above?

Shapes and Formulas: Summary

Shapes	Formulas
a, c, h, b (triangle)	Triangle Area = $\frac{1}{2}$ of the base x the height $A = \frac{1}{2} bh$ Perimeter = $a + b + c$

Shapes	Formulas
	Square Area = length x width $A = lw$ Perimeter = side + side + side + side $P = 4s$
	Rectangle Area = length × width $A = lw$ Perimeter = 2 × length + 2 × width $P = 2l + 2w$
	Parallelogram and Rhombus Area = base × height $A = bh$ Perimeter = 2 × length + 2 × width $P = 2l + 2w$
	Trapezoid Area = the sum of the two bases divided by 2 x height $A = \dfrac{(b_1 + b_2)}{2}$ Perimeter = $a + b_1 + b_2 + c$ $P = a + b_1 + b_2 + c$
	Circle The distance around the circle is a circumference (C). The length of a line segment passing through the center with end points on the circle is the diameter (d). The length of a line segment connecting the center to a Point on the circle is the radius (r). The diameter is twice the length of the radius ($d = 2r$). $C = \pi d = 2\pi r$ $A = \pi r^2$ $\pi = 3.14$ or $\dfrac{22}{7}$

Shapes and Formulas: Summary

Shapes	Formulas
s (cube)	**Cube** Volume = side × side × side $V = s^3$
h, *w*, *l* (rectangular solid)	**Rectangular Solid** Volume = length × width × height $V = lwh$
r, *h* (cylinder)	**Cylinder** Volume = πr^2 × height $V = \pi r^2 h$
r (sphere)	**Sphere** Volume = $\dfrac{4}{3} \pi r^3$ $V = \dfrac{4}{3} \pi r^3$

Answers to "On Your Own" Practice Sets

On Your Own—Angles

1. B

2. 180°

3. 143°

4. 74°

5. 24°

6. 156°

7. 43°

8. 140°

9. 150°

10. 110°

On Your Own—Triangles

1. 60°

2. 4 inches

3. 40°

4. 15 cm

5. 60°

6. b

7. 2 cm; 3 cm

8. 35°

On Your Own—Quadrilaterals

1. 360°

2. 16 inches

3. 360°

4. 60°

5. 90°

On Your Own—Perimeter and Area

1. 8 inches

2. 6 sq inches

3. 24 inches

4. 32 sq inches

5. 45 cm

6. 100 sq cm

On Your Own—Circles: Circumference and Area

1. 63.9 cm

2. 314 sq cm

On Your Own—Volume

1. 729 m^2

2. 576 units^2

3. 226.08 sq inches

4. 532.33 sq cm

CHAPTER 12
How to Solve Word Problems

Introduction to Word Problems

What is a word problem? Basically it is a description of a real-life situation that requires a mathematical solution. To solve a word problem, you need to translate the situation into mathematical terms and then calculate the answer.

Many of the math questions on the SSAT and ISEE are word problems. To do well, you need to learn good word problem–solving skills. The following pages will show you many different kinds of word problems. For each kind, you'll learn how to translate the facts of the problem into mathematical terms. Then you'll see how to use those terms to set up an equation. Finally, you'll see how to solve that equation for the missing piece of information that you're looking for.

How to Tackle Word Problems

Here are some helpful suggestions for dealing with word problems.

- Read the problem all the way through before you start making any calculations. That way, you will better understand what the problem is about and what you are supposed to find out.
- Be sure you understand what the problem is asking. Are you supposed to find a distance? How fast something is moving? When someone will arrive at point *A*? How much something costs? How many items you can buy if you have a certain amount of money? How much older Kim is than Kay? Draw a picture if that helps.
- List the information that the problem gives you. Note any units of measure (meters, pounds, feet per second, and the like).
- Look for key words in the problem that define relationships or indicate what mathematical operation you need to use. (See the list of key words that follows.)
- Figure out what unit of measure you must use to express your answer. Cubic meters? Centimeters per second? Dollars? Minutes? Number of items?
- Weed out unnecessary information that will not help you solve the problem.

- Use the information you have gathered to create an equation to help you solve the problem.
- Solve the equation.

Key Words

Many word problems contain key words that tell you what mathematical operation you need to use to solve the problem. It pays to know these key words, so be sure you study the following list.

Key Words	Example Phrases
These Key Words Tell You to ADD	
Increased by	If the temperature is increased by
More than	If the bicycle costs $75 more than
Sum	If the sum of the paychecks is
Total	The total number of payments equals
Added	If a is added to b
Plus	If the interest plus the principle is
Combined	If the volume of the cube is combined with
In all	How many pounds in all
Successive	The cost of 8 successive phone bills
These Key Words Tell You to SUBTRACT	
Less than	The interest payment was less than
Difference	The difference between the time it takes to
Are left	How many pieces of pie are left if
Fewer than	If there are 15 fewer scholarships this year than
Minus	Some number minus 36
Reduced by	If the federal budget is reduced by
These Key Words Tell You to MULTIPLY	
Times	There are 3 times as many red tiles as blue tiles.
Product	The product of a and b is
Increased by a factor of	If the speed is increased by a factor of
Decreased by a factor of	If the temperature is decreased by a factor of
At	If you buy 12 cameras at $249 each
Per	If a ferry can carry 20 cars per trip, how many cars can it carry in 6 trips?
Total	If you spend $10 a week on movies for a total of 5 weeks
Twice	The house covers twice as many square feet as

Key Words

Key Words	Example Phrases
These Key Words Tell You to DIVIDE	
Quotient	What is the quotient if the numerator is 500?
Divided equally among	If 115 tickets are divided equally among 5 groups
Divided into equal groups	If the students were divided into 6 equal groups
Ratio of	If the ratio of oxygen to hydrogen is
Per	If a ferry can carry 24 cars per trip, how many trips will it take to carry 144 cars?
Percent	What percent of 100 is 30?
Half	If half the profits go to charity, then how much
These Key Words Tell You to Use an EQUALS SIGN	
Is	If the total bill is $19.35
Sells for	If the car sells for $26,000
Gives	If multiplying a^2 and b^2 gives c^2

On Your Own—Key Words

For each of the following phrases, indicate what operation is appropriate.

1. How many are left? _____
2. What is the ratio of 6 to 3? _____
3. What is the total? _____
4. How much is twice the amount? _____
5. If it sells for _____

Setting Up an Equation and Solving for an Unknown

Before you start tackling word problems, you need to know how to set up an equation and solve for an unknown. For each problem, you will be given certain pieces of information (*what you know*). You first need to translate this information into mathematical terms. Then you can use those terms to set up an equation. An *equation* is nothing more than a mathematical expression that indicates that one mathematical term is equal to another. The terms in an equation are shown on opposite sides of an equals sign. The missing piece of information that you are looking for (*what you need to find*) is called the *unknown*. In your equation, you can represent an unknown by a letter such as x or a.

In the pages that follow, you will see how to set up equations for many different kinds of word problems. The process of solving an equation for an unknown is pretty simple. Work through these examples until you get perfectly comfortable with the process.

Examples

Solve for x.

$25x = 200$

This equation is read, "25 times some unknown number x equals 200." Your task is to determine what number x is. Here is how to solve this equation.

Divide both sides of the equation by 25:

$$\frac{25x}{25} = \frac{200}{25}$$

$$x = \frac{200}{25}$$

$$x = 8$$

Solve for x:

$$\frac{x}{5} = \frac{3}{45}$$

To solve this type of problem, cross-multiply (45 times x and 3 times 5).

$45x = 15$

$$x = \frac{15}{45} = \frac{1}{3} = 0.33$$

Solve for x:

$$\frac{10}{x} = \frac{50}{350}$$

To solve this problem, cross-multiply (10 times 350 and 50 times x).

$50x = 3500$

$x = 70$

To check your answer, merely substitute 70 back into the equation and see if it works.

$\dfrac{10}{70} = \dfrac{50}{350}$ Reduce the fractions to $\dfrac{1}{7} = \dfrac{1}{7}$ or cross-multiply (10 times 350 and 70 times 50) making $3{,}500 = 3{,}500$. Either way, you are correct.

Types of Arithmetic Word Problems

In the pages that follow, you will learn about many different kinds of word problems that you are likely to see on the ASVAB Arithmetic Reasoning test. For each kind, you will see how to use the information you are given to set up an equation. Then you will see how to solve the equation for the unknown that is the answer to the problem. The following chart shows the different kinds of word problems discussed in this chapter.

Simple Interest	Percent Change
Compound Interest	Numbers and Number Relationships
Ratio and Proportion	Age
Motion	Measurement
Percent	

Simple Interest

Interest is an amount paid for the use of money. *Interest rate* is the percent paid per year. *Principal* is the amount of money on which interest is paid. *Simple interest* is interest that is computed based only on the principal, the interest rate, and the time. To calculate simple interest, use this formula:

Interest = Principal × Rate × Time.

$$I = prt$$

Examples

Martina has $300 in a savings account that pays simple interest at a rate of 3% per year. How much interest will she earn on that $300 if she keeps it in the account for 5 years?

Procedure

What must you find? Amount of simple interest.
What are the units? Dollars.
What do you know? Rate = 3% per year; time = 5 years; principal = $300.
Create an equation and solve.

$$I = (\$300)(0.03)(5)$$
$$I = \$45$$

Five years ago, Robin deposited $500 in a savings account that pays simple interest. She made no further deposits, and today the account is worth $750. What is the rate of interest?

Procedure

What must you find? Rate of simple interest.
What are the units? Percent per year.
What do you know? Interest = $250 ($750 − $500); principal = $500; time = 5 years.
Create an equation and solve.

$$250 = (500)(x)(5)$$
$$250 = 2500x$$
$$\frac{250}{2500} = x$$

$$x = \frac{250}{2500} = 0.10 \text{ or } 10\%$$

1. Sheena has $500 in a savings account that pays simple interest at a rate of 2% per year. How much interest will she earn on that $500 if she keeps it in the account for 5 years?

2. Five years ago, Kevin deposited $1,000 in a savings account that pays simple interest. He made no further deposits, and today the account is worth $1,250. What is the rate of interest?

3. Two years ago, Peggy borrowed $5,000 to purchase a car. The interest rate is 2.5%. After two years, how much interest has she paid?

Compound Interest

Compound interest is the interest paid on the principal and also on any interest that has already been paid. To calculate compound interest, you can use the formula $I = prt$, but you must calculate the interest for each time period and then combine them for a total.

Example

Ricardo bought a $1,000 savings bond that earns 5% interest compounded annually. How much interest will he earn in two years?

Procedure

What must you find? Amount of compound interest.
What are the units? Dollars.
What do you know? Principal = $1000; rate = 5%; time = 2 years.
Create an equation and solve.
To find the compound interest, calculate the amount earned the first year. Add that amount to the principal, then calculate the interest earned in the second year. Total the amount of interest earned in the two years.

Year 1: $I = prt$
$I = (\$1,000)(0.05)(1)$

$$I = \$50$$

New principal = $1,050
Year 2: $I = prt$
$I = (\$1,050)(0.05)(1)$

$$I = \$52.50$$

So the total compound interest paid in two years is $50 + $52.50 = $102.50.

On Your Own—Compound Interest

1. Kerry bought a $500 savings bond that earns 8% interest compounded annually. How much will the bond be worth in two years?

2. Leo invested in a savings account that earned 3.5% annually. How much will the account be worth in 3 years?

Ratio and Proportion

On the SSAT or ISEE you may encounter word problems that will require you to work with ratios and proportions.

Example

Kim reads an average of 150 pages per week. At that rate, how many weeks will it take him to read 1,800 pages?

Procedure

What must you find? How long it will take to read 1,800 pages.
What are the units? Weeks.
What do you know? 150 pages read each week; 1,800 pages to be read.
Set up a proportion and solve.

$$\frac{\text{Number of pages}}{1\ \text{week}} = \frac{\text{Number of pages}}{x\ \text{weeks}}$$

Substitute values into the equation.

$$\frac{150\ \text{pages}}{1\ \text{week}} = \frac{1,800\ \text{pages}}{x\ \text{weeks}}$$

Cross-multiply:

$150x = 1,800$
$x = 12$ weeks

It takes 8 hours to fill a swimming pool that holds 3,500 gallons of water. At that rate, how many hours will it take to fill a pool that holds 8,750 gallons?

Procedure

What must you find? How long it will take to fill the 8,750-gallon pool.
What are the units? Hours.
What do you know? Number of hours for 3,500 gallons.
Set up a proportion and solve.

$$\frac{\text{Number of gallons}}{\text{Number of hours}} = \frac{\text{Number of gallons}}{\text{Number of hours}}$$

$$\frac{3,500\ \text{gallons}}{8\ \text{hours}} = \frac{8,750\ \text{gallons}}{x}$$

Cross-multiply:
$3500x = (8)(8,750)$
$x = 20$ hours

An airplane travels the 1,700 miles from Phoenix to Nashville in 2.5 hours. Flying at the same speed, the plane could travel the 2,550 miles from Phoenix to Boston in how many hours?

Procedure

What must you find? Time it would take to fly 2,550 miles.
What are the units? Hours.
What do you know? The plane traveled 1,700 miles in 2.5 hours.
Set up a proportion and solve.

$$\frac{\text{Number of miles}}{\text{Number of hours}} = \frac{\text{Number of miles}}{\text{Number of hours}}$$

Substitute values.

$$\frac{1,700 \text{ miles}}{2.5 \text{ hours}} = \frac{2,550 \text{ miles}}{x}$$

Cross-multiply:

$1,700x = (2.5)(2,550)$
$1,700x = 6,375$
$x = 3.75$ hours

On Your Own—Ratio and Proportion

1. Jerry reads an average of 75 pages per week. At that rate, how many weeks will it take him to read 1,000 pages?
2. It takes 2 minutes to fill a balloon that holds 4,000 units of helium. At that rate, how many minutes will it take to fill a balloon that holds 6,000 units of helium?
3. An empty swimming pool can hold 5,000 gallons of water. If a hose can fill the pool at 250 gallons every $\frac{1}{2}$ hour, how long will it take to fill the pool?

Motion

Motion problems deal with how long it will take to get from point a to point b if you are traveling at a certain steady rate. To solve them, use this formula:

Distance = Rate × Time or $d = rt$

Example

If a racing boat travels at a steady rate of 80 miles per hour, how many miles could it travel in 3.5 hours?

Procedure

What must you find? Distance traveled in 3.5 hours.
What are the units? Miles.
What do you know? Rate = 80 miles per hour; time = 3.5 hours.
Create an equation and solve.

$d = rt$

Substitute values into the formula:

$d = (80)(3.5)$
$d = 280$ miles

On Your Own—Motion

1. If a motorcycle travels at a steady rate of 40 miles per hour, how many miles could it travel in 4.5 hours?
2. If a jet travels at 450 miles per hour, how long will it take for the jet to travel 5,940 miles?

Percent

There are likely to be word problems involving percent on both the SSAT and ISEE.

Examples

Lilly's bill at a restaurant is $22.00 and she wants to leave a 15% tip. How much money should her tip be?

Procedure

What must you find? Amount of tip.
What are the units? Dollars and cents.
What do you know? Total bill = $22.00; percent of tip = 15.
Create an equation and solve.
Tip = 15% × 22.00.
Substitute and solve.
$t = (0.15)(22.00)$
$t = \$3.30$

Frederick earns $1,500 per month at his job, but 28% of that amount is deducted for taxes. What is his monthly take-home pay?

Procedure

What must you find? Monthly take-home pay.
What are the units? Dollars and cents.
What do you know? Monthly pay before taxes = $1,500; percent deducted = 28%.
Create an equation and solve.

Take-home pay is 1500 minus 28% × 1,500
$T = 1500 - (1500 \times 0.28)$

$$T = 1,500 - (420)$$
$$T = \$1,080$$

40 is 80% of what number?

Procedure

What must you find? Number of which 40 is 80%.
What are the units? Numbers.
What do you know? 40 is 80% of some larger number.
Create an equation and solve.

$40 = 0.8x$
$0.8x = 40$

$$x = \frac{40}{0.8}$$

$x = 50$

On Your Own—Percent

1. If your gross monthly pay is \$3,000 and 32% is removed for taxes and insurance, what is your net pay?
2. If you invest \$1,000 in a mutual fund that has a 0.5% fee, how much is the fee?

Percent Change

Some word problems may ask you to calculate the percent of change from one number or amount to another.

Examples

Samantha now earns \$300 per month working at a cosmetics store, but starting next month her monthly salary will be \$375. Her raise will be what percent increase over her current salary?

Procedure

What must you find? Percent change from current salary.
What are the units? Percent.
What do you know? Current pay = \$300/month; pay after the raise = \$375/month.
Create an equation and solve.

$$\text{Percent change} = \frac{\text{Amount of change}}{\text{Starting point}}$$

Substitute values and solve:

$$\text{Percent change} = \frac{(375 - 300)}{300}$$

$$\text{Percent change} = \frac{75}{300}$$

Percent change = 0.25 or 25%

On his 16th birthday, Brad was 60 inches tall. On his 17th birthday he was 65 inches tall. What was the percent increase in Brad's height during the year?

Procedure

What must you find? Percent change in height.
What are the units? Percent.
What do you know? Starting height = 60 inches; height after a year = 65 inches.
Create an equation and solve.

$$\text{Percent change} = \frac{\text{Amount of change}}{\text{Starting point}}$$

Substitute values and solve.

$$\text{Percent change} = \frac{5 \text{ inches}}{60 \text{ inches}}$$

Percent change = 0.08 or 8%

At a certain store, every item is discounted by 15% off the original price. If Kevin buys a CD originally priced at $15.00 and a baseball cap originally priced at $11.50, how much money will he save?

Procedure

What must you find? Total amount saved.
What are the units? Dollars and cents.
What do you know? Percent change = 15%; original price for two items = $15.00 + $11.50 = $26.50.
Create an equation and solve.

$$\text{Percent change} = \frac{\text{Amount of change}}{\text{Starting point}}$$

Substitute values and solve.

$$0.15 = \frac{x}{26.50}$$

$x = 0.15 \, (26.50)$
$x = \$3.98$

On Your Own—Percent Change

1. A magazine has reduced its subscription price from $15.00 per month to $13.00 per month. What is the percent reduction?
2. The tuition for college was increased from $10,000 per year to $12,500 per year. What is the percent increase?
3. A car went on a 12% "end of the year" sale. The car's original price was $25,000. What is the sale price?

Numbers and Number Relationships

Pay attention to the key words in this type of word problem.

Examples

If the sum of two numbers is 45 and one number is 5 more than the other, what are the two numbers?

Procedure

What must you find? Value of each number.
What are the units? Numbers.
What do you know? The sum of two numbers is 45; one number is 5 more than the other.
Create an equation and solve.

Let x be the smaller number.
$x + (x + 5) = 45$
Solve for x:

$x + x + 5 = 45$
$2x = 40$
$x = 20$

So the two numbers are 20 and $20 + 5 = 25$.

One number is twice the size of another and the two numbers together total 150. What are the two numbers?

Procedure

What must you find? Value of each number.
What are the units? Numbers.
What do you know? One number is twice the size of the other and the sum of the numbers is 150.
Create an equation and solve.

Let x be the smaller number.
$x + 2x = 150$
$3x = 150$
$x = 50$

So the smaller number is 50 and the larger number is 100.

Age

Some word problems ask you to calculate a person's age given certain facts.

Examples

Jessica is 26 years old. Two years ago she was twice as old as her brother Ned. How old is Ned now?

Procedure

What must you find? Ned's age now.
What are the units? Years.
What do you know? When Jessica was 24, she was 2 times as old as Ned.
Create an equation and solve.
Prepare an equation that shows the relationship.
Let x = Ned's age two years ago.
$2x = 24$
$x = 12$
Ned's age two years later = $12 + 2 = 14$ years.

On Your Own—Numbers and Number Relationships

1. One number is 3 times another number less 12. If the first number is 108, what is the second number?
2. Aaron is 30 years old. If his sister Angela is half his age plus 2 years, how old is Angela?

Measurement

Some word problems will ask you to use what you know about units of measure to solve problems. If necessary, review the table of units of measure in Chapter 9.

Example

How many cups of milk are in 5 pints of milk?

Procedure

What must you find? The number of cups of milk in 5 pints.
What are the units? Cups.
What do you know? According to the chart in Chapter 9, there are 2 cups in 1 pint.
Create an equation and solve.

Let x = the number of cups in 5 pints
5 pints = x cups
1 pint = 2 cups
5×1 pint = 5×2 cups (Multiply both sides of the equation by 5.)
5 pints = 10 cups = x cups
$x = 10$
So there are 10 cups in 5 pints.

On Your Own—Measurement

1. If Candice lives 2 miles from Thomas, how many feet is the distance?
2. A football field is 100 yards. If a ship is 4 football fields long, how many feet long is the ship?

Geometry Word Problems

Word problems on the SSAT or ISEE may also deal with geometry concepts such as perimeter, area, and volume. To solve these problems, you may also need to use information about different units of measure. To review units of measure, see Chapter 9.

Just as with other kinds of word problems, you can solve geometry problems by following a specific procedure. In the examples that follow, pay special attention to the procedure outlined in each solution. Follow this same procedure whenever you need to solve this kind of word problem.

Examples

Sally is buying wood to make a rectangular picture frame measuring 11 in × 14 in. The wood costs 25 cents per inch. How much will Sally have to pay for the wood?

Procedure

What must you find? Cost of the wood for the frame.
What are the units? Dollars and cents.
What do you know? Cost of the wood per inch; shape of the frame, measure of the frame.
Create an equation and solve.

Length of wood needed for rectangular frame $= 2l + 2w$

Substitute values and solve:

Length of wood $= 2(14) + 2 (11)$
Length of wood $= 28 + 22 = 50$ in

If each inch costs 0.25, then $0.25 \times 50 = \$12.50$

Sergei is planting rose bushes in a rectangular garden measuring 12 ft × 20 ft. Each rosebush needs 8 ft^2 of space. How many rose bushes can Sergei plant in the garden?

Procedure

What must you find? Number of rose bushes that can be planted in the garden.
What are the units? Numbers.
What do you know? Shape of the garden, garden length and width, amount of area needed for each rose bush.
Create an equation and solve.

$A = lw$
Substitute values and solve.
$A = 12 \times 20 = 240$ ft^2
Each rose bush needs 8 ft^2
$240 \div 8 = 30$
Sergei can plant 30 rose bushes in the garden.

1. A floor is 10 feet long and 12 feet wide. Chris wants to lay tiles that are 10 inches square on the floor. How many tiles will he need?

2. Ian has a front lawn that is 300 feet by 120 feet. If 1 pound of fertilizer is needed for every 600 square feet, how many pounds of fertilizer are needed?

3. Gerry wants to inflate an exercise ball. The ball has a radius of 15 inches. If a pump can push 5 cubic inches of air every second, how many seconds will it take to inflate the ball?

4. A grey wolf needs 10.75 square miles of land to live. If a national park measures 20 miles by 60 miles of land, about how many grey wolves can be supported?

5. A garden is shaped like a triangle with a base of 40 feet and a height of 25 feet. If Ralph wants to plant lemon trees, each of which requires about 15 square feet of growing space, what is the maximum number of trees he can plant?

Answers to "On Your Own" Practice Sets

On Your Own—Key Words

1. subtract

2. divide

3. add

4. multiply

5. equals

On Your Own—Simple Interest

1. $50

2. 5%

3. $250

On Your Own—Compound Interest

1. $583.20

2. $5938.43

On Your Own—Ratio and Proportion

1. 13.33 weeks

2. 3 minutes

3. 20 half hours or 10 hours

On Your Own—Motion

1. 180 miles

2. 13.2 hours

On Your Own—Percent

1. $2040.00

2. $50.00

On Your Own—Percent Change

1. about 13%

2. 25%

3. $22,000

On Your Own—Numbers and Number Relationships

1. 40

2. 17

On Your Own—Measurement

1. 10,560 feet

2. 1,200 feet

On Your Own—Geometry

1. 172.8 tiles

2. 60 pounds

3. 2,826 seconds

4. about 112 wolves

5. 33 trees

How to Solve Quantitative Comparisons (ISEE Only)

Quantitative comparisons are another type of math question that appears only on the ISEE. If you are taking the SSAT, you can skip this chapter.

On the ISEE, quantitative comparisons appear only on the upper level and middle level versions of the test. If you are taking the lower level version, you will not see this question type.

On the upper level versions of the ISEE, quantitative comparison questions appear in the Quantitative Reasoning section, where they make up 15 of the 35 total questions.

Format of Quantitative Comparison Questions

Each quantitative comparison question consists of two mathematical quantities shown side by side, one in column A and the other in column B. Some problems present additional information relating to the two quantities that you need to consider when choosing your answer. This additional information will appear in the center, between column A and column B. Your task is to evaluate the two quantities and determine whether one quantity is greater than the other, whether the two are the same, or whether it is impossible to determine if one is greater than the other. Quantitative comparison problems may be drawn from arithmetic, algebra, or geometry.

Sample Quantitative Comparison Question Explained

Let's look at a sample question to see what is involved. Quantitative comparison questions have their own special set of directions. Read the directions, then study the question that follows.

Directions: For each of the following quantities, two quantities are given—one in column A, the other in column B. Compare the two quantities and mark your answer sheet as follows:

(A) if the quantity in column A is greater
(B) if the quantity in column B is greater
(C) if the quantities are equal
(D) if the relationship cannot be determined from the information given

Notes

- Information concerning one or both of the compared quantities will be centered above the two columns for some items.
- Symbols that appear in both columns represent the same thing in column A and in column B.
- Letters such as x, n, and k are symbols for real numbers.
- Figures are drawn to scale unless otherwise noted.

Column A		Column B

1.

$$3x - 4 = 2$$
$$3y + 15 = 9$$

x $\qquad\qquad\qquad\qquad\qquad\qquad\qquad\qquad\qquad$ y

In the problem, you are asked to compare x and y. The centered information tells you about x and y. If you solve the two equations, you can find values for x and y as follows:

$3x - 4 = 2$
$3x = 2 + 4$
$3x = 6$
$x = 2$

$3y + 15 = 9$
$3y = 9 - 15$
$3y = -6$
$y = -2$

Now that you have values for x and y, you can compare the two quantities. If $x = 2$ and $y = -2$, then x is greater than y. Since x is the quantity in column A, the correct answer is choice A, "The quantity in Column A is greater."

How to Solve Quantitative Comparison Questions

Here is a six-step strategic plan that you can use to solve quantitative comparison questions.

1. Look carefully at the two quantities. Ask yourself: Are they fractions or percents? Algebraic expressions? Geometric measures? Is the quantity in column A the same kind of quantity as the one in column B?
2. Look to see if there is any information centered between the two columns that might help you solve the problem. If so, how does it apply to the given quantities?
3. Think of how you might restate one or both of the quantities so that you are comparing like terms. Maybe you will need to perform an arithmetic calculation. Maybe you will need to substitute values into

an algebraic expression. Maybe you will need to find a geometric measure.

4. Carry out your plan. Restate one or both quantities so that you can compare like terms. Then compare.

5. Be sure to mark your answer correctly. Mark choice A if the quantity in column A is larger. Mark choice B if the quantity in column B is larger. Mark choice C if the two quantities are equal. Mark choice D if the relationship cannot be determined.

6. If the two quantities are algebraic expressions and values are not specified, keep in mind that your answer must be true for any values you substitute for unknowns. If the relationship between the quantities is different for different values, you must mark choice D as your answer.

Try the six-step strategy to help you answer the quantitative comparison questions that follow. Then compare your answer to the solution that follows each question.

Sample Quantitative Comparison Question Set Explained

Directions: For each of the following quantities, two quantities are given—one in column A, the other in column B. Compare the two quantities and mark your answer sheet as follows:

(A) if the quantity in column A is greater
(B) if the quantity in column B is greater
(C) if the quantities are equal
(D) if the relationship cannot be determined from the information given

Notes

- Information concerning one or both of the compared quantities will be centered above the two columns for some items.
- Symbols that appear in both columns represent the same thing in column A and in column B.
- Letters such as x, n, and k are symbols for real numbers.
- Figures are drawn to scale unless otherwise noted.

Column A	Column B
1.	Sequence: 100, 90, 180, 170, 340, …
seventh term in sequence	eighth term in sequence

1. A is correct.
The sequence follows the rule: Starting with the first number, subtract 10, then double. The seventh term will be 660. The eighth term will be 650.

2. C is correct.

$2^{-4} = \dfrac{1}{2^4}; 2^4 = 2 \times 2 \times 2 \times 2 = 16;$ so, $\dfrac{1}{2^4} = \dfrac{1}{16}.$

$\left(\dfrac{1}{4}\right)^2 = \dfrac{1}{4} \times \dfrac{1}{4} = \dfrac{1}{16}$

3. $\hspace{4cm}$ $a, b,$ and c are integers.
$$a > 0 > b > c$$

$\hspace{1.5cm}$ a/b $\hspace{6cm}$ a/c

3. B is correct.

Since $a > 0$, it is a positive integer. Since and b and c are less then zero, they are both negative integers. The quotient of a positive integer divided by a negative integer is a negative rational number. So, a/b and a/c *are* negative rational numbers.

Since both have the same numerator, the negative rational number that has the greater denominator will be greater.

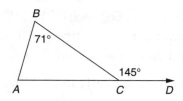

4.

$\hspace{1.5cm}$ $m\angle A$ $\hspace{6cm}$ $m\angle B$

4. A is correct.
$\angle BCA$ and $\angle BCD$ are supplementary angles.
Therefore, $m\angle BCA + m\angle BCD = 180°$.
$m\angle BCA + 145 = 180°$
$m\angle BCD = 35°$

The sum of the measures of the three angles in a triangle is equal to 180.
$m\angle A + m\angle B + m\angle C = 180°$
$m\angle A + 71° + 35° = 180°$
$m\angle A + 106° = 180°$
$m\angle A = 74°$

5. $\hspace{4cm}$ $x < 0 < y$

$\hspace{1.5cm}$ $[x^2 - 1]$ $\hspace{6cm}$ $[2y + 1]$

5. D is correct.
A number less than 0 is a negative number. So, x is a negative number. The square of a negative number is a positive number. Without knowing the absolute values of x and y, there is insufficient information to determine the answer to this question.

6. width of a rectangle   length of the side of a square
    that has a perimeter of 20 feet   that has a perimeter of 24 feet

6. D is correct.
You can determine that the length of the side of the square is 6 ft, since $4s = 24$. However, you cannot determine the width of the rectangle, since you do not know its length.

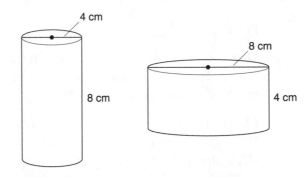

7.

volume of cylinder 1   volume of cylinder 2

7. B is correct.
Substitute values for r and h into the formula: $V = \pi r^2 h$.
Cylinder 1
$h = 8$ cm; $d = 4$ cm, so $r = 2$ cm

$V = \pi r^2 h$
$ = \pi(2)^2 8$
$ = 32\pi$

Cylinder 2
$h = 4$ cm; $d = 8$ cm, so $r = 4$ cm

$V = \pi r^2 h$
$ = \pi(4)^2 4$
$ = 64\pi$

8. $y = 2x^2 + 4x + 5$

    y, when $x = -2$ y, when $x = 0$

8. C is correct.
$y = 2x^2 + 4x + 5$ $y = 2x^2 + 4x + 5$
$y = 2(-2)^2 + 4(-2) + 5$ $y = 2(0)^2 + 4(0) + 5$
$y = 8 - 8 + 5$ $y = 0 + 0 + 5$
$y = 5$ $y = 5$

On Your Own

Now take the time to apply what you have just learned about quantitative comparison questions to see how well you can do on Practice Set A. When you are finished, use the answer key to score your work.

Review the strategies and tips discussed above and then try Practice Set B. Remember that the more you practice with these items, the easier they will become for you to answer correctly.

Practice Set A

Directions: For each of the following quantities, two quantities are given—one in column A, the other in column B. Compare the two quantities and mark your answer sheet as follows:

(A) if the quantity in column A is greater
(B) if the quantity in column B is greater
(C) if the quantities are equal
(D) if the relationship cannot be determined from the information given

Notes

- Information concerning one or both of the compared quantties will be centered above the two columns for some items.
- Symbols that appear in both columns represent the same thing in Column A as in column B.
- Letters such as $x, n,$ and k are symbols for real numbers.
- Figures are drawn to scale unless otherwise noted.

Column A		Column B
1.	$\dfrac{9}{a} = \dfrac{36}{8}$	
$\dfrac{2}{a}$		$\dfrac{a}{2}$
2.	$x + y = 5$ $3x + 2y = 12$	
x		y
3.	p is a prime number c is a composite number	
The sum of the factors of p		The sum of the factors of c
4. percent increase from 20 to 25		percent increase from 50 to 60
5. 0.6		$\dfrac{2}{3}$
6.	$-5m - 2 = 3$ $4n + 12 = 8$	
m		n

7. A 13-foot ladder is leaning against a building. The top of the ladder reaches 12 feet up the building. The distance of the bottom of the ladder is from the base of the building is a.

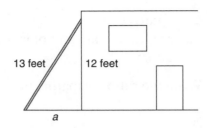

13 feet   12 feet

a

a	10 feet
8. 8,047	$(8 \times 10^2) + (4 \times 10^1) + (7 \times 10^0)$
9. $100/\sqrt{25}$	$2\sqrt{16}$
10. number of fluid ounces in 15 gallons	number of hours in 3 weeks

Answers and Explanations

1. C is correct.

$$\frac{9}{a} = \frac{36}{8}$$

$36a = 72$

$a = 2$

$$\frac{2}{a} = \frac{2}{2} = 1$$

$$\frac{a}{2} = \frac{2}{2} = 1$$

2. B is correct.

Solve the first equation for y.

$x + y = 5 \quad y = 5 - x$

Substitute the expression for y into the second equation.

$3x + 2y = 12$

$3x + 2(5 - x) = 12$

Solve for x.

$3x + 10 - 2x = 12$

$x + 10 = 12$

$x = 2$

Substitute the value for x into the first equation and solve for y.

$x + y = 5$

$2 + y = 5$

$\quad y = 3$

3. D is correct.

A prime number is a whole number greater than 1 that has only two factors, the number itself and 1. A composite number is a whole number greater than 1, that has other factors beside 1 and itself. However, the size of the factors is not known, so the answer to the question posed cannot be answered.

4. A is correct.

Subtract to find amount of increase.

$25 - 20 = 5$ $60 - 50 = 10$

Write the ratio comparing the amount of increase to the original amount.

$\dfrac{5}{20} = \dfrac{1}{4}$ $\dfrac{10}{50} = \dfrac{1}{5}$

Express the ratio as a percent.

$\dfrac{1}{4} = 25\%$ $\dfrac{1}{5} = 20\%$

5. C is correct.

Let $n = 0.6$.

Since one digit repeats multiply by 10. $10n = 6.6$

Subtract the original equation.

$$10n = 6.6$$
$$\underline{- \; n = 0.6}$$
$$9n = 6.0$$

Solve the equation.

$9n = 6$

$n = \dfrac{6}{9} = \dfrac{2}{3}$

6. C is correct.

$-5m - 2 = 3$ $4n + 12 = 8$

$-5m = 5$ $4n = -4$

$m = -1$ $n = -1$

7. B is correct.

The ladder, wall of building, and ground form a right triangle. Using the Pythagorean theorem,

$a^2 = c^2 - b^2$

$a^2 = 13^2 - 12^2$

$a^2 = 169 - 144$

$a^2 = 25$

$a = 5$ feet

8. A is correct.

$(8 \times 10^2) + (4 \times 10^1) + (7 \times 10^0)$

$= (8 \times 100) + (4 \times 10) + (7 \times 1) = 847$

9. A is correct.

$\frac{100}{\sqrt{25}} = \frac{100}{5} = 20$

$2\sqrt{16} = 2(4) = 8$

10. B is correct.

32 fl oz = 1 gal

15 • 32 = 480 fl oz in 15 gal

24 hours = 1 day

7 days = 1 week

7 • 24 = 168 hours in 1 week

3 • 168 = 504 hours in 3 weeks

Practice Set B

1.　　　　　　Parallelogram *MNPQ* is shown below.

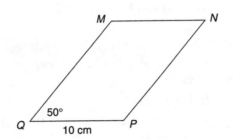

Length of *MN*	Length of *PN*

2.　　　　　　　　$10 > t > -2$

$3t$ 　　　　　　　　　　　　　　　　　$-4t$

3.　　　　　　　　$\frac{5}{12} = \frac{y}{144}$

$\frac{y}{2}$ 　　　　　　　　　　　　　　　$90 - y$

4.　　percent decrease from 53 to 37.　　percent decrease from 72 to 50.4

5.　　　　　　　　*j* and *k* are integers

$j < k < 0$

$j + k$ 　　　　　　　　　　　　　　　　$k - j$

6.

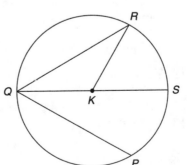

number of different chords
drawn

number of different radii
drawn

7.   The average weight of Bertha, Sue, and Myra is 105 pounds.

| The sum of Sue's and Bertha's weight | The sum of Myra's and Sue's weight |

8.
$$d = 125\% \text{ of } 800$$
$$g = 0.2\% \text{ of } 50{,}000$$

d g

9. a, b, and c are integers
$$b > a, \text{ and } c > a$$

$a/b \bullet a/c$ 1

10.   The number of congruent   The number of congruent
sides in an equilateral triangle   angles in a right triangle

Answers and Explanations

1. D is correct.
Since the figure is a parallelogram, opposite sides are congruent. So the length of $\overline{MN}$ is 10 cm. However, the length of $\overline{PN}$ cannot be determined.

2. D is correct.
Since t could be any value from 10 to −2, it is impossible to determine which algebraic expression is greater.

3. C is correct.
$$\frac{5}{12} = \frac{y}{144}$$
$$12y = 5 \bullet 144$$
$$12y = 720$$
$$y = 60$$
$$\frac{y}{2} = \frac{60}{2} = 30$$
$$90 - y = 90 - 60 = 30$$

4. C is correct.
Subtract to find amount of increase.
$53 - 37.1 = 15.9$ $72 - 50.4 = 21.6$

Write the ratio comparing the amount of decrease to the original amount.
$$\frac{15.9}{53}$$ $$\frac{21.6}{72}$$
Express the ratio as a percent by dividing.
$15.9 \div 53 = 0.3 = 30\%$ $21.6 \div 72 = 0.3 = 30\%$

5. B is correct.

Since both j and k are integers < 0, they are negative integers. Since $j < k$, then $j + k$ which represents the sum of two negative integers will always be a negative integer, and $k - j$ which represents the difference between the greater integer and the lesser integer will always be a positive integer. All positive integers are greater than all negative integers.

6. C is correct.

A chord is any line segment with both end points on a circle. There are 3 chords drawn in the circle: $\overline{QP}$, $\overline{QR}$, and $\overline{QS}$.

A radius is a line segment that has one end point in the center of the circle, and another end point on the circle. There are 3 radii drawn in the circle: $\overline{KQ}$, $\overline{KR}$, and $\overline{KS}$.

7. D is correct.

There is no information about the weights of each girl in order to determine and compare the sums of any two girls' weights.

8. A is correct.

125% of 800 = 1.25 • 800 = 1,000
0.2% of 50,000 = 0.002 • 50,000 = 100

9. B is correct.

Since b and c are greater than a, the rational numbers a/b and a/c are each less than 1. The product of any two rational numbers each less than 1, is less than 1.

10. A is correct.

There are 3 congruent sides in an equilateral triangle. A right isosceles triangle has 2 congruent 45 °angles.

PART IV

PRACTICE TESTS FOR THE SSAT

SSAT Practice Test I

The following practice test is designed to be just like the real SSAT. It matches the actual test in content coverage and level of difficulty. The test is in five sections: Verbal, Quantitative I, Reading Comprehension, Quantitative II, and the Essay.

This practice test will be an accurate reflection of how you'll do on test day if you treat it as the real examination. Here are some hints on how to take the test under conditions similar to those of the actual exam:

- Find a quiet place to work and set aside a period of approximately 3 hours when you will not be disturbed.
- Work on only one section at a time, and use your watch or a timer to keep track of the time limits for each test part.

- Tear out your answer sheet and mark your answers by filling in the ovals for each question.
- Write your essay on the pages provided.
- Become familiar with the directions for each part of the test. You'll save time on the actual test day by already being familiar with this information.

At the end of the test you'll find Answer Keys for each section and explanations for every question. Check your answers against the keys to find out how you did on each section of the test and what test topics you might need to study more. Then review the explanations, paying particular attention to the ones for the questions you answered incorrectly.

SSAT Practice Test I

ANSWER SHEET

Section 1: Verbal

1. Ⓐ Ⓑ Ⓒ Ⓓ Ⓔ	21. Ⓐ Ⓑ Ⓒ Ⓓ Ⓔ	41. Ⓐ Ⓑ Ⓒ Ⓓ Ⓔ
2. Ⓐ Ⓑ Ⓒ Ⓓ Ⓔ	22. Ⓐ Ⓑ Ⓒ Ⓓ Ⓔ	42. Ⓐ Ⓑ Ⓒ Ⓓ Ⓔ
3. Ⓐ Ⓑ Ⓒ Ⓓ Ⓔ	23. Ⓐ Ⓑ Ⓒ Ⓓ Ⓔ	43. Ⓐ Ⓑ Ⓒ Ⓓ Ⓔ
4. Ⓐ Ⓑ Ⓒ Ⓓ Ⓔ	24. Ⓐ Ⓑ Ⓒ Ⓓ Ⓔ	44. Ⓐ Ⓑ Ⓒ Ⓓ Ⓔ
5. Ⓐ Ⓑ Ⓒ Ⓓ Ⓔ	25. Ⓐ Ⓑ Ⓒ Ⓓ Ⓔ	45. Ⓐ Ⓑ Ⓒ Ⓓ Ⓔ
6. Ⓐ Ⓑ Ⓒ Ⓓ Ⓔ	26. Ⓐ Ⓑ Ⓒ Ⓓ Ⓔ	46. Ⓐ Ⓑ Ⓒ Ⓓ Ⓔ
7. Ⓐ Ⓑ Ⓒ Ⓓ Ⓔ	27. Ⓐ Ⓑ Ⓒ Ⓓ Ⓔ	47. Ⓐ Ⓑ Ⓒ Ⓓ Ⓔ
8. Ⓐ Ⓑ Ⓒ Ⓓ Ⓔ	28. Ⓐ Ⓑ Ⓒ Ⓓ Ⓔ	48. Ⓐ Ⓑ Ⓒ Ⓓ Ⓔ
9. Ⓐ Ⓑ Ⓒ Ⓓ Ⓔ	29. Ⓐ Ⓑ Ⓒ Ⓓ Ⓔ	49. Ⓐ Ⓑ Ⓒ Ⓓ Ⓔ
10. Ⓐ Ⓑ Ⓒ Ⓓ Ⓔ	30. Ⓐ Ⓑ Ⓒ Ⓓ Ⓔ	50. Ⓐ Ⓑ Ⓒ Ⓓ Ⓔ
11. Ⓐ Ⓑ Ⓒ Ⓓ Ⓔ	31. Ⓐ Ⓑ Ⓒ Ⓓ Ⓔ	51. Ⓐ Ⓑ Ⓒ Ⓓ Ⓔ
12. Ⓐ Ⓑ Ⓒ Ⓓ Ⓔ	32. Ⓐ Ⓑ Ⓒ Ⓓ Ⓔ	52. Ⓐ Ⓑ Ⓒ Ⓓ Ⓔ
13. Ⓐ Ⓑ Ⓒ Ⓓ Ⓔ	33. Ⓐ Ⓑ Ⓒ Ⓓ Ⓔ	53. Ⓐ Ⓑ Ⓒ Ⓓ Ⓔ
14. Ⓐ Ⓑ Ⓒ Ⓓ Ⓔ	34. Ⓐ Ⓑ Ⓒ Ⓓ Ⓔ	54. Ⓐ Ⓑ Ⓒ Ⓓ Ⓔ
15. Ⓐ Ⓑ Ⓒ Ⓓ Ⓔ	35. Ⓐ Ⓑ Ⓒ Ⓓ Ⓔ	55. Ⓐ Ⓑ Ⓒ Ⓓ Ⓔ
16. Ⓐ Ⓑ Ⓒ Ⓓ Ⓔ	36. Ⓐ Ⓑ Ⓒ Ⓓ Ⓔ	56. Ⓐ Ⓑ Ⓒ Ⓓ Ⓔ
17. Ⓐ Ⓑ Ⓒ Ⓓ Ⓔ	37. Ⓐ Ⓑ Ⓒ Ⓓ Ⓔ	57. Ⓐ Ⓑ Ⓒ Ⓓ Ⓔ
18. Ⓐ Ⓑ Ⓒ Ⓓ Ⓔ	38. Ⓐ Ⓑ Ⓒ Ⓓ Ⓔ	58. Ⓐ Ⓑ Ⓒ Ⓓ Ⓔ
19. Ⓐ Ⓑ Ⓒ Ⓓ Ⓔ	39. Ⓐ Ⓑ Ⓒ Ⓓ Ⓔ	59. Ⓐ Ⓑ Ⓒ Ⓓ Ⓔ
20. Ⓐ Ⓑ Ⓒ Ⓓ Ⓔ	40. Ⓐ Ⓑ Ⓒ Ⓓ Ⓔ	60. Ⓐ Ⓑ Ⓒ Ⓓ Ⓔ

Section 2: Quantitative I

1. Ⓐ Ⓑ Ⓒ Ⓓ Ⓔ	11. Ⓐ Ⓑ Ⓒ Ⓓ Ⓔ	21. Ⓐ Ⓑ Ⓒ Ⓓ Ⓔ
2. Ⓐ Ⓑ Ⓒ Ⓓ Ⓔ	12. Ⓐ Ⓑ Ⓒ Ⓓ Ⓔ	22. Ⓐ Ⓑ Ⓒ Ⓓ Ⓔ
3. Ⓐ Ⓑ Ⓒ Ⓓ Ⓔ	13. Ⓐ Ⓑ Ⓒ Ⓓ Ⓔ	23. Ⓐ Ⓑ Ⓒ Ⓓ Ⓔ
4. Ⓐ Ⓑ Ⓒ Ⓓ Ⓔ	14. Ⓐ Ⓑ Ⓒ Ⓓ Ⓔ	24. Ⓐ Ⓑ Ⓒ Ⓓ Ⓔ
5. Ⓐ Ⓑ Ⓒ Ⓓ Ⓔ	15. Ⓐ Ⓑ Ⓒ Ⓓ Ⓔ	25. Ⓐ Ⓑ Ⓒ Ⓓ Ⓔ
6. Ⓐ Ⓑ Ⓒ Ⓓ Ⓔ	16. Ⓐ Ⓑ Ⓒ Ⓓ Ⓔ	
7. Ⓐ Ⓑ Ⓒ Ⓓ Ⓔ	17. Ⓐ Ⓑ Ⓒ Ⓓ Ⓔ	
8. Ⓐ Ⓑ Ⓒ Ⓓ Ⓔ	18. Ⓐ Ⓑ Ⓒ Ⓓ Ⓔ	
9. Ⓐ Ⓑ Ⓒ Ⓓ Ⓔ	19. Ⓐ Ⓑ Ⓒ Ⓓ Ⓔ	
10. Ⓐ Ⓑ Ⓒ Ⓓ Ⓔ	20. Ⓐ Ⓑ Ⓒ Ⓓ Ⓔ	

Section 3: Reading Comprehension

1. (A) (B) (C) (D) (E) 17. (A) (B) (C) (D) (E) 33. (A) (B) (C) (D) (E)
2. (A) (B) (C) (D) (E) 18. (A) (B) (C) (D) (E) 34. (A) (B) (C) (D) (E)
3. (A) (B) (C) (D) (E) 19. (A) (B) (C) (D) (E) 35. (A) (B) (C) (D) (E)
4. (A) (B) (C) (D) (E) 20. (A) (B) (C) (D) (E) 36. (A) (B) (C) (D) (E)
5. (A) (B) (C) (D) (E) 21. (A) (B) (C) (D) (E) 37. (A) (B) (C) (D) (E)
6. (A) (B) (C) (D) (E) 22. (A) (B) (C) (D) (E) 38. (A) (B) (C) (D) (E)
7. (A) (B) (C) (D) (E) 23. (A) (B) (C) (D) (E) 39. (A) (B) (C) (D) (E)
8. (A) (B) (C) (D) (E) 24. (A) (B) (C) (D) (E) 40. (A) (B) (C) (D) (E)
9. (A) (B) (C) (D) (E) 25. (A) (B) (C) (D) (E)
10. (A) (B) (C) (D) (E) 26. (A) (B) (C) (D) (E)
11. (A) (B) (C) (D) (E) 27. (A) (B) (C) (D) (E)
12. (A) (B) (C) (D) (E) 28. (A) (B) (C) (D) (E)
13. (A) (B) (C) (D) (E) 29. (A) (B) (C) (D) (E)
14. (A) (B) (C) (D) (E) 30. (A) (B) (C) (D) (E)
15. (A) (B) (C) (D) (E) 31. (A) (B) (C) (D) (E)
16. (A) (B) (C) (D) (E) 32. (A) (B) (C) (D) (E)

Section 4: Quantitative II

1. (A) (B) (C) (D) (E) 11. (A) (B) (C) (D) (E) 21. (A) (B) (C) (D) (E)
2. (A) (B) (C) (D) (E) 12. (A) (B) (C) (D) (E) 22. (A) (B) (C) (D) (E)
3. (A) (B) (C) (D) (E) 13. (A) (B) (C) (D) (E) 23. (A) (B) (C) (D) (E)
4. (A) (B) (C) (D) (E) 14. (A) (B) (C) (D) (E) 24. (A) (B) (C) (D) (E)
5. (A) (B) (C) (D) (E) 15. (A) (B) (C) (D) (E) 25. (A) (B) (C) (D) (E)
6. (A) (B) (C) (D) (E) 16. (A) (B) (C) (D) (E)
7. (A) (B) (C) (D) (E) 17. (A) (B) (C) (D) (E)
8. (A) (B) (C) (D) (E) 18. (A) (B) (C) (D) (E)
9. (A) (B) (C) (D) (E) 19. (A) (B) (C) (D) (E)
10. (A) (B) (C) (D) (E) 20. (A) (B) (C) (D) (E)

SECTION 1

Time: 30 Minutes

60 Questions

This section includes two different types of questions: synonyms and analogies. There are directions and a sample question for each question type.

Directions: Each of the following questions consists of a word in capital letters followed by five words or phrases. Select the one word or phrase that means most nearly the same as the word in capital letters.

Sample Question:

ESSENTIAL:
(A) dire
(B) confusing
(C) vital
(D) expert
(E) honest

Correct Answer: C

---

1. NOVICE:
   (A) burden
   (B) agreement
   (C) beggar
   (D) beginner
   (E) expression

2. FABRICATE:
   (A) stitch
   (B) fasten
   (C) falsify
   (D) deter
   (E) decorate

3. FRIENDLY:
   (A) congenital
   (B) amiable
   (C) sanctimonious
   (D) ambivalent
   (E) responsive

4. GENRE:
   (A) proposal
   (B) category
   (C) purpose
   (D) principle
   (E) generation

5. SUMMIT:
   (A) conference
   (B) valley
   (C) essence
   (D) nadir
   (E) outline

6. DEFTLY:
   (A) wilfully
   (B) closely
   (C) quickly
   (D) randomly
   (E) skillfully

GO ON TO THE NEXT PAGE.

7. PROSPER:
   - (A) accomplish
   - (B) strive
   - (C) affect
   - (D) gather
   - (E) thrive

8. SPURN:
   - (A) cross
   - (B) return
   - (C) betray
   - (D) reject
   - (E) hinder

9. COMPLIMENTARY:
   - (A) secondary
   - (B) free
   - (C) charming
   - (D) attractive
   - (E) matched

10. VISAGE:
   - (A) encounter
   - (B) station
   - (C) face
   - (D) bandage
   - (E) wound

11. RESPITE:
   - (A) pause
   - (B) presumption
   - (C) recluse
   - (D) blockage
   - (E) susceptibility

12. REGRETFUL:
   - (A) bewildered
   - (B) credulous
   - (C) desultory
   - (D) contrite
   - (E) dubious

13. FRUGAL:
   - (A) inadequate
   - (B) shrewd
   - (C) economical
   - (D) balanced
   - (E) equitable

14. IMPLY:
   - (A) suggest
   - (B) implore
   - (C) greet
   - (D) reminisce
   - (E) appeal

15. INCITE:
   - (A) insist
   - (B) dispel
   - (C) maintain
   - (D) assert
   - (E) provoke

16. MEAGER:
   - (A) paltry
   - (B) stunted
   - (C) timid
   - (D) sloppy
   - (E) frigid

17. PREDICTION:
   - (A) predecessor
   - (B) forecast
   - (C) predicament
   - (D) prejudice
   - (E) display

18. FACET:
   - (A) goal
   - (B) endeavor
   - (C) tactic
   - (D) aspect
   - (E) ambition

19. ABSOLVE:
   - (A) admonish
   - (B) accede
   - (C) opine
   - (D) clear
   - (E) affirm

20. DESTROY:
   - (A) inveigh
   - (B) subvert
   - (C) rescind
   - (D) sanction
   - (E) abjure

GO ON TO THE NEXT PAGE.

21. MOURN:
    (A) replete
    (B) whimper
    (C) argue
    (D) disapprove
    (E) grieve

22. POISONOUS:
    (A) dangerous
    (B) hurtful
    (C) toxic
    (D) devious
    (E) ruthless

23. APLOMB:
    (A) omen
    (B) ascent
    (C) epitome
    (D) confidence
    (E) atonement

24. CORROBORATION:
    (A) confirmation
    (B) announcement
    (C) bulletin
    (D) tribulation
    (E) ordeal

25. ERRATIC:
    (A) mistaken
    (B) immaculate
    (C) unpredictable
    (D) opportune
    (E) inadvertent

26. CREDIBLE:
    (A) languid
    (B) believable
    (C) forthright
    (D) fallible
    (E) enviable

27. ABSCOND:
    (A) abolish
    (B) choose
    (C) leave
    (D) remove
    (E) steal

28. CALM:
    (A) rest
    (B) inspire
    (C) exalt
    (D) soothe
    (E) commend

29. IRRITABLE:
    (A) voluble
    (B) timorous
    (C) transitory
    (D) turgid
    (E) petulant

30. TRAVESTY:
    (A) disaster
    (B) mockery
    (C) misfortune
    (D) adage
    (E) opinion

GO ON TO THE NEXT PAGE.

Directions: The questions that follow ask you to find relationships between words. For each question select the answer choice that best completes the meaning of the sentence.

Sample Question:

> Swim is to pool as
> (A) fork is to plate
> (B) sweep is to broom
> (C) clean is to kitchen
> (D) sleep is to bed
> (E) trot is to horse
>
> Correct Answer: D
> Choice D is correct because a pool is a place to swim just as a bed is a place to sleep.

31. Safe is to dangerous as
    (A) taste is to smell
    (B) bland is to spicy
    (C) dry is to fire
    (D) multiplication is to divide
    (E) lazy is to exercise

32. Star is to sky as
    (A) mountain is to valley
    (B) cloud is to sun
    (C) fish is to ocean
    (D) dream is to sleep
    (E) fit is to shoe

33. Cut is to wound as
    (A) storm is to snow
    (B) brick is to building
    (C) drink is to thirst
    (D) save is to money
    (E) cry is to tears

34. Camera is to picture as
    (A) breeze is to fan
    (B) paint is to frame
    (C) brush is to hair
    (D) phone is to call
    (E) horse is to gallop

35. Lumens is to brightness as
    (A) velocity is to speed
    (B) decibels is to volume
    (C) pint is to liquid
    (D) mile is to kilometer
    (E) measure is to depth

36. Book is to writer as
    (A) needle is to doctor
    (B) cavity is to dentist
    (C) truck is to driver
    (D) crop is to farmer
    (E) script is to actor

37. Frigid is to tropical as
    (A) raw is to cooked
    (B) detergent is to clean
    (C) snow is to sunshine
    (D) sleek is to stylish
    (E) beach is to sandy

38. Los Angeles is to California as
    (A) Phoenix is to New Mexico
    (B) Philadelphia is to Pittsburgh
    (C) Houston is to Texas
    (D) state is to country
    (E) Denver is to America

39. Menu is to diner as catalog is to
    (A) cashier
    (B) order
    (C) seller
    (D) purchase
    (E) shopper

40. Cuff is to collar as mouse is to
    (A) keyboard
    (B) cheese
    (C) cat
    (D) trap
    (E) rodent

GO ON TO THE NEXT PAGE.

41. Snake is to belly as
    (A) monkey is to tail
    (B) bear is to hands
    (C) horse is to legs
    (D) pig is to snout
    (E) person is to feet

42. Carat is to diamond as
    (A) calorie is to heat
    (B) liquid is to volume
    (C) perimeter is to inches
    (D) unit is to measurement
    (E) gram is to pound

43. Book is to read as data is to
    (A) analyze
    (B) prove
    (C) submit
    (D) foretell
    (E) conclude

44. Burnish is to polish as
    (A) search is to find
    (B) wash is to rinse
    (C) peel is to scrape
    (D) shine is to glisten
    (E) reinforce is to strengthen

45. Fresh is to rancid as
    (A) heat is to boil
    (B) ripe is to rotten
    (C) molten is to lava
    (D) shed is to discard
    (E) cooked is to burnt

46. Fire is to heat as
    (A) cold is to snow
    (B) lamp is to light
    (C) cool is to breeze
    (D) wax is to melt
    (E) music is to listen

47. Browsing is to shopping as
    (A) skimming is to reading
    (B) nodding is to agreeing
    (C) walking is to running
    (D) hiking is to climbing
    (E) seeing is to recognizing

48. Recital is to pianist as exhibit is to
    (A) museum
    (B) clay
    (C) auction
    (D) artist
    (E) gallery

49. Song is to medley as
    (A) series is to book
    (B) collection is to displays
    (C) gumball is to machines
    (D) picture is to collage
    (E) survey is to lists

50. Exercise is to sweat as
    (A) wander is to meander
    (B) reduce is to budget
    (C) harvest is to produce
    (D) accept is to refuse
    (E) vote is to confirm

51. Stamen is to flower as
    (A) computer is to monitor
    (B) lens is to eye
    (C) socket is to cord
    (D) spiral is to notebook
    (E) pillow is to sleep

52. Map is to cartographer as
    (A) club is to golfer
    (B) book is to librarian
    (C) car is to mechanic
    (D) building is to architect
    (E) cake is to baker

53. Baby is to crawling as
    (A) rock is to skipping
    (B) trout is to fishing
    (C) frog is to jumping
    (D) parent is to driving
    (E) bird is to nesting

54. Eraser is to chalkboard as
    (A) mop is to floor
    (B) keyboard is to computer
    (C) ballpoint is to pen
    (D) towel is to soap
    (E) machine is to washing

GO ON TO THE NEXT PAGE.

55. Eager is to fervent as
    (A) tedious is to bored
    (B) glum is to sad
    (C) pleased is to ecstatic
    (D) enraged is to mad
    (E) remorse is to sorrow

56. Bread is to moldy as
    (A) whisker is to hairy
    (B) disease is to sickly
    (C) blood is to scab
    (D) steel is to rusty
    (E) running is to sweaty

57. Dog is to collie as lizard is to
    (A) cage
    (B) chameleon
    (C) reptile
    (D) pet
    (E) desert

58. Chisel is to carving as
    (A) thread is to sewing
    (B) clay is to sculpting
    (C) wheel is to driving
    (D) blender is to mixing
    (E) recipe is to cooking

59. Drop is to break as
    (A) spill is to tip
    (B) stumble is to fall
    (C) adorn is to decorate
    (D) stitch is to sew
    (E) drive is to crash

60. Ruby is to red as amber is to
    (A) brown
    (B) green
    (C) pink
    (D) blue
    (E) purple

STOP!
If you finish before time is up, check your work on this section only.

Directions: For each of the following questions, mark the letter of your choice on the answer sheet.

1. If $6 + 12 +$ ____ $= 5 + 11 + 6$, then ____ $=$
   (A) 2
   (B) 3
   (C) 4
   (D) 5
   (E) 6

2. $4 \times 3 \times 6 \times 2$ is equal to the product of 24 and
   (A) 6
   (B) 7
   (C) 8
   (D) 9
   (E) 11

3. If $2/3$ of a number is 24, then $1/4$ of the same number is
   (A) 20
   (B) 16
   (C) 13
   (D) 12
   (E) 9

4. A box of chocolates has 45 pieces. If 9 pieces have nuts in them, what percent of the chocolates are without nuts?
   (A) 20%
   (B) 45%
   (C) 79%
   (D) 80%
   (E) 84%

5. In the Northshore Swimming Club, 6 of 48 members are females. What is the ratio of females to all club members?
   (A) $\frac{3}{16}$
   (B) $\frac{1}{15}$
   (C) $\frac{1}{4}$
   (D) $\frac{1}{8}$
   (E) $\frac{1}{12}$

6. Two numbers together add to 375. One number is twice the size of the other. What are the two numbers?
   (A) 25, 50
   (B) 50, 100
   (C) 75, 150
   (D) 95, 190
   (E) 125, 250

7. $6^{3}/4\% =$
   (A) 67.5
   (B) 6.75
   (C) 0.675
   (D) 0.0675
   (E) 0.00675

GO ON TO THE NEXT PAGE.

8. A club collected $1,085.00. If 75% of that came from membership dues, how much money came from sources other than membership?
   (A) $271.25
   (B) $338.75
   (C) $365.75
   (D) $425.05
   (E) $442.25

9. A right angle is an angle that measures
   (A) exactly 90°
   (B) greater than 90°
   (C) less than 90°
   (D) 45°
   (E) 30°

10. In the equilateral triangle shown, what is the measure of each angle?

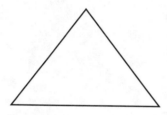

   (A) 60°
   (B) 90°
   (C) 120°
   (D) 140°
   (E) 180°

11. If $12a + 4a - 7a = 27$, $a =$
    (A) 1
    (B) 2
    (C) 3
    (D) 4
    (E) 5

12. It costs n dollars to buy 10 boxes of crackers. At the same rate, how many dollars will it cost to buy 25 boxes of crackers?
    (A) $2.5n$
    (B) $25n$
    (C) $2n/5$
    (D) $5n/2$
    (E) $250n$

13. In the figure below, if ∠1 is 33°, what is the measure of ∠2?

    (A) 56°
    (B) 110°
    (C) 130°
    (D) 147°
    (E) 180°

14. Paul has a garden that is 4 meters by 7 meters. If he uses 2 ounces of fertilizer per square meter, how many ounces must he use?
    (A) 21 oz
    (B) 42 oz
    (C) 44 oz
    (D) 50 oz
    (E) 56 oz

15. Steve is measuring the growth of a tomato plant. The chart below indicates his measurements for the past five weeks. Based on the information in the chart, what should he predict will be the height of the plant at week 6?

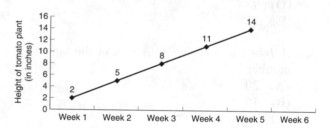

    (A) 15 inches
    (B) 17 inches
    (C) 18 inches
    (D) 21 inches
    (E) 24 inches

16. A student buys a sandwich for 80 cents, milk for 20 cents, and pie for 30 cents. How much did the meal cost?
    (A) $1.00
    (B) $1.20
    (C) $1.30
    (D) $1.40
    (E) $1.50

GO ON TO THE NEXT PAGE.

17. On a test with 75 questions, Cassidy answered 45 correctly. What percent did she answer correctly?
(A) 60%
(B) 72%
(C) 84%
(D) 89%
(E) 92%

18. Which of the following is NOT equal to a whole number?
(A) $\frac{16}{4}$

(B) $6 \times \frac{2}{3}$

(C) $4 \div \frac{1}{4}$

(D) $\frac{1}{3} \times 4$

(E) $3 + 2$

19. Jake spent one-fifth of his life in school. If he is now 55, how many years did he spend in school?
(A) 9
(B) 11
(C) 13
(D) 15
(E) 17

20. What is the perimeter of the following rectangle?

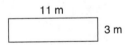

(A) 12 m
(B) 18 m
(C) 24 m
(D) 28 m
(E) 30 m

21. Bobby's test scores for social studies are 93, 76, 91, 83, and 72. What is his average score?
(A) 83
(B) 87
(C) 91
(D) 93
(E) 94

22. Riverside School has 150 fewer students than twice the number of students at Hillside School. If Riverside School has 500 students, how many students attend Hillside School?
(A) 125
(B) 150
(C) 250
(D) 300
(E) 325

23. A ladder is placed against a building. If the ladder makes a 55° angle with the ground, what is the measure of the angle that the ladder makes with the building?
(A) 25°
(B) 30°
(C) 35°
(D) 40°
(E) 45°

24. Ashley buys 48 apples. There are 12 Red Delicious applies and 16 Granny Smith apples. What fraction of the apples are not Red Delicious or Granny Smith?
(A) $\frac{1}{5}$

(B) $\frac{1}{4}$

(C) $\frac{1}{3}$

(D) $\frac{5}{12}$

(E) $\frac{7}{12}$

25. What is the total cost of a $750 television, including an 8% sales tax?
(A) $765
(B) $784
(C) $79218
(D) $810
(E) $824

STOP!
If you finish before time is up, check your work on this section only.

SECTION 3
Time: 40 Minutes
40 Questions

Directions: Each reading passage is followed by questions about it. Answer the questions that follow a passage on the basis of what is stated or implied in that passage. For each question, select the answer you think is best and record your choice by filling in the corresponding oval on the answer sheet.

Volcanoes are mountains, but they are very different from other mountains; they are not formed by folding and crumpling or by uplift and erosion. Instead, volcanoes are built by the accu-
5 mulation of their own eruptive products—lava, bombs (crusted over lava blobs), ashflows, and tephra (airborne ash and dust). A *volcano* is most commonly a conical hill or mountain built around a vent that connects with reservoirs of molten
10 rock below the surface of the Earth. The term volcano also refers to the opening or vent through which the molten rock and associated gases are expelled.

Deep within the Earth it is so hot that some
15 rocks slowly melt and become a thick flowing substance called *magma*. Because it is lighter than the solid rock around it, magma rises and collects in magma chambers. Eventually some of the magma pushes through vents and fissures in
20 the Earth's surface and a volcanic eruption occurs. Magma that has erupted is called *lava*.

Some volcanic eruptions are explosive and others are not. How explosive an eruption is depends on how runny or sticky the magma is.
25 If magma is thin and runny, gases can escape easily from it. When this type of magma erupts, it flows out of the volcano. Because they move slowly enough for people to get out of their way, lava flows rarely kill people. They can, however,
30 cause considerable destruction to buildings in their path. If magma is thick and sticky, gases cannot escape easily. Pressure builds up until the gases escape violently and explode. In this type of eruption, the magma blasts into the air and breaks
35 apart into pieces called *tephra*. Tephra can range in size from tiny particles of ash to house-size

boulders. Large-sized tephra typically falls back to the ground on or close to the volcano and progressively smaller fragments are carried away
40 from the vent by wind. Volcanic ash, the smallest tephra fragments, can travel hundreds to thousands of kilometers downwind from a volcano.

1. A primary difference between volcanoes and other mountains is in
   (A) their height
   (B) their ruggedness
   (C) their age
   (D) where they are located
   (E) how they are formed

2. A volcanic eruption is likely to be most explosive if magma
   (A) is thin and runny
   (B) is thick and sticky
   (C) rises and collects in magma chambers
   (D) pushes out through fissures in the Earth's surface
   (E) becomes lava

3. The author uses italic print primarily to
   (A) emphasize words that are used in an unusual way
   (B) indicate words that are difficult to pronounce
   (C) point out foreign words
   (D) highlight important terms that are defined in the text
   (E) indicate words that are not necessary to understanding the passage

GO ON TO THE NEXT PAGE.

4. All of the following can be explicitly answered by the passage EXCEPT:
   (A) What factors contribute to hot temperatures deep inside the Earth?
   (B) Why are some volcanic eruptions explosive while others are not?
   (C) As dangerous as eruptions can be, why do lava flows rarely kill people?
   (D) Why does magma rise and collect in chambers?
   (E) Why does pressure build up in magma that is thick and sticky?

5. This passage would most likely appear in
   (A) a newspaper
   (B) a science textbook
   (C) an adventure novel
   (D) a travel brochure
   (E) a safety manual

6. Which of the following statements is NOT true of tephra?
   (A) It can range in size from tiny particles of ash to huge boulders.
   (B) It can travel thousands of kilometers from a volcano.
   (C) It can be found trapped in magma.
   (D) Large tephra falls on or close to a volcano.
   (E) It is the term for rock fragments erupted into the air by volcanoes.

The following speech was delivered by Frederick Douglass at a meeting of the Anti-Slavery Society in Pittsburgh in 1863.

I am one of those who believe that it is the mission of this war to free every slave in the United States. I am one of those who believe that we should consent to no peace which shall not be
5   an Abolition peace. I am, moreover, one of those who believe that the work of the American Anti-Slavery Society will not have been completed until the black men of the South, and the black men of the North, shall have been admitted, fully
10 and completely, into the body politic of America. I look upon slavery as going the way of all the earth. It is the mission of the war to put it down.

I know it will be said that I ask you to make the black man a voter in the South. It is said that
15 the colored man is ignorant, and therefore he shall not vote. In saying this, you lay down a rule for the black man that you apply to no other class

of your citizens. If he knows enough to be hanged, he knows enough to vote. If he knows an honest
20 man from a thief, he knows much more than some of our white voters. If he knows enough to take up arms in defence of this Government and bare his breast to the storm of rebel artillery, he knows enough to vote.

25 All I ask, however, in regard to the blacks, is that whatever rule you adopt, whether of intelligence or wealth, as the condition of voting for whites, you shall apply it equally to the black man. Do that, and I am satisfied, and eternal justice
30 is satisfied; liberty, fraternity, equality, are satisfied, and the country will move on harmoniously.

7. According to Douglass, the mission of the Civil War is to
   (A) destroy the Confederacy
   (B) punish the rebel soldiers
   (C) end slavery
   (D) preserve the Union
   (E) create a new class of citizens

8. Douglass believes the work of the Anti-Slavery Society should not be considered complete until
   (A) slavery is abolished
   (B) black men in the South are able to vote
   (C) blacks can move freely between the South and the North
   (D) black men of the North and South have the right to vote
   (E) all conditions for voting are ended

9. What does Douglass mean by calling for black men to be admitted "fully and completely into the body politic of America"(lines 9–10)?
   (A) They must have the same rights and privileges as all other citizens.
   (B) They must be able to vote.
   (C) They must be able to run for office.
   (D) They must take up arms to defend the Government.
   (E) They must be considered a separate class of citizens.

GO ON TO THE NEXT PAGE.

10. The purpose of Douglass's speech was to
    (A) inform members of the society of the horrors of slavery
    (B) convince listeners to adopt fair and equal voting requirements
    (C) inform listeners of the progress of the war
    (D) convince members of the society that slavery should be ended
    (E) explain how the right to vote would create harmony

The great Pullman was whirling onward with such dignity of motion that a glance from the window seemed simply to prove that the plains of Texas were pouring eastward. Vast flats of green
5 grass, dull-hued spaces of mesquite and cactus, little groups of frame houses, woods of light and tender trees, all were sweeping into the east, sweeping over the horizon, a precipice.

A newly married pair had boarded this coach
10 at San Antonio. The man's face was reddened from many days in the wind and sun, and a direct result of his new black clothes was that his brick-colored hands were constantly performing in a most conscious fashion. From time to time he
15 looked down respectfully at his attire. He sat with a hand on each knee, like a man waiting in a barber's shop. The glances he devoted to other passengers were furtive and shy.

The bride was not pretty, nor was she very
20 young. She wore a dress of blue cashmere, with small reservations of velvet here and there and with steel buttons abounding. She continually twisted her head to regard her puff sleeves, very stiff, straight, and high. They embarrassed her.
25 It was quite apparent that she had cooked, and that she expected to cook, dutifully. The blushes caused by the careless scrutiny of some passengers as she had entered the car were strange to see upon this plain, under-class countenance,
30 which was drawn in placid, almost emotionless lines.

They were evidently very happy. "Ever been in a parlor-car before?" he asked, smiling with delight.
35 "No," she answered, "I never was. It's fine, ain't it?"

"Great! And then after a while we'll go forward to the diner and get a big layout. Finest meal in the world. Charge a dollar."

40 "Oh, do they?" cried the bride. "Charge a dollar? Why, that's too much—for us—ain't it, Jack?"

"Not this trip, anyhow," he answered bravely. "We're going to go the whole thing."
Stephen Crane from
"The Bride Comes to Yellow Sky"

11. The tone of the passage suggests that the author regards the newly married couple with
    (A) embarrassment
    (B) disrespect
    (C) sympathy
    (D) sorrow
    (E) scorn

12. Which word best describes the newlywed couple?
    (A) well-to-do
    (B) sad
    (C) frightened
    (D) unsophisticated
    (E) unpleasant

13. When this passage takes place, the bride and groom were most probably
    (A) in a hotel
    (B) at a train station
    (C) on a stagecoach
    (D) in a diner
    (E) on a train

14. As it is used in line 18 the word "furtive" most nearly means
    (A) stealthy
    (B) steady
    (C) focused
    (D) friendly
    (E) unabashed

15. The narrator of this story is
    (A) the groom
    (B) the bride
    (C) a participant in the story
    (D) an outside observer
    (E) an adult looking back on his life

GO ON TO THE NEXT PAGE.

16. The main purpose of this passage is to
    (A) express an opinion
    (B) analyze information
    (C) introduce characters and setting
    (D) resolve a crisis
    (E) set up a conflict between two characters

17. By saying, "It was quite apparent that she had cooked, and that she expected to cook, dutifully," the author is suggesting that the bride
    (A) expects to eat out regularly
    (B) has led a life of hard work
    (C) has never eaten in a restaurant before
    (D) wants to learn more about cooking
    (E) will learn to cook her husband's favorite foods

Over two decades ago, scientists in the Agricultural Research Service Vegetable Crops Research Unit at Madison, Wisconsin, began a quest to breed carrots packed with beta-carotene—
5   an orange pigment used by the body to create vitamin A. Thanks largely to their work, today's carrots provide consumers with 75 percent more beta-carotene than those available 25 years ago.
    The researchers, led by plant geneticist
10 Philipp Simon, haven't limited themselves to the color orange. They've selectively bred a rainbow of carrots—purple, red, yellow, even white. Scientists are learning that these plant pigments perform a range of protective duties in the
15 human body.
    Red carrots derive their color mainly from lycopene, a type of carotene believed to guard against heart disease and some cancers. Yellow carrots accumulate xanthophylls, pigments similar
20 to beta-carotene that support good eye health. Purple carrots possess an entirely different class of pigments—anthocyanins—which act as powerful antioxidants.
    While colored carrots are unusual, they're not
25 exactly new. "Purple and yellow carrots were eaten more than 1,000 years ago in Afghanistan and 700 years ago in western Europe," says Simon. "But the carrot-breeding process has gone on intensively for just 50 years."
30 In nature, different strains of carrots contain varying types and amounts of carotenoids—the pigments responsible for orange, yellow, and red colors. To assist seed companies and growers who wish to produce nutrient-rich carrots, Simon and
35 his lab are working to map all the genes that play

a part in synthesizing carotenoids in major carrot lines. Simon now knows of 20 genes that are involved. But determining a particular gene's role in generating carotenoids is not that straightforward.
40 Aside from enhancing the nutritional value of carrots—as well as onions, garlic, and cucumbers—researchers at Simon's laboratory also work to improve the vegetable's culinary quality and appeal.
45 With their compelling health benefits and a thumbs-up from taste testers, Simon's colorful carrots will be a great addition to supermarket produce aisles once consumers create a demand for them.

18. The main purpose of this passage is to
    (A) explain why carrots can be various colors
    (B) point out the health benefits of carotenoids
    (C) report on enhancements to the nutritional value of carrots
    (D) explore ways to increase carrot production
    (E) encourage people to buy carrots of various colors

19. The author's tone can best be described as
    (A) argumentative
    (B) emotional
    (C) sentimental
    (D) informative
    (E) optimistic

20. According to the passage, carrots have been bred in all of the following colors EXCEPT:
    (A) yellow
    (B) green
    (C) white
    (D) red
    (E) purple

21. The type of carotene that gives carrots a red color is
    (A) lycopene
    (B) xanthophyll
    (C) anthocyanin
    (D) beta-carotene
    (E) antioxidant

GO ON TO THE NEXT PAGE.

22. Which of the following is true of colored carrots?
    (A) They first appeared about 50 years ago.
    (B) They do not equal regular carrots in nutritive value.
    (C) They are not as tasty as traditional carrots.
    (D) They were first bred by scientists at the Agricultural Research Service Vegetable Crops Research Unit.
    (E) They derive their color from varying types and amounts of carotenoids.

23. This passage can best be described as
    (A) a short story
    (B) a biography
    (C) a research report
    (D) propaganda
    (E) an editorial

> From the outskirts of the town,
> Where of old the mile-stone stood,
>   Now a stranger, looking down
>   I behold the shadowy crown
> 5 Of the dark and haunted wood
>
>   Is it changed, or am I changed?
> Ah! the oaks are fresh and green,
>   But the friends with whom I ranged
>   Through their thickets are estranged
> 10 By the years that intervene.
>
>   Bright as ever flows the sea,
> Bright as ever shines the sun,
>   But alas! they seem to me
>   Not the sun that used to be,
> 15 Not the tides that used to run.
>
> —Henry Wadsworth Longfellow
> "Changed"

24. The author's tone is best described as
    (A) lighthearted
    (B) optimistic
    (C) nostalgic
    (D) hostile
    (E) humorous

25. This poem is written from the point of view of
    (A) a frightened child
    (B) a disinterested adult
    (C) a sympathetic outside observer
    (D) a sad observer of a transformation
    (E) an adult recalling a childhood dream

26. In line 5, the author most probably refers to the woods as "haunted" in order to
    (A) make the narrator seem foolish and superstitious
    (B) hint at the narrator's acceptance of death
    (C) reveal the narrator's belief in spirits
    (D) set a dark and gloomy mood
    (E) indicate the woods were filled with memories

27. Which of the following best expresses the theme of this poem?
    (A) the power of the sun
    (B) the passage of time
    (C) the fluctuation of the tide
    (D) autumn
    (E) nature's renewal

The Statue of Liberty was a gift to the people of the United States from the people of France in recognition of the friendship established between the two nations during the American Revolution.
5 Over the years, the Statue of Liberty has come to symbolize freedom and democracy, as well as this international friendship.
Sculptor Frederic Auguste Bartholdi was commissioned to design a sculpture with the year
10 1876 in mind for completion, to commemorate the centennial of the American Declaration of Independence. Alexandre Gustave Eiffel (designer of the Eiffel Tower) was called in to address the structural issues of Bartholdi's colossal sculpture.
15 The Statue was a joint effort between America and France and it was agreed upon that the American people would build the pedestal, and the French people would be responsible for the Statue and its assembly here in the United States.
20 Lack of funds was a problem on both sides of the Atlantic Ocean. In France, public fees, various forms of entertainment, and a lottery were among the methods used to raise funds. In the United States, benefit theatrical events, art exhibitions,
25 auctions and prize fights helped to provide the needed funds. When fundraising for the pedestal lagged, Joseph Pulitzer (noted for the Pulitzer Prize) used the editorial pages of his newspaper *The World* to aid in the fundraising effort.
30 Pulitzer's campaign of harsh criticism against both the rich, who had failed to finance the pedestal construction, and the middle class, who

GO ON TO THE NEXT PAGE.

were content to rely upon the wealthy to provide the funds, was successful in motivating the people
35 of America to donate.

Financing for the pedestal was completed in August 1885, and pedestal construction was finished in April of 1886. The Statue was completed in France in July, 1884 and arrived in New York
40 Harbor in June of 1885 on board the French frigate *Isere*. In transit, the Statue was reduced to 350 individual pieces and packed in 214 crates. The Statue was re-assembled on her new pedestal in four months time. On October 28th 1886,
45 in front of thousands of spectators, President Grover Cleveland accepted the Statue on behalf of the United States. She was a centennial gift ten years late.

28. According to the passage, the Statue of Liberty was intended to celebrate the
(A) Centennial of the Declaration of Independence
(B) end of the Civil War
(C) end of hostilities between France and the United States
(D) start of the twentieth century
(E) dawn of a new era of international cooperation

29. In line 13, which word can be substituted for "address" without changing the meaning of the sentence?
(A) speak to
(B) focus on
(C) forward
(D) lecture
(E) label

30. From his actions, it can be inferred that Joseph Pulitzer's attitude toward the Statue of Liberty was
(A) openly hostile
(B) extremely cautious
(C) enthusiastically supportive
(D) completely neutral
(E) overly critical

31. According to the passage, the Statue of Liberty symbolizes
I. democracy
II. freedom
III. international friendship
IV. a treaty between the United States and France

(A) I only
(B) II only
(C) I and III only
(D) I, II, and III only
(E) I, II, III, and IV

32. According to the passage, all of the following are true EXCEPT:
(A) The United States agreed to finance and build the pedestal.
(B) Bartholdi needed help with structural issues of the statue.
(C) Joseph Pulitzer was instrumental in raising money for the pedestal.
(D) The designer of the Eiffel Tower was called in to help raise funds for the project.
(E) The statue was completed in France before the pedestal was fully funded.

33. The main purpose of the passage is to
(A) inform the reader about the history of the Statue of Liberty
(B) describe how Bartholdi designed the Statue of Liberty
(C) compare fundraising efforts in the United States and France
(D) defend the use of newspaper editorials to help raise funds for the project
(E) explain how the Statue was assembled on her pedestal

34. This passage would most likely appear in a
(A) short story
(B) novel
(C) newspaper
(D) engineering journal
(E) textbook

GO ON TO THE NEXT PAGE.

At the end of what seemed a tedious while, I had managed to pack my head full of islands, towns, bars, "points," and bends; and a curiously inanimate mass of lumber it was, too. However, inasmuch as I could shut my eyes and reel off a good long string of these names without leaving out more than ten miles of river in every fifty, I began to feel that I could take a boat down to New Orleans if I could make her skip those little gaps. But of course my complacency could hardly get start enough to lift my nose a trifle into the air, before Mr. Bixby would think of something to fetch it down again. One day he turned on me suddenly with this settler: —

"What is the shape of Walnut Bend?"

He might as well have asked me my grandmother's opinion of protoplasm. I reflected respectfully, and then said I didn't know it had any particular shape. My gunpowdery chief went off with a bang, of course, and then went on loading and firing until he was out of adjectives.

I had learned long ago that he only carried just so many rounds of ammunition, and was sure to subside into a very placable and even remorseful old smooth-bore as soon as they were all gone. That word "old" is merely affectionate; he was not more than thirty-four. I waited. By and by he said, —

"My boy, you've got to know the *shape* of the river perfectly. It is all there is left to steer by on a very dark night. Everything else is blotted out and gone. But mind you, it hasn't the same shape in the night that it has in the day-time."

"How on earth am I ever going to learn it, then?"

"How do you follow a hall at home in the dark? Because you know the shape of it. You can't see it."

"Do you mean to say that I've got to know all the million trifling variations of shape in the banks of this interminable river as well as I know the shape of the front hall at home?"

"On my honor you've got to know them *better* than any man ever did know the shapes of the halls in his own house."

"I wish I was dead!"

Mark Twain from *Life on the Mississippi*

35. When the narrator says, "my complacency could hardly get start enough to lift my nose a trifle into the air, before Mr. Bixby would think of something to fetch it down again," he means
(A) Whenever the narrator picked his head up, Mr. Bixby was there to tell him to keep his eyes on the river.
(B) Just as he thought he was learning the river, Bixby would demonstrate how little the narrator actually knew.
(C) No one can name all the islands, towns, bars, points, and bends of the Mississippi River.
(D) No other pilot knew the river as well as Mr. Bixby did.
(E) The narrator could never hope to know the river as well as Bixby did.

36. Why does the narrator compare Bixby's question about the shape of Walnut Bend to asking about his grandmother's opinion of protoplasm?
(A) Only his grandmother could answer Bixby's question.
(B) Both are questions that have no real answer.
(C) Both are questions the narrator cannot answer.
(D) Walnut Bend has the same shape as protoplasm.
(E) Bixby does not know the narrator's grandmother.

37. What is the meaning of "gunpowdery" in line 19?
(A) loud
(B) smoky
(C) strong
(D) explosive
(E) gritty

38. Which of the following best describes the narrator's reaction to the information that he will need to know the shape of the river perfectly even at night?
(A) anger
(B) regret
(C) amazement
(D) enthusiasm
(E) despair

GO ON TO THE NEXT PAGE.

39. The tone of this passage can best be described as
   (A) humorous
   (B) serious
   (C) angry
   (D) analytical
   (E) tense

40. This passage can best be described as
   (A) a news item
   (B) propaganda
   (C) an autobiography
   (D) a research report
   (E) a textbook excerpt

STOP!
If you finish before time is up, check your work on this section only.

Time: 30 Minutes
25 Questions

Directions: For each of the following questions, mark the letter of your choice on the answer sheet.

1. What is 2% of 5,000?
   (A) 10
   (B) 80
   (C) 100
   (D) 105
   (E) 110

2. $3.5 \times 0.93 =$
   (A) 2.886
   (B) 2.965
   (C) 3.255
   (D) 3.311
   (E) 3.405

3. Which of the following is NOT equal to a whole number?
   (A) $\frac{32}{4}$
   (B) $4 \times \frac{8}{16}$
   (C) $8 \div \frac{1}{8}$
   (D) $\frac{5}{12} \times 8$
   (E) $6.4 + 11.6$

4. $62\frac{1}{2}\% =$
   (A) 625
   (B) 62.5
   (C) 6.25
   (D) 0.625
   (E) 0.0625

5. It costs m dollars to buy 60 nails. At the same rate, how many dollars will it cost to buy 24 nails?
   (A) $\frac{m}{5}$
   (B) $\frac{2m}{5}$
   (C) $2m$
   (D) $5m$
   (E) $10m$

6. If $\frac{5}{12}$ of a number is 50, then $\frac{1}{2}$ of the same number is
   (A) 72
   (B) 70
   (C) 64
   (D) 60
   (E) 56

7. $4^2 + 3(2 - 6) =$
   (A) 4
   (B) 12
   (C) −4
   (D) −8
   (E) −12

8. What is the mean of the following numbers?
   24, 34, 12, 16, 34, 104, 890
   (A) 48
   (B) 64
   (C) 148
   (D) 152
   (E) 160

9. If $\frac{2}{25} = \frac{n}{500}$, what is n?
   (A) 20
   (B) 40
   (C) 60
   (D) 80
   (E) 100

10. If $6 \times 8 \div$ ____ $= 5 \times 4 + 4$, then ____ $=$
    (A) 2
    (B) 3
    (C) 4
    (D) 5
    (E) 6

GO ON TO THE NEXT PAGE.

11. $48 \div 6 \times 8 \times 8$ is equal to the product of 16 and
    (A) 16
    (B) 18
    (C) 24
    (D) 28
    (E) 32

12. $2 + {}^4\!/_{25} =$
    (A) 2.225
    (B) 2.16
    (C) 2.24
    (D) 2.45
    (E) 2.40

13. At the amusement park, Karen uses $^1\!/_3$ of her tickets for rides and $^1\!/_6$ of her tickets for food. What fraction of her tickets is left?
    (A) $\dfrac{1}{6}$

    (B) $\dfrac{1}{4}$

    (C) $\dfrac{1}{2}$

    (D) $\dfrac{2}{3}$

    (E) $\dfrac{3}{5}$

14. $12 \div 3^{3}/_4 =$
    (A) $1\dfrac{4}{5}$

    (B) $2\dfrac{2}{3}$

    (C) $2\dfrac{7}{16}$

    (D) $3\dfrac{5}{8}$

    (E) $3\dfrac{9}{13}$

15. Rosa buys a blouse for $23.95. The sales tax is 6.5%. What is the total cost of the blouse, including the sales tax?
    (A) $24.35
    (B) $24.78
    (C) $25.20
    (D) $25.51
    (E) $26.92

16. Kyle can ride his bike 30 km in 2 hours. At the same rate, how far can he ride in 7 hours?
    (A) 90 km
    (B) 105 km
    (C) 125 km
    (D) 130 km
    (E) 150 km

17. The distance around a rectangular park is 1 mile. If the width of the park is 880 feet, what is its length?
    (A) 720 ft
    (B) 840 ft
    (C) 1,250 ft
    (D) 1,510 ft
    (E) 1,760 ft

18. $10 \times (0.38 + 3.5) + 5.2 =$
    (A) 15.25
    (B) 24.15
    (C) 32.40
    (D) 44
    (E) 46.5

19. Daryl rents a computer by the hour. The rental company charges $25 + $6 per hour. Which equation represents this situation?
    (A) $25 + 6h$
    (B) $6h - 25$
    (C) $6(25 + h)$
    (D) $\dfrac{6}{h} + 25$

    (E) $h + \dfrac{25}{h}$

20. The temperature at midnight was $-12°C$. It rose $2°C$ each hour. What was the temperature at 11:00 A.M.?
    (A) $-2°C$
    (B) $4°C$
    (C) $8°C$
    (D) $10°C$
    (E) $12°C$

21. How many yards are in 4 miles?
    (A) 6,460
    (B) 6,720
    (C) 6,884
    (D) 7,040
    (E) 7,225

GO ON TO THE NEXT PAGE.

22. $25\frac{3}{5} \times 1\frac{1}{2} =$

    (A) $28\frac{4}{5}$

    (B) $30\frac{5}{3}$

    (C) $32\frac{2}{3}$

    (D) $35\frac{1}{3}$

    (E) $38\frac{2}{5}$

23. $23.4 \div 6 =$
    (A) 39
    (B) 3.9
    (C) 0.39
    (D) 0.039
    (E) 0.0039

24. $11\frac{1}{2} - 9\frac{3}{4} =$

    (A) $2\frac{1}{8}$

    (B) 2

    (C) $1\frac{7}{8}$

    (D) $1\frac{3}{4}$

    (E) $1\frac{1}{2}$

25. Each edge of a cube measures 5 in. What is the volume?
    (A) 10 in^3
    (B) 25 in^3
    (C) 100 in^3
    (D) 125 in^3
    (E) 250 in^3

STOP!
If you finish before time is up, check your work on this section only.

SECTION 5
Time: 25 Minutes

Directions: You will have 25 minutes to plan and write an essay on the topic below. Read the topic carefully. Jot down some brief notes on the scratch paper provided and organize your thoughts before you begin to write. Write your final essay on the ruled lines below. Write or print legibly, using the black pen that will be given to you at the test center. A copy of your essay will be sent to each school that will be receiving your test results.

Topic: Haste makes waste.

Assignment: Do you agree or disagree with the topic statement? Support your position with examples from your own experience, the experience of others, current events, history, or literature.

_____

_____

_____

_____

_____

_____

_____

Answer Key

Section 1 Verbal

1.	D	21.	E	41.	E
2.	C	22.	C	42.	A
3.	B	23.	D	43.	A
4.	B	24.	A	44.	E
5.	A	25.	C	45.	B
6.	E	26.	B	46.	B
7.	E	27.	C	47.	A
8.	D	28.	D	48.	D
9.	B	29.	E	49.	D
10.	C	30.	B	50.	C
11.	A	31.	B	51.	B
12.	D	32.	C	52.	E
13.	C	33.	E	53.	C
14.	A	34.	D	54.	A
15.	E	35.	B	55.	C
16.	A	36.	D	56.	D
17.	B	37.	A	57.	B
18.	D	38.	C	58.	D
19.	D	39.	E	59.	B
20.	B	40.	A	60.	A

Section 2 Quantitative I

1.	C	10.	A	19.	B
2.	A	11.	C	20.	D
3.	E	12.	A	21.	A
4.	D	13.	D	22.	E
5.	D	14.	E	23.	C
6.	E	15.	B	24.	D
7.	D	16.	C	25.	D
8.	A	17.	A		
9.	A	18.	D		

Section 3 Reading Comprehension

1.	E	15.	D	29.	B
2.	B	16.	C	30.	C
3.	D	17.	B	31.	D
4.	A	18.	C	32.	D
5.	B	19.	D	33.	A
6.	C	20.	B	34.	E
7.	C	21.	A	35.	B
8.	D	22.	E	36.	C
9.	A	23.	C	37.	D
10.	B	24.	C	38.	E
11.	C	25.	D	39.	A
12.	D	26.	E	40.	C
13.	E	27.	B		
14.	A	28.	A		

Section 4 Quantitative II

1.	C	10.	A	19.	A
2.	C	11.	E	20.	D
3.	D	12.	B	21.	D
4.	D	13.	C	22.	E
5.	B	14.	E	23.	B
6.	D	15.	D	24.	D
7.	A	16.	B	25.	D
8.	C	17.	E		
9.	B	18.	D		

Answers and Explanations

Section 1 Verbal

1. **D is correct.** A *novice* is a person new to a field or activity—a *beginner*.

2. **C is correct.** To *fabricate* is to concoct in order to deceive—in other words, to *falsify*.

3. **B is correct.** *Friendly* means agreeable in disposition, good-natured and likable, or *amiable*.

4. **B is correct.** A *genre* is a type or class. The choice that best fits this definition is *category*.

5. **A is correct.** A *summit* is a *conference* or meeting of high-level officials, typically called to shape a course of action.

6. **E is correct.** To do something *deftly* is to do it quickly and *skillfully*.

7. **E is correct.** To *prosper* is to be fortunate or successful, especially in terms of one's health or finances—in other words, to *thrive*.

8. **D is correct.** To *spurn* is to *reject* disdainfully or contemptuously; *scorn*.

9. **B is correct.** *Complimentary* means given *free* to repay a favor or as an act of courtesy.

10. **C is correct.** *Visage* is the *face* or facial expression of a person; *countenance*.

11. **A is correct.** A *respite* is a usually short interval of rest or relief—in other words, a *pause*.

12. **D is correct.** *Regretful* means feeling troubled, remorseful, or *contrite* for one's sins or offenses.

13. **C is correct.** *Frugal* means thrifty or *economical*.

14. **A is correct.** To *imply* is to *suggest*, express, or indicate indirectly.

15. **E is correct.** To *incite* is to *provoke* or urge on.

16. **A is correct.** *Meager* means deficient in quantity, fullness, or extent; scanty or *paltry*.

17. **B is correct.** A *prediction* is a foretelling or a *forecast*.

18. **D is correct.** A *facet* is one of numerous *aspects*, as of a subject.

19. **D is correct.** To *absolve* is to *clear* someone of guilt or blame.

20. **B is correct.** To *subvert* means to overthrow or *destroy* something.

21. **E is correct.** To *mourn* is to feel or express grief or sorrow—in other words, to *grieve*.

22. **C is correct.** *Poisonous* means capable of harming or killing by or as if by poison; venomous or *toxic*.

23. **D is correct.** *Aplomb* is self-assurance or *confidence*.

24. **A is correct.** *Corroboration* is ratification or *confirmation* that some statement or fact is true.

25. **C is correct.** Behavior that is *erratic* lacks consistency, regularity, or uniformity; in other words it is *unpredictable*.

26. **B is correct.** *Credible* means plausible or *believable*.

27. **C is correct.** To *abscond* is to *leave* quickly and secretly and hide oneself, often to avoid arrest or prosecution.

28. **D is correct.** To *calm* is to make or become calm or quiet—in other words, to *soothe*.

29. **E is correct.** *Irritable* means easily provoked, impatient, ill-tempered, or *petulant*.

30. **B is correct.** A *travesty* is a debased or grotesque likeness or a *mockery*.

31. **B is correct.** *Safe* is the opposite of *dangerous* just as *bland* is the opposite of *spicy*. Only choice B provides two adjectives that are opposite in meaning. Choices D and E cannot be correct because the words in each pair are not the same part of speech.

32. **C is correct.** A *star* is found in the *sky* in the same way that a *fish* is found in the *ocean*.

33. **E is correct.** This analogy pairs an activity with a result. Of the answer choices, only choice E has the same relationship as the original word pair: To *cut* produces a *wound* as to *cry* produces *tears*.

34. **D is correct.** This stem provides a usage sequence by pairing *camera* with *picture*. Choice A comes close to being right but reverses the order by placing *breeze* before *fan*. Only choice D follows the logic of the stem and places the words in the correct order: a *camera* is used to take a *picture* just as a *phone* is used to make a *call*.

35. **B is correct.** This sequence tests your knowledge of relationships between units of measurement. *Lumens* are a measure of *brightness* just as *decibels* are a measure of *volume*.

36. **D is correct.** *Books* are produced by *writers* much as *crops* are produced by *farmers*. No other choice offers a product made by a particular worker. *Doctors* do not make *needles* (choice A); *dentists* do not produce *cavities* (choice B); *drivers* do not build *trucks* (choice C); and *actors* do not write *scripts* (choice E).

37. **A is correct.** *Frigid* is the opposite of *tropical*, and *raw* is the opposite of *cooked*. No other answer choice offers the proper contrast.

38. **C is correct.** This analogy tests your knowledge of places and locations. Los Angeles is a city in California just as Houston is a city in Texas. Choice A is incorrect because Phoenix is in Arizona, not New Mexico. Philadelphia and Pittsburgh (choice B) are both cities in Pennsylvania. Choice E is incorrect because it pairs a city with a country, not a state.

39. **E is correct.** The relationship in this sequence is one of individual to object. A *diner* uses a *menu* in the way that a *shopper* would use a *catalog*. One provides a list of options for the other.

40. **A is correct.** This sequence offers a part-to-part relationship. A *cuff* is a part of a shirt in the same way that a *collar* is a part of a shirt. Similarly, a *mouse* is part of a computer in the same way that a *keyboard* is part of a computer.

41. **E is correct.** Initially, this relationship in this sequence may strike you as one of part to whole. However, you will need to take the analogy one step further in order to arrive at the correct answer. The *belly* is the part of the *snake* used for traveling just as *feet* are the part of a *person* used for traveling. Don't be fooled by choice C; a *horse* travels on its feet, just like a person.

42. **A is correct.** The relationship that this sequence is testing is one of measurement units. A *diamond* is measured in *carats* and *heat* is measured in *calories*. Choices C and D provide the right descriptions, however both answer choices invert the correct order.

43. **A is correct.** This is another example of an object-to-activity analogy. People *read books* in much the same way that they *analyze data*.

44. **E is correct.** This sequence provides another example of an activity-to-result analogy. When you *burnish* an object, you *polish* it. Similarly, when you *reinforce* an object, you *strengthen* it.

45. **B is correct.** The relationship in this question is one of contrasts. *Fresh* is the opposite of *rancid*, just as *ripe* is the opposite of *rotten*. No other answer choice offers a comparable contrast.

46. **B is correct.** A *fire* produces *heat* much the same way that a *lamp* gives off *light*. Choice B is the only option that presents a similar relationship.

47. **A is correct.** The relationship in this sequence is one of degrees of contrast. *Browsing* denotes inspecting something in a leisurely and casual manner in the same way that *skimming* a book does. Both *shopping* and *reading* require a greater degree of commitment.

48. **D is correct.** The relationship presented in this sequence is one of usage. As a showcase for talent, a *recital* is used by a *pianist* in much the same way that an *exhibit* is used by an *artist*.

49. **D is correct.** This is a part-to-whole analogy. A *song* is a part of a *medley* as a *picture* is part of a *collage*. Choice A may seem correct, but the terms are reversed. A *book* can be part of a *series*, but a *series* cannot be a part of a *book*.

50. **C is correct.** The relationship in this question is one of an activity (*exercise*) and a result (*sweat*). Only choice C provides a comparable relationship.

51. **B is correct.** This analogy is one of a part to a whole. The *stamen* is a part of the *flower* in much the same way the *lens* is a part of the *eye*. Choice A is almost correct, except that it offers the whole before the part. Choice B is the only answer choice that presents a logical sequence in the right order.

52. **E is correct.** Flip the words: a *cartographer* makes *maps*. Similarly, a *baker* makes *cakes*. No other option presents the same relationship.

53. **C is correct.** A *baby* travels by *crawling* much the same way a *frog* travels by *jumping*. A *rock* only travels across the water by *skipping* (choice A) when thrown by a person. The correct answer does not rely on an outside influence.

54. **A is correct.** This analogy is one of usage. An *eraser* is used to clean a *chalkboard*, and in a similar way, a *mop* is used to clean a *floor*.

55. **C is correct.** This is an analogy of degrees of similarity. Flip the words and you will see that *fervent* is a more intense feeling than *eager* just as *ecstatic* is a more intense feeling than *pleased*. Choice D may seem correct, but the words appear in reverse order, from more intense to less intense. To be correct, *mad* would need to come before *enraged*.

56. **D is correct.** When *bread* deteriorates or gets old, it becomes *moldy*. Similarly, when *steel* becomes old or is left to deteriorate in the elements it becomes *rusty*.

57. **B is correct.** Again, flip the words around and you will see that a *collie* is a particular type of *dog*, just as a *chameleon* is a particular type of *lizard*. Choice C is incorrect because *reptile* is too general.

58. **D is correct.** This sequence presents an object-to-activity analogy, also known as a tool-to-function analogy. A *chisel* is used for *carving* in the same way that a *blender* is used for *mixing*. No other option provides an appropriate comparison. Choices A and B are both incorrect for the same reason; they are used respectively in each activity, but are not the tool used to perform the activity. Choice C is incorrect because a car is used for driving, and choice E is incorrect because a stove or oven is used for cooking.

59. **B is correct.** This sequence is another example of an activity to a result analogy. When you *drop* something, it can *break*. Similarly, when you *stumble* you can *fall*. Choices A, C, and D are all synonyms, and choice E is too big a stretch.

60. **A is correct.** The relationship presented in this sequence is one of part to whole. *Ruby* is a shade of *red*, and *amber* is a shade of orange or *brown*. Since *orange* is not an option, choice A is the correct answer.

1. **C is correct.** $5 + 11 + 6 = 22$; $6 + 12 = 18$; and $22 - 18 = 4$.

2. **A is correct.** $4 \times 3 \times 6 \times 2 = 144$; $144 \div 24 = 6$.

3. **E is correct.**
$\frac{2}{3}x = 24$
$\frac{1}{3}x = 12$
$x = 36$
$\frac{1}{4}x = 9$

4. **D is correct.** This problem needs to be completed in two steps. First, you need to determine what percent of chocolates have nuts and then subtract that from 100% to determine what percent do not have nuts. Dividing 9 by 45 gives the percent that have nuts, which is 20%. Subtracting that number from 100% gives the correct answer: 80% of the chocolates do not have nuts.

5. **D is correct.** To find the ratio of one number to another, create a fraction to show the relationship. In this problem there are 6 female club members in a total of 48 club members. The fraction that shows the relationship is $\frac{6}{48}$. This fraction can be simplified to $\frac{1}{8}$, the correct answer.

6. **E is correct.** Set this up as an equation. A number plus 2 times that number is 300.
$x + 2x = 375$
Solve for x.
$3x = 375$
$x = 125$
So one number is 125 and the other is twice that or 250.

7. **D is correct.** $6\frac{3}{4}\% = 0.0675$.

8. **A is correct.** Multiply $1,085.00 by 0.25 to get $271.25.

9. **A is correct.** By definition, a right angle is one that measures 90°.

10. **A is correct.** In an equilateral triangle, all three angles are equal. Since the sum of the angles in a triangle is 180°, each angle must be $180 \div 3 = 60°$.

11. **C is correct.** Solve the equation.
$12a + 4a - 7a = 27$
$16a - 7a = 27$
$9a = 27$
$a = 3$

12. **A is correct.** It costs n dollars to buy 10 boxes. Since $25 = 2.5 \times 10$, it will cost $2.5n$ dollars to buy 25 boxes.

13. **D is correct.** A straight angle measures 180°. So if $\angle 1$ is 33°, the other angle must measure $180° - 33° = 147°$.

14. **E is correct.** Calculate the number of square meters in the garden and then determine how many ounces of fertilizer are needed. The area of a rectangle is calculated by multiplying the length × the width. So the area of the garden is $4 \times 7 = 28 \ m^2$. Paul needs 2 oz of fertilizer for every square meter, so $2 \times 28 = 56$ oz.

15. **B is correct.** According to the chart, the plant is growing 3 inches taller each week. So in week 6, it should be $14 + 3 = 17$ inches tall.

16. **C is correct.** $0.80 + $0.20 + $0.30 = $1.30

17. **A is correct.** To calculate the percent, divide the number of items answered correctly by the total number of items. $45 \div 75 = 0.60$. To change that to a percent, move the decimal point two places to the right and add the percent sign to get 60%.

18. **D is correct.** $^{16}/_4 = 4$; $6 \times ^2/_3 = ^{12}/_3 = 4$; $4 \div ^1/_4 = 4 \times ^4/_1 = 16$; $3 + 2 = 5$. However, $^1/_3 \times 4 = ^4/_3$, which is not a whole number.

19. **B is correct.** In this problem you need to find $^1/_5$ of 55. $55 \div 5 = 11$.

20. **D is correct.** To find the perimeter of a rectangle, add the lengths of the four sides. In this instance, 11 meters + 11 meters + 3 meters + 3 meters = 28 meters, the correct answer.

21. **A is correct.** To find the average, add the numbers and divide by the number of numbers. In this problem the numbers add to 415. Dividing that by 5 gives an average of 83.

22. **E is correct.** Create an equation:

    Riverside = 2 × Hillside −150
    $500 = 2x - 150$
    $750 = 2x$
    $325 = x$

23. **C is correct.** In this problem you know two of the three angles, one measuring 55° and the other measuring 90°, since the building forms a 90° angle with the ground. Together those two angles measure 145°. Since a triangle has a total of 180°, the third angle must measure $180° - 145° = 35°$.

24. **D is correct.** 12 Red Delicious apples + 16 Granny Smith apples = 28 apples. $48 - 28 = 20$ apples that are not Red Delicious or Granny Smith. $^{20}/_{48} = ^5/_{12}$.

25. **D is correct.** 8% of $750 = 0.08 \times 750 = \$60$. $\$750 + \$60 = \$810$.

Section 3 Reading Comprehension

1. **E is correct.** As stated in the first two sentences, "Volcanoes are mountains, but they are very different from other mountains; they are not formed by folding and crumpling or by uplift and erosion. Instead, volcanoes are built by the accumulation of their own eruptive products—lava, bombs (crusted over lava blobs), ashflows, and tephra (airborne ash and dust)."

2. **B is correct.** As stated in the third paragraph, "How explosive an eruption is depends on how runny or sticky the magma is. . . .If magma is thick and sticky, gases cannot escape easily. Pressure builds up until the gases escape violently and explode." Choice A is wrong because if magma is thin and runny, "gases can escape easily from it," and when this type of magma erupts, "it flows out of the volcano." Choices C and D are both true of magma, but neither indicates how explosive an eruption will be. Choice E is wrong because magma that has erupted is called lava, regardless of the explosiveness of the eruption.

3. **D is correct.** The words in italics are scientific terms for which the author provides definitions within the text. ("A *volcano* is most commonly a conical hill or mountain built around a vent that connects with reservoirs of molten rock below the surface of the Earth." "Magma that has erupted is called *lava*.")

4. **A is correct.** The passage states that "Deep within the Earth it is so hot that some rocks slowly melt and become a thick flowing substance called *magma*." However, the passage does not mention the factors that contribute to hot temperatures deep inside the Earth. Choice B is answered in lines 22–37. Choice C is answered in lines 26–27. Choice D is answered in lines 16–18. Choice E is answered in lines 31–33.

5. **B is correct.** This passage explains how volcanoes are formed and the nature of volcanic eruptions using the scientific terminology and strictly factual presentation typical of information presented in a science textbook.

There is nothing timely about the information, so it is not likely to be from a newspaper article as in choice A. There is no evidence of a plot or characters, so you can easily eliminate choice C. The passage does not describe a particular volcano or its surroundings, so it is unlikely to be from a travel brochure as in choice D, and there is no mention of safety, so choice E cannot be correct.

6. **C is correct.** During a volcanic eruption, magma blasts into the air and breaks apart into pieces called tephra; thus choice E is true. As explained in the last paragraph, tephra can vary greatly in size (choice A), it can travel hundreds to thousands of kilometers downwind from a volcano (choice B), and large tephra typically falls back to the ground on or close to the volcano (choice D). Gases, not tephra, may be trapped in magma; therefore choice C is the only choice that is NOT true of tephra.

7. **C is correct.** Douglass makes this point in the very first sentence when he says, "I am one of those who believe that it is the mission of this war to free every slave in the United States." Choices A, B, and D might all be consequences of the Civil War, but in this speech Douglass mentions only freeing every slave in the United States as the mission of the war.

8. **D is correct.** Douglass believed that "the work of the American Anti-Slavery Society will not have been completed until the black man of the South, and the black men of the North, shall have been admitted, fully and completely, into the body politic of America." He specifically mentions that voting rights should be extended equally to all black men. He does not advocate voting rights only for black men in the South (choice B) and he does not mention that voting rights should be extended to everyone (choice E). Douglass advocates the abolition of slavery as the "mission of the war," but he believes that the work of the Anti-Slavery Society should go beyond this goal to the greater goal of setting the same conditions for voting for black men and white men.

9. **A is correct.** The *body politic* means "the people of a politically organized nation or state." To be fully and completely admitted to the body politic means to have all the rights accorded to any other citizen of the nation or state. Choices B, C, and D are rights and duties that are included in choice A. If black men were considered as a separate class of citizens, they would not be "fully and completely" admitted to the body politic.

10. **B is correct.** The passage is written in the first person and offers the views of the author on the subject of slavery and voting rights. The last paragraph makes it clear that the author is trying to convince members of the society that "whatever rule you adopt, whether of intelligence or wealth, as the condition of voting for whites, you shall apply it equally to the black man." He goes on to say that if they say that "I am satisfied, and eternal justice is satisfied; liberty, fraternity, equality, are satisfied, and the country will move on harmoniously." As stated in the italic text at the start of the article, this speech was given at a meeting of the Anti-Slavery Society. It is unlikely that members of an Anti-Slavery Society would need to be convinced that slavery should be ended so choice D can be eliminated. Choices A and C can also be eliminated because the passage is a statement of the author's opinions on the subject, not just an objective presentation of information about the horrors of slavery (choice A) or the progress of the war (choice C). Choice E is not correct because, while the passage mentions that granting voting rights to blacks will help the country "move on harmoniously," it does not explain how this will happen.

11. **C is correct.** The author describes the newly married pair as uncomfortable in their new clothes, unused to taking trips in a "fine" parlor-car, and embarrassed by the scrutiny of other passengers. He seems to like the unsophisticated couple and to be sympathetic toward their situation. The bride and groom may be embarrassed, but the author is not, so choice A is incorrect. Choices B, D, and E are all incorrect because nothing in the passage supports the idea that the author regards the couple with *disrespect* (meaning "discourtesy" or "rudeness"), *sorrow* (meaning "sadness"), or *scorn* (meaning "contempt" or "disdain").

12. **D is correct.** Both the bride and the groom were unaccustomed to wearing new clothes. The groom's face was "reddened from many days in the wind and sun." The bride had never traveled in a parlor car and she was clearly more used to cooking than to eating in a dining car. All of these clues point to the fact that the newlyweds were *unsophisticated* (meaning "innocent") country people. The fact that the bride thinks that a dollar is too much for them to spend on a meal indicates that the couple are not wealthy or well-to-do, so choice A is wrong. The passage mentions that the couple "were evidently very happy." so choice B is wrong. Although the couple are described as being shy and embarrassed by the attention of other passengers, there is nothing to support the idea that they were either frightened (choice C) or unpleasant (choice E).

13. **E is correct.** The story takes place on a train crossing the plains of Texas. You can tell this from the fact that the groom asks his bride, "Have you ever been in a parlor-car before?" and then mentions that they will "go forward to the diner and get a big layout." Parlor-cars and dining cars are found on trains. Although the passage states that the newly married pair "had boarded this coach at San Antonio," the coach that is referred to is a car on a train, not a stage coach, so choice C is wrong. The groom mentions that "after a while we'll go forward to the diner," but, at the time this passage takes place, they have not yet gone to the diner to eat, so choice D is wrong. The couple have already boarded the train, so they cannot be in a hotel (choice A) or at a train station (choice B).

14. **A is correct.** Lines 17–18 states that "The glances he devoted to other passengers were furtive and shy." From this sentence you can tell that *furtive* must be something that goes with *shy*. Neither *friendly* nor *unabashed* (meaning "unembarrassed" or "not shy") works well with shy, so you can eliminate choices D and E. Similarly, you can eliminate choice C because *focused* means "clear and sharp," which is not commonly associated with *shy*. That leaves choice A, which is correct. A *furtive* glance is a secret or stealthy glance.

15. **D is correct.** The story is told in the third person by someone who is not a participant in the story. Therefore you can eliminate choices A, B, and C. In a story told by someone looking back on his life, the story would most likely be told in the first person (using "I" and "me" throughout). Because this story is told by someone who can see everything that is happening in the tale, but is not himself participating in the tale, it is most likely the work of an outside observer

16. **C is correct.** This passage is actually the beginning of a short story. Its purpose is to introduce the characters and setting of the story to come. The passage is purely descriptive. There is no attempt to express an opinion (choice A), analyze information (choice B), or resolve a crisis (choice D). At this point in the story there is no conflict between the major characters. In fact, the bride and groom are described as "evidently very happy."

17. **B is correct.** If you can tell by simply looking at the bride that "she had cooked, and that she expected to cook, dutifully," then the bride most probably has the red, rough hands indicative of a life of hard work. Just looking at a person is unlikely to reveal whether that person expects to eat out regularly or has ever eaten in a restaurant before, so choices A and C are incorrect. Similarly, it is impossible to tell what a person wants to or might expect to learn about cooking by observation alone, so choices D and E are also incorrect.

18. **C is correct.** The purpose of this passage is to report on the work done by scientists to breed carrots with enhanced nutritional value. The researchers have selectively bred carrots in a rainbow of colors and studied the effects of the various plant pigments on the human body.

19. **D is correct.** The passage is intended to inform readers of developments in carrot breeding. The passage does not argue a point, nor does it contain any emotionally charged language; thus choices A and B can be eliminated. Nothing about the passage could be termed sentimental and although the last sentence offers the opinion that colorful carrots will be a good addition to supermarket produce aisles, this is not enough to describe the entire passage as optimistic.

20. **B is correct.** As stated in lines 11–12, researchers have "selectively bred a rainbow of carrots—purple, red, yellow, even white." The only choice not mentioned is green.

21. **A is correct.** As stated in lines 16–17, "Red carrots derive their color mainly from lycopene, a type of carotene believed to guard against heart disease and some cancers." Xanthophyll (choice B) is found in yellow carrots. Anthocyanin (choice C) is the pigment found in purple carrots. Beta-carotene (choice D) is the pigment found in orange carrots. An antioxidant (choice E) is a substance that slows down oxidation and helps check deterioration.

22. **E is correct.** As stated in the passage, "In nature, different strains of carrots contain varying types and amounts of carotenoids—the pigments responsible for orange, yellow, and red colors." Choices A and D are incorrect because the passage states that colored carrots were eaten "more than 1,000 years ago in Afghanistan and 700 years ago in western Europe." Choice B is wrong because it is contradicted by the statement that "today's carrots provide consumers with 75 percent more beta-carotene than those available 25 years ago." Choice C is wrong because the last sentence says the colorful carrots get "a thumbs-up from taste testers."

23. **C is correct.** The passage reports on the work of agricultural research scientists as they attempt to breed nutrient-rich carrots. It has no characters or plot so it cannot be a short story. It is not the story of someone's life, so it cannot be a biography. It is not written for the purpose of promoting some doctrine or cause, so it does not fall into the category of propaganda. It is not primarily an expression of the opinion of the author, so it is not an editorial.

24. **C is correct.** Tone is the author's attitude toward a topic. It is created through details and language. The sense of this poem is that the narrator has returned to a place he once knew and finds himself "now a stranger" and laments the fact that nothing is as it used to be: "Not the sun that used to be, Not the tides that used to run." The best description of this tone is nostalgic, meaning "sentimental" or "evidencing bittersweet longing for things of the past." Words such as "shadowy crown," "dark and haunted wood," and "alas" are not consistent with a lighthearted, optimistic, or humorous tone so you can rule out choices A, B, and E. The author's tone may be sad, but it is not hostile or angry as in choice D.

25. **D is correct.** The narrator of this poem is clearly an adult returning to a scene of his youth and feeling a sense of sadness at the transformation he observes. Old friends are "estranged," the sun is "not the sun that used to be," and the tides are "not the tides that used to run." Choice A is incorrect because the narrator is an adult, not a child. Choice B is incorrect because the narrator is not indifferent to what he sees. Choice C is incorrect because the narrator is not an outside observer as evidenced by the use of the pronoun "I" throughout. Choice E is incorrect because the narrator is recalling actual sights from his childhood, not dreams.

26. **E is correct.** The author's choice of the word *haunted*, which means "inhabited by the spirit of people and times gone by," serves to underscore the idea of memories of friendships past. Choices A and B do not fit the poem at all. Choice C reflects one meaning of the word *haunted*, but misses the point that the poem is about memories, not spirits. Choice D is incorrect because the poem is sad and nostalgic, not dark and gloomy.

27. **B is correct.** The theme of the poem is the main idea the poem conveys. In this case, the theme is the passage of time. The poem mentions both the sun (choice A) and the tide (choice C), but each shows only that time has passed. There is no mention of autumn (choice D) in this poem. In fact, the only reference to the season is the description of the oaks as "fresh and green," an indication of spring rather than fall. The poem is not about renewal (choice E), but rather about the changes brought about by the passage of time.

28. **A is correct.** As stated in the second paragraph, the sculpture was commissioned to be completed in 1876, "to commemorate the centennial of the American Declaration of Independence." Choice B is incorrect because the Statue commemorated the friendship between the United States and France during the Revolutionary War, not the Civil War. Choice C is incorrect because the passage mentions only friendship between France and the United States; there is no mention of hostility between the two nations. Choice D is incorrect because the Statue was supposed to have been completed in 1876, which is 24 years before the start of the twentieth century. Choice E is wrong because there is no mention of a new era of international cooperation.

29. **B is correct.** Eiffel was called in to *attend to* or *focus on* the structural issues of the sculpture. All of the choices are synonyms for the word *address*, but only choice B fits the context of this sentence.

30. **C is correct.** When Pulitzer saw that fundraising for the pedestal was lagging, he "used the editorial pages of his newspaper *The World* to aid in the fundraising effort." He criticized the rich for failing to give enough to finance the pedestal, and he criticized the middle class for relying on the rich to provide all the funds needed for the pedestal. These actions imply that Pulitzer was enthusiastic in his support of the Statue and did his best to convince others to support it as well.

31. **D is correct.** As stated in the first paragraph, the Statue was a gift to the people of the United States "in recognition of the friendship established between the two nations during the American Revolution." Over the years, however, "the Statue of Liberty has come to symbolize freedom and democracy as well as this international friendship." There is no mention in the passage of a treaty between the United States and France.

32. **D is correct.** Alexandre Gustave Eiffel, who designed the Eiffel Tower, was called in "to address the structural issues of Bartholdi's colossal sculpture," not to help raise money for the project. Choice A is mentioned in line 17. Choice B is mentioned in lines 12–14. Choice C is mentioned in lines 27–35. Choice E can be ascertained by noting that the statue was completed in France in July 1884 and financing for the pedestal was completed in August 1885, more than a year later.

33. **A is correct.** This passage is entirely devoted to telling the history of the Statue of Liberty from design to financing to completion. It does not describe how Bartholdi designed the statue (choice B), but only tells that he did so with the help of Eiffel. It mentions fundraising in the United States and France (choice C), but is not devoted to comparing them. Likewise, it mentions how Pulitzer used newspaper editorials to increase donations (choice D), but makes no attempt to defend this practice. Only one sentence in the entire passage is devoted to assembling the statue on her pedestal (choice E).

34. **E is correct.** This informational article is most likely to be found in a textbook. Choices A and B are easily eliminated because the passage is fact, not fiction. Choice C is incorrect because the passage tells of events that happened long ago, not timely current events as would be reported in a newspaper article. The passage does not describe the engineering aspects of the Statue, so choice D is not a likely choice.

35. **B is correct.** Bixby never gave the narrator a chance to become complacent about what he had learned. There were always more twists and turns to be studied and more shapes to be learned. The narrator may have thought that Bixby knew the river better than any other pilot, but that is not the meaning of this particular quote.

36. **C is correct.** The narrator is comparing his knowledge of the shape of Walnut Bend to his knowledge of his grandmother's opinion of protoplasm. Since it is highly unlikely that the narrator knows anything about his grandmother's opinion of protoplasm (or even whether she has any such opinion), you can infer that he also knows nothing about the shape of Walnut Bend.

37. **D is correct.** In describing Bixby's response to the narrator's not knowing the shape of Walnut Bend, the author says, "My gunpowdery chief went off with a bang, of course, and then went on loading and firing until he was out of adjectives." The word that best describes something that goes off with a bang and keeps on firing until the ammunition runs out is *explosive*.

38. **E is correct.** Upon learning that he must know all the variations of shape in the banks of the river as well as he knows "the shape of the front hall at home," the narrator replies, "I wish I was dead!" This reaction can best be described as "hopelessness" or "despair."

39. **A is correct.** Tone is the writer's attitude toward a topic. It is revealed through the writer's word choice. Statements such as "a curiously inanimate mass of lumber it was" and "He might as well have asked me my grandmother's opinion of protoplasm" help to reveal the humor with which the author regards the situation.

40. **C is correct.** The passage is written in the first person and appears to describe events that occurred in the life of the author. These are characteristic of autobiographical writing.

Section 4 Quantitative II

1. **C is correct.** 2% is the equivalent of 0.02; $0.02 \times 5,000 = 100$.

2. **C is correct.**
$$\begin{array}{r} 3.5 \\ \times\, 0.93 \\ \hline 1\,05 \\ 31\,5 \\ \hline 3.255 \end{array}$$

3. **D is correct.** $^{32}/_4 = 8$; $4 \times {}^8/_{16} = {}^{32}/_{16} = 2$; $8 \div {}^1/_8 = 8 \times {}^8/_1 = 64$; $6.4 + 11.6 = 18$. However, ${}^5/_{12} \times 8 = {}^{40}/_{12} = 3{}^1/_3$, which is not a whole number.

4. **D is correct.** $62{}^1/_2\% = 0.625$.

5. **B is correct.** It costs m dollars to buy 60 nails. 24 nails are ${}^2/_5$ of 60, so the cost of 24 nails will be ${}^2/_5 \times m = {}^{2m}/_5$ dollars.

6. **D is correct.**
$5/_{12}x = 50$
$1/_{12}x = 10$
$x = 120$
$1/_2 x = 60$

7. **A is correct.** Perform operations in the parentheses first, then the exponents, and then the remaining operations.
$16 + 3(-4)$
$16 + (-12) = 4$

8. **C is correct.** When calculating the average or mean, add the numbers and then divide by the number of numbers. The sum of 24, 36, 18, 30, 90, and 690 is 888, divided by 6 is 148.

9. **B is correct.** This item is set up as a proportion. To solve for n, cross-multiply so that the problem becomes $25n = 1,000$. $n = 1,000 \div 25 = 40$.

10. **A is correct.** $5 \times 4 + 4 = 24$. $6 \times 8 = 48$, and $48 \div 24 = 2$.

11. **E is correct.** $48 \div 6 \times 8 \times 8 = 512$. $512 \div 16 = 32$.

12. **B is correct.** $2 + 4/_{25} = 2.16$
The fraction $4/_{25} = 16/_{100} = 0.16$, so $2 + 4/_{25} = 2.16$.

13. **C is correct.** $1/_3 + 1/_6 = 2/_6 + 1/_6 = 3/_6$.
$3/_6 = 1/_2$, so if Karen has used $1/_2$ of her tickets, $1/_2$ are left.

14. **E is correct.**
$12 \div 3^3/_4 = 12/_1 \div 13/_4$
$= 12/_1 \times 4/_{13}$
$= 48/_{13} = 3^9/_{13}$

15. **D is correct.** $\$23.95 \times 0.065 = \$1.56$. $\$23.95 + \$1.56 = \$25.51$.

16. **B is correct.** Set up a proportion:
$30/_2 = n/_7$
$n = 105$

17. **E is correct.** 1 mile = 5,280 ft. If the width of the park is 880 feet, then two sides of the park measure $880 + 880 = 1,760$ ft. $5,280 - 1,760 = 3,520$. The other two sides of the park must each measure one-half of 3,520 ft. $3,520 \div 2 = 1,760$ ft.

18. **D is correct.**
$10 \times (0.38 + 3.5) + 5.2$
$= (10 \times 0.38) + (10 \times 3.5) + 5.2$
$= 3.8 + 35 + 5.2$
$= 44$

19. **A is correct.** The rental company charges $\$25 + \$6$ per hour. The equation that represents this situation is $25 + 6h$ where h = number of hours.

20. **D is correct.** From midnight to 11:00 A.M. there are 11 hours. If the temperature rose 2°C each hour, then it rose 22°C.
$(-12) + 22 = 10°C$

21. **D is correct.** 1 mile = 5,280 ft., so 4 miles = 21,120 ft. 1 yd = 3 ft, so $21,120 \div 3 = 7,040$ yd.

22. **E is correct.**

$$25\tfrac{3}{5} \times 1\tfrac{1}{2}$$
$$= \tfrac{128}{5} \times \tfrac{3}{2}$$
$$= \tfrac{384}{10} = 38\tfrac{4}{10} = 38\tfrac{2}{5}$$

23. **B is correct.**

$$23.4 \div 6 = 3.9$$

24. **D is correct.**

$$11\tfrac{1}{2} - 9\tfrac{3}{4} = 11\tfrac{2}{4} - 9\tfrac{3}{4}$$
$$= 10\tfrac{6}{4} - 9\tfrac{3}{4}$$
$$= 1\tfrac{3}{4}$$

25. **D is correct.** Find the volume by multiplying length $\times$ width $\times$ height. Since all of these dimensions on a cube are the same, multiply:

$$5 \times 5 \times 5 = 125 \text{ in}^3$$

SSAT Practice Test II

The following practice test is designed to be just like the real SSAT. It matches the actual test in content coverage and level of difficulty. The test is in five sections: Verbal, Quantitative I, Reading Comprehension, Quantitative II, and the Essay.

This practice test will be an accurate reflection of how you'll do on test day if you treat it as the real examination. Here are some hints on how to take the test under conditions similar to those of the actual exam:

- Find a quiet place to work and set aside a period of approximately 3 hours when you will not be disturbed.
- Work on only one section at a time, and use your watch or a timer to keep track of the time limits for each test part.

- Tear out your answer sheet and mark your answers by filling in the ovals for each question.
- Write your essay on the pages provided.
- Become familiar with the directions for each part of the test. You'll save time on the actual test day by already being familiar with this information.

At the end of the test you'll find Answer Keys for each section and explanations for every question. Check your answers against the keys to find out how you did on each section of the test and what test topics you might need to study more. Then review the explanations, paying particular attention to the ones for the questions you answered incorrectly.

SSAT Practice Test II

ANSWER SHEET

Section 1: Verbal

1. (A) (B) (C) (D) (E)	21. (A) (B) (C) (D) (E)	41. (A) (B) (C) (D) (E)
2. (A) (B) (C) (D) (E)	22. (A) (B) (C) (D) (E)	42. (A) (B) (C) (D) (E)
3. (A) (B) (C) (D) (E)	23. (A) (B) (C) (D) (E)	43. (A) (B) (C) (D) (E)
4. (A) (B) (C) (D) (E)	24. (A) (B) (C) (D) (E)	44. (A) (B) (C) (D) (E)
5. (A) (B) (C) (D) (E)	25. (A) (B) (C) (D) (E)	45. (A) (B) (C) (D) (E)
6. (A) (B) (C) (D) (E)	26. (A) (B) (C) (D) (E)	46. (A) (B) (C) (D) (E)
7. (A) (B) (C) (D) (E)	27. (A) (B) (C) (D) (E)	47. (A) (B) (C) (D) (E)
8. (A) (B) (C) (D) (E)	28. (A) (B) (C) (D) (E)	48. (A) (B) (C) (D) (E)
9. (A) (B) (C) (D) (E)	29. (A) (B) (C) (D) (E)	49. (A) (B) (C) (D) (E)
10. (A) (B) (C) (D) (E)	30. (A) (B) (C) (D) (E)	50. (A) (B) (C) (D) (E)
11. (A) (B) (C) (D) (E)	31. (A) (B) (C) (D) (E)	51. (A) (B) (C) (D) (E)
12. (A) (B) (C) (D) (E)	32. (A) (B) (C) (D) (E)	52. (A) (B) (C) (D) (E)
13. (A) (B) (C) (D) (E)	33. (A) (B) (C) (D) (E)	53. (A) (B) (C) (D) (E)
14. (A) (B) (C) (D) (E)	34. (A) (B) (C) (D) (E)	54. (A) (B) (C) (D) (E)
15. (A) (B) (C) (D) (E)	35. (A) (B) (C) (D) (E)	55. (A) (B) (C) (D) (E)
16. (A) (B) (C) (D) (E)	36. (A) (B) (C) (D) (E)	56. (A) (B) (C) (D) (E)
17. (A) (B) (C) (D) (E)	37. (A) (B) (C) (D) (E)	57. (A) (B) (C) (D) (E)
18. (A) (B) (C) (D) (E)	38. (A) (B) (C) (D) (E)	58. (A) (B) (C) (D) (E)
19. (A) (B) (C) (D) (E)	39. (A) (B) (C) (D) (E)	59. (A) (B) (C) (D) (E)
20. (A) (B) (C) (D) (E)	40. (A) (B) (C) (D) (E)	60. (A) (B) (C) (D) (E)

Section 2: Quantitative I

1. (A) (B) (C) (D) (E)	11. (A) (B) (C) (D) (E)	21. (A) (B) (C) (D) (E)
2. (A) (B) (C) (D) (E)	12. (A) (B) (C) (D) (E)	22. (A) (B) (C) (D) (E)
3. (A) (B) (C) (D) (E)	13. (A) (B) (C) (D) (E)	23. (A) (B) (C) (D) (E)
4. (A) (B) (C) (D) (E)	14. (A) (B) (C) (D) (E)	24. (A) (B) (C) (D) (E)
5. (A) (B) (C) (D) (E)	15. (A) (B) (C) (D) (E)	25. (A) (B) (C) (D) (E)
6. (A) (B) (C) (D) (E)	16. (A) (B) (C) (D) (E)	
7. (A) (B) (C) (D) (E)	17. (A) (B) (C) (D) (E)	
8. (A) (B) (C) (D) (E)	18. (A) (B) (C) (D) (E)	
9. (A) (B) (C) (D) (E)	19. (A) (B) (C) (D) (E)	
10. (A) (B) (C) (D) (E)	20. (A) (B) (C) (D) (E)	

Section 3: Reading Comprehension

1. Ⓐ Ⓑ Ⓒ Ⓓ Ⓔ   17. Ⓐ Ⓑ Ⓒ Ⓓ Ⓔ   33. Ⓐ Ⓑ Ⓒ Ⓓ Ⓔ
2. Ⓐ Ⓑ Ⓒ Ⓓ Ⓔ   18. Ⓐ Ⓑ Ⓒ Ⓓ Ⓔ   34. Ⓐ Ⓑ Ⓒ Ⓓ Ⓔ
3. Ⓐ Ⓑ Ⓒ Ⓓ Ⓔ   19. Ⓐ Ⓑ Ⓒ Ⓓ Ⓔ   35. Ⓐ Ⓑ Ⓒ Ⓓ Ⓔ
4. Ⓐ Ⓑ Ⓒ Ⓓ Ⓔ   20. Ⓐ Ⓑ Ⓒ Ⓓ Ⓔ   36. Ⓐ Ⓑ Ⓒ Ⓓ Ⓔ
5. Ⓐ Ⓑ Ⓒ Ⓓ Ⓔ   21. Ⓐ Ⓑ Ⓒ Ⓓ Ⓔ   37. Ⓐ Ⓑ Ⓒ Ⓓ Ⓔ
6. Ⓐ Ⓑ Ⓒ Ⓓ Ⓔ   22. Ⓐ Ⓑ Ⓒ Ⓓ Ⓔ   38. Ⓐ Ⓑ Ⓒ Ⓓ Ⓔ
7. Ⓐ Ⓑ Ⓒ Ⓓ Ⓔ   23. Ⓐ Ⓑ Ⓒ Ⓓ Ⓔ   39. Ⓐ Ⓑ Ⓒ Ⓓ Ⓔ
8. Ⓐ Ⓑ Ⓒ Ⓓ Ⓔ   24. Ⓐ Ⓑ Ⓒ Ⓓ Ⓔ   40. Ⓐ Ⓑ Ⓒ Ⓓ Ⓔ
9. Ⓐ Ⓑ Ⓒ Ⓓ Ⓔ   25. Ⓐ Ⓑ Ⓒ Ⓓ Ⓔ
10. Ⓐ Ⓑ Ⓒ Ⓓ Ⓔ   26. Ⓐ Ⓑ Ⓒ Ⓓ Ⓔ
11. Ⓐ Ⓑ Ⓒ Ⓓ Ⓔ   27. Ⓐ Ⓑ Ⓒ Ⓓ Ⓔ
12. Ⓐ Ⓑ Ⓒ Ⓓ Ⓔ   28. Ⓐ Ⓑ Ⓒ Ⓓ Ⓔ
13. Ⓐ Ⓑ Ⓒ Ⓓ Ⓔ   29. Ⓐ Ⓑ Ⓒ Ⓓ Ⓔ
14. Ⓐ Ⓑ Ⓒ Ⓓ Ⓔ   30. Ⓐ Ⓑ Ⓒ Ⓓ Ⓔ
15. Ⓐ Ⓑ Ⓒ Ⓓ Ⓔ   31. Ⓐ Ⓑ Ⓒ Ⓓ Ⓔ
16. Ⓐ Ⓑ Ⓒ Ⓓ Ⓔ   32. Ⓐ Ⓑ Ⓒ Ⓓ Ⓔ

Section 4: Quantitative II

1. Ⓐ Ⓑ Ⓒ Ⓓ Ⓔ   11. Ⓐ Ⓑ Ⓒ Ⓓ Ⓔ   21. Ⓐ Ⓑ Ⓒ Ⓓ Ⓔ
2. Ⓐ Ⓑ Ⓒ Ⓓ Ⓔ   12. Ⓐ Ⓑ Ⓒ Ⓓ Ⓔ   22. Ⓐ Ⓑ Ⓒ Ⓓ Ⓔ
3. Ⓐ Ⓑ Ⓒ Ⓓ Ⓔ   13. Ⓐ Ⓑ Ⓒ Ⓓ Ⓔ   23. Ⓐ Ⓑ Ⓒ Ⓓ Ⓔ
4. Ⓐ Ⓑ Ⓒ Ⓓ Ⓔ   14. Ⓐ Ⓑ Ⓒ Ⓓ Ⓔ   24. Ⓐ Ⓑ Ⓒ Ⓓ Ⓔ
5. Ⓐ Ⓑ Ⓒ Ⓓ Ⓔ   15. Ⓐ Ⓑ Ⓒ Ⓓ Ⓔ   25. Ⓐ Ⓑ Ⓒ Ⓓ Ⓔ
6. Ⓐ Ⓑ Ⓒ Ⓓ Ⓔ   16. Ⓐ Ⓑ Ⓒ Ⓓ Ⓔ
7. Ⓐ Ⓑ Ⓒ Ⓓ Ⓔ   17. Ⓐ Ⓑ Ⓒ Ⓓ Ⓔ
8. Ⓐ Ⓑ Ⓒ Ⓓ Ⓔ   18. Ⓐ Ⓑ Ⓒ Ⓓ Ⓔ
9. Ⓐ Ⓑ Ⓒ Ⓓ Ⓔ   19. Ⓐ Ⓑ Ⓒ Ⓓ Ⓔ
10. Ⓐ Ⓑ Ⓒ Ⓓ Ⓔ   20. Ⓐ Ⓑ Ⓒ Ⓓ Ⓔ

Time: 30 Minutes
60 Questions

This section includes two different types of questions: synonyms and analogies. There are directions and a sample question for each question type.

Directions: Each of the following questions consists of a word in capital letters followed by five words or phrases. Select the one word or phrase that means most nearly the same as the word in capital letters.

Sample Question:

ESSENTIAL:
(A) dire
(B) confusing
(C) vital
(D) expert
(E) honest

Correct Answer: C

---

1. SHAME:
   (A) grief
   (B) anguish
   (C) suffering
   (D) remorse
   (E) humiliation

2. TELL:
   (A) censure
   (B) preclude
   (C) dissuade
   (D) divulge
   (E) contrive

3. CONCISE:
   (A) clever
   (B) brief
   (C) small
   (D) exclusive
   (E) subdued

4. INQUIRY:
   (A) testimony
   (B) subpoena
   (C) investigation
   (D) verification
   (E) statement

5. ATTITUDE:
   (A) disposition
   (B) dissension
   (C) charisma
   (D) exemption
   (E) dispensation

6. TEDIOUSLY:
   (A) tremendously
   (B) delicately
   (C) relentlessly
   (D) fearlessly
   (E) tiresomely

GO ON TO THE NEXT PAGE.

7. DEPLETE:
   (A) deride
   (B) reduce
   (C) deprecate
   (D) discredit
   (E) elicit

8. CAUTIOUS:
   (A) discreet
   (B) anxious
   (C) startled
   (D) scared
   (E) stricken

9. SPARSE:
   (A) spatial
   (B) thin
   (C) spastic
   (D) vivid
   (E) lifeless

10. AVERSION:
    (A) model
    (B) portrayal
    (C) dislike
    (D) history
    (E) arrangement

11. BENEFACTOR:
    (A) composer
    (B) contributor
    (C) agent
    (D) connoisseur
    (E) demagogue

12. DORMANT:
    (A) inactive
    (B) restful
    (C) covert
    (D) durable
    (E) arbitrary

13. MALCONTENT:
    (A) sickly
    (B) troublesome
    (C) dissatisfied
    (D) malicious
    (E) foolhardy

14. SATISFY:
    (A) please
    (B) appease
    (C) consume
    (D) imbibe
    (E) dissipate

15. MERIT:
    (A) deserve
    (B) require
    (C) necessitate
    (D) pardon
    (E) base

16. PROMINENT:
    (A) excellent
    (B) accomplished
    (C) admirable
    (D) extensive
    (E) conspicuous

17. OBJECTIVE:
    (A) interest
    (B) forbearance
    (C) observation
    (D) concern
    (E) intention

18. BREACH:
    (A) admission
    (B) representation
    (C) felony
    (D) violation
    (E) security

19. LAMENT:
    (A) remark
    (B) acknowledge
    (C) regret
    (D) explain
    (E) declare

20. RECTIFY:
    (A) start
    (B) give
    (C) examine
    (D) fix
    (E) advance

GO ON TO THE NEXT PAGE.

21. SUBMERGE:
   (A) submit
   (B) subscribe
   (C) immerse
   (D) subsist
   (E) clarify

22. PERMANENT:
   (A) historical
   (B) indelible
   (C) delectable
   (D) permissive
   (E) conspicuous

23. ABYSS:
   (A) island
   (B) chamber
   (C) niche
   (D) hole
   (E) division

24. ORDER:
   (A) imbroglio
   (B) judgment
   (C) decree
   (D) appraisal
   (E) verdict

25. SHREWD:
   (A) poignant
   (B) astute
   (C) copious
   (D) specious
   (E) tactile

26. CLANDESTINE:
   (A) secret
   (B) criminal
   (C) familiar
   (D) apprehensive
   (E) disgraceful

27. COERCE:
   (A) twist
   (B) mislead
   (C) perceive
   (D) chastise
   (E) compel

28. DILATE:
   (A) embellish
   (B) impede
   (C) deflate
   (D) enlarge
   (E) prevent

29. INANE:
   (A) ridiculous
   (B) deficient
   (C) practical
   (D) cumbersome
   (E) indulgent

30. PLETHORA:
   (A) quandary
   (B) resonance
   (C) excess
   (D) separation
   (E) veneer

GO ON TO THE NEXT PAGE.

Directions: The questions that follow ask you to find relationships between words. For each question select the answer choice that best completes the meaning of the sentence.

Sample Question:

> Swim is to pool as
> (A) fork is to plate
> (B) sweep is to broom
> (C) clean is to kitchen
> (D) sleep is to bed
> (E) trot is to horse
>
> Correct Answer: D
> Choice D is correct because a pool is a place to swim just as a bed is a place to sleep.

---

31. Insult is to compliment as
    (A) puzzle is to vex
    (B) difficulty is to enjoy
    (C) brood is to worry
    (D) assure is to console
    (E) please is to annoy

32. Wolf is to pack as
    (A) lamb is to sheep
    (B) kitten is to mother
    (C) goose is to gaggle
    (D) school is to fish
    (E) cattle is to herd

33. Announce is to inform as
    (A) dig is to hole
    (B) fold is to box
    (C) finger is to point
    (D) wrap is to conceal
    (E) water is to extinguish

34. Shovel is to dig as
    (A) launch is to rocket
    (B) blade is to cut
    (C) sneeze is to cold
    (D) eye is to blink
    (E) bowling is to ball

35. Liter is to volume as
    (A) gram is to mass
    (B) ounce is to pound
    (C) centimeter is to kilometer
    (D) inches is to ruler
    (E) radius is to diameter

36. Tourist is to sightseeing as analyst is to
    (A) traveling
    (B) curing
    (C) ruins
    (D) science
    (E) examining

37. Whisper is to scream as
    (A) holler is to yell
    (B) calm is to water
    (C) pester is to bother
    (D) glance is to stare
    (E) carry is to gather

38. Rock is to quarry as
    (A) rust is to iron
    (B) coal is to mine
    (C) pan is to gold
    (D) metal is to alloy
    (E) water is to ice

39. Spider is to web as
    (A) teller is to bank
    (B) bird is to nest
    (C) horse is to track
    (D) pasture is to cow
    (E) school is to student

40. Seat is to steering wheel as handle bar is to
    (A) hand
    (B) steer
    (C) rider
    (D) bike
    (E) brake

GO ON TO THE NEXT PAGE.

41. Drive is to street as
    (A) walk is to path
    (B) run is to school
    (C) eat is to snack
    (D) fly is to bird
    (E) study is to book

42. Mile is to distance as minute is to
    (A) rate
    (B) quickness
    (C) time
    (D) hour
    (E) speed

43. Kick is to foot as
    (A) back is to float
    (B) swim is to arms
    (C) chew is to mouth
    (D) grind is to mill
    (E) content is to book

44. Feed is to nourish as
    (A) trap is to bury
    (B) giggle is to laugh
    (C) travel is to skate
    (D) water is to hydrate
    (E) throw is to fetch

45. Plum is to prune as
    (A) pear is to pineapple
    (B) hen is to rooster
    (C) cream is to milk
    (D) corn is to pop
    (E) grape is to raisin

46. Maple tree is to syrup as
    (A) coffee is to bean
    (B) orange is to juice
    (C) seed is to grass
    (D) chip is to chocolate
    (E) wheat is to bread

47. Envious is to jealous as
    (A) melancholic is to mournful
    (B) distressed is to dismayed
    (C) entertained is to amused
    (D) happy is to joyful
    (E) sorry is to regretful

48. Knitter is to needles as
    (A) teacher is to test
    (B) diver is to ocean
    (C) chef is to apron
    (D) singer is to recording
    (E) boxer is to gloves

49. Claw is to cat as
    (A) tail is to donkey
    (B) shell is to turtle
    (C) fang is to snake
    (D) talon is to eagle
    (E) hand is to clock

50. Surprise is to startle
    (A) choose is to grab
    (B) inflate is to breathe
    (C) destroy is to ruin
    (D) need is to want
    (E) mix is to bake

51. Scene is to play as
    (A) stage is to screen
    (B) projector is to movie
    (C) car is to engine
    (D) chapter is to book
    (E) award is to actor

52. Aquatic is to water as terrestrial is to
    (A) outer space
    (B) island
    (C) rocket
    (D) land
    (E) planet

53. Passenger is to bus as
    (A) cargo is to ship
    (B) pilot is to plane
    (C) bicycle is to motorist
    (D) motor is to boat
    (E) freight is to rail

54. Seed is to rind as
    (A) socket is to plug
    (B) bark is to branch
    (C) spark is to light
    (D) knob is to door
    (E) propeller is to plane

GO ON TO THE NEXT PAGE.

55. Malign is to disparage as
    (A) elate is to enjoy
    (B) irritate is to bother
    (C) emulate is to deprecate
    (D) ask is to say
    (E) ponder is to worry

56. Shoreline is to ocean as
    (A) horizon is to sunrise
    (B) wave is to water
    (C) lake is to river
    (D) current is to tide
    (E) border is to country

57. Shark is to hammerhead as bear is to
    (A) arctic
    (B) cub
    (C) moose
    (D) polar
    (E) paw

58. Sociologist is to behavior as
    (A) ballerina is to slipper
    (B) writer is to computer
    (C) zoologist is to tree
    (D) chef is to meal
    (E) archaeologist is to artifact

59. Hold is to grip as
    (A) jump is to bounce
    (B) jog is to sprint
    (C) drive is to fast
    (D) speak is to tell
    (E) talk is to speech

60. Player is to team as
    (A) guide is to tour
    (B) membership is to club
    (C) actor is to cast
    (D) herd is to pack
    (E) principal is to school

STOP!
If you finish before time is up, check your work on this section only.

Directions: For each of the following questions, mark the letter of your choice on the answer sheet.

1. Louisa went to the grocery store and bought a package of hamburger patties for $6.16, a package of buns for $2.10, a container of mustard for $1.78, a jar of relish for $2.16, and a bag of charcoal for $5.35. What was her total bill?
   (A) $12.64
   (B) $14.74
   (C) $16.15
   (D) $17.55
   (E) $19.65

2. A teacher has assigned 315 pages of reading. If Jessica starts reading on Monday and reads 65 pages each day, on what day will she complete the assignment?
   (A) Wednesday
   (B) Thursday
   (C) Friday
   (D) Saturday
   (E) Sunday

3. Renee deposits $4,000 in a saving account that earns 2% simple interest per year. How much interest will she earn after 2 years?
   (A) $100
   (B) $160
   (C) $165
   (D) $180
   (E) $195

4. Rachel flies 2,880 miles in 9 hours. What is the average speed of her airplane?
   (A) 285 miles/hour
   (B) 315 miles/hour
   (C) 320 miles/hour
   (D) 340 miles/hour
   (E) 355 miles/hour

5. An acute angle is an angle that measures
   (A) exactly 90°
   (B) greater than 90°
   (C) less than 90°
   (D) exactly 120°
   (E) more than 120°

6. Al has 3 times as much money as Bill. Bill has 2 times as much money as Charlie. If Charlie has $12.55, how much money does Al have?
   (A) $33.75
   (B) $75.30
   (C) $82.20
   (D) $88.35
   (E) $96.40

7. Alex's car gets an average of 26 miles per gallon of gas on the highway. If he drives 858 miles, how many gallons of gas will he use?
   (A) 33 gallons
   (B) 57 gallons
   (C) 78 gallons
   (D) 84 gallons
   (E) 92 gallons

GO ON TO THE NEXT PAGE.

8. In the figure shown, the two outer rays form a right angle. If angle 1 measures 65°, what is the measure of angle 2?

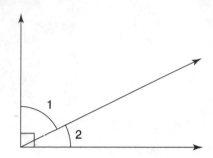

(A) 120°
(B) 90°
(C) 60°
(D) 35°
(E) 25°

9. Will has $12,444.12 in his checking account. He writes checks for $8,204.94 and $890.99. How much is left in Will's account?
(A) $989.65
(B) $2,259.30
(C) $2,867.30
(D) $2,945.60
(E) $3,348.19

10. Paula is 3 years older than Lindsey, who is 2 years younger than Dave. If Paula is 17, how old is Dave?
(A) 16
(B) 17
(C) 19
(D) 21
(E) 23

11. In a recent election, Rebecca received 14% of the votes. If 7,000 votes were cast, how many votes did Rebecca receive?
(A) 680
(B) 980
(C) 1,080
(D) 1,220
(E) 1,460

12. In the figure shown, if angle 2 measures 45°, what is the measure of angle 4?

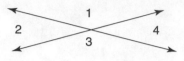

(A) 135°
(B) 75°
(C) 45°
(D) 35°
(E) 25

13. If ¼ of a number is 12, then ⅙ of the same number is
(A) 16
(B) 15
(C) 12
(D) 9
(E) 8

14. Figure WXYZ is a parallelogram. Which of the following is NOT necessarily true?

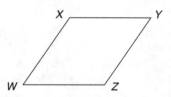

(A) Side WX is parallel to side ZY.
(B) Side XY is parallel to side WZ.
(C) ∠W has the same measure as ∠Y.
(D) Side WX is the same length as side XY.
(E) ∠X has the same measure as ∠Z.

15. Renee wants to carpet her living room. The rectangular room measures 15 feet × 18 feet. How many square yards of carpet must Renee purchase?
(A) 20 yd²
(B) 30 yd²
(C) 32 yd²
(D) 35 yd²
(E) 40 yd²

GO ON TO THE NEXT PAGE.

16. In an equilateral triangle what is the measure of each angle?
    (A) 30°
    (B) 45°
    (C) 60°
    (D) 90°
    (E) 110°

17. Last month, the librarian at a certain library kept track of all books checked out. The graph below shows the results by type of book. Which type of book was checked out least?

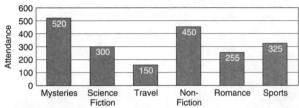

Number of Library Books Checked Out of Local Libraries

    (A) Mysteries
    (B) Science fiction
    (C) Travel
    (D) Nonfiction
    (E) Sports

18. If $9 + 3 +$ _____ $= 8 + 6 + 4$, then ___ $=$
    (A) 2
    (B) 3
    (C) 4
    (D) 5
    (E) 6

19. $2 \times 3 \times 5 \times 6$ is equal to the product of 30 and
    (A) 6
    (B) 7
    (C) 8
    (D) 9
    (E) 11

20. Which of the following is NOT equal to a whole number?
    (A) $\dfrac{20}{5}$
    (B) $5 \times \dfrac{3}{4}$
    (C) $6 \div \dfrac{1}{6}$
    (D) $\dfrac{3}{5} \times 10$
    (E) $7 + 5$

21. $4\,{}^3/_{10}\% =$
    (A) 43
    (B) 4.3
    (C) 0.43
    (D) 0.043
    (E) 0.0043

22. It costs d dollars to buy 6 chocolate bars. At the same rate, how many dollars will it cost to buy 15 chocolate bars?
    (A) $2.5d$
    (B) $25d$
    (C) $\dfrac{2d}{5}$
    (D) $\dfrac{5d}{2}$
    (E) $250d$

23. In the triangle shown, $\angle ACB$ measures 55° and $\angle CAB$ measures 65°. What is the measure of $\angle CBA$?

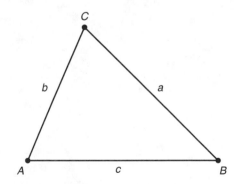

    (A) 50°
    (B) 60°
    (C) 80°
    (D) 90°
    (E) 110°

GO ON TO THE NEXT PAGE.

24. There are 15 black marbles and 10 white marbles in a bag. If you pick a marble from the bag without looking, what are your chances of picking a white marble?

(A) $\dfrac{1}{25}$

(B) $\dfrac{3}{25}$

(C) $\dfrac{2}{5}$

(D) $\dfrac{3}{5}$

(E) $\dfrac{4}{5}$

25. $^3/_4 - {}^5/_{12} =$

(A) $\dfrac{1}{12}$

(B) $\dfrac{3}{12}$

(C) $\dfrac{1}{3}$

(D) $\dfrac{2}{3}$

(E) $\dfrac{3}{4}$

STOP!
If you finish before time is up, check your work on this section only.

Each reading passage is followed by questions about it. Answer the questions that follow a passage on the basis of what is stated or implied in that passage. For each question, select the answer you think is best and record your choice by filling in the corresponding oval on the answer sheet.

> At the Thirteenth Annual Convention of the National Negro Business League in 1912, no women were included on the schedule of speakers. Madam C. J. Walker, a highly successful inventor
>
> 5 and distributor of hair care products for African-American women, shocked the participants when she walked up and claimed the podium from moderator Booker T. Washington:
>
> "Surely you are not going to shut the door
> 10 in my face. I feel that I am in a business that is a credit to the womanhood of our race. I am a woman who started in business seven years ago with only $1.50. This year (up to the 19th day of this month . . .) I had taken in $18,000. (Prolonged
> 15 applause). This makes a grand total of $63,049 made in my hair business in Indianapolis. (Applause.) I have been trying to get before you business people to tell you what I am doing. I am a woman that came from the cotton fields of the
> 20 South; I was promoted from there to the wash-tub (laughter); then I was promoted to the cook kitchen, and from there I promoted myself into the business of manufacturing hair goods and preparations . . . I am not ashamed of my past; I am
> 25 not ashamed of my humble beginning. Don't think that because you have to go down in the wash-tub that you are any less a lady! (Prolonged applause.)"

1. The purpose of Madam Walker's speech was to
   (A) demonstrate her hair products to the league
   (B) lash out at Booker T. Washington for ignoring her
   (C) make the members of the league take notice of her business success
   (D) influence the members of the league to admit more women
   (E) encourage black women to go into business for themselves

2. As reflected in her speech, Madam Walker's attitude is best described as
   (A) envious
   (B) proud
   (C) reverent
   (D) cautious
   (E) fearful

3. The reaction of the members of the league to Madam Walker's speech can be described as
   (A) indifferent
   (B) angry
   (C) sad
   (D) favorable
   (E) critical

GO ON TO THE NEXT PAGE.

4. The reference to her promotion from the cotton fields to the wash tub to the cook kitchen is used to
(A) show how far she has come
(B) establish a connection with her audience
(C) suggest that hard work is not ladylike
(D) debunk a myth about African-American women
(E) make people feel sorry for her

5. What does Madam Walker means when she says, "Don't think that because you have to go down in the wash-tub that you are any less a lady" (lines 25–27)?
(A) Ladies should not have to scrub and cook.
(B) Getting down on your knees to scrub is hard work for a lady.
(C) It is not ladylike to work with your hands.
(D) Very few ladies get ahead in the business world.
(E) There is nothing demeaning about hard work.

On March 20, 1980, a series of small earthquakes signaled the awakening of Mount St. Helens from a 123-year slumber. Over the next two months more than 10,000 earthquakes followed as magma
5 moved into the volcano, wedging the volcano apart at a rate of five feet per day. Heat from a rising plume of volcanic ash melted glacial ice creating cement-like slurries of rock and ash called mudflows. Superheated avalanches of hot gas,
10 magma caused a visible swelling of the volcano's north flank creating a feature that scientists called "the bulge."

Many geologists weren't surprised by Mount St. Helens' awakening. In the 1950s, geologists
15 had begun an extensive study of the deposits around Mount St. Helens. In 1975, they published a report predicting that Mount St. Helens was the volcano in the lower 48 states most likely to erupt by the end of the century.
20 On the morning of May 18, 1980, a magnitude 5.1 earthquake triggered the collapse of the summit and north flank of Mount St. Helens and formed the largest landslide in recorded history. Gas-rich magma and super-heated groundwater
25 trapped inside the volcano were suddenly released in a powerful lateral blast. In less than three minutes, 230 square miles of forest lay flattened. The hot gas and magma melted the snow and ice that covered the volcano. The resulting floodwater

30 mixed with the rock and debris to create concrete-like mudflows that scoured river valleys surrounding the mountain.

A plume of volcanic ash and pumice billowed out of the volcano reaching a height of 15 miles
35 and transformed day into night across Eastern Washington. Avalanches of super-heated gas and pumice, called pyroclastic flows, swept down the flanks of the volcano. While the landslide and lateral blast were over within minutes, the
40 eruption column, mudflows and pyroclastic flows continued throughout the day and following night. By the following morning major eruptive activity had ceased and the landscape appeared to be a gray wasteland.

6. The primary purpose of this passage is to
(A) offer general information about volcanoes
(B) describe a specific volcanic eruption
(C) offer specific advice about what to do when a volcano erupts
(D) provide historical background about volcanoes
(E) appeal for action to protect the environment

7. The first sentence implies that
(A) Mount St. Helens had never before erupted
(B) Mount St. Helens erupts every 123 years
(C) Mount St. Helens last erupted in 1857
(D) no records exist for eruptions that occurred more than 123 years ago
(E) no one suspected that Mount St. Helens could erupt

8. As used in line 7, "rising" most nearly means
(A) growing
(B) maturing
(C) approaching
(D) ascending
(E) advancing

GO ON TO THE NEXT PAGE.

9. The statement that "Many geologists weren't surprised by Mount St. Helens' awakening," (lines 13–14) primarily suggests that
   (A) geologists were able to predict when Mount St. Helens would erupt
   (B) the assumptions geologists had made about Mount St. Helens were being proven
   (C) the longer a volcano remains dormant, the more likely it is to become active
   (D) nothing is surprising to geologists
   (E) the heat rising from the volcanic ash had provided an important clue to the geologists

10. The author describes the events of May 18, 1980, mainly by means of
    (A) scientific analysis
    (B) detached and impartial observation
    (C) vivid language and dramatic images
    (D) presentation of facts in chronological order
    (E) presentation of details in spatial order

11. By calling the landscape "a gray wasteland" (line 44), the author implies that
    (A) the landscape was covered with a blanket of dirty snow
    (B) the landscape was littered with garbage and other waste matter
    (C) the trees were all covered with gray ash
    (D) the sun could not penetrate the forest
    (E) the landscape had been striped bare and covered in volcanic ash

It was Paul's afternoon to appear before the faculty of the Pittsburgh High School to account for his various misdemeanors. He had been suspended a week ago, and his father had called
5 the Principal's office and confessed his perplexity about his son. Paul entered the faculty room suave and smiling. His clothes were a trifle out-grown, and the tan velvet on the collar of his open overcoat was frayed and worn; but for all that
10 there was something of the dandy about him, and he wore an opal pin in his neatly knotted black four-in-hand, and a red carnation in his buttonhole. This latter adornment the faculty somehow felt was not properly significant of the
15 contrite spirit befitting a boy under the ban of suspension.
Paul was tall for his age and very thin, with high, cramped shoulders and a narrow chest. His eyes were remarkable for a certain hysterical
20 brilliancy, and he continually used them in a conscious, theatrical sort of way, peculiarly offensive in a boy. The pupils were abnormally large, as though he were addicted to belladonna, but there was a glassy glitter about them which that drug
25 does not produce.
When questioned by the Principal as to why he was there Paul stated, politely enough, that he wanted to come back to school. This was a lie, but Paul was quite accustomed to lying; found it,
30 indeed, indispensable for overcoming friction. His teachers were asked to state their respective charges against him, which they did with such a rancor and aggrievedness as evinced that this was not a usual case. Disorder and impertinence were
35 among the offenses named, yet each of his instructors felt that it was scarcely possible to put into words the real cause of the trouble, which lay in a sort of hysterically defiant manner of the boy's; in the contempt which they all knew he felt
40 for them, and which he seemingly made not the least effort to conceal. Once, when he had been making a synopsis of a paragraph at the black-board, his English teacher had stepped to his side and attempted to guide his hand. Paul had started
45 back with a shudder and thrust his hands violently behind him. The astonished woman could scarcely have been more hurt and embarrassed had he struck at her. The insult was so involuntary and definitely personal as to be unforgettable. In one
50 way and another he had made all his teachers, men and women alike, conscious of the same feeling of physical aversion. In one class he habitually sat with his hand shading his eyes; in another he always looked out of the window during the recitation;
55 in another he made a running commentary on the lecture, with humorous intention.
Willa Cather from "Paul's Case: A Study in Temperament"

12. This passage can best be characterized as
    (A) an amusing story about a high school escapade
    (B) a fond remembrance of the narrator's youth
    (C) a penetrating examination of a young man's character
    (D) a polite appeal for forgiveness
    (E) an astute description of the relationship between a father and son

GO ON TO THE NEXT PAGE.

13. In line 10, the expression "there was something of the dandy about him" means that Paul
    (A) was afraid of appearing before the faculty
    (B) was in need of new clothes
    (C) did not care how he looked
    (D) paid great attention to his clothes
    (E) was hard on his clothes

14. The red carnation in Paul's buttonhole in lines 12–13 made the faculty feel that Paul
    (A) did not take his suspension seriously enough
    (B) did not really want to come back to school
    (C) was trying to impress the principal
    (D) thought he should be forgiven
    (E) was sincere in his desire to improve his behavior

15. In the eyes of the faculty, Paul's most serious offense was his
    (A) insulting remarks made in class
    (B) inability to control his temper
    (C) failure to complete his assignments
    (D) obvious contempt for his teachers
    (E) lack of attention in class

16. Which adjective best describes Paul?
    (A) contrite
    (B) funny
    (C) defiant
    (D) violent
    (E) embarrassed

17. As used in line 33, the word "rancor" means
    (A) turmoil
    (B) bitterness
    (C) remorse
    (D) resistance
    (E) dismay

18. In lines 45–46, Paul shuddered and threw his hands behind him because
    (A) his teacher had touched his hand
    (B) he could not answer the teacher's question
    (C) his teacher had hurt him
    (D) he was afraid of the teacher
    (E) he wanted to strike the teacher

The Homestead Act of 1862 has been called one the most important pieces of legislation in the history of the United States. Designed to spur Western migration, the Homestead Act culminated a twenty-year battle to distribute public lands to citizens willing to farm. Opposition to the Act came from Northern businessmen, who feared it would lower property values and reduce the supply of cheap labor, and from Southerners, who feared homesteaders would add to the voices calling for the abolition of slavery. With Southerners out of the picture in 1862, the legislation finally passed and was signed into law by Abraham Lincoln. Under this Act, 270 million acres, or 10% of the area of the United States, was claimed and settled.

A homesteader had only to be the head of a household and at least 21 years of age to claim a 160-acre parcel of land. Settlers from all walks of life, including newly arrived immigrants, farmers without land of their own from the East, single women and former slaves came to meet the challenge of "proving up" and keeping this "free land." Homesteaders were required to live on the land, build a home, make improvements, and farm for 5 years before they were eligible to "prove up." A total filing fee of $18 was the only money required, but settlers paid a big price in sacrifice and hard work.

People interested in Homesteading first had to file their intentions at the nearest Land Office where they paid a fee of $10 to claim the land temporarily, and a $2 commission to the land agent. The homesteader then returned to the land to begin the process of building a home and farming the land, both requirements for "proving up." After five years of living on and working the land, the homesteader had to find two neighbors or friends willing to vouch for the truth of his or her statements about the land's improvements and sign the "proof" document. With the successful completion of this final form and payment of a $6 fee, the homesteader received the patent (or deed) for the land, signed with the name of the current President of the United States.

GO ON TO THE NEXT PAGE.

19. The primary purpose of the passage is to
    (A) discuss the reasons for westward expansion in the United States
    (B) explain the provisions of the Homestead Act
    (C) point out the difficulties of homesteading
    (D) argue in favor of extending the Homestead Act
    (E) explain the importance of "proving up"

20. In line 30, "file" most nearly means
    (A) arrange in order
    (B) classify
    (C) sharpen
    (D) record
    (E) finish

21. In order to acquire land under the Homestead Act, claimants had to meet all of the following conditions EXCEPT:
    (A) be a head of household
    (B) be at least 21 years of age
    (C) be a native-born U.S. citizen
    (D) farm the land for five years
    (E) build a house on the land

22. How much U.S. land was transferred to individuals under the terms of the Homestead Act?
    (A) 160 acres per person
    (B) 320 acres per family
    (C) 1.6 million acres
    (D) 270 million acres
    (E) 30% of all U.S. land

23. The author calls the Homestead Act one of the most important pieces of legislation in United States history because it
    (A) helped settle the West
    (B) provided cheap labor
    (C) lowered land values
    (D) helped to end slavery
    (E) passed after a twenty year battle

Manatees and dugongs, also known as sea cows, belong to the scientific order Sirenia. In ancient mythology, "siren" was a term used for monsters or sea nymphs who lured sailors and

5   their ships to treacherous rocks and shipwreck with mesmerizing songs. Throughout history, sailors sometimes thought they were seeing mermaids when they were probably seeing

---

manatees or dugongs. With a little imagination,
10 manatees have an uncanny resemblance to human form that could only increase after long months at sea. In fact, manatees and dugongs may have helped to perpetuate the myth of mermaids. Like the mythological creatures for which they
15 were named, all sirenians living on earth today are vulnerable to extinction

Manatees and dugongs are the only completely aquatic mammals that are herbivores. Unlike the other marine mammals (dolphins, whales, seals,
20 sea lions, sea otters, walruses, and polar bears) sirenians eat only seagrasses and other aquatic vegetation. Unlike other marine mammals, sirenians have an extremely low metabolism and zero tolerance for cold water. Like dolphins and
25 whales, manatees and dugongs are totally aquatic mammals that never leave the water—not even to give birth. The combination of these factors means that sirenians are restricted to warm shallow coastal waters, estuaries, and rivers, with
30 healthy ecosystems that support large amounts of seagrass and other vegetation.

The average adult manatee is about three meters (9.8 feet) long and weighs between 362–544 kilograms (800–1,200 pounds). It is
35 estimated that a manatee can eat about 10–15% of its body weight in vegetation daily. So, for example, a 453-kilogram (1,000-pound) manatee would probably eat between 45–68 kilograms (100–150 pounds) of sea grass and water hyacinths
40 a day!

24. Paragraph 1 is primarily concerned with
    (A) the origin of the scientific classification Sirenia
    (B) the similarities between manatees and mermaids
    (C) how manatees cause shipwrecks
    (D) a comparison between manatees and dugongs
    (E) the imagination of manatees

25. As used in line 6, "mesmerizing" most nearly means
    (A) discordant
    (B) mellifluous
    (C) high pitched
    (D) hypnotic
    (E) mysterious

GO ON TO THE NEXT PAGE.

26. The passage supports which of the following conclusions?
    (A) Manatees are like other marine mammals in their diet.
    (B) All sirenians are endangered.
    (C) Because of their low metabolism manatees tolerate cold water well.
    (D) Mermaids were classified as sirenians.
    (E) Manatees leave the water only to give birth.

27. The author develops paragraph 2 by presenting
    (A) two sides of an issue
    (B) a thesis followed by specific examples
    (C) a description of similarities and differences
    (D) an opinion and reasons why it is held
    (E) a hypothesis and data to prove it

28. According to the passage, manatees prefer the shallow coastal waters of Florida because of which of the following?
    I. availability of vegetation
    II. favorable water temperatures
    III. safety

    (A) I only
    (B) II only
    (C) III only
    (D) I and II only
    (E) I, II, and III

29. Which of the following represents the number of pounds of food an average adult manatee consumes in a day?
    (A) 10–15
    (B) 100–150
    (C) 352–544
    (D) 800–1000
    (E) 1000–1200

Day had broken cold and gray, exceedingly cold and gray, when the man turned aside from the main Yukon trail and climbed the high earth-bank, where a dim and little-traveled trail
5 led eastward through the fat spruce timberland. It was a steep bank, and he paused for breath at the top, excusing the act to himself by looking at his watch. It was nine o'clock. There was no sun nor hint of sun, though there was not a cloud in
10 the sky. It was a clear day, and yet there seemed

an intangible pall over the face of things, a subtle gloom that made the day dark, and that was due to the absence of sun. This fact did not worry the man.
    As he turned to go on, he spat speculatively.
15 There was a sharp, explosive crackle that startled him. He spat again. And again, in the air, before it could fall to the snow, the spittle crackled. He knew that at fifty below spittle crackled on the snow, but this spittle had crackled in the air.
20 Undoubtedly it was colder than fifty below—how much colder he did not know. But the temperature did not matter. He was bound for the old claim on the left fork of Henderson Creek, where the boys were already. They had come over across the
25 divide from the Indian Creek country, while he had come the roundabout way to take a look at the possibilities of getting out logs in the spring from the islands in the Yukon.
    At the man's heels trotted a dog, a big native
30 husky, the proper wolf-dog, gray-coated and without any visible or temperamental difference from its brother, the wild wolf. The animal was depressed by the tremendous cold. It knew that it was no time for travelling. Its instinct told it a
35 truer tale than was told to the man by the man's judgment. It experienced a vague but menacing apprehension that subdued it and made it slink along at the man's heels, and that made it question eagerly every unwonted movement of the man as
40 if expecting him to go into camp or to seek shelter somewhere and build a fire.
    Jack London from "To Build a Fire"

30. In the first paragraph the author establishes a mood of
    (A) promise
    (B) serenity
    (C) hostility
    (D) foreboding
    (E) regret

31. As used in line 1, "broken" most nearly means
    (A) dawned
    (B) separated
    (C) shattered
    (D) interrupted
    (E) cracked

GO ON TO THE NEXT PAGE.

32. The statement that "It was a steep bank, and he paused for breath at the top, excusing the act to himself by looking at his watch," (lines 6–8) suggests that the man
(A) was worried about running late
(B) was not accustomed to hiking in the Yukon
(C) was disoriented by the extreme cold
(D) had traveled farther than he thought
(E) expected to see the sun

33. The discussion of spitting into the air (lines 14–19) serves primarily to suggest
(A) the strangeness of the landscape
(B) the severity of the cold
(C) the courage of the man
(D) the frustration of the dog
(E) the gloom of the day

34. In lines 15–16, the author includes the detail that the sharp, explosive crackle "startled him" primarily to emphasize
(A) the man's fragile state of mind
(B) how eerily quiet it had become
(C) that the temperature was dropping
(D) the danger the man was in
(E) that it was colder than the man thought

35. Which word best describes how the author regards the man in the story?
(A) clever
(B) cautious
(C) foolish
(D) ambitious
(E) ruthless

36. With which of the following statements is the author most likely to agree?
(A) The man is right to press on.
(B) The dog is unfazed by the cold.
(C) The man is jealous of the dog.
(D) The dog is wiser than the man.
(E) The sun will make the day more bearable.

I was asked not long ago to tell something about the sports and pastimes that I engaged in during my youth. Until that question was asked it had never occurred to me that there was no
5   period of my life that was devoted to play. From the time that I can remember anything, almost every day of my life has been occupied in some kind of labor; though I think I would now be a

more useful man if I had had time for sports.
10   During the period that I spent in slavery I was not large enough to be of much service, still I was occupied most of the time in cleaning the yards, carrying water to the men in the fields, or going to the mill, to which I used to take the corn, once a
15   week, to be ground. The mill was about three miles from the plantation. This work I always dreaded. The heavy bag of corn would be thrown across the back of the horse, and the corn divided about evenly on each side; but in some way,
20   almost without exception, on these trips, the corn would so shift as to become unbalanced and would fall off the horse, and often I would fall with it. As I was not strong enough to reload the corn upon the horse, I would have to wait,
25   sometimes for many hours, till a chance passer-by came along who would help me out of my trouble. The hours while waiting for someone were usually spent in crying. The time consumed in this way made me late in reaching the mill, and by the time
30   I got my corn ground and reached home it would be far into the night. The road was a lonely one, and often led through dense forests. I was always frightened. The woods were said to be full of soldiers who had deserted from the army, and I
35   had been told that the first thing a deserter did to a Negro boy when he found him alone was to cut off his ears. Besides, when I was late in getting home I knew I would always get a severe scolding or a flogging.
Booker T. Washington from *Up from Slavery: An Autobiography*

37. In line 2, "engaged" means most nearly
(A) pledged
(B) occupied
(C) meshed
(D) participated
(E) reserved

38. The author's "trouble" in line 26 is
(A) not being able to have the corn ground at the mill
(B) having to travel alone in the dark
(C) not being able to reload the corn that had fallen off the horse
(D) not knowing the way through the woods
(E) facing a flogging for being late

GO ON TO THE NEXT PAGE.

39. The author was always frightened on his way home from the mill for all of the following reasons EXCEPT:
   (A) There were few people on the road at night.
   (B) The woods were full of soldiers.
   (C) He feared having his ears cut off.
   (D) He knew he would be flogged for being late.
   (E) He thought he might be kidnapped.

40. The author's attitude toward his youth is best described as
   (A) affectionate nostalgia
   (B) analytical detachment
   (C) open hostility
   (D) deep sorrow
   (E) righteous indignation

STOP!
If you finish before time is up, check your work on this section only.

Time: 30 Minutes
25 Questions

Directions: For each of the following questions, mark the letter of your choice on the answer sheet.

1. If $16 \div 4 \times \underline{\quad} = 5 \times 8 - 16$, then $\underline{\quad} =$
   (A) 2
   (B) 3
   (C) 4
   (D) 5
   (E) 6

2. $42 \div 7 \times 8 \times 5$ is equal to the product of 12 and
   (A) 16
   (B) 20
   (C) 24
   (D) 28
   (E) 32

3. Which of the following is NOT equal to a whole number?
   (A) $\dfrac{30}{5}$

   (B) $4 \times \dfrac{12}{16}$

   (C) $16 \div \dfrac{1}{16}$

   (D) $\dfrac{5}{9} \times 8$

   (E) $10.2 + 12.8$

4. $46\frac{3}{4}\% =$
   (A) 467.5
   (B) 46.75
   (C) 4.675
   (D) 0.4675
   (E) 0.04675

5. It costs m dollars to buy 48 notepads.
   At the same rate, how many dollars will it cost to buy 30 notepads?

   (A) $\dfrac{m}{8}$

   (B) $\dfrac{5m}{8}$

   (C) $5m$

   (D) $\dfrac{8m}{5}$

   (E) $10m$

6. If $\frac{3}{7}$ of a number is 18, then $\frac{1}{2}$ of the same number is
   (A) 32
   (B) 30
   (C) 28
   (D) 24
   (E) 21

7. 60 is approximately what percent of 90?
   (A) 30%
   (B) 33%
   (C) 45%
   (D) 67%
   (E) 70%

8. $\sqrt[3]{216} =$
   (A) 3
   (B) 5
   (C) 6
   (D) 11
   (E) 12

GO ON TO THE NEXT PAGE.

9. In the following figure, if ∠6 measures 90°, what is the measure of ∠1?

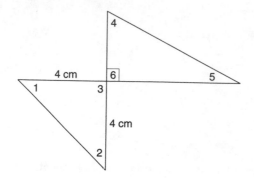

(A) 25°
(B) 35°
(C) 45°
(D) 55°
(E) 58°

10. Each edge of a cube measures 8 cm. What is the volume?
(A) 64 cm³
(B) 176 cm³
(C) 384 cm³
(D) 420 cm³
(E) 512 cm³

11. $-10 - (-5 - 4) =$
(A) −4
(B) −3
(C) −1
(D) 1
(E) 3

12. $^3/_4 + ^1/_2 + ^2/_3 - ^5/_6 =$

(A) $1\frac{1}{12}$

(B) $1\frac{1}{3}$

(C) $1\frac{5}{6}$

(D) $2\frac{1}{6}$

(E) $2\frac{1}{4}$

13. Karen is driving to a town 175 miles away. If she drives at a steady speed of 50 miles per hour, how long will the trip take?
(A) 2 hours 50 minutes
(B) 3 hours

(C) 3 hours 10 minutes
(D) 3 hours 30 minutes
(E) 3 hours 50 minutes

14. The number of students who won awards at the science fair this year was 2 more than 3 times as many as last year. If 20 students won awards this year, how many won awards last year?
(A) 18
(B) 15
(C) 12
(D) 8
(E) 6

15. If $3.4a + 8.7a = 38.72$, $a =$
(A) 2.9
(B) 3.2
(C) 3.5
(D) 3.9
(E) 4.6

16. $12 + -6 \times 3 =$
(A) 21
(B) 6
(C) −6
(D) −12
(E) −21

17. A clock is showing 3:00. How many degrees is the angle formed between the minute and hour hands?
(A) 30°
(B) 60°
(C) 90°
(D) 120°
(E) 180°

18. The area of a carpet is 216 square feet. What is the area in square yards?
(A) 18 yd²
(B) 24 yd²
(C) 28 yd²
(D) 34 yd²
(E) 36 yd²

19. A truck travels 126 miles in 3 hours. At that speed, in how many hours will the truck reach its destination, 924 miles away?
(A) 22 hours
(B) 24 hours
(C) 25.5 hours
(D) 28 hours
(E) 30.5 hours

GO ON TO THE NEXT PAGE.

20. 18 is what percent of 144?
    (A) 8%
    (B) 12.5%
    (C) 14%
    (D) 16.75%
    (E) 22%

21. In a dresser drawer there are 3 pairs of white socks, 5 pairs of black socks, and 4 pairs of blue socks. If you pick a pair without looking, what are the chances that you will pick a blue pair?
    (A) $\dfrac{1}{12}$
    (B) $\dfrac{1}{6}$
    (C) $\dfrac{1}{4}$
    (D) $\dfrac{1}{3}$
    (E) $\dfrac{7}{12}$

22. What is the least common multiple of 3, 4, and 18?
    (A) 18
    (B) 24
    (C) 36
    (D) 54
    (E) 72

23. What is the greatest common factor of 16, 24, 96, and 120?

    (A) 2
    (B) 4
    (C) 8
    (D) 12
    (E) 36

24. Order from least to greatest:
    3/5, 1¹/₂, 0.8
    (A) $1\dfrac{1}{2}, 0.8, \dfrac{3}{5}$
    (B) $0.8, \dfrac{3}{5}, 1\dfrac{1}{2}$
    (C) $1\dfrac{1}{2}, \dfrac{3}{5}, 0.8$
    (D) $0.8, 1\dfrac{1}{2}, \dfrac{3}{5}$
    (E) $\dfrac{3}{5}, 0.8, 1\dfrac{1}{2}$

25. ⁷/₁₂ + ⁵/₆ + ¹/₄ =
    (A) $1\dfrac{1}{6}$
    (B) $1\dfrac{1}{4}$
    (C) $1\dfrac{1}{2}$
    (D) $1\dfrac{2}{3}$
    (E) $1\dfrac{5}{6}$

STOP!
If you finish before time is up, check your work on this section only.

SECTION 5
Time: 25 Minutes

Directions: You will have 25 minutes to plan and write an essay on the topic below. Read the topic carefully. Jot down some brief notes on the scratch paper provided and organize your thoughts before you begin to write. Write your final essay on the ruled lines below. Write or print legibly, using the black pen that will be given to you at the test center. A copy of your essay will be sent to each school that will be receiving your test results.

Topic: Every cloud has a silver lining.

Assignment: Do you agree or disagree with the topic statement? Support your position with examples from your own experience, the experience of others, current events, history, or literature.

_____

_____

_____

_____

_____

_____

_____

_____

_____

_____

_____

_____

_____

_____

Answer Key

Section 1 Verbal

1.	E	21.	C	41.	A
2.	D	22.	B	42.	C
3.	B	23.	D	43.	C
4.	C	24.	C	44.	D
5.	A	25.	B	45.	E
6.	E	26.	A	46.	B
7.	B	27.	E	47.	A
8.	A	28.	D	48.	E
9.	B	29.	A	49.	D
10.	C	30.	C	50.	C
11.	B	31.	E	51.	D
12.	A	32.	C	52.	D
13.	C	33.	D	53.	A
14.	B	34.	B	54.	B
15.	A	35.	A	55.	B
16.	E	36.	E	56.	E
17.	E	37.	D	57.	D
18.	D	38.	B	58.	E
19.	C	39.	B	59.	B
20.	D	40.	E	60.	C

Section 2 Quantitative I

1.	D	10.	A	19.	A
2.	C	11.	B	20.	B
3.	B	12.	C	21.	D
4.	C	13.	E	22.	A
5.	C	14.	D	23.	B
6.	B	15.	B	24.	C
7.	A	16.	C	25.	C
8.	E	17.	C		
9.	E	18.	E		

Section 3 Reading Comprehension

1.	C	15.	D	29.	B
2.	B	16.	C	30.	D
3.	D	17.	B	31.	A
4.	A	18.	A	32.	B
5.	E	19.	B	33.	B
6.	B	20.	D	34.	E
7.	C	21.	C	35.	C
8.	D	22.	D	36.	D
9.	B	23.	A	37.	D
10.	C	24.	A	38.	C
11.	E	25.	D	39.	E
12.	C	26.	B	40.	B
13.	D	27.	C		
14.	A	28.	D		

Section 4 Quantitative II

1.	E	10.	E	19.	A
2.	B	11.	C	20.	B
3.	D	12.	A	21.	D
4.	D	13.	D	22.	C
5.	B	14.	E	23.	C
6.	E	15.	B	24.	E
7.	D	16.	C	25.	D
8.	C	17.	C		
9.	C	18.	B		

Answers and Explanations

Section 1 Verbal

1. **E is correct.** *Shame* is a painful emotion caused by a strong sense of guilt, embarrassment, unworthiness, or disgrace. Another word for shame is *humiliation*.

2. **D is correct.** To *divulge* something is to make it known, especially something private or a secret—to *tell*.

3. **B is correct.** *Concise* is an adjective meaning expressing much in few words; clear and succinct—in other words, *brief*.

4. **C is correct.** An *inquiry* is a close examination of a matter in a search for information or truth. An *inquiry* is synonymous with an *investigation*.

5. **A is correct.** Like *disposition*, an *attitude* is a state of mind or feeling.

6. **E is correct.** To do something *tediously* is the same as doing it *tiresomely* by reason of length, slowness, dullness, or boredom.

7. **B is correct.** To *deplete* something is to decrease the fullness of it; use it up; or empty it out—in other words, to *reduce* it.

8. **A is correct.** *Cautious* describes someone who is careful, tentative, restrained, or guarded. Another way to describe such a person would be to say that she or he is *discreet*.

9. **B is correct.** *Sparse* is an adjective describing conditions that are not thick or dense. *Thin* is synonymous with *sparse*.

10. **C is correct.** An *aversion* is an avoidance of a thing, situation, or behavior because it has been associated with an unpleasant or painful stimulus. If you have an aversion to something, you have a fixed, intense *dislike* for it.

11. **B is correct.** A *benefactor* is someone who gives aid, especially financial aid—in other words, a *contributor*.

12. **A is correct.** When something is *dormant* it is lying asleep, or as if asleep. That is, it is *inactive*.

13. **C is correct.** If someone is described as *malcontent*, he is *dissatisfied* with existing conditions.

14. **B is correct.** To *appease* means to *satisfy* or relieve.

15. **A is correct.** To *merit* means to earn or *deserve*.

16. **E is correct.** If something is *prominent*, it is immediately noticeable—in other words, *conspicuous*.

17. **E is correct.** An *objective* is something worked toward or striven for. *Intention* is synonymous with *objective*.

18. **D is correct.** A *breach* is a *violation* or infraction, as of a law, a legal obligation, or a promise.

19. **C is correct.** To *lament* is to *regret* deeply, or to express grief for or about.

20. **D is correct.** To *rectify* means to set right or correct by calculation or adjustment—in other words, to *fix*.

21. **C is correct.** To *submerge* something is to place it under water or to cover it with water. *Submerge* is synonymous with *immerse*.

22. **B is correct.** Something that is *indelible* is impossible to remove, erase, or wash away. Therefore, it is *permanent*.

23. **D is correct.** An *abyss* is an immeasurably deep chasm, depth, or void—a *hole*.

24. **C is correct.** An *order* is an authoritative indication to be obeyed; a command or direction. Similarly, a *decree* is an authoritative order having the force of law.

25. **B is correct.** A *shrewd* person is characterized by keen awareness, sharp intelligence, and often a sense of the practical. As well, a person described as *astute* has or shows discernment, awareness, and intelligence.

26. **A is correct.** *Clandestine* is an adjective meaning kept or done in *secret*, often to conceal an illicit or improper purpose.

27. **E is correct.** To *coerce* someone is to force that person to act or think in a certain way by use of pressure, threats, or intimidation. *Compel* can be used synonymously with *coerce*.

28. **D is correct.** To *dilate* something is to make it larger or wider, or to cause it to expand—in other words, to *enlarge*.

29. **A is correct.** *Inane* describes one that lacks sense or substance—*ridiculous*.

30. **C is correct.** A *plethora* is an abundance or an *excess*.

31. **E is correct.** To *insult* someone is the opposite of what you would do if you were to *compliment* someone, just as to *please* someone is the opposite of what you would do if you were to *annoy* someone. Only choice E provides two verbs that are opposite in meaning. The verbs presented in choices A, C, and D are synonymous with each other, and the word pair in choice B are not the same parts of speech.

32. **C is correct.** This stem provides a part-to-whole sequence by pairing a *wolf* with a *pack*, the name given to a group of wolves. Choice A is incorrect because a group of sheep is called a flock, and choice D is incorrect because the analogy is presented backward. For choice E to be correct, it would have to read "cow is to herd." Choice C is the only correct answer because a group of *geese* is often referred to as a *gaggle*.

33. **D is correct.** This question tests your knowledge of synonym pairs. *Announce* and *inform* are synonyms in much the same way that *wrap* and *conceal* are synonyms. No other answer choice offers two words that have similar meanings.

34. **B is correct.** The relationship in this sequence is one of usage. A *shovel* is used to *dig*, as well; a *blade* is used to *cut*. Choice D is incorrect because an eye is used to see, not blink.

35. **A is correct.** This sequence tests your knowledge of relationships between units of measurement. Flip the words: *volume* can be measured in *liters*, just as *mass* can be measured in *grams*.

36. **E is correct.** This stem provides an individual-to-activity sequence by pairing *tourist* with *sightseeing*. Your task is to complete the analogy by deciding what activity an *analyst* performs. Choices C and D are easily eliminated because they are not verbs. As well, analysts aren't known for extensive traveling or curing people of ailments. Clearly, *examining* (choice E) is the only correct answer.

37. **D is correct.** This question tests your knowledge of degrees of contrast. A *whisper* is less intense than a *scream* just as a *glance* is less intense than a *stare*. The words provided in choices A and C are too close in meaning to one another, and both lack the proper contrast.

38. **B is correct.** This sequence gauges your knowledge of items to the places they are found. *Rocks* come from a *quarry*. Similarly, *coal* comes from a *mine*. No other choice represents a comparable analogy.

39. **B is correct.** This stem analogizes an animal or insect with its habitat. As you can see from the introduction, a *spider's* domain is its *web* just as a *bird's* domain is its *nest*. Choice D is incorrect because the sequence is inverted.

40. **E is correct.** This sentence tests your aptitude in recognizing part-to-part analogies by beginning with a *seat* and a *steering wheel* which are both parts of a vehicle. Similarly, the correct answer (choice E) reflects that a *handle bar* and a *brake* are both parts of a bicycle.

41. **A is correct.** This is a fairly straightforward usage sequence that analogizes an activity (*driving*) to the location it takes place (*street*). You should be able to infer that a person would *drive* on the *street* just as they would *walk* on a *path*. Ask yourself: how could the other choices be made correct? You might conclude that you would substitute *track* for *school* (choice B), *snack* for *school* (choice C), *sky* for *bird* (D), and *library* for *book* (choice E).

42. **C is correct.** This is another measurement question that provides you with the stem that *miles* measure *distance*. Of all the available choices, the only one that is correct is that *minutes* measure *time* in the same way that *miles* measure *distance*.

43. **C is correct.** This sequence tests your knowledge of parts to activities. You should be able to discount choices B and D immediately because choice B uses the plural form *arms*, and choice D provides a location rather than a body part. Choice E is incorrect as well because neither word is a verb. Of the remaining choices, you could possibly make an argument for choice A except for the fact that the noun and verb are in reverse order. Choice C is correct because, like the stem, you use your *mouth* to *chew* just as you use your *foot* to *kick*.

44. **D is correct.** This stem presents an activity-to-result analogy. When you *feed* something you *nourish*. Similarly, when you *water* something you *hydrate* it. Only choice D presents this type of complementary relationship.

45. **E is correct.** To answer this analogy correctly, you will need to know that a *prune* is actually a dried *plum*. Of the answer choices available, only choice E is correct; a *raisin* is actually a dried *grape*.

46. **B is correct.** This is another type of food analogy that involves some knowledge on your part. To answer this question correctly, you will need to know that *maple trees* produce *syrup* in much the same way that *oranges* produce *juice*. That is, the product comes directly from the source. Of the choices, you should be able to conclude that coffee does not produce beans (choice A); a chip does not produce chocolate (choice D); and although wheat produces bread, bread does not come directly from this source. Similarly, choice C is incorrect because it is not a better answer than choice B. Both syrup and juice are consumed by people, while grass is typically not.

47. **A is correct.** This sequence presents another analogy in degrees of contrast. As you can see from the stem, *envious* is less extreme than *jealous* much the same way that *melancholic* is less extreme than *mournful*. All the other answer choices present word pairs that are similar in meaning to one another; however, only choice A provides enough of a contrast between the mild and more extreme.

48. **E is correct.** This analogy is one of individual to object. A *knitter* uses *needles* just as a *boxer* uses *gloves* as the tools of a trade. As well, there is the point that both of these people use these tools with their hands, and also that only choice E complements the plural needles with the plural gloves; all the other answer choices provide singular options rather than plural.

49. **D is correct.** At first, this stem may appear to be a simple part-to-whole analogy, but in order to arrive at the correct answer, you will have to take it a step further. *Talon* is the name given to the claw of a predatory animal. Therefore, the correct answer is that *claw* is to *cat* as *talon* is to *eagle*. Choice C may seem correct, but it would be difficult to argue that it is a better answer than choice D.

50. **C is correct.** This is another question that tests your knowledge of synonym pairs. *Surprise* and *startle* are synonymous just as *destroy* and *ruin* are synonymous. Choice A is incorrect because you need not necessarily grab something in order to choose it, and choice D is incorrect because need and want are often easily confused with one another.

51. **D is correct.** The relationship in this sequence is one part to whole. A *scene* is part of a *play* in much the same way that a *chapter* is a part of a *book*. Choice C may seem correct; however, on closer inspection you'll notice that the relationship is inverted.

52. **D is correct.** This analogy tests your knowledge of adjectives used to describe nouns. *Aquatic* is an adjective used to describe something consisting of, relating to, or being in water. *Terrestrial* is an adjective used to describe something of, relating to, or composed of land. So the correct answer is choice D; *aquatic* is to *water* as *terrestrial* is to *land*.

53. **A is correct.** This sequence offers a part-to-whole analogy with a bit of a twist because the correct answer is a bit different from the stem. Flip the words if you have trouble discerning the right answer: a *bus* carries *passengers*. Similarly, a *ship* carries *cargo*. Keep in mind that just because the bus carries people and the ship carries things, no other option presents the relationship of a vessel carrying anything.

54. **B is correct.** The analogy presented in this stem is one of part to part. A *seed* is part of a piece of fruit in the same way that the *rind* is part of a piece of fruit. Similarly, *bark* is part of a tree just as a *branch* is part of a tree.

55. **B is correct.** This sequence presents another test of your knowledge of synonym pairs. Both *malign* and *disparage* are verbs that denote speaking unfavorably of someone just as *irritate* and *bother* are verbs that denote annoying someone. No other choice offers a pair of words that share the same meaning.

56. **E is correct.** This part-to-whole analogy goes a step further in testing your aptitude for comparisons. A *shoreline* borders the *ocean* and separates land from water just as a *border* separates one *country* from another.

57. **D is correct.** This is another part-to-whole analogy. If you have trouble arriving at the correct response, flip the words: a *hammerhead* is a type of *shark* just as *polar* is a type of *bear*. Choice B is incorrect because a cub is a young bear, not a specific type of bear.

58. **E is correct.** This analogy asks you to make a correlation between an individual and what that individual studies. *Sociologists* study *behavior* just as an *archaeologist* would study an *artifact*. The other answers are incorrect because a ballerina does not study a slipper (choice A); a writer may use a computer but would not study one (choice B); a zoologist studies animals, not trees (choice C); and a chef prepares meals rather than studying them (choice D).

59. **B is correct.** This sequence presents an analogy of contrasts and asks you to find the degree of difference. To *hold* something denotes a less intense commitment to the object than to *grip* something does. Similarly, *jogging* denotes putting less effort into running than *sprinting* does.

60. **C is correct.** By now you should be familiar with perhaps the most easily recognizable analogy: part to whole. A *player* is part of a *team* just as an *actor* is part of a *cast*. Choice E may seem correct, because a principal is part of a school. However, both player and actor seem to imply that no special status is given to either. A principal, as we all know, is the leader of the school, and it would be difficult to argue that choice E is a better answer than choice C.

Section 2 Quantitative I

1. **D is correct.** This is a simple addition problem. Add the amounts to get the total of $17.55.

2. **C is correct.** If Jessica has 315 pages of reading and reads 65 pages each day, on Monday she has read 65 pages, on Tuesday she has read 2(65) or 130 pages, on Wednesday she has read 3(65) or 195 pages, and on Thursday she has read 4(65) or 260 pages. On Friday, Jessica would need to read only 55 pages to complete the assignment. Another way to do this is to divide 315 by 65 to get 4.85. If Monday is 1, Tuesday is 2, Wednesday is 3, and Thursday is 4, then Friday would be 5. On Friday Jessica would complete the assignment.

3. **B is correct.** Simple interest problems use the formula $I = prt$ where I is the amount of interest, p is the principal or the amount saved or invested, r is the rate of interest, and t is the amount of time that the interest is accruing. In this problem, you are asked to find the interest, given that the principal is $4,000, the rate of interest is 2%, and the amount of time is 2 years. Substituting this information into the formula, you get $I = 4,000(0.02)(2) = 160 in interest.

4. **C is correct.** 2,880 ÷ 9 = 320 miles per hour.

5. **C is correct.** By definition, an acute angle is one that measures less than 90°.

6. **B is correct.** Create equations to solve this problem.
   Al = 3(Bill)
   Bill = 2(Charlie)
   Charlie = $12.55
   Solve for Al.
   Substitute what you know into the formulas.
   Bill = 2($12.55)
   Bill = $25.10
   To find Al, substitute what you know about Bill.
   Al = 3($25.10)
   Al = $75.30

7. **A is correct.** In this problem you need to calculate the number of 26-mpg units there are in 858. Do this by dividing 858 by 26.
   858 ÷ 26 = 33 gallons

8. **E is correct.** A right angle measures 90°. If angle 1 measures 65°, then angle 2 must measure 90° − 65° = 25°.

9. **E is correct.** Add the amount of the checks and subtract the total from the current amount in the checking account.
   $12,444.12 − ($8,204.94 + $890.99) = $3,348.19

10. **A is correct.** Create equations to solve this problem.
    Paula = Lindsey + 3
    Lindsey = Dave − 2
    You are told that Paula is 17. Substitute that information into the first equation.
    17 = Lindsey + 3
    Lindsey = 14
    Substitute that into the second equation.
    14 = Dave − 2
    Dave = 16

11. **B is correct.** To calculate 14% of 7,000, multiply 7,000 by 0.14.
    7,000(0.14) = 980 votes

12. **C is correct.** When two straight lines intersect as shown, they form opposite vertical angles. Those angles have the same measure, so if angle 2 measures 45°, then angle 4 must also measure 45°.

13. **E is correct.**
    $\frac{1}{4}x = 12$
    $x = 48$
    $\frac{1}{6}x = 8$

14. **D is correct.** In a parallelogram, opposite sides are parallel and opposite angles are equal. However, adjacent sides are not necessarily the same length.

15. **B is correct.** The area of the room is 15 × 18 = 270 ft². One square yard = 9 square feet, so 270 ft² ÷ 9 = 30 yd².

16. **C is correct.** An equilateral triangle has three equal angles. A triangle has a total of 180°, so each angle must be 180° ÷ 3 = 60°.

17. **C is correct.** According to the graph, only 150 travel books were checked out during the month. This was the fewest for any of the categories listed.

18. **E is correct.** $8 + 6 + 4 = 18$; $9 + 3 = 12$; and $18 - 12 = 6$.

19. **A is correct.** $2 \times 3 \times 5 \times 6 = 180$; $180 \div 30 = 6$.

20. **B is correct.** $^{20}\!/_5 = 4$; $6 \div {}^1\!/_6 = 6 \times {}^6\!/_1 = 36$; $^3\!/_5 \times 10 = {}^{30}\!/_5 = 6$; $7 + 5 = 12$. However, $5 \times {}^3\!/_4 = {}^{15}\!/_4 = 3{}^3\!/_4$, which is not a whole number.

21. **D is correct.** $4{}^3\!/_{10}\% = 0.043$.

22. **A is correct.** It costs d dollars to buy 6 chocolate bars. Since $15 = 2.5 \times 6$, it will cost $2.5d$ dollars to buy 15 chocolate bars.

23. **B is correct.** The angles in a triangle total $180°$. The two given angles measure $55° + 65° = 120°$. Thus the remaining angle must measure $180° - 120° = 60°$.

24. **C is correct.** There are $10 + 15 = 25$ marbles in the bag. If you pick one without looking, your chances of picking a white marble are $^{10}\!/_{25}$ or $^2\!/_5$.

25. **C is correct.** $^3\!/_4 - {}^5\!/_{12} = {}^9\!/_{12} - {}^5\!/_{12} = {}^5\!/_{12} = {}^1\!/_3$

Section 3 Reading Comprehension

1. **C is correct.** As she says in lines 17–18, "I have been trying to get before you business people to tell you what I am doing." Choice A can be eliminated because Madam Walker was not trying to demonstrate her products to the members of the league, but merely to make them aware of what she was doing and how well she was doing. Choice B is wrong because Madam Walker was addressing her remarks to the entire league, not just to Booker T. Washington. Choices D and E are wrong because there is no support in the passage for either choice.

2. **B is correct.** Madam Walker came to the podium uninvited and boasted of her business success. She tells how she came from "the cotton fields" to the "wash-tub" to the "cook kitchen" and finally to head of a thriving business. She says "I am not ashamed of my past; I am not ashamed of my humble beginning." Clearly, she is proud of her accomplishments.

3. **D is correct.** The reactions of the audience are indicated in parentheses throughout the speech. The fact that the audience reacted with applause, laughter and prolonged applause indicates that their reaction was favorable. It is unlikely that the audience would applaud and laugh if they were indifferent (choice A), angry (choice B), sad (choice C), or critical (choice E) of the speech.

4. **A is correct.** Walker uses the reference to her promotions from farm laborer, to laundress, to cook to show just how far she has come to get to her current position as head of a company that has made more than $63,000 (a great deal of money in 1912) in only seven years.

5. **E is correct.** Madam Walker says, "I am not ashamed of my past; I am not ashamed of my humble beginning. Don't think that because you have to go down in the wash-tub that you are any less a lady!" By this she means that hard work, like washing and scrubbing, is nothing to be ashamed of. Nor does it diminish a woman's status as a lady who is entitled to be treated with respect.

6. **B is correct.** The entire passage discusses the 1980 eruption of Mount St. Helens. The information provided is specific to a particular volcano, so choices A and D are incorrect. The passage does not tell readers what to do when a volcano erupts, nor does it appeal for action to protect the environment, so choices C and E are wrong.

7. **C is correct.** A 123-year slumber means that Mount St. Helens had no eruptions going back 123 years from 1980. That puts the last eruption at 1857. Choice A is wrong because if Mount St. Helens had been "sleeping" for 123 years, it must have been active 123 years ago. Choice B is wrong because there is nothing to support the idea that Mount St. Helens erupts every 123 years. Choice D is wrong because there is no mention of when

geologists began keeping records of volcanic eruptions. Choice E is wrong because if Mount St. Helens erupted 123 years ago, it could always erupt again.

8. **D is correct.** *Rising* is used in the following sentence: "Heat from a rising plume of volcanic ash melted glacial ice creating cement-like slurries of rock and ash called mudflows." Each of the answer choices is a possible meaning for *rising*. However, in context, the best meaning is *ascending*.

9. **B is correct.** The passage states that the geologists were not surprised by Mount St. Helens' awakening because they had been studying Mount St. Helens for many years and in 1975 they "published a report predicting Mount St. Helens was the volcano in the lower 48 states most likely to erupt by the end of the century." Thus, the assumptions they had made about Mount St. Helens based on extensive studies of deposits found around the volcano were proving to be correct. Choice A is wrong because the geologists predicted only that Mount St. Helens was the volcano "most likely to erupt by the end of the century." They did not predict when it would erupt, but only that it was most likely to erupt. The passage provides no information to support either choice C or choice D. Choice E describes an event leading up to the actual eruption, but it has nothing to do with why the geologists were not surprised by the volcano's awakening.

10. **C is correct.** The author's use of vivid language is illustrated by such words as "triggered," "blast," "flattened," "scoured," "billowed," and "swept." Examples of dramatic images include these: "In less than three minutes, 230 square miles of forest lay flattened," ". . .concrete-like mudflows that scoured river valleys," "A plume of volcanic ash and pumice billowed out of the volcano reaching a height of 15 miles and transformed day into night."

11. **E is correct.** A wasteland is barren land with no vegetation. The author mentions in lines 23–32 that the landslides flattened the forest and concrete-like mudflows scoured river valleys surrounding the mountain. Choice A is wrong because the landscape was covered in volcanic ash, not snow. Choice B is wrong because a wasteland is barren, not covered in waste matter. Choice C is wrong because the trees had been flattened and swept away. Choice D is wrong because the forest was no longer standing.

12. **C is correct.** The entire passage focuses on Paul's attitude and his demeanor. The red carnation in his buttonhole, the fact that he "was quite accustomed to lying," the contempt he shows for his teachers, all are evidence of the author's penetrating look at the character of the young man in question.

13. **D is correct.** A dandy is a man who is very concerned about his appearance and so pays great attention to his clothes. This description fits Paul who, even though his clothes were a trifle outgrown and the collar of his overcoat was frayed, still wore an opal pin in his necktie and a red carnation in his buttonhole.

14. **A is correct.** The faculty felt that the red carnation "was not properly significant of the contrite spirit befitting a boy under the ban of suspension." His jaunty dress made them feel that Paul was not sufficiently humbled by his suspension or sorry about his actions.

15. **D is correct.** As stated in lines 37–39, the real cause of the trouble "lay in a sort of hysterically defiant manner of the boy's; in the contempt which they all knew he felt for them, and which he seemingly made not the least effort to conceal." The insult mentioned in the passage is not a remark, but rather the way in which Paul "started back with a shudder and thrust his hands violently behind him" when his English teacher tried to guide his hand, so choice A is wrong. There is no mention of Paul's inability to control his temper or failure to complete assignments, so choices B and C are wrong. The passage mentions that Paul looked out the window during recitation, which indicates that he was inattentive in class (choice E), but this offense is minor in comparison to the obvious contempt he displayed toward his teachers.

16. **C is correct.** Paul is described as having a "defiant manner," which means he is impertinent, insolent, or boldly resistant to authority. There is no evidence in the passage that Paul is either *contrite* (remorseful) or *embarrassed* (ashamed), so choices A and E are wrong. He moves his hands violently behind him when the English teacher attempts to guide his hand, but his actions in general cannot be described as violent, so choice D is wrong. He comments on the lecture "with humorous intention," but there is no indication that others find him funny, so choice B is wrong.

17. **B is correct.** As stated in lines 31–33, the teachers stated the charges against Paul with "rancor and aggrievedness." *Rancor* means "bitterness" or "malice." Neither *turmoil*, which means "confusion," nor *resistance*,

which means "opposition," makes sense in relation to stating a case, so choices A and D are wrong. *Remorse* (choice C), which means "regret" and *dismay* (choice E), which means "discouragement" or "despair," do not fit the context of the passage.

18. **A is correct.** This story is presented as an example of the contempt which all the teachers knew Paul felt for them and which he seemed to make no effort to conceal. Paul shuddered and thrust his hands violently behind him when the English teacher attempted to guide his hand as he worked at the blackboard. "The insult was so involuntary and definitely personal as to be unforgettable. In one way and another he had made all his teachers, men and women alike, conscious of the same feeling of physical aversion." Paul's reaction had nothing to do with not being able to answer the question (choice B) or being hurt by the teacher (choice C). Likewise, there is no indication that he was afraid of the teacher (choice D) or that he wanted to strike the teacher (choice E). The passage says only that the teacher "could scarcely have been more hurt and embarrassed had he struck at her."

19. **B is correct.** This informative passage tells about the Homestead Act of 1862, including the provisions of the Act and the part it played in the settling of the American West. Choice A is wrong because the passage focuses on the Homestead Act, not on the settling of the West. Choice C is wrong because, although the passage briefly mentions the hard work and sacrifices of homesteaders, this is not the primary purpose of the entire passage. Choice D is wrong because the passage says nothing about extending the Act, and Choice E is wrong because "proving up" is just one of the provisions of the Homestead Act.

20. **D is correct.** *File* is used in the following sentence: "People interested in Homesteading first had to file their intentions at the nearest Land Office where they paid a fee of $10 to claim the land . . ." Although each of the choices is a possible meaning for the word *file*, the one that makes sense in the context of this sentence is *record* (choice D).

21. **C is correct.** As stated in paragraph 2, "A homesteader had only to be the head of a household and at least 21 years of age to claim a 160-acre parcel of land." Also, homesteaders were required "to live on the land, build a home, make improvements, and farm for 5 years before they were eligible to 'prove up.'" There is no mention of settlers having to be native-born citizens. In fact, the passage specifically mentions "newly arrived immigrants" as would-be homesteaders.

22. **D is correct.** As stated in paragraph 1, "Under this Act 270 million acres, or 10% of the area of the United States, was claimed and settled." Choice A is wrong because each homesteader could claim a 160-acre parcel of land, but that does not means that every person was entitled to 160 acres of land. Choice E is wrong because the passage states that 10 percent, not 30 percent, of all U.S. lands passed into the hands of individuals.

23. **A is correct.** The Homestead Act was designed "to spur Western migration." As a result of this Act, "270 million acres, or 10% of the area of the United States, was claimed and settled." Thus the Act served its purpose of helping settle the West.

24. **A is correct.** The first paragraph tells how manatees and dugongs came to be called sirenians because of their resemblance to the sirens, or sea nymphs, of Greek mythology. Choice B is wrong because, although the passage mentions that sailors—particularly those who have spent many months at sea—may have mistaken a manatee for a mermaid, it does not provide specific similarities between manatees and mermaids. Choice C is wrong because it was the sirens of mythology who are said to have caused shipwrecks. Choice D is wrong because the passage does not compare manatees and dugongs, except to say that both are sirenians. Choice E is wrong because it is the observer of the manatee, not the manatee itself, who might imagine that the manatee looks like a mermaid.

25. **D is correct.** The second sentence of the passage tells how the sirens "lured sailors and their ships to treacherous rocks and shipwreck with mesmerizing songs." *Mesmerizing* means "captivating," spellbinding," or "hypnotic."

26. **B is correct.** The last sentence of paragraph 1 ("Like the mythological creatures for which they were named, all sirenians living on earth today are vulnerable to extinction.") supports the idea that all sirenians are endangered. Information in the passage contradicts each of the other answer choices.

27. **C is correct.** Lines 11–15 ("Unlike . . . birth.") of the passage are devoted to listing the ways in which sirenians are different from and similar to other marine mammals.

28. **D is correct.** As stated in the passage, "sirenians eat only seagrasses and other aquatic vegetation." These grasses grow best in shallow waters where sunlight can penetrate. Additionally, "sirenians have an extremely low metabolism and zero tolerance for cold water"; therefore, they need the warmer temperatures of Florida's coastal waters. There is no mention of safety in the passage and, in fact, these very waters are also attractive to people in speedy powerboats, who pose the biggest danger to slow-moving manatees.

29. **B is correct.** The average adult manatee "weighs between 362–544 kilograms (800–1,200 pounds)" and eats "between 45–68 kilograms (100–150 pounds) of sea grass and water hyacinths a day!"

30. **D is correct.** Mood is the pervading spirit or feeling of a passage as transmitted by the author's choice of words. In this passage the day is described as "exceedingly cold and gray" with "no sun nor hint of sun, though there was not a cloud in the sky." There was "an intangible pall over the face of things, a subtle gloom that made the day dark." And yet, despite these warning signs, the man was not worried. Taken together this information imparts a sense of impending misfortune or foreboding.

31. **A is correct.** All of the choices are definitions of the word *broken*, but only choice A makes sense in context. The day was cold and gray when it came into being or dawned.

32. **B is correct.** Clearly, the facts that the man is traveling a little-used trail, is unconcerned about the extremely cold temperature, and does not notice that the dog seems almost hesitant to follow, indicate that the man is not accustomed to such activity. Choices A and D are wrong because the passage makes no mention of when the man is expected to meet the others, so it cannot be inferred that he is either behind or ahead of schedule. Choice C is wrong because, even though it is extremely cold out, there is no evidence, at this point, that the man is disoriented. Choice E is wrong, because although the passage makes note of the sun's absence, there is nothing to indicate the man expected to see it.

33. **B is correct.** The man knew that "at fifty below spittle crackled on the snow." Obviously he wanted to test the temperature of the air. When he found that this spittle "had crackled in the air," he realized that the temperature was even lower than fifty below, which indicates severe cold.

34. **E is correct.** The man was startled because he was not expecting to hear his spittle crackle before it fell to the snow. The passage goes on to say that the man knew "that at fifty below spittle crackled on the snow, but this spittle had crackled in the air. Undoubtedly it was colder than fifty below."

35. **C is correct.** The day is described as "exceedingly cold and gray." The man determines that "it was colder than fifty below," and yet he continues to travel on. Even the dog "was depressed by the tremendous cold. It knew that it was no time for traveling." Under these circumstances, the best description of the man's actions is foolish.

36. **D is correct.** As stated in lines 32–33, "The animal was depressed by the tremendous cold. It knew that it was no time for travelling. Its instinct told it a truer tale than was told to the man by the man's judgment." These statements clearly support choice D.

37. **D is correct.** Each of the answer choices is a meaning of the word *engaged*. However, only *participated* makes sense in place of the word *engaged* in this sentence: "I was asked not long ago to tell something about the sports and pastimes that I engaged in during my youth."

38. **C is correct.** The author's "trouble" was not being strong enough to get the corn back up on the horse once it had fallen off. Thus he was forced to wait until someone older and stronger came along to help before he could continue on his way to the mill. Choice A is wrong because the author does eventually get the corn to the mill to be ground. Choice B is wrong because, although the author mentions being afraid to travel at night, this is not the trouble referred to in line 15. Choice D is wrong because the author seems to know his way, and choice E is wrong because the mention of flogging comes much later in the passage.

39. **E is correct.** There is no mention of kidnapping in the passage. Choice A is wrong because the passage states "the road was a lonely one," and this contributed to the author's fear. Choice B is wrong because the passage

says "the woods were said to be full of soldiers who had deserted from the army," another reason for his fear. Choice C is wrong because the author had been told that "the first thing a deserter did to a Negro boy when he found him alone was to cut off his ears." Choice D is wrong because the author knew that when he was late he would "always get a severe scolding or a flogging."

40. **B is correct.** The author recounts the events of his youth analytically, He tells that "there was no period of my life that was devoted to play," and mentions, "From the time that I can remember anything, almost every day of my life has been occupied in some kind of labur." He relates his experience in taking the corn to the mill to be ground, and although he says he dreaded it and mentions crying as he waited for help, he relates the experience in a detached and matter-of-fact way. Certainly the author shows no longing to return to the days of his youth, so choice A cannot be correct. The language of the passage is too straightforward to be described as hostile or indignant, thus eliminating choices C and E. And, while his story may seem sad to readers, the author does not appear to be consumed by sorrow over the days of his youth.

Section 4 Quantitative II

1. **E is correct.** $5 \times 8 - 16 = 24$; $16 \div 4 = 4$, and $24 \div 4 = 6$.

2. **B is correct.** $42 \div 7 \times 8 \times 5 = 240$; $240 \div 12 = 20$.

3. **D is correct.** $30/5 = 6$; $4 \times 12/16 = 48/16 = 3$; $16 \div 1/16 = 16 \times 16/1 = 256$; $10.2 + 12.8 = 23$. However, $5/9 \times 8 = 40/9 = 4\,4/9$, which is not a whole number.

4. **D is correct.** $46\,3/4\% = 0.4675$.

5. **B is correct.** It costs m dollars to buy 48 notepads. 30 notepads are $5/8$ of 48, so the cost of 30 notepads will be $5/8 \times m = 5m/8$ dollars.

6. **E is correct.**
   $3/7x = 18$
   $1/7x = 6$
   $x = 42$
   $1/2x = 21$

7. **D is correct.** $60 = x\%$ of 90
   $60 = 90x$ Solve for x.
   $x = \dfrac{60}{90} =$
   $x = \dfrac{6}{9} =$
   $x = \dfrac{2}{3} =$ Divide 2 by 3 to get 0.6666 or 67%

8. **C is correct.** The cube root is the number that, when multiplied by itself three times, results in the original number. In this case, $6 \times 6 \times 6 = 216$, so 6 is the correct answer.

9. **C is correct.** In this problem $\angle 6$ measures 90°. Thus $\angle 3$ also measures 90° Because the two sides of the triangle are equal, it is an isosceles triangle. That makes $\angle 1$ and $\angle 2$ equal. Since $\angle 3 = 90°$, that leaves 90° to be split equally between $\angle 1$ and $\angle 2$. So each angle measures 45°.

10. **E is correct.** To find the volume, multiply length × width × height. Since the object is a cube, all these dimensions are the same.
    $8 \times 8 \times 8 = 512$ cm³

11. **C is correct.**
$-10 - (-5 - 4)$
$= -10 - (-9)$
$= -10 + 9 = -1$

12. **A is correct.**
$3/4 + 1/2 + 2/3 - 5/6$
$= 9/12 + 6/12 + 8/12 - 10/12$
$= 23/12 - 10/12$
$= 13/12$
$= 1\,1/12$

13. **D is correct.** Use the formula $d = r \times t$ where d = distance, r = rate, and t = time.
$d = r \times t$
$175 = 50 \times t$
$t = 175/50$
$t = 3.5$ hours = 3 hours 30 minutes

14. **E is correct.** Let n be the number of students who won awards last year. Set up an equation:
$3n + 2 = 20$
$3n = 18$
$n = 6$

15. **B is correct.**
$3.4a + 8.7a = 38.72$
$12.1a = 38.72$
$a = 3.2$

16. **C is correct.**
$12 + -6 \times 3$
$= 12 + (-18)$
$= -6$

17. **C is correct.** At 3:00, the minute and hour hands on a clock form a right angle, which measures 90°.

18. **B is correct.** 9 ft² = 1 yd²; 216 ÷ 9 = 24.

19. **A is correct.** Set up a proportion:
$3/126 = x/924$
$3 \times 924 = 126x$
$2772 = 126x$
$2772/126 = x$
$22 = x$

20. **B is correct.** Set up a proportion:
$18/144 = x/100$
$(100 \times 18) = (144 \times x)$
$1800 = 144x$
$1800/144 = x$
$x = 12.5$

21. **D is correct.** The total number of pairs in the drawer is 3 + 5 + 4 = 12. If there are 4 pairs of blue socks, then the chances of picking a blue pair are $4/12$ or $1/3$.

22. **C is correct.** The least common multiple of a group of numbers is the least whole number (greater than 0) that is a multiple of all of the numbers. The least common multiple of 3, 4, and 18 is 36 (3×12, 4×9, 2×18).

23. **C is correct.** The greatest common factor of a group of numbers is the largest whole number that is a factor of all the numbers. The greatest common factor of 16, 24, 96, and 120 is 8.

24. **E is correct.** Convert to equivalent expressions. $3/5 = 6/10$; $0.8 = 8/10$; $1 1/2 = 1 5/10 = 15/10$. $6/10 < 8/10 < 15/10$.

25. **D is correct.** Convert to equivalent expressions: $5/6 = 10/12$; $1/4 = 3/12$;
$7/12 + 10/12 + 3/12 = 20/12 = 1 8/12 = 1 2/3$

SSAT Practice Test III

The following practice test is designed to be just like the real SSAT. It matches the actual test in content coverage and level of difficulty. The test is in five sections: Verbal, Quantitative I, Reading Comprehension, Quantitative II, and the Essay.

This practice test will be an accurate reflection of how you'll do on test day if you treat it as the real examination. Here are some hints on how to take the test under conditions similar to those of the actual exam:

- Find a quiet place to work and set aside a period of approximately 3 hours when you will not be disturbed.
- Work on only one section at a time, and use your watch or a timer to keep track of the time limits for each test part.

- Tear out your answer sheet and mark your answers by filling in the ovals for each question.
- Write your essay on the pages provided.
- Become familiar with the directions for each part of the test. You'll save time on the actual test day by already being familiar with this information.

At the end of the test you'll find Answer Keys for each section and explanations for every question. Check your answers against the keys to find out how you did on each section of the test and what test topics you might need to study more. Then review the explanations, paying particular attention to the ones for the questions you answered incorrectly.

SSAT Practice Test III

ANSWER SHEET

Section 1: Verbal

1. Ⓐ Ⓑ Ⓒ Ⓓ Ⓔ	21. Ⓐ Ⓑ Ⓒ Ⓓ Ⓔ	41. Ⓐ Ⓑ Ⓒ Ⓓ Ⓔ
2. Ⓐ Ⓑ Ⓒ Ⓓ Ⓔ	22. Ⓐ Ⓑ Ⓒ Ⓓ Ⓔ	42. Ⓐ Ⓑ Ⓒ Ⓓ Ⓔ
3. Ⓐ Ⓑ Ⓒ Ⓓ Ⓔ	23. Ⓐ Ⓑ Ⓒ Ⓓ Ⓔ	43. Ⓐ Ⓑ Ⓒ Ⓓ Ⓔ
4. Ⓐ Ⓑ Ⓒ Ⓓ Ⓔ	24. Ⓐ Ⓑ Ⓒ Ⓓ Ⓔ	44. Ⓐ Ⓑ Ⓒ Ⓓ Ⓔ
5. Ⓐ Ⓑ Ⓒ Ⓓ Ⓔ	25. Ⓐ Ⓑ Ⓒ Ⓓ Ⓔ	45. Ⓐ Ⓑ Ⓒ Ⓓ Ⓔ
6. Ⓐ Ⓑ Ⓒ Ⓓ Ⓔ	26. Ⓐ Ⓑ Ⓒ Ⓓ Ⓔ	46. Ⓐ Ⓑ Ⓒ Ⓓ Ⓔ
7. Ⓐ Ⓑ Ⓒ Ⓓ Ⓔ	27. Ⓐ Ⓑ Ⓒ Ⓓ Ⓔ	47. Ⓐ Ⓑ Ⓒ Ⓓ Ⓔ
8. Ⓐ Ⓑ Ⓒ Ⓓ Ⓔ	28. Ⓐ Ⓑ Ⓒ Ⓓ Ⓔ	48. Ⓐ Ⓑ Ⓒ Ⓓ Ⓔ
9. Ⓐ Ⓑ Ⓒ Ⓓ Ⓔ	29. Ⓐ Ⓑ Ⓒ Ⓓ Ⓔ	49. Ⓐ Ⓑ Ⓒ Ⓓ Ⓔ
10. Ⓐ Ⓑ Ⓒ Ⓓ Ⓔ	30. Ⓐ Ⓑ Ⓒ Ⓓ Ⓔ	50. Ⓐ Ⓑ Ⓒ Ⓓ Ⓔ
11. Ⓐ Ⓑ Ⓒ Ⓓ Ⓔ	31. Ⓐ Ⓑ Ⓒ Ⓓ Ⓔ	51. Ⓐ Ⓑ Ⓒ Ⓓ Ⓔ
12. Ⓐ Ⓑ Ⓒ Ⓓ Ⓔ	32. Ⓐ Ⓑ Ⓒ Ⓓ Ⓔ	52. Ⓐ Ⓑ Ⓒ Ⓓ Ⓔ
13. Ⓐ Ⓑ Ⓒ Ⓓ Ⓔ	33. Ⓐ Ⓑ Ⓒ Ⓓ Ⓔ	53. Ⓐ Ⓑ Ⓒ Ⓓ Ⓔ
14. Ⓐ Ⓑ Ⓒ Ⓓ Ⓔ	34. Ⓐ Ⓑ Ⓒ Ⓓ Ⓔ	54. Ⓐ Ⓑ Ⓒ Ⓓ Ⓔ
15. Ⓐ Ⓑ Ⓒ Ⓓ Ⓔ	35. Ⓐ Ⓑ Ⓒ Ⓓ Ⓔ	55. Ⓐ Ⓑ Ⓒ Ⓓ Ⓔ
16. Ⓐ Ⓑ Ⓒ Ⓓ Ⓔ	36. Ⓐ Ⓑ Ⓒ Ⓓ Ⓔ	56. Ⓐ Ⓑ Ⓒ Ⓓ Ⓔ
17. Ⓐ Ⓑ Ⓒ Ⓓ Ⓔ	37. Ⓐ Ⓑ Ⓒ Ⓓ Ⓔ	57. Ⓐ Ⓑ Ⓒ Ⓓ Ⓔ
18. Ⓐ Ⓑ Ⓒ Ⓓ Ⓔ	38. Ⓐ Ⓑ Ⓒ Ⓓ Ⓔ	58. Ⓐ Ⓑ Ⓒ Ⓓ Ⓔ
19. Ⓐ Ⓑ Ⓒ Ⓓ Ⓔ	39. Ⓐ Ⓑ Ⓒ Ⓓ Ⓔ	59. Ⓐ Ⓑ Ⓒ Ⓓ Ⓔ
20. Ⓐ Ⓑ Ⓒ Ⓓ Ⓔ	40. Ⓐ Ⓑ Ⓒ Ⓓ Ⓔ	60. Ⓐ Ⓑ Ⓒ Ⓓ Ⓔ

Section 2: Quantitative I

1. Ⓐ Ⓑ Ⓒ Ⓓ Ⓔ	11. Ⓐ Ⓑ Ⓒ Ⓓ Ⓔ	21. Ⓐ Ⓑ Ⓒ Ⓓ Ⓔ
2. Ⓐ Ⓑ Ⓒ Ⓓ Ⓔ	12. Ⓐ Ⓑ Ⓒ Ⓓ Ⓔ	22. Ⓐ Ⓑ Ⓒ Ⓓ Ⓔ
3. Ⓐ Ⓑ Ⓒ Ⓓ Ⓔ	13. Ⓐ Ⓑ Ⓒ Ⓓ Ⓔ	23. Ⓐ Ⓑ Ⓒ Ⓓ Ⓔ
4. Ⓐ Ⓑ Ⓒ Ⓓ Ⓔ	14. Ⓐ Ⓑ Ⓒ Ⓓ Ⓔ	24. Ⓐ Ⓑ Ⓒ Ⓓ Ⓔ
5. Ⓐ Ⓑ Ⓒ Ⓓ Ⓔ	15. Ⓐ Ⓑ Ⓒ Ⓓ Ⓔ	25. Ⓐ Ⓑ Ⓒ Ⓓ Ⓔ
6. Ⓐ Ⓑ Ⓒ Ⓓ Ⓔ	16. Ⓐ Ⓑ Ⓒ Ⓓ Ⓔ	
7. Ⓐ Ⓑ Ⓒ Ⓓ Ⓔ	17. Ⓐ Ⓑ Ⓒ Ⓓ Ⓔ	
8. Ⓐ Ⓑ Ⓒ Ⓓ Ⓔ	18. Ⓐ Ⓑ Ⓒ Ⓓ Ⓔ	
9. Ⓐ Ⓑ Ⓒ Ⓓ Ⓔ	19. Ⓐ Ⓑ Ⓒ Ⓓ Ⓔ	
10. Ⓐ Ⓑ Ⓒ Ⓓ Ⓔ	20. Ⓐ Ⓑ Ⓒ Ⓓ Ⓔ	

Section 3: Reading Comprehension

1. Ⓐ Ⓑ Ⓒ Ⓓ Ⓔ   17. Ⓐ Ⓑ Ⓒ Ⓓ Ⓔ   33. Ⓐ Ⓑ Ⓒ Ⓓ Ⓔ
2. Ⓐ Ⓑ Ⓒ Ⓓ Ⓔ   18. Ⓐ Ⓑ Ⓒ Ⓓ Ⓔ   34. Ⓐ Ⓑ Ⓒ Ⓓ Ⓔ
3. Ⓐ Ⓑ Ⓒ Ⓓ Ⓔ   19. Ⓐ Ⓑ Ⓒ Ⓓ Ⓔ   35. Ⓐ Ⓑ Ⓒ Ⓓ Ⓔ
4. Ⓐ Ⓑ Ⓒ Ⓓ Ⓔ   20. Ⓐ Ⓑ Ⓒ Ⓓ Ⓔ   36. Ⓐ Ⓑ Ⓒ Ⓓ Ⓔ
5. Ⓐ Ⓑ Ⓒ Ⓓ Ⓔ   21. Ⓐ Ⓑ Ⓒ Ⓓ Ⓔ   37. Ⓐ Ⓑ Ⓒ Ⓓ Ⓔ
6. Ⓐ Ⓑ Ⓒ Ⓓ Ⓔ   22. Ⓐ Ⓑ Ⓒ Ⓓ Ⓔ   38. Ⓐ Ⓑ Ⓒ Ⓓ Ⓔ
7. Ⓐ Ⓑ Ⓒ Ⓓ Ⓔ   23. Ⓐ Ⓑ Ⓒ Ⓓ Ⓔ   39. Ⓐ Ⓑ Ⓒ Ⓓ Ⓔ
8. Ⓐ Ⓑ Ⓒ Ⓓ Ⓔ   24. Ⓐ Ⓑ Ⓒ Ⓓ Ⓔ   40. Ⓐ Ⓑ Ⓒ Ⓓ Ⓔ
9. Ⓐ Ⓑ Ⓒ Ⓓ Ⓔ   25. Ⓐ Ⓑ Ⓒ Ⓓ Ⓔ
10. Ⓐ Ⓑ Ⓒ Ⓓ Ⓔ   26. Ⓐ Ⓑ Ⓒ Ⓓ Ⓔ
11. Ⓐ Ⓑ Ⓒ Ⓓ Ⓔ   27. Ⓐ Ⓑ Ⓒ Ⓓ Ⓔ
12. Ⓐ Ⓑ Ⓒ Ⓓ Ⓔ   28. Ⓐ Ⓑ Ⓒ Ⓓ Ⓔ
13. Ⓐ Ⓑ Ⓒ Ⓓ Ⓔ   29. Ⓐ Ⓑ Ⓒ Ⓓ Ⓔ
14. Ⓐ Ⓑ Ⓒ Ⓓ Ⓔ   30. Ⓐ Ⓑ Ⓒ Ⓓ Ⓔ
15. Ⓐ Ⓑ Ⓒ Ⓓ Ⓔ   31. Ⓐ Ⓑ Ⓒ Ⓓ Ⓔ
16. Ⓐ Ⓑ Ⓒ Ⓓ Ⓔ   32. Ⓐ Ⓑ Ⓒ Ⓓ Ⓔ

Section 4: Quantitative II

1. Ⓐ Ⓑ Ⓒ Ⓓ Ⓔ   11. Ⓐ Ⓑ Ⓒ Ⓓ Ⓔ   21. Ⓐ Ⓑ Ⓒ Ⓓ Ⓔ
2. Ⓐ Ⓑ Ⓒ Ⓓ Ⓔ   12. Ⓐ Ⓑ Ⓒ Ⓓ Ⓔ   22. Ⓐ Ⓑ Ⓒ Ⓓ Ⓔ
3. Ⓐ Ⓑ Ⓒ Ⓓ Ⓔ   13. Ⓐ Ⓑ Ⓒ Ⓓ Ⓔ   23. Ⓐ Ⓑ Ⓒ Ⓓ Ⓔ
4. Ⓐ Ⓑ Ⓒ Ⓓ Ⓔ   14. Ⓐ Ⓑ Ⓒ Ⓓ Ⓔ   24. Ⓐ Ⓑ Ⓒ Ⓓ Ⓔ
5. Ⓐ Ⓑ Ⓒ Ⓓ Ⓔ   15. Ⓐ Ⓑ Ⓒ Ⓓ Ⓔ   25. Ⓐ Ⓑ Ⓒ Ⓓ Ⓔ
6. Ⓐ Ⓑ Ⓒ Ⓓ Ⓔ   16. Ⓐ Ⓑ Ⓒ Ⓓ Ⓔ
7. Ⓐ Ⓑ Ⓒ Ⓓ Ⓔ   17. Ⓐ Ⓑ Ⓒ Ⓓ Ⓔ
8. Ⓐ Ⓑ Ⓒ Ⓓ Ⓔ   18. Ⓐ Ⓑ Ⓒ Ⓓ Ⓔ
9. Ⓐ Ⓑ Ⓒ Ⓓ Ⓔ   19. Ⓐ Ⓑ Ⓒ Ⓓ Ⓔ
10. Ⓐ Ⓑ Ⓒ Ⓓ Ⓔ   20. Ⓐ Ⓑ Ⓒ Ⓓ Ⓔ

Time: 30 Minutes
60 Questions

This section includes two different types of questions: synonyms and analogies. There are directions and a sample question for each question type.

Directions: Each of the following questions consists of a word in capital letters followed by five words or phrases. Select the one word or phrase that means most nearly the same as the word in capital letters.

Sample Question:

> ESSENTIAL:
> (A) dire
> (B) confusing
> (C) vital
> (D) expert
> (E) honest
>
> Correct Answer: C

1. BIAS:
   (A) preference
   (B) conversion
   (C) resolution
   (D) predicament
   (E) conclusion

2. INHABIT:
   (A) continue
   (B) confirm
   (C) surround
   (D) dwell
   (E) exhibit

3. GENEROUS:
   (A) beneficial
   (B) precocious
   (C) sociable
   (D) garrulous
   (E) benevolent

4. AGGREGATE:
   (A) median
   (B) agent
   (C) organization
   (D) total
   (E) equipment

5. IMPLEMENT:
   (A) idea
   (B) detail
   (C) instrument
   (D) component
   (E) property

6. GRACIOUSLY:
   (A) gratefully
   (B) kindly
   (C) easily
   (D) comfortably
   (E) readily

GO ON TO THE NEXT PAGE.

7. MEANDER:
   (A) manage
   (B) exercise
   (C) review
   (D) wander
   (E) delete

8. CONCUR:
   (A) alleviate
   (B) conspire
   (C) agree
   (D) contribute
   (E) congeal

9. AGILE:
   (A) able
   (B) provocative
   (C) listless
   (D) nimble
   (E) willful

10. ADDITION:
    (A) inclusion
    (B) nucleus
    (C) origin
    (D) antecedent
    (E) inception

11. PROCLIVITY:
    (A) effulgence
    (B) inclination
    (C) finesse
    (D) resurgence
    (E) weakness

12. PERSISTENT:
    (A) intelligent
    (B) perceptible
    (C) considerable
    (D) pretentious
    (E) determined

13. TEMPERATE:
    (A) sweet
    (B) moderate
    (C) peckish
    (D) warm
    (E) memorable

14. ENCOURAGE:
    (A) foster
    (B) conduct
    (C) determine
    (D) develop
    (E) cope

15. SCOLD:
    (A) scream
    (B) incense
    (C) berate
    (D) seethe
    (E) infuriate

16. IRREGULAR:
    (A) irrelevant
    (B) eccentric
    (C) irrespective
    (D) sporadic
    (E) preternatural

17. COMMENCEMENT:
    (A) justification
    (B) beginning
    (C) announcement
    (D) experience
    (E) conclusion

18. POROUS:
    (A) confident
    (B) ruinous
    (C) soluble
    (D) permeable
    (E) clever

19. CRITICIZE:
    (A) abuse
    (B) disparage
    (C) avenge
    (D) impale
    (E) hinder

20. ACQUIRE:
    (A) abstain
    (B) prefer
    (C) taste
    (D) produce
    (E) procure

GO ON TO THE NEXT PAGE.

21. DELUGE:
    (A) defer
    (B) delineate
    (C) overwhelm
    (D) thrash
    (E) facilitate

22. VENERABLE:
    (A) respected
    (B) bright
    (C) varied
    (D) trivial
    (E) measured

23. OBVIOUSLY:
    (A) substantially
    (B) momentously
    (C) allegedly
    (D) comprehensively
    (E) apparently

24. CERTAINTY:
    (A) agreement
    (B) conjecture
    (C) suspicion
    (D) assurance
    (E) belief

25. INCESSANT:
    (A) annoyed
    (B) disturbed
    (C) constant
    (D) lachrymose
    (E) irrevocable

26. VAGUE:
    (A) obsolete
    (B) nebulous
    (C) precocious
    (D) vexed
    (E) ponderous

27. SIGNIFY:
    (A) indicate
    (B) dedicate
    (C) assail
    (D) ratify
    (E) imagine

28. ACQUIESCE:
    (A) compare
    (B) remit
    (C) negotiate
    (D) comply
    (E) suffer

29. DIVISIVE:
    (A) factious
    (B) contiguous
    (C) variegated
    (D) diverse
    (E) prolific

30. ACCORD:
    (A) violation
    (B) description
    (C) recognition
    (D) settlement
    (E) condition

GO ON TO THE NEXT PAGE.

Directions: The questions that follow ask you to find relationships between words. For each question select the answer choice that best completes the meaning of the sentence.

Sample Question:

Swim is to pool as
(A) fork is to plate
(B) sweep is to broom
(C) clean is to kitchen
(D) sleep is to bed
(E) trot is to horse

Correct Answer: D
Choice D is correct because a pool is a place to swim just as a bed is a place to sleep.

---

31. Moist is to arid as sublime is to
    (A) majestic
    (B) dull
    (C) bright
    (D) foreboding
    (E) deserted

32. Saddle is to horse as
    (A) dog is to leash
    (B) cat is to collar
    (C) car is to driver
    (D) surfer is to surfboard
    (E) cushion is to chair

33. Jazz is to music as
    (A) projector is to film
    (B) brush is to paint
    (C) sing is to perform
    (D) tap is to dance
    (E) novel is to fiction

34. Kangaroo is to hop as snake is to
    (A) rattle
    (B) bite
    (C) swallow
    (D) coil
    (E) slither

35. Bowling is to lane as
    (A) soccer is to field
    (B) tennis is to net
    (C) rink is to hockey
    (D) kitchen is to dinner
    (E) court is to basketball

36. Water is to wave as
    (A) shell is to egg
    (B) cloud is to sky
    (C) fire is to flame
    (D) galaxy is to planet
    (E) tree is to leaf

37. Brief is to time as short is to
    (A) cake
    (B) travel
    (C) stop
    (D) substantial
    (E) distance

38. Square is to cube as circle is to
    (A) sphere
    (B) pyramid
    (C) cylindrical
    (D) round
    (E) perimeter

39. Select is to choose as
    (A) accept is to deny
    (B) pardon is to excuse
    (C) smile is to laugh
    (D) rid is to leave
    (E) squander is to skimp

40. Teaspoon is to tablespoon as pint is to
    (A) measure
    (B) liter
    (C) cup
    (D) quart
    (E) volume

GO ON TO THE NEXT PAGE.

41. Darkness is to light as
    (A) garment is to dry
    (B) color is to contrast
    (C) gap is to hole
    (D) calm is to quiet
    (E) silence is to sound

42. Husk is to corn as
    (A) shell is to nut
    (B) stem is to apple
    (C) egg is to yolk
    (D) sunflower is to seed
    (E) drain is to water

43. Order is to sequence as
    (A) number is to line
    (B) schedule is to plan
    (C) beginning is to end
    (D) manage is to discipline
    (E) wedding is to marriage

44. Dock is to boat as
    (A) sea is to submarine
    (B) hangar is to airplane
    (C) trailer is to truck
    (D) lot is to parking
    (E) car is to garage

45. Compass is to circle as ruler is to
    (A) angle
    (B) rectangle
    (C) line
    (D) straight
    (E) measure

46. Skin is to hair as
    (A) shower is to cap
    (B) meow is to kitten
    (C) sand is to beach
    (D) stem is to petal
    (E) volume is to sound

47. Sugar is to cake as
    (A) seat is to stadium
    (B) tennis is to racket
    (C) thumb is to finger
    (D) smile is to teeth
    (E) bird is to wing

48. Chill is to freeze as giggle is to
    (A) smile
    (B) smirk
    (C) guffaw
    (D) hysterical
    (E) gasp

49. Silk is to worm as
    (A) honey is to bee
    (B) corn is to pop
    (C) bread is to wheat
    (D) egg is to chicken
    (E) frog is to croak

50. Dawn is to dusk as
    (A) shriek is to scream
    (B) start is to finish
    (C) drink is to eat
    (D) study is to learn
    (E) copy is to trace

51. Astronomer is to stars as biologist is to
    (A) earth
    (B) water
    (C) stars
    (D) rocks
    (E) life

52. Weaving is to loom as
    (A) brick is to building
    (B) diving is to swim
    (C) singing is to song
    (D) cooking is to stove
    (E) rolling is to ball

53. Celsius is to Fahrenheit as kilometer is to
    (A) distance
    (B) mile
    (C) gallon
    (D) inch
    (E) yard

54. Express is to state as
    (A) communicate is to write
    (B) restructure is to rebuild
    (C) defy is to intimidate
    (D) shorten is to abbreviate
    (E) tease is to mock

GO ON TO THE NEXT PAGE.

55. Hang is to dry as soak is to
    (A) vanquish
    (B) annihilate
    (C) saturate
    (D) roust
    (E) render

56. Salamander is to amphibian as kangaroo is to
    (A) pouch
    (B) land
    (C) koala
    (D) mammal
    (E) hop

57. Median is to highway as
    (A) diameter is to circle
    (B) tower is to signal
    (C) seam is to stitch
    (D) tree is to axe
    (E) razor is to beard

58. Filter is to coffeepot as
    (A) bandage is to wound
    (B) screen is to window
    (C) hole is to cover
    (D) lid is to pot
    (E) bottle is to cap

59. Stream is to drop as boulder is to
    (A) fountain
    (B) gorge
    (C) pebble
    (D) mountain
    (E) crater

60. Find is to locate as
    (A) convey is to exemplify
    (B) puzzle is to quiz
    (C) dig is to diminish
    (D) disguise is to masquerade
    (E) perceive is to interject

STOP!
If you finish before time is up, check your work on this section only.

Time: 30 Minutes
25 Questions

Directions: For each of the following questions, mark the letter of your choice on the answer sheet.

1. Andre had a birthday party and spent $12.98 on balloons, $47.23 on party favors, $22.97 on a cake, $14.77 on ice cream, and $15.00 on invitations. How much did Andre spend on the party?
   (A) $87.25
   (B) $112.95
   (C) $125.20
   (D) $127.30
   (E) $131.50

2. Bob's iPod contains 800 songs. If 240 songs are either jazz or rap songs, what percent of his collection is jazz or rap?
   (A) 12%
   (B) 15%
   (C) 20%
   (D) 25%
   (E) 30%

3. Matt took a bike trip. On the first day he rode 15 miles. On the second day he rode 35 miles, and the third day he rested. On the fourth day he rode 57 miles, and on the fifth day he rode 43 miles. What is the average number of miles that he rode per day?
   (A) 25
   (B) 27
   (C) 30
   (D) 32
   (E) 34

4. Aaron has 256 cans of soup that he needs to pack into boxes that hold 30 cans each. How many cans of soup are left over after he fills as many boxes as he can?
   (A) 4
   (B) 16
   (C) 18
   (D) 22
   (E) 24

5. An obtuse angle is an angle that measures
   (A) less than 90°
   (B) exactly 90°
   (C) between 90° and 180°
   (D) exactly 180°
   (E) greater than 180°

6. Two numbers add to 1,500. One number is 4 times the size of the other. What are the two numbers?
   (A) 300, 1,200
   (B) 200, 1,300
   (C) 500, 1,000
   (D) 750, 750
   (E) 800, 700

7. A box of laundry soap contains 200 oz. If the cost for 5 ounces is 10 cents, how much does the box of soap cost?
   (A) $2.80
   (B) $3.10
   (C) $3.60
   (D) $3.80
   (E) $4.00

GO ON TO THE NEXT PAGE.

8. A computer is priced at $1,800. Next week it will be on sale for $270 less. What percent of the current price will Blythe save if she buys the computer next week?
   (A) 10%
   (B) 12%
   (C) 15%
   (D) 20%
   (E) 25%

9. In the figure shown, lines *AB* and *CD* are parallel and ∠1 measures 120°. What is the measure of ∠2?

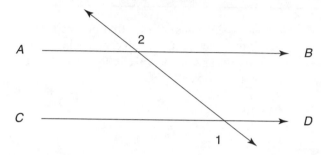

   (A) 40°
   (B) 60°
   (C) 75°
   (D) 90°
   (E) 120°

10. High school students were asked to pick their favorite kind of birthday party. The results are shown in the chart below. Which kind of party did the fewest students pick?

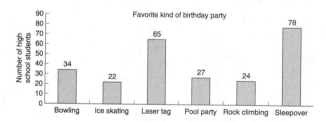

   (A) bowling
   (B) ice skating
   (C) laser tag
   (D) rock climbing
   (E) sleepover

11. It costs *m* dollars to buy 24 cookies. At the same rate, how many dollars will it cost to buy 6 cookies?
    (A) $\frac{m}{4}$

    (B) $\frac{m}{6}$

    (C) 4*m*
    (D) 6*m*
    (E) 24*m*

12. 18 ÷ ³/₄ =
    (A) 3
    (B) 6
    (C) 12
    (D) 24
    (E) 30

13. A rectangular garden is 40 yards long and 15 yards wide. Darryl runs once around the edge of the garden. How far does Darryl run?
    (A) 55 yards
    (B) 80 yards
    (C) 100 yards
    (D) 110 yards
    (E) 120 yards

14. In the figure shown, if ∠1 measures 35°, what is the measure of ∠2?

    (A) 145°
    (B) 95°
    (C) 65°
    (D) 45°
    (E) 35°

15. If 4 × 3 × _____ = 5 × 4 + 4, then _____ =
    (A) 2
    (B) 3
    (C) 4
    (D) 5
    (E) 6

16. 6 × 2 × 5 × 7 is equal to the product of 60 and
    (A) 6
    (B) 7
    (C) 8
    (D) 9
    (E) 11

GO ON TO THE NEXT PAGE.

17. Which of the following is NOT equal to a whole number?

   (A) $\dfrac{24}{6}$

   (B) $6 \times \dfrac{8}{16}$

   (C) $9 \div \dfrac{1}{9}$

   (D) $\dfrac{3}{5} \times 8$

   (E) $7.4 + 5.6$

18. $71\frac{1}{5}\% =$
   (A) 712
   (B) 71.2
   (C) 7.12
   (D) 0.712
   (E) 0.0712

19. In the rectangle shown, side a measures 13 cm and side b measures 36 cm. What is the perimeter of the rectangle?

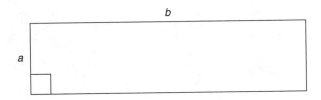

   (A) 49 cm
   (B) 98 cm
   (C) 196 cm
   (D) 469 cm
   (E) 512 cm

20. If ⅗ of a number is 18, then ½ of the same number is
   (A) 16
   (B) 15
   (C) 12
   (D) 9
   (E) 8

21. If Joanne tosses a 1–6 number cube, what is the probability that the cube number facing up will be even?

   (A) $\dfrac{1}{6}$

   (B) $\dfrac{1}{5}$

   (C) $\dfrac{1}{4}$

   (D) $\dfrac{1}{3}$

   (E) $\dfrac{1}{2}$

22. A $400 television is on sale for 15% off. What is the sale price?
   (A) $390
   (B) $385
   (C) $375
   (D) $350
   (E) $340

23. $16 \div -4 \times 2 =$
   (A) 10
   (B) 8
   (C) −4
   (D) −8
   (E) −12

24. In the triangle shown, side a is 4 ft long, side b is 6 ft long, and side c is 8 ft long. What is the area of the triangle?

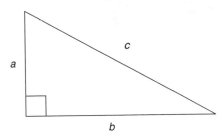

   (A) 12 ft²
   (B) 18 ft²
   (C) 24 ft²
   (D) 36 ft²
   (E) 42 ft²

GO ON TO THE NEXT PAGE.

25. Donna is d years old. Frank is f years old.
    Frank is 4 years younger than Donna.
    Which equation represents the relationship
    between Donna's and Frank's age?

    (A) $d = \dfrac{f}{4}$

    (B) $d = 4 - f$
    (C) $f = d - 4$
    (D) $f = 4 - d$

    (E) $d = \dfrac{4}{f}$

STOP!

If you finish before time is up, check your work on this section only.

Time: 40 Minutes
40 Questions

Directions: Each reading passage is followed by questions about it. Answer the questions that follow a passage on the basis of what is stated or implied in that passage. For each question, select the answer you think is best and record your choice by filling in the corresponding oval on the answer sheet.

"The President shall from time to time give to Congress information of the State of the Union and recommend to their Consideration such measures as he shall judge necessary and expedient."
5 Article II, Sec. 3, U.S. Constitution

On a cold January morning in 1790, George Washington personally delivered the first state of the union address to a joint meeting of the two bodies of Congress at Federal Hall in New York
10 City, which was then the provisional capital of the United States. Since Washington's first speech to Congress, U.S. Presidents have "from time to time" given Congress an assessment of the condition of the union. Presidents have used the opportunity
15 to present their goals and agenda through broad ideas or specific details. The annual message or "State of the Union" message's length, frequency, and method of delivery have varied from President to President and era to era.
20 In 1801, Thomas Jefferson discontinued the practice of delivering the address in person, regarding it as too monarchial for the new republic. Instead, Jefferson wrote out his address and sent it to Congress to be read by a clerk. This practice
25 continued for the next 112 years. The first president to revive Washington's spoken precedent was Woodrow Wilson in 1913.

For many years, the speech was referred to as "the President's Annual Message to Congress."
30 The term "State of the Union" did not become widely used until after 1935 when Franklin Delano Roosevelt began using the phrase.

With the advent of radio and television, the President's annual message has become not only
35 a conversation between the President and Congress but also an opportunity for the President to

communicate with the American people at the same time. Calvin Coolidge's 1923 speech was the first to be broadcast on radio. Harry S. Truman's
40 1947 address was the first to be broadcast on television. Lyndon Johnson's address in 1965 was the first delivered in the evening, and George W. Bush's 2002 address was the first to be broadcast live on the World Wide Web.

1. The author most likely included the quotation from the U.S. Constitution in lines 1–4 in order to
    (A) show how well the author knows the Constitution
    (B) illustrate the wording used in the Constitution
    (C) explain the reason for the State of the Union address
    (D) demonstrate how different Presidents have interpreted the same provision
    (E) point out the difference between a constitutional duty and a custom

2. The phrase "from time to time" in line 1 has been interpreted to mean
    (A) once in a while
    (B) in a timely manner
    (C) annually
    (D) at a convenient time
    (E) when time allows

GO ON TO THE NEXT PAGE.

3. U.S. presidents deliver State of the Union messages primarily because they
   (A) are following a tradition started by George Washington
   (B) are required to do so by the U.S. Constitution
   (C) need to fulfill campaign promises
   (D) want to thank their supporters
   (E) are trying to unify opposing factions

4. Thomas Jefferson's State of the Union address differed from Washington's address in that Jefferson
   (A) spoke first to the Senate and then to the House of Representatives
   (B) presented more frequent messages than did Washington
   (C) broadcast his message on radio
   (D) did not deliver his address in person
   (E) had his speech printed in the newspaper

5. In the first half of the twentieth century, the State of the Union address was forever changed by
   (A) the advent of radio and television
   (B) Thomas Jefferson
   (C) Lyndon Johnson
   (D) moving the site of the speech from New York to Washington, D.C.
   (E) newspaper coverage of the speech

6. Which of the following questions is answered by the information in the passage?
   (A) How many presidents have delivered spoken State of the Union messages?
   (B) When is the State of the Union message delivered?
   (C) How long is the average State of the Union message?
   (D) Why did Woodrow Wilson revive the spoken State of the Union message?
   (E) Which president delivered the first televised State of the Union message?

While they cannot be seen from the air, or felt aboard an ocean-going ship, tsunamis can cause as great a loss of life and property as their other natural disaster cousins—tornadoes and hurricanes.
5   The tsunami that occurred on December 26, 2004 was the worst tsunami ever recorded in terms of lives lost. Triggered by a powerful earthquake in the Indian Ocean, it ravaged the shores of Indonesia,

10   Sri Lanka, India, and Thailand, and even hit the east coast of Africa more than 2,300 miles away.

A tsunami is a series of ocean waves generated by any rapid large-scale disturbance of the sea water. Most tsunamis are generated by earth-
15   quakes, but they may also be caused by volcanic eruptions, landslides, undersea slumps or meteor impacts. In 1963 the term "tsunami" was adopted internationally to describe this natural phenom-enon. A Japanese word, it is the combination of the characters *tsu* (harbor) and *nami* (wave).
20   Tsunamis are often mistakenly called "tidal waves." However, the tides have nothing to do with the formation of tsunamis.

The waves radiate outward in all directions from the disturbance and can propagate across
25   entire ocean basins. For example, in 1960, an earthquake in Chile caused a tsunami that swept across the Pacific to Japan. Tsunami waves are distinguished from ordinary ocean waves by their great length between peaks, often exceeding
30   100 miles in the deep ocean, and by the long amount of time between these peaks, ranging from five minutes to an hour.

In the deep ocean, a tsunami is barely notice-able, causing only a small rising and falling of the
35   sea surface as it passes. Only as it approaches land does a tsunami become a hazard. As the tsunami approaches land and shallow water, the waves slow down and become compressed, causing them to grow in height. In the best of cases, the tsunami
40   comes onshore like a quickly rising tide and causes a gentle flooding of low-lying coastal areas.

In the worst of cases, a bore will form. A bore is a wall of turbulent water that can be several meters high and can rush onshore with great
45   destructive power. Behind the bore is a deep and fast-moving flood that can pick up and sweep away almost anything in its path. Minutes later, the water will drain away as the trough of the tsunami wave arrives, sometimes exposing great
50   patches of the sea floor. But then the water will rush in again as before, causing additional damage.

This destructive cycle may repeat many times before the hazard finally passes. Persons caught in the path of a tsunami have little chance to
55   survive. They can be easily crushed by debris or they may simply drown. Children and the elderly are particularly at risk, as they have less mobility, strength and endurance.

GO ON TO THE NEXT PAGE.

5

7. The main purpose of this passage is to
   (A) describe the tsunami of 2004
   (B) point out the differences between tsunamis and tidal waves
   (C) explain the origin of the term "tsunami"
   (D) provide general information about tsunamis
   (E) tell how to survive a tsunami

8. The passage names all of the following as possible causes of a tsunami EXCEPT:
   (A) earthquakes
   (B) volcanic eruptions
   (C) landslides
   (D) meteor impacts
   (E) tornadoes

9. The author cites the 1960 tsunami in Japan to show
   (A) how far a tsunami can reach
   (B) how devastating a tsunami can be
   (C) the importance of detecting a tsunami early
   (D) how quickly a tsunami can travel
   (E) the need for international cooperation in preventing tsunamis

10. Which of the following best describes the difference between a tsunami wave and a regular ocean wave?
    (A) Tsunami waves are more than 100 miles apart in the deep ocean, while regular ocean waves follow closely one after the other.
    (B) The length between peaks and the amount of time between peaks is greater in tsunami waves than it is in regular ocean waves.
    (C) Regular ocean waves are more harmful to young children, while tsunami waves are more are more likely to endanger the elderly.
    (D) Tsunami waves are more likely to affect boats in deep water than are regular ocean waves.
    (E) Tsunami waves are highest in deep water, while regular ocean waves are highest near the shore.

11. The style of the passage is most like that found in
    (A) a personal letter
    (B) an adventure novel
    (C) a weather report
    (D) a science textbook
    (E) a news article

12. A tsunami becomes a hazard as it approaches land because
    (A) the waves compress and grow higher in shallow water
    (B) the waves speed up as they approach the shore
    (C) the water drains away, exposing the sea floor
    (D) people get too close to the shore
    (E) beaches are popular with children and the elderly

13. As used in paragraph 5, the word "bore" means
    (A) hollow, cylindrical chamber
    (B) dull person
    (C) gauge
    (D) hole made by a drill
    (E) dangerous wave

To an Athlete Dying Young

The time you won your town the race
We chaired you through the market-place;
Man and boy stood cheering by,
And home we brought you shoulder-high.

5   Today, the road all runners come,
Shoulder-high we bring you home,
And set you at your threshold down,
Townsman of a stiller town.

Smart lad, to slip betimes away
10 From fields where glory does not stay,
And early though the laurel grows
It withers quicker than the rose.

Eyes the shady night has shut
Cannot see the record cut,
15 And silence sounds no worse than cheers
After earth has stopped the ears.

Now you will not swell the rout
Of lads that wore their honors out
Runners whom renown outran
20 And the name died before the man.

GO ON TO THE NEXT PAGE.

So set, before its echoes fade,
The fleet foot on the sill of shade,
And hold to the low lintel up
The still-defended challenge-cup.

25 And round that early-laurelled head
Will flock to gaze the strength less dead,
And find unwithered on its curls
The garland briefer than a girl's.

—A. E. Housman

14. The athlete described in this poem is most likely a
    (A) tennis player
    (B) swimmer
    (C) runner
    (D) football player
    (E) girl

15. The setting for this poem is a
    (A) victory celebration
    (B) funeral
    (C) field of laurels
    (D) rose garden
    (E) championship race

16. The "stiller town" referred to in line 8 means
    (A) old age
    (B) a country village
    (C) home
    (D) death
    (E) a quiet town

17. The author admires the athlete for
    (A) winning his race
    (B) bringing home a laurel wreath
    (C) setting a new record
    (D) returning to his hometown
    (E) dying young

18. The author is likely to agree with which of the following statements?
    I. Glory is a fleeting thing.
    II. It is best to die at the peak of one's fame.
    III. An athlete's fame lives on even after retirement.

    (A) I only
    (B) II only
    (C) III only
    (D) I and II only
    (E) I, II, and III

The earthquake shook down in San Francisco hundreds of thousands of dollars worth of walls and chimneys. But the conflagration that followed burned up hundreds of millions of dollars' worth of property. There is no estimating within hundreds of millions the actual damage wrought. Not in history has a modern imperial city been so completely destroyed. San Francisco is gone. Nothing remains of it but memories and a fringe of dwelling-houses on its outskirts. Its industrial section is wiped out. Its business section is wiped out. Its social and residential section is wiped out. The factories and warehouses, the great stores and newspaper buildings, the hotels and the palaces of the nabobs, are all gone. Remains only the fringe of dwelling-houses on the outskirts of what was once San Francisco.

Within an hour after the earthquake shock the smoke of San Francisco's burning was a lurid tower visible a hundred miles away. And for three days and nights this lurid tower swayed in the sky, reddening the sun, darkening the day, and filling the land with smoke.

On Wednesday morning at a quarter past five came the earthquake. A minute later the flames were leaping upward. In a dozen different quarters south of Market Street, in the working-class ghetto, and in the factories, fires started. There was no opposing the flames. There was no organization, no communication. All the cunning adjustments of a twentieth century city had been smashed by the earthquake. The streets were humped into ridges and depressions, and piled with the debris of fallen walls. The steel rails were twisted into perpendicular and horizontal angles. The telephone and telegraph systems were disrupted. And the great water-mains had burst. All the shrewd contrivances and safeguards of man had been thrown out of gear by thirty seconds' twitching of the earth-crust.

By Wednesday afternoon, inside of twelve hours, half the heart of the city was gone. At that time I watched the vast conflagration from out on the bay. It was dead calm. Not a flicker of wind stirred. Yet from every side wind was pouring in upon the city. East, west, north, and south, strong winds were blowing upon the doomed city. The heated air rising made an enormous suck. Thus did the fire of itself build its own colossal chimney through the atmosphere. Day and night this dead

GO ON TO THE NEXT PAGE.

calm continued, and yet, near to the flames, the wind was often half a gale, so mighty was the suck.

Wednesday night saw the destruction of the very heart of the city. Dynamite was lavishly used, and many of San Francisco proudest structures were crumbled by man himself into ruins, but there was no withstanding the onrush of the flames. Time and again successful stands were made by the fire-fighters, and every time the flames flanked around on either side or came up from the rear, and turned to defeat the hard-won victory.

Jack London from
"The Story of an Eyewitness"

19. The first paragraph of the passage establishes a mood of
(A) awe and disbelief
(B) desperate longing
(C) uncontrolled outrage
(D) cautious optimism
(E) heartfelt pity

20. The author describes the effects of the earthquake by relying on
(A) scientific knowledge
(B) comparisons to similar events in history
(C) confirmed statistical data
(D) vivid images appealing primarily to the sense of sight
(E) insights based largely on interviews with residents

21. In line 15, "nabob" most nearly means
(A) knave
(B) wealthy person
(C) elected official
(D) native son
(E) descendant of royalty

22. The statement that "All the cunning adjustments of a twentieth century city had been smashed by the earthquake" (lines 30–32) suggests primarily that
(A) the city had been reduced to a primitive existence
(B) the earthquake destroyed many of the city's newest buildings
(C) numerous irreplaceable mechanisms were lost during the earthquake
(D) only necessities such as plumbing and electricity remained intact
(E) many people died as a result of the earthquake

23. Which best describes the overall organization of the passage?
(A) a discussion of opposing viewpoints
(B) a description of events in spatial order
(C) a description of events in chronological order
(D) an enumeration of facts supported by statistical data
(E) a statement of opinion backed up by reasons

24. The primary purpose of the passage is to
(A) present a scientific explanation of the San Francisco earthquake
(B) provide an eyewitness report of the San Francisco earthquake
(C) convey the despair of San Francisco residents as they watched the destruction of their city
(D) describe the conditions that allowed the fires to spread
(E) praise the efforts of fire-fighters who battled bravely to put out the fires

Over 200 years ago, English physician Edward Jenner observed that milkmaids stricken with a viral disease called cowpox were rarely victims of a similar disease, smallpox. This observation led to the development of the first vaccine. In an experiment that was to prove a revelation, Jenner took a few drops of fluid from a pustule of a woman who had cowpox and injected the fluid into a healthy young boy who had never had cowpox or smallpox. Six weeks later, Jenner injected the boy with fluid from a smallpox pustule. Miraculously, the boy remained free of the dreaded smallpox.

In those days, a million people died from smallpox each year in Europe alone, most of them children. Those who survived were often left with grim reminders of their ordeals: blindness, deep scars, and deformities. When Jenner laid the foundation for modern vaccines in 1796, he started on a course that would ease the suffering of people around the world for centuries to come. By the beginning of the 20th century, vaccines for rabies, diphtheria, typhoid fever, and plague were in use, in addition to the vaccine for smallpox. By 1980, an updated version of Jenner's vaccine led to the total eradication of smallpox.

GO ON TO THE NEXT PAGE.

Since Jenner's time, vaccines have been developed against more than 20 infectious diseases such as influenza, pneumonia, whooping cough, rubella, meningitis, and hepatitis B. Due to tremendous advances in molecular biology, scientists are using novel approaches to develop vaccines against deadly diseases that still plague humankind.

Scientists use vaccines to "trick" the human immune system into producing antibodies or immune cells that protect against the real disease-causing organism. Weakened microbes, killed microbes, inactivated toxins, and purified proteins or polysaccharides derived from microbes are the most common components used in vaccine development strategies. As science advances, researchers are developing even better vaccines.

25. Which of the following best describes smallpox in the years before 1796?
    (A) It struck a million people a year in Europe alone.
    (B) It was common among milkmaids.
    (C) It was spread by cows.
    (D) It killed more than a million Europeans a year.
    (E) The few who survived the disease were left unharmed.

26. According to the passage vaccines have been developed for all of the following diseases EXCEPT:
    (A) pneumonia
    (B) scarlet fever
    (C) typhoid fever
    (D) rubella
    (E) meningitis

27. According to the passage, which of the following are components used in vaccine development?
    I. inactivated toxins
    II. weakened microbes
    III. purified proteins

    (A) I only
    (B) II only
    (C) III only
    (D) I and II only
    (E) I, II, and III

28. The vaccine produced by Jenner in 1796
    (A) completely eradicated smallpox
    (B) was effective only against cowpox
    (C) served as the basis for modern vaccines
    (D) could be used against rabies
    (E) wiped out typhoid fever

29. Which of the following best describes how vaccines work?
    (A) They directly attack the disease-causing organism.
    (B) They fool the body into producing antibodies that protect against the real disease-causing organism.
    (C) They contain deadly disease-producing organisms that are injected directly into the blood stream.
    (D) They contain antibodies that protect the body from deadly diseases.
    (E) They cause allergic reactions in most people.

The crimson hand, which at first had been strongly visible upon the marble paleness of Georgiana's cheek, now grew more faintly outlined. She remained not less pale than ever; but the birthmark, with every breath that came and went, lost somewhat of its former distinctness. Its presence had been awful; its departure was more awful still. Watch the stain of the rainbow fading out of the sky, and you will know how the mysterious symbol passed away.

"By Heaven! It is well-nigh gone!" said Aylmer to himself, in almost irrepressible ecstasy. "I can scarcely trace it now. Success! Success! And now it is like the faintest rose color. The lightest flush of blood across her cheek would overcome it. But she is so pale!"

He drew aside the window curtain and suffered the light of natural day to fall into the room and rest upon her cheek. At the same time he heard a gross, hoarse chuckle, which he had long known as his servant Aminadab's expression of delight.

"Ah, clod! ah, earthly mass!" cried Aylmer, laughing in a sort of frenzy. "You have served me well! Matter and spirit—earth and heaven—have both done their part in this! Laugh, thing of the senses! You have earned the right to laugh."

These exclamations broke Georgiana's sleep. She slowly unclosed her eyes and gazed into the

GO ON TO THE NEXT PAGE.

mirror which her husband had arranged for that purpose. A faint smile flitted over her lips when she recognized how barely perceptible was now that crimson hand which had once blazed with such disastrous brilliancy as to scare away all their happiness. But then her eyes sought Aylmer's face with a trouble and anxiety that he could by no means account for.

"My poor Aylmer!" murmured she.

"Poor? Nay, richest, happiest, most favored!" exclaimed he. "My peerless bride, it is successful! You are perfect!"

"My poor Aylmer," she repeated with a more than human tenderness, "you have aimed loftily; you have done nobly. Do not repent that with so high and pure a feeling, you have rejected the best the earth could offer. Aylmer, dearest Aylmer, I am dying!"

Nathaniel Hawthorne from "The Birthmark"

30. The birthmark on Georgiana's face had the shape of a
    (A) rainbow
    (B) rose
    (C) hand
    (D) butterfly
    (E) sun

31. It can be reasonably inferred from the story that Aylmer
    (A) is a poor man
    (B) does not love his wife
    (C) is trying to kill his wife
    (D) has performed an operation on his wife
    (E) is dying

32. Which of the following best describes what happens to the mark on Georgiana's cheek?
    (A) It takes a new shape.
    (B) It becomes very faint.
    (C) It stays the same.
    (D) It grows larger.
    (E) It turns a deep red color.

33. Which word best describes how Aylmer regards Georgiana at the end of the passage?
    (A) flawless
    (B) amusing
    (C) tiresome
    (D) brilliant
    (E) undesirable

34. Georgiana's feelings toward Aylmer could best be described as
    (A) bitter
    (B) angry
    (C) happy
    (D) tender
    (E) uncaring

35. Which is the best expression of the main idea of this passage?
    (A) Love is blind.
    (B) Birthmarks should be removed.
    (C) Perfection cannot be achieved on earth.
    (D) Beauty is in the eye of the beholder.
    (E) All's well that ends well.

The summers we spent in the country, now at one place, now at another. We children, of course, loved the country beyond anything. We disliked the city. We were always wildly eager to get to the country when spring came, and very sad when in the late fall the family moved back to town. In the country we of course had all kinds of pets—cats, dogs, rabbits, a coon, and a sorrel Shetland pony named General Grant. When my younger sister first heard of the real General Grant, by the way, she was much struck by the coincidence that some one should have given him the same name as the pony. (Thirty years later my own children had *their* pony Grant.) In the country we children ran barefoot much of the time, and the seasons went by in a round of uninterrupted and enthralling pleasures—supervising the haying and harvesting, picking apples, hunting frogs successfully and woodchucks unsuccessfully, gathering hickory-nuts and chestnuts for sale to patient parents, building wigwams in the woods, and sometimes playing Indians in too realistic manner by staining ourselves (and incidentally our clothes) in liberal fashion with poke-cherry juice. Thanksgiving was an appreciated festival, but it in no way came up to Christmas. Christmas was an occasion of literally delirious joy. In the evening we hung up our stockings—or rather the biggest stockings we could borrow from the grown-ups—and before dawn we trooped in to open them while sitting on father's and mother's bed; and the bigger presents were arranged, those for each child on its own table, in the drawing-room, the doors to which were thrown open after breakfast. I never knew

GO ON TO THE NEXT PAGE.

any one else have what seemed to me such attractive Christmases, and in the next generation I tried to reproduce them exactly for my own children.

Theodore Roosevelt from *An Autobiography*

36. This passage serves mainly to
    (A) recount the author's experience working on a farm in summer
    (B) provide a description of the author's summer home
    (C) describe the joys of being in the country
    (D) convey the author's love of family celebrations
    (E) explain the significance of the pony's name

37. In lines 8–13, the author includes the story of the pony's name primarily to
    (A) show his love for animals
    (B) poke good-hearted fun at his sister
    (C) point up the difficulty of raising a pony
    (D) show his love for his own children.
    (E) emphasize the friendship between the Roosevelt and Grant families

38. All of the following can be explicitly answered by information in the passage EXCEPT:
    (A) Where did the author and his siblings prefer to spend their childhood summers?
    (B) What types of pets did the author and his siblings have in the country?
    (C) How did the author and his siblings spend their time in the country?
    (D) Where did the author and his siblings stay while in the country?
    (E) How did the author feel about Thanksgiving?

39. The statement that "I never knew any one else have what seemed to me such attractive Christmases, and in the next generation I tried to reproduce them exactly for my own children" (lines 34–38) primarily suggests that the author
    (A) wanted his children to follow his example
    (B) missed the Christmases from his childhood
    (C) went to great lengths trying to recreate his childhood
    (D) carried on certain traditions because he thought his children would enjoy them, too
    (E) wanted his children to know the value of carrying on traditions

40. The passage is told from the point of view of
    (A) an adult looking back fondly on his own life
    (B) a child describing his life
    (C) an adult describing another person's life
    (D) a child describing events that happened to someone else
    (E) an adult filled with regret over the passing of time

STOP!
If you finish before time is up, check your work on this section only.

Time: 30 Minutes
25 Questions

Directions: For each of the following questions, mark the letter of your choice on the answer sheet.

1. If $28 \div 4 \times$ _____ $= 8 \times 9 - 16$, then ___ =
   (A) 2
   (B) 3
   (C) 6
   (D) 7
   (E) 8

2. $72 \div 9 \times 6 \times 12$ is equal to the product of 18 and
   (A) 16
   (B) 20
   (C) 24
   (D) 28
   (E) 32

3. Which of the following is NOT equal to a whole number?
   (A) $\dfrac{42}{7}$
   (B) $9 \times \dfrac{7}{16}$
   (C) $14 \div \dfrac{1}{14}$
   (D) $\dfrac{8}{12} \times 9$
   (E) $22.3 + 13.7$

4. $102\,^{3}\!/_{4}\% =$
   (A) 102.75
   (B) 10.275
   (C) 1.0275
   (D) 0.10275
   (E) 0.010275

5. It costs m dollars to buy 64 cans of soda. At the same rate, how many dollars will it cost to buy 48 cans?
   (A) $\dfrac{m}{4}$
   (B) $\dfrac{3m}{4}$
   (C) $3m$
   (D) $\dfrac{4m}{3}$
   (E) $5m$

6. If $^{7}\!/_{16}$ of a number is 42, then $^{1}\!/_{2}$ of the same number is
   (A) 58
   (B) 56
   (C) 52
   (D) 48
   (E) 44

7. $^{2}\!/_{3} \div ^{5}\!/_{6} =$
   (A) $\dfrac{4}{5}$
   (B) $\dfrac{5}{18}$
   (C) $\dfrac{15}{6}$
   (D) $2\dfrac{1}{2}$
   (E) $3\dfrac{5}{6}$

GO ON TO THE NEXT PAGE.

8. If the following is a right triangle and ∠2 measures 59°, what is the measure of ∠1?

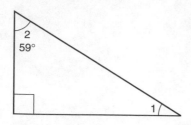

(A) 26°
(B) 31°
(C) 43°
(D) 52°
(E) 56°

9. $^1/_2 + ^1/_4 + ^3/_{16} =$

(A) $\dfrac{3}{5}$

(B) $\dfrac{5}{6}$

(C) $\dfrac{7}{8}$

(D) $\dfrac{15}{16}$

(E) $1\dfrac{1}{8}$

10. $^{15}/_{16} + 4^3/_8 =$

(A) $5\dfrac{1}{16}$

(B) $5\dfrac{5}{16}$

(C) $5\dfrac{9}{16}$

(D) $6\dfrac{1}{16}$

(E) $6\dfrac{1}{8}$

11. What is the greatest common factor of 75, 90, and 120?
(A) 5
(B) 10
(C) 15
(D) 20
(E) 25

12. What is the least common multiple of 13, 26, and 2?
(A) 2
(B) 6
(C) 7
(D) 13
(E) 26

13. $^{18}/_{25} =$
(A) 0.54
(B) 0.63
(C) 0.66
(D) 0.68
(E) 0.72

14. Which pair of fractions is equivalent?

(A) $\dfrac{2}{3}, \dfrac{5}{6}$

(B) $\dfrac{9}{12}, \dfrac{5}{6}$

(C) $\dfrac{3}{4}, \dfrac{7}{8}$

(D) $\dfrac{4}{10}, \dfrac{2}{5}$

(E) $\dfrac{2}{3}, \dfrac{5}{9}$

15. A fence along a road is divided into sections that are each 5 meters long. If the fence is 0.5 kilometers long, how many sections are there?
(A) 10
(B) 50
(C) 100
(D) 250
(E) 500

16. The drama club is spending $224 to put on a play. They plan to sell tickets at $3.00 each. If they sell n tickets, which of the following represents their profit after expenses?
(A) $3n - 224$

(B) $224 + \dfrac{n}{3}$

(C) $3n + 224$
(D) $224(n + 3)$

(E) $\dfrac{(n + 3)}{224}$

GO ON TO THE NEXT PAGE.

17. Christine spends 2 days a week painting houses and 3 days a week doing carpentry. If she earns $300 a day for painting and $240 a day for carpentry, how much does she earn in a week?
    (A) $1,280
    (B) $1,320
    (C) $1,360
    (D) $1,440
    (E) $1,460

18. The number of sixth-grade students in the hill school is 8 more than $\frac{1}{6}$ of the whole student body. If there are 144 students in the school, how many are in sixth grade?
    (A) 26
    (B) 30
    (C) 32
    (D) 36
    (E) 40

19. One kilometer is approximately equal to 0.6 mile. How many kilometers are in 8 miles?
    (A) about 6
    (B) about 7
    (C) about 11
    (D) about 13
    (E) about 15

20. $12 + (-8) + (-9) + 6 =$
    (A) −6
    (B) −3
    (C) 0
    (D) 1
    (E) 3

21. $-36 \div -12 =$
    (A) −12
    (B) −6
    (C) −3
    (D) 1
    (E) 3

22. At 6:00 o'clock, what is the measure of the angle formed by the minute and hour hands on a clock?
    (A) 45°
    (B) 90°
    (C) 120°
    (D) 180°
    (E) 360°

23. A clock shows 2:05. What time is it when 4 hours 58 minutes have passed?
    (A) 7:03
    (B) 6:54
    (C) 6:46
    (D) 6:38
    (E) 5:50

24. A circle has a radius of 1.35 meters. Wire costs 2¢ per centimeter. How much will it cost to stretch a wire between two points on the circle if it passes through the center?
    (A) $5.40
    (B) $5.56
    (C) $5.64
    (D) $5.72
    (E) $5.80

25. If Tino rides his bike at a steady speed of 9 miles per hour, how far will he ride in 3 hours 40 minutes?
    (A) 27 miles
    (B) 33 miles
    (C) 36 miles
    (D) 39 miles
    (E) 42 miles

STOP!
If you finish before time is up, check your work on this section only.

SECTION 5
Time: 25 Minutes

Directions: You will have 25 minutes to plan and write an essay on the topic below. Read the topic carefully. Jot down some brief notes on the scratch paper provided and organize your thoughts before you begin to write. Write your final essay on the ruled lines below. Write or print legibly, using the black pen that will be given to you at the test center. A copy of your essay will be sent to each school that will be receiving your test results.

Topic: Two heads are better than one.

Assignment: Do you agree or disagree with the topic statement? Support your position with examples from your own experience, the experience of others, current events, history, or literature.

_____

_____

_____

_____

_____

_____

_____

_____

_____

_____

_____

_____

_____

_____

_____

_____

_____

_____

_____

_____

_____

Answer Key

Section 1 Verbal

1.	A	21.	C	41.	E
2.	D	22.	A	42.	A
3.	E	23.	E	43.	B
4.	D	24.	D	44.	B
5.	C	25.	C	45.	C
6.	B	26.	B	46.	D
7.	D	27.	A	47.	A
8.	C	28.	D	48.	C
9.	D	29.	A	49.	A
10.	A	30.	D	50.	B
11.	B	31.	B	51.	E
12.	E	32.	E	52.	D
13.	B	33.	D	53.	B
14.	A	34.	E	54.	D
15.	C	35.	A	55.	C
16.	D	36.	C	56.	D
17.	B	37.	E	57.	A
18.	D	38.	A	58.	B
19.	B	39.	B	59.	C
20.	E	40.	D	60.	D

Section 2 Quantitative I

1.	B	10.	B	19.	B
2.	E	11.	A	20.	B
3.	C	12.	D	21.	E
4.	B	13.	D	22.	E
5.	C	14.	A	23.	D
6.	A	15.	A	24.	A
7.	E	16.	B	25.	C
8.	C	17.	D		
9.	E	18.	D		

Section 3 Reading Comprehension

1.	C	15.	B	29.	B
2.	C	16.	D	30.	C
3.	B	17.	E	31.	D
4.	D	18.	D	32.	B
5.	A	19.	A	33.	A
6.	E	20.	D	34.	D
7.	D	21.	B	35.	C
8.	E	22.	A	36.	C
9.	A	23.	C	37.	B
10.	B	24.	B	38.	D
11.	D	25.	D	39.	D
12.	A	26.	B	40.	A
13.	E	27.	E		
14.	C	28.	C		

Section 4 Quantitative II

1.	E	10.	B	19.	D
2.	E	11.	C	20.	D
3.	B	12.	E	21.	E
4.	C	13.	E	22.	D
5.	B	14.	D	23.	A
6.	D	15.	C	24.	A
7.	A	16.	A	25.	B
8.	B	17.	B		
9.	D	18.	C		

Answers and Explanations

Section 1 Verbal

1. **A is correct.** A *bias* is a *preference* or an inclination, especially one that inhibits impartial judgment.

2. **D is correct.** To *inhabit* is to live in or reside in—in other words, to *dwell*.

3. **E is correct.** *Generous* is an adjective meaning liberal in giving or sharing. Similarly, *benevolent* is an adjective meaning characterized by or suggestive of doing good, often in regard to charity.

4. **D is correct.** *Aggregate* is a *total*, constituting or amounting to a whole.

5. **C is correct.** An *implement*, used here as a noun, is a tool or *instrument* used in doing work—for instance, *a gardening implement*.

6. **B is correct.** To behave *graciously* is to behave in a *kindly* or warm manner.

7. **D is correct.** To *meander* is to move aimlessly and idly without a fixed direction—in other words, to *wander*.

8. **C is correct.** To *concur* is to be of the same opinion—to *agree*.

9. **D is correct.** *Agile* is an adjective used to describe someone or something that is quick, light, and moves with ease. The choice that best fits this definition is *nimble*.

10. **A is correct.** *Addition* is the act or process of adding something extra to a thing; something added. Similarly, *inclusion* is the act or state of being included; something included.

11. **B is correct.** *Proclivity* is a noun meaning a natural propensity, predisposition, or *inclination*.

12. **E is correct.** When someone is *persistent*, that person refuses to give up or let go—in other words, is *determined*.

13. **B is correct.** *Temperate* is an adjective meaning *moderate* in degree or quality.

14. **A is correct.** To *encourage* is to give support to or to cultivate. Similarly, to *foster* is to promote the development and growth of.

15. **C is correct.** To *scold* is to reprimand or to criticize harshly and usually angrily—in other words, to *berate*.

16. **D is correct.** *Irregular* is an adjective used to describe something that occurs at an uneven rate, occurrence, or duration. *Sporadic* can be used synonymously with *irregular*.

17. **B is correct.** A *commencement* is a *beginning* or a start.

18. **D is correct.** *Porous* is an adjective used to describe something that permits the passage of gas or liquid through pores or small spaces. *Permeable*, meaning that which can be permeated or penetrated, especially by liquid or gases, is its synonym.

19. **B is correct.** To *criticize* is to find fault with. Similarly, to *disparage* is to speak of in a slighting or disrespectful way.

20. **E is correct.** To *acquire* is to gain possession of. *Procure*, which means to obtain or acquire, is its synonym.

21. **C is correct.** To *deluge* is to *overwhelm* with a large number or amount.

22. **A is correct.** *Venerable* is an adjective, usually used to describe a person who commands respect by virtue of age, character, dignity, or position. A person who is described as venerable could similarly be described as *respected*.

23. **E is correct.** *Obviously* is defined as easily perceived or understood. *Apparently*, its synonym, is defined as readily understood.

24. **D is correct.** A *certainty* is something that is clearly established or assured—in other words, an *assurance*.

25. **C is correct.** *Incessant* describes something that continues without interruption—something that is *constant*.

26. **B is correct.** *Vague*, like *nebulous*, describes something that is not clearly expressed or is inexplicit.

27. **A is correct.** To *signify* is to make known, as with a sign or word—in other words, to *indicate*.

28. **D is correct.** To *acquiesce* is to consent or to *comply* passively or without protest.

29. **A is correct.** *Divisive* is an adjective used to describe something creating dissension or discord. Similarly, *factious* describes something of, relating to, produced by, or characterized by internal dissension.

30. **D is correct.** An *accord* is a *settlement* or compromise of conflicting opinions.

Explanations for Analogies

31. **B is correct.** The relationship in this question is one of contrasts. *Moist* is the opposite of *arid* just as *sublime* (meaning "inspiring awe" or "impressive") is the opposite of *dull*. Only choice B provides an adjective that is opposite in meaning.

32. **E is correct.** This sequence presents an analogy of part to whole, but it also wants you to take the comparison a step further and consider usage when discerning the right answer. A *saddle* sits atop a *horse* in much the same way that a *cushion* sits atop a *chair*.

33. **D is correct.** This stem provides another part-to-whole analogy. *Jazz* is a style of *music* just as *tap* is style of *dance*. No other answer choice offers a specific style of a thing paired with a broader reference to that thing.

34. **E is correct.** This is a fairly straightforward usage sequence that analogizes an activity (hop) to the animal that performs it. A *kangaroo hops* from one place to another just as a *snake slithers* from one place to another. *Coil* (choice D) is incorrect because it is the activity the snake performs in order to sleep or rest.

35. **A is correct.** This is a fairly straightforward usage sequence that analogizes an event (bowling) to the location it takes place (lane). You should be able to infer that *bowling* occurs on a *lane* just as *soccer* occurs on a *field*.

36. **C is correct.** Flip the words if you have trouble understanding this stem: *wave* is to *water* as *flame* is to *fire*. No other choice pairs a noun with another noun that suggests its form and motion. *Fire* takes the form of a *flame*; similarly, *water* can take the form of a *wave*.

37. **E is correct.** This sequence tests your familiarity of adjectives used to describe levels of contrast with nouns. A *brief* amount of *time* describes a short duration just as a *short distance* describes an abbreviated trip. No other answer choice matches the context of the stem with regard to describing a term of measurement.

38. **A is correct.** A *square* represented in three-dimensional form takes the shape of a *cube* just as a *circle* represented in three-dimensional form takes the shape of a *sphere*. Choice C is incorrect because *cylindrical* is an adjective which describes something of, relating to, or having the shape of a cylinder, not a noun.

39. **B is correct.** This is another question that tests your knowledge of synonym pairs. *Select* and *choose* are synonymous just as *pardon* and *excuse* are synonymous. Choice C is incorrect because, although both words denote pleasure or happiness, they are not synonymous. Choice E is incorrect because squander means "to fail to take advantage of," and skimp means "to provide for or supply inadequately."

40. **D is correct.** To answer this measurement analogy correctly, it will help you to know that an amount consisting of a *teaspoon* is less than an amount consisting of a *tablespoon*. So, following the pattern the stem establishes,

you will need to know which choice represents a greater measure than a *pint*. Choice B is incorrect because, although a liter is greater than *a pint*, this is a metric measurement. The other three measurements the stem provides are U.S. Customary measurements; therefore choice B is not a better answer than choice D. Choice C is incorrect because a cup is a measurement which is less than a pint, not more.

41. **E is correct.** This question provides another example of an analogy that tests your knowledge of contrasts of degrees. *Darkness* is the absence of *light* just as *silence* is the absence of *sound*. None of the other relationships offers a combination that defines one word by the absence of another; *garment* is not the absence of *dry* (choice A); *color* is not the absence of *contrast* (choice B); *gap* is not the absence of *hole* (C); and *calm* is not the absence of *quiet* (choice D).

42. **A is correct.** The relationship presented in this sequence is one of part to whole; however, this analogy goes a step further, and you will need to discern how in order to arrive at the correct answer. The *husk* is the outer covering of an ear of *corn* just as a *shell* is the outer covering of a *nut*. Therefore, choice A is correct. No other option presents this type of part-to-whole relationship.

43. **B is correct.** This sequence provides another example of an analogy involving words that are synonymous with one another. After reading the stem you should realize that *order* and *sequence* are synonyms. In order to select the correct answer, you will have to choose the option that also contains two words with similar meanings. *Schedule* and *plan* (choice B) is the only correct answer.

44. **B is correct.** Flip the words if you have difficulty with this sequence. A *boat* is kept at a *dock*, and similarly, a *plane* is kept in a *hangar*. Choice E may seem correct, but be careful; a closer look will reveal that this choice has *car* and *garage* in the incorrect order.

45. **C is correct.** This type of sequence is known as a usage analogy. Typically with this type of comparison, the stem will provide an instrument and a function of that instrument. You should be able to infer from the stem that a *compass* is used to draw a *circle*. Similarly, a *ruler* is used to draw a *line*.

46. **D is correct.** This question presents a part-to-part analogy. *Skin* and *hair* are both parts of the human body just as both *stem* and *petal* are parts of a flower. No other option presents two pieces that are part of a whole.

47. **A is correct.** The relationship presented in this sequence is one of part to whole. *Sugar* is one ingredient (part) of a *cake* just as a *seat* is one part of a *stadium*. Choice E is incorrect because, as it is written, the whole (bird) precedes the part (wing).

48. **C is correct.** This question tests your knowledge of degrees of contrast. To *chill* something is less extreme than to *freeze* it. Similarly, to *giggle* is less extreme than to *guffaw* (meaning "to laugh heartily and boisterously").

49. **A is correct.** By now, you have seen several types of analogies involving objects or individuals and activities. There is the object-to-activity analogy (*chisel* is to *carve*), as well as the individual-to-activity analogy (*tourist* is to *sightsee*). The sequence presented here is another variation, this time involving insects. To answer this question correctly, you will need to know that *worm* and *silk* appear in the stem because silk is produced by a species of worm. Similarly, *honey* is produced by *bees*.

50. **B is correct.** This question tests your knowledge of opposites. *Dawn* represents the beginning of daylight just as *dusk* represents the end of daylight. Only choice B offers a comparable contrast.

51. **E is correct.** This analogy asks you to make a correlation between an individual and what that individual studies. An *astronomer* studies the *stars* just as a *biologist* studies *life*.

52. **D is correct.** This is another usage sequence that analogizes an activity (weaving) to the apparatus used in that activity (loom). So choice D is correct because a *stove* is used for *cooking* just as a *loom* is used for *weaving*. No other option pairs an activity with an object used in that activity.

53. **B is correct.** This is a type of measurement question that compares metric measurements with U.S. Customary measurements. *Celsius* is the how temperature is measured with the metric system just as *Fahrenheit* is how temperature is measured with the U.S. Customary system. Similarly, *kilometers* are how long distances are

measured with the metric system just as *miles* are how long distances are measured with the U.S. Customary system.

54. **D is correct.** To *state* something is to *express* it just as to *shorten* something is to *abbreviate* it. No other option provides a pair of words with meanings that are synonymous.

55. **C is correct.** This type of sequence is referred to as an activity-to-result analogy. One way to dry something (clothes, for instance) is by hanging them. Therefore, *hang* is the activity and *dry* is the result. Similarly, when you *soak* something in water (say, a towel) the result is that you *saturate* it.

56. **D is correct.** To have a better chance at answering this part-to-whole analogy correctly, it will help if you know that a salamander is scientifically classified as an amphibian (meaning it can live on land or in water). Indeed, knowing this should make it easier for you to conclude that if a *salamander* is an *amphibian* then a *kangaroo* must be a *mammal*.

57. **A is correct.** A *median* divides two sides of the *highway*. In a similar sense, a *diameter* divides two sides of a *circle*.

58. **B is correct.** The *filter* in a *coffeepot* allows the liquid coffee to pass through but keeps out the coffee grounds. Similarly, a *screen* on a *window* allows air to pass through while keeping out larger pieces of debris, such as leaves.

59. **C is correct.** This sequence presents a relationship that is one of degree, with the first word being much larger than the second. A *stream* is a much larger body of water than a single *drop*. As well, a *boulder* is a much larger rock than a *pebble*.

60. **D is correct.** The analogy in this sentence is one of similarities. When you *find* an item you are looking for, you have *located* it. Likewise, when you *masquerade*, you *disguise* yourself as someone else. No other option offers a pair of words that share a similar meaning.

Section 2 Quantitative I

1. **B is correct.** This is a simple addition problem. Add the amounts of $12.98, $47.23, $22.97, $14.77, $15.00 to get the total of $112.95.

2. **E is correct.** To calculate the percent, divide the number of jazz and rap songs by the total number of songs. $256 \div 800 = 0.30$ To change that to a percent, move the decimal point two places to the right and add the percent sign to get the correct answer of 30%.

3. **C is correct.** To find the average, add up the numbers and divide by the number of numbers. In this instance the number of miles Matt rode adds to 150. The number of days is 5, so the average number of miles per day he rode is $150 \div 5 = 30$. Don't make the mistake of dividing by 4 because on one day Matt's number of miles was 0. That number needs to be used in calculating the average.

4. **B is correct.** If Aaron has 256 cans of soup to pack into boxes of 30, he can fill $256 \div 30 = 8$ boxes with 16 cans of soup left over.

5. **C is correct.** By definition, an obtuse angle is one that measures between 90° and 180°.

6. **A is correct.** You are told that two numbers add to 1,500 and that one of the two is 4 times the size of other. Create an equation:

$x + 4x = 1,500$
Solve for x.
$5x = 1,500$
$x = 300$
$4x = 1,200$
So the two numbers are 300 and 1,200.

7. **E is correct.** To calculate the answer, divide 200 by 5.
$$200 \div 5 = 40$$

   Multiply:
   $$40 \times \$0.10 = \$4.00$$

8. **C is correct.** Use the following formula: $\text{Percent of change} = \dfrac{\text{Amount of change}}{\text{Starting point.}}$

   In this problem we know that the amount of change is \$270 and the starting price of the computer is \$1,800. Substitute that information into the formula:

   Percent of change = \$270/\$1,800 = 0.15.

   Change that number to a percent by moving the decimal place two places to the right and add the percent sign. 0.15 = 15%

9. **E is correct.** Angles 1 and 2 are on opposite sides of the transversal, are outside the two parallel lines, and are not adjacent. They are therefore opposite exterior angles, which by definition have the same measure.

10. **B is correct.** According to the graph, ice skating was the least popular kind of party. It was picked by only 22 students, the fewest for any of the party types listed.

11. **A is correct.** It costs m dollars to buy 24 cookies. 6 cookies are $1/4$ of 24, so the cost of 6 cookies will be $1/4 \times m = m/4$ dollars.

12. **D is correct.** $18 \div {}^3/_4 = {}^{18}/_1 \div {}^3/_4 = {}^{18}/_1 \times {}^4/_3 = {}^{72}/_3 = 24$.

13. **D is correct.** The edge of the garden is its perimeter. To find the perimeter of a rectangle, add the lengths of the sides: 40 + 15 + 40 + 15 = 110 yards.

14. **A is correct.** The two angles together form a straight angle, which measures 180°. Therefore, $\angle 2 = 180° - 35° = 145°$.

15. **A is correct.** $5 \times 4 + 4 = 24$; $4 \times 3 = 12$; and $24 \div 12 = 2$.

16. **B is correct.** $6 \times 2 \times 5 \times 7 = 420$; $420 \div 60 = 7$.

17. **D is correct.** ${}^{24}/_6 = 4$; $6 \times {}^8/_{16} = {}^{48}/_{16} = 3$; $9 \div {}^1/_9 = 9 \times {}^9/_1 = 81$; $7.4 + 5.6 = 13$. However, ${}^3/_5 \times 8 = {}^{24}/_5 = 4\,{}^4/_5$, which is not a whole number.

18. **D is correct.** $71{}^1/_5\% = 0.712$.

19. **B is correct.** To find the perimeter, add the lengths of the sides: 13 + 36 + 13 + 36 = 98 cm.

20. **B is correct.**
    $${}^3/_5 x = 18$$
    $${}^1/_5 x = 6$$
    $$x = 30$$
    $${}^1/_2 x = 15$$

21. **E is correct.** Of the 6 numbers on the cube, 3 are even. So the probability that the number facing up will be even is ${}^3/_6$ or ${}^1/_2$.

22. **E is correct.** 15% of \$400 = 0.15 × 400 = \$60. \$400 − \$60 = \$340.

23. **D is correct.** $16 \div -4 = -4$.
    $$-4 \times 2 = -8$$

24. **A is correct.** To find the area of a triangle, use the formula $A = (^1/_2)bh$ where b is the base of the triangle and h is the height. Because the triangle shown is a right triangle, side a is the height. Substituting into the formula: $A = (^1/_2)(6)(4) = 12$ ft^2.

25. **C is correct.** If Frank is 4 years younger than Donna, the relationship between their two ages can be expressed by the equation $f = d - 4$.

Section 3 Reading Comprehension

1. **C is correct.** The quotation shows that the president has a duty to report to Congress on the State of the Union and to recommend necessary and expedient measures. This annual message to Congress came to be known as the State of the Union. Choice A is wrong because the use of the quotation does not necessarily indicate that the author is knowledgeable about the Constitution, but only about this particular provision. Choice B is wrong because, although the quotation does illustrate the actual wording of this section of the Constitution, it is not intended to illustrate the wording of the entire Constitution. Choice D is wrong because there is no demonstration of different interpretations of this provision. The differences cited are in the form, content and delivery method of the message, not in the need to report to Congress. Choice E is wrong because the passage does not distinguish between constitutional duty and custom. The report on the State of the Union is mandated by the Constitution.

2. **C is correct.** The Constitution requires the president to give Congress information on the state of the union "from time to time." Throughout the passage, the State of the Union message is referred to as the president's "annual message." Clearly, the phrase "time to time" has come to mean "annually."

3. **B is correct.** This information is found in the opening quote from the U.S. Constitution, which says that presidents have a constitutional duty to "give to Congress information of the State of the Union."

4. **D is correct.** Thomas Jefferson thought Washington's oral presentation was "too monarchial for the new republic," so Jefferson "wrote out his address and sent it to Congress to be read by a clerk."

5. **A is correct.** As stated in the last paragraph, "With the advent of radio and television, the President's annual message has become not only a conversation between the President and Congress but also an opportunity for the President to communicate with the American people at the same time." Choices B and C are wrong because Thomas Jefferson was president in the nineteenth century and Lyndon Johnson in the second half of the twentieth century. Choice D is wrong because Congress moved to Washington, D.C. in 1800, and choice E is wrong because newspaper coverage of the State of the Union message began long before the start of the twentieth century.

6. **E is correct.** As stated in the last paragraph, "Harry S. Truman's 1947 address was the first to be broadcast on television." None of the other questions is answered by information in the passage.

7. **D is correct.** Since there is no mention of how to survive a tsunami, choice E can be easily eliminated. Although the passage touches upon the tsunami of 2004 (choice A), the difference between a tsunami and a tidal wave (choice B), and the origin of the word "tsunami" (choice C), each of these choices is too narrow to cover the overall purpose of the passage, which is to provide information about tsunamis in general.

8. **E is correct.** As stated in the second paragraph, "Most tsunamis are generated by earthquakes, but they may also be caused by volcanic eruptions, landslides, undersea slumps or meteor impacts." Tornadoes are mentioned along with hurricanes, not as a cause of tsunamis, but rather as another kind of natural disaster.

9. **A is correct.** The author mentions the 1960 tsunami in Japan in the third paragraph: "The waves radiate outward in all directions from the disturbance and can propagate across entire ocean basins. For example, in 1960, an earthquake in Chile caused a tsunami that swept across the Pacific to Japan." The words "for example" indicate that the reference to Japan is intended to show how far the waves radiated from the earthquake in Chile.

10. **B is correct.** The answer to this question is found in paragraph 3 which says, "Tsunami waves are distinguished from ordinary ocean waves by their great length between peaks, often exceeding 100 miles in the deep ocean, and by the long amount of time between these peaks, ranging from five minutes to an hour." Choice A is wrong because the passage does not mention that regular waves follow closely one after the other. Choice C is wrong because it has no support in the passage. Choice D is wrong because the passage states that in deep water "a tsunami is barely noticeable, causing only a small rising and falling of the sea surface as it passes." Choice E is wrong because tsunami waves grow in height as they approach land and shallow water.

11. **D is correct.** This passage is full of the kind of strictly factual scientific information most likely to be found in a science textbook. Choice A can be eliminated because the passage has none of the folksy qualities of a personal letter. Choice B cannot be correct because the passage is clearly fact, not fiction. Choice C is wrong because the passage describes a natural disaster, not the weather, and choice E is wrong because the passage merely mentions the tsunami of 2004, but does not go on to provide the details of that particular event as a news article would.

12. **A is correct.** The answer to this question can be found in paragraph 4: "As the tsunami approaches land and shallow water, the waves slow down and become compressed, causing them to grow in height." In the best of cases the tsunami comes ashore like a rising tide causing flooding of coastal areas. In the worst of cases, a wall of turbulent water several meters high rushes ashore with great destructive power.

13. **E is correct.** All of the choices are meanings of the word "bore." However, only choice E is correct in context. As stated in the second sentence of paragraph 5, "A bore is a wall of turbulent water that can be several meters high and can rush onshore with great destructive power."

14. **C is correct.** Line 1 mentions that the athlete "won your town the race." "Runners" are also mentioned in lines 5 and 19, and line 22 mentions "the fleet of foot." All of these references make it obvious that the athlete in this poem is a runner. Choice E cannot be correct because the author addresses the athlete as "Smart lad" in line 9.

15. **B is correct.** The setting is revealed in lines 5–8: "Today, the road all runners come, Shoulder-high we bring you home, And set you at your threshold down, Townsman of a stiller town." These words describe a funeral procession for a young champion being carried to his grave. Lines 1–4 describe a victory celebration that happened at some earlier point in time. The word "today" in line 5 indicates that the poem takes place at the funeral for a young athlete.

16. **D is correct.** The second stanza describes a funeral. The athlete is carried to his gravesite and in death becomes a "townsman of a stiller town."

17. **E is correct.** The author calls the athlete a "smart lad" to die before his glory fades (lines 9–10). Lines 17–20 praise the athlete for not becoming one of those "lads that wore their honors out," meaning an athlete who continues to compete even though he can no longer keep up.

18. **D is correct.** Lines 11–12 ("And early though the laurel grows/It withers quicker than the rose") express the poet's belief that, although the athlete's glory came early, it will not last. In other words, glory withers and dies as quickly as a rose, and statement I is correct. Statement II is confirmed by lines 9–10 ("Smart lad, to slip betimes away/From fields where glory does not stay") as well as lines 17–20 ("Now you will not swell the rout/Of lads that wore their honors out/Runners whom renown outran/And the name died before the man."). Nothing in the poem supports statement III.

19. **A is correct.** The constant repetition of "gone" and "wiped out" in lines 8–15 serves to emphasize the author's inability to believe that such devastation could possibly occur. "San Francisco is *gone* . . . Its industrial section is *wiped out*. Its business section is *wiped out*. Its social and residential section is *wiped out*. The factories and warehouses, the great stores and newspaper buildings, the hotels and the palaces of the nabobs, are all *gone*." Choices B, D, and E are wrong because there are no words in the paragraph that support a mood of desperate longing, cautious optimism, or heartfelt pity. Choice C is possible; however, the mood of the paragraph is much closer to awe and disbelief than it is to uncontrolled outrage, so choice A is a better answer.

20. **D is correct.** Here are just a few examples of the vivid images provided by the author: " the smoke of San Francisco's burning was a lurid tower visible a hundred miles away . . ." "The streets were humped into ridges

and depressions, and piled with the debris of fallen walls." "The steel rails were twisted into perpendicular and horizontal angles."

21. **B is correct.** A *nabob* is "a rich and important person." Choice A is wrong because a *knave* is "a rascal "or "a rogue." Choice E is wrong because although the passage mentions "the palaces of nabobs," a nabob does not have to be of royal blood. Choices C and D have nothing to do with the word "nabob."

22. **A is correct.** The passage tells mainly of the massive destruction the San Francisco earthquake caused; roads and rail systems were destroyed, telephone and telegraph systems were "disrupted," and the "water-mains had burst." Thus, the statement conveys the idea that all modern conveniences had been lost, and the city had been reduced to living without twentieth-century amenities.

23. **C is correct.** The passage is arranged in chronological order. This is evident in the first few words of paragraphs 3, 4, and 5. Paragraph 3 starts with the words "On Wednesday morning," paragraph 4 starts with "By Wednesday afternoon," and paragraph 5 starts with "Wednesday night."

24. **B is correct.** As evidenced by lines 42–44 ("At that time I watched the vast conflagration from out on the bay."), the author was an eyewitness to the earthquake. His primary purpose for writing this passage was to report what he saw during that terrible time. Choice A is wrong because the passage provides no scientific explanation telling how earthquakes occur. Choice C is wrong because the passage describes the events of the earthquake, but does not go into the feelings of the residents. Choice D is wrong because only one paragraph of the account is devoted to the winds that helped the fire spread. Choice E is wrong because the author's praise for the firefighters' efforts is only one small part of the account, not its entire focus.

25. **D is correct.** As stated in the second paragraph, "In those days, a million people died from smallpox each year in Europe alone . . .". Choice A is wrong because the passage states that a million people died from smallpox. Since some people did survive smallpox, it can be assumed that the disease struck many more than a million people each year. Choices B and C are wrong because milkmaids contracted cowpox, not smallpox, from the cows. Choice E is wrong because the passage states that those who survived "were often left with grim reminders of their ordeals: blindness, deep scars, and deformities."

26. **B is correct.** Choices A, D, and E are all mentioned in paragraph 3: "Since Jenner's time, vaccines have been developed against more than 20 infectious diseases such as influenza, pneumonia, whooping cough, rubella, rabies, meningitis, and hepatitis B." Choice C is mentioned in paragraph 2, "By the beginning of the 20th century, vaccines for rabies, diphtheria, typhoid fever, and plague were in use, in addition to the vaccine for smallpox." The only answer choice not mentioned is choice B, scarlet fever.

27. **E is correct.** As stated in the last paragraph, "Weakened microbes, killed microbes, inactivated toxins, and purified proteins or polysaccharides derived from microbes are the most common components used in vaccine development strategies."

28. **C is correct.** The answer to this question is found in the second paragraph, which states that "Jenner laid the foundation for modern vaccines" and "started on a course that would ease the suffering of people around the world for centuries to come." Choice A is wrong because it was not until 1980 that "an updated version of Jenner's vaccine led to the total eradication of smallpox." Choice B is wrong because Jenner used cowpox-producing organisms to make the vaccine that protected people from the more deadly smallpox. Choices D and E are wrong because although Jenner's work was the basis for the development of vaccines for rabies and typhoid fever, the vaccine Jenner produced in 1796 was for smallpox only.

29. **B is correct.** According to the last paragraph, "Scientists use vaccines to 'trick' the human immune system into producing antibodies or immune cells that protect against the real disease-causing organism." Choice A is wrong because the vaccine does not directly attack the disease-causing organism, instead it causes the body to produce antibodies against the disease-causing organism. Choice C is wrong because vaccines contain "weakened microbes, killed microbes, inactivated toxins, and purified proteins or polysaccharides derived from microbes," not deadly disease-producing organisms. Choice D is wrong because the vaccine does not contain antibodies, rather it triggers the body to produce antibodies. Choice E is wrong because although some people may have an allergic reaction to some vaccines, vaccines do not work by producing an allergic reaction.

30. **C is correct.** The first sentence describes the birthmark as a "crimson hand, which at first had been strongly visible upon the marble paleness of Georgiana's cheek." The birthmark fades like "the stain of the rainbow fading out of the sky," but it is not shaped like a rainbow, so choice A is incorrect. The birthmark fades to "the faintest rose color," but is not described as having the shape of a rose, so choice B is incorrect. There is nothing in the passage to suggest that the birthmark is shaped like a butterfly or a sun, so choices D and E are both incorrect.

31. **D is correct.** The first paragraph tells that the birthmark is fading. In the second paragraph Aylmer says, "Success! Success!" indicating that he is responsible for making the birthmark fade. Thus the most reasonable assumption is that Alymer had performed some kind of operation on his wife to remove her birthmark. The presence of a servant indicates that Aylmer is not a poor man, making choice A incorrect. Choices B and C can be eliminated because all the evidence indicates that Aylmer is striving to help his wife by removing the birthmark that "had once blazed with such disastrous brilliancy as to scare away all their happiness." Choice E is wrong because it is Georgiana, not Aylmer, who is dying.

32. **B is correct.** Georgiana gazes into the mirror and sees "how barely perceptible was now that crimson hand which had once blazed with such disastrous brilliancy as to scare away all their happiness." A mark that is barely perceptible is very faint.

33. **A is correct.** When Georgiana awakens, Alymer calls her his "peerless bride" and proclaims, "You are perfect!" The best synonym for "perfect" is "flawless."

34. **D is correct.** Even though Georgiana knows she is dying as a result of Aylmer's attempt to remove her birthmark, she speaks to Alymer "with more than human tenderness," calling him "My poor Aylmer" and "dearest Aylmer." Her words do not indicate that she is bitter (choice A) or angry (choice B). She may be happy to see that the birthmark is gone, but that does not describe her feelings toward Aylmer, so choice C is wrong. Because she is tender and loving toward her husband, she would not be described as uncaring; thus, choice E is wrong.

35. **C is correct.** Aylmer's attempt to make his wife perfect resulted in destroying her, thus illustrating the fact that perfection cannot be achieved on earth. Choice A is wrong because if love were blind Aylmer would not have attempted to remove the birthmark. Choice B is wrong because the passage proves the opposite to be true. Choice D is wrong because the effect of the birthmark was "to scare away all their happiness." Choice E is wrong because the story did not end well; it ended with Georgiana's death.

36. **C is correct.** Most of the passage is devoted to a description of the "enthralling pleasures" of life in the country. Choices A and B are wrong because neither one is covered in the passage. Choices D and E are wrong because each is covered by only one small part of the passage and is not the focus of the passage as a whole.

37. **B is correct.** The tone of the passage is one of carefree joy and happiness. Making fun of his sister for not knowing that General Grant was a real person is just one example of the light-heartedness of the entire passage.

38. **D is correct.** Although the author states that "summers we spent in the country" and we children "loved the country beyond anything," he never specifically mentions where the family stays while in the country. The only reference to where they stayed is the very vague "now at one place, now at another." Choice A is answered in lines 4–6: "We were always wildly eager to get to the country when spring came, and very sad when in the late fall the family moved back to town." Choice B is answered in lines 7–9 where the author mentions such pets as "cats, dogs, rabbits, a coon, and a sorrel Shetland pony named General Grant." Choice C is answered in lines 17–19 where the author states that they spent their time in the country "supervising haying and harvesting, picking apples, hunting frogs successfully and woodchucks unsuccessfully." Choice E is answered in lines 24–26 where the author states that "Thanksgiving was an appreciated festival, but it in no way came up to Christmas."

39. **D is correct.** The statement primarily suggests that the author recreated the Christmases of his youth primarily because he wanted his own children to feel the same joy that he had experienced as a child. Choice A is wrong because there is no mention made that the author was setting an example that he wanted his children to follow. Choice B is wrong because the author never states that he misses the Christmases of his youth. Rather, he is reminiscing about some of his favorite childhood memories. Choice C is wrong because the passage does

not imply that the author is trying to reproduce his entire childhood, but merely the Christmases of his past. Choice E is wrong because there is no evidence that the author wanted his children to know the value of carrying on traditions.

40. **A is correct.** The passage is narrated by an adult looking back with obvious fondness on his own happy childhood. The author tells of wonderful summers spent in the country. He also mentions something that happens "thirty years later" when he has children of his own. These clues are enough to determine that the passage was written by an adult and that it concerns his own life. Choices B and D are wrong because the passage is written from the point of view of an adult, not a child. Choice C is wrong because the passage is written in the first person, using pronouns such as *I* and *we*, which usually indicate that the passage is autobiographical. Choice E is wrong because the author recalls his childhood with fondness, not regret.

Section 4 Quantitative II

1. **E is correct.** $8 \times 9 - 16 = 56$; $28 \div 4 = 7$; and $56 \div 7 = 8$.

2. **E is correct.** $72 \div 9 \times 6 \times 12 = 576$; $576 \div 18 = 32$.

3. **B is correct.** $^{42}/_7 = 6$; $14 \div ^1/_{14} = 14 \times ^{14}/_1 = 196$; $^8/_{12} \times 9 = ^{72}/_{12} = 6$. $22.3 + 13.7 = 36$. However, $9 \times ^7/_{16} = {}^{63}/_{16} = 3\,^{15}/_{16}$, which is not a whole number.

4. **C is correct.** $102^3/_4\% = 1.0275$.

5. **B is correct.** It costs m dollars to buy 64 cans of soda. 48 cans are $^3/_4$ of 64, so the cost of 40 cans of soda will be $3/4 \times m = 3m/4$ dollars.

6. **D is correct.**
$$\frac{7}{16}x = 42$$
$$\frac{1}{16}x = 6$$
$$x = 96$$
$$\frac{1}{2}x = 48$$

7. **A is correct.** When dividing fractions, invert and multiply. See if you can simplify the fractions.
$$\frac{2}{3} \div \frac{5}{6} = \frac{2}{3} \times \frac{6}{5} \quad \text{Multiply}$$
$$= \frac{12}{15} \quad \text{Simplify}$$
$$= \frac{4}{5}$$

8. **B is correct.** A right triangle has one angle that measures $90°$. If a second angle measures $49°$, that accounts for $139°$ of the total $180°$ in the triangle. $180° - 139° = 31°$

9. **D is correct.** Convert to equivalent expressions: $^1/_2 = ^8/_{16}$; $^1/_4 = ^4/_{16}$;
$^8/_{16} + ^4/_{16} + ^3/_{16} = ^{15}/_{16}$

10. **B is correct.** Convert to equivalent expressions:
$4^3/_8 = ^{35}/_8 = ^{70}/_{16}$
$^{15}/_{16} + ^{70}/_{16} = ^{85}/_{16} = 5\,^5/_{16}$

11. **C is correct.** The greatest common factor of a group of numbers is the greatest whole number that is a factor of all the numbers. The greatest common factor of 75, 90, and 120 is 15.

12. **E is correct.** The least common multiple of a group of numbers is the least whole number, greater than 0, that is a multiple of all of the numbers. The least common multiple of 13, 26, and 2 is 26.

13. **E is correct.** $^{18}/_{25} = {}^{72}/_{100} = 0.72$.

14. **D is correct.** $^4/_{10}$ can be simplified to $^2/_5$.

15. **C is correct.** 0.5 km = 500 meters; 500 ÷ 5 = 100.

16. **A is correct.** If the club sells n tickets at $3.00 each, the amount they will earn is $3n$. Their profit after paying $224 in expenses is $3n - 224$.

17. **B is correct.** (2 × $300) + (3 × $240) = $600 + $720 = $1,320

18. **C is correct.** Set up an equation. If x = number of students in sixth grade,
$$x = \frac{144}{6} + 8$$
$$x = 24 + 8$$
$$x = 32$$

19. **D is correct.** 8 ÷ 0.6 = 13.33, so there are about 13 kilometers in 8 miles.

20. **D is correct.** $12 + (-8) + (-9) + 6 = 4 + (-9) + 6 = -5 + 6 = 1$.

21. **E is correct.** $-36 \div -12 = 3$. Check: $3 \times -12 = -36$.

22. **D is correct.** At 6:00 o'clock, the minute hand points straight up and the hour hand points straight down. Together, they form a straight angle that measures 180°.

23. **A is correct.** When 4 hours have passed, the time is 6:05. After another 58 minutes the time is 7:03.

24. **A is correct.** A wire stretched between two points on a circle and passing through the center will form a diameter of the circle. Diameter = radius × 2. If the radius is 1.35 m, the diameter = 2(1.35) = 2.7 m = 270 cm. If wire costs 2¢/cm, the cost of the wire stretching across the circle will be 270 × 2¢ = 540¢ = $5.40.

25. **B is correct.** Use the formula $r \times t = d$ where r = rate, t = time, and d = distance.
3 hours 40 minutes = $3^2/_3$ hours.
$$r \times t = d$$
$$9 \times 3^2/_3 = 33 \text{ miles}$$

PART V

PRACTICE TESTS FOR THE ISEE

ISEE Practice Test I

(Lower Level: For Candidates for Grades 5 and 6)

The following practice test is designed to be just like the real ISEE that you will take if you are applying for admission to grades 5 or 6. It matches the actual test in content coverage and level of difficulty. The test is in five sections: Verbal Reasoning, Quantitative Reasoning, Reading Comprehension, Mathematics Achievement, and the Essay.

This practice test will be an accurate reflection of how you'll do on test day if you treat it as the real examination. Here are some hints on how to take the test under conditions similar to those of the actual exam:

- Find a quiet place to work and set aside a period of approximately 3 hours when you will not be disturbed.
- Work on only one section at a time, and use your watch or a timer to keep track of the time limits for each test part.
- Tear out your answer sheet and mark your answers by filling in the ovals for each question.
- Write your essay on the pages provided.
- Become familiar with the directions for each part of the test. You'll save time on the actual test day by already being familiar with this information.

At the end of the test you'll find Answer Keys for each section and explanations for every question. Check your answers against the keys to find out how you did on each section of the test and what test topics you might need to study more. Then review the explanations, paying particular attention to the ones for the questions that you answered incorrectly.

ISEE Practice Test I

ANSWER SHEET

Note: If there are more answer lines than there are questions in a section, leave the extra answer lines blank.

Section 1: Verbal Reasoning

1. Ⓐ Ⓑ Ⓒ Ⓓ	17. Ⓐ Ⓑ Ⓒ Ⓓ	33. Ⓐ Ⓑ Ⓒ Ⓓ
2. Ⓐ Ⓑ Ⓒ Ⓓ	18. Ⓐ Ⓑ Ⓒ Ⓓ	34. Ⓐ Ⓑ Ⓒ Ⓓ
3. Ⓐ Ⓑ Ⓒ Ⓓ	19. Ⓐ Ⓑ Ⓒ Ⓓ	35. Ⓐ Ⓑ Ⓒ Ⓓ
4. Ⓐ Ⓑ Ⓒ Ⓓ	20. Ⓐ Ⓑ Ⓒ Ⓓ	36. Ⓐ Ⓑ Ⓒ Ⓓ
5. Ⓐ Ⓑ Ⓒ Ⓓ	21. Ⓐ Ⓑ Ⓒ Ⓓ	37. Ⓐ Ⓑ Ⓒ Ⓓ
6. Ⓐ Ⓑ Ⓒ Ⓓ	22. Ⓐ Ⓑ Ⓒ Ⓓ	38. Ⓐ Ⓑ Ⓒ Ⓓ
7. Ⓐ Ⓑ Ⓒ Ⓓ	23. Ⓐ Ⓑ Ⓒ Ⓓ	39. Ⓐ Ⓑ Ⓒ Ⓓ
8. Ⓐ Ⓑ Ⓒ Ⓓ	24. Ⓐ Ⓑ Ⓒ Ⓓ	40. Ⓐ Ⓑ Ⓒ Ⓓ
9. Ⓐ Ⓑ Ⓒ Ⓓ	25. Ⓐ Ⓑ Ⓒ Ⓓ	
10. Ⓐ Ⓑ Ⓒ Ⓓ	26. Ⓐ Ⓑ Ⓒ Ⓓ	
11. Ⓐ Ⓑ Ⓒ Ⓓ	27. Ⓐ Ⓑ Ⓒ Ⓓ	
12. Ⓐ Ⓑ Ⓒ Ⓓ	28. Ⓐ Ⓑ Ⓒ Ⓓ	
13. Ⓐ Ⓑ Ⓒ Ⓓ	29. Ⓐ Ⓑ Ⓒ Ⓓ	
14. Ⓐ Ⓑ Ⓒ Ⓓ	30. Ⓐ Ⓑ Ⓒ Ⓓ	
15. Ⓐ Ⓑ Ⓒ Ⓓ	31. Ⓐ Ⓑ Ⓒ Ⓓ	
16. Ⓐ Ⓑ Ⓒ Ⓓ	32. Ⓐ Ⓑ Ⓒ Ⓓ	

Section 2: Quantitative Reasoning

1. Ⓐ Ⓑ Ⓒ Ⓓ	13. Ⓐ Ⓑ Ⓒ Ⓓ	25. Ⓐ Ⓑ Ⓒ Ⓓ
2. Ⓐ Ⓑ Ⓒ Ⓓ	14. Ⓐ Ⓑ Ⓒ Ⓓ	26. Ⓐ Ⓑ Ⓒ Ⓓ
3. Ⓐ Ⓑ Ⓒ Ⓓ	15. Ⓐ Ⓑ Ⓒ Ⓓ	27. Ⓐ Ⓑ Ⓒ Ⓓ
4. Ⓐ Ⓑ Ⓒ Ⓓ	16. Ⓐ Ⓑ Ⓒ Ⓓ	28. Ⓐ Ⓑ Ⓒ Ⓓ
5. Ⓐ Ⓑ Ⓒ Ⓓ	17. Ⓐ Ⓑ Ⓒ Ⓓ	29. Ⓐ Ⓑ Ⓒ Ⓓ
6. Ⓐ Ⓑ Ⓒ Ⓓ	18. Ⓐ Ⓑ Ⓒ Ⓓ	30. Ⓐ Ⓑ Ⓒ Ⓓ
7. Ⓐ Ⓑ Ⓒ Ⓓ	19. Ⓐ Ⓑ Ⓒ Ⓓ	31. Ⓐ Ⓑ Ⓒ Ⓓ
8. Ⓐ Ⓑ Ⓒ Ⓓ	20. Ⓐ Ⓑ Ⓒ Ⓓ	32. Ⓐ Ⓑ Ⓒ Ⓓ
9. Ⓐ Ⓑ Ⓒ Ⓓ	21. Ⓐ Ⓑ Ⓒ Ⓓ	33. Ⓐ Ⓑ Ⓒ Ⓓ
10. Ⓐ Ⓑ Ⓒ Ⓓ	22. Ⓐ Ⓑ Ⓒ Ⓓ	34. Ⓐ Ⓑ Ⓒ Ⓓ
11. Ⓐ Ⓑ Ⓒ Ⓓ	23. Ⓐ Ⓑ Ⓒ Ⓓ	35. Ⓐ Ⓑ Ⓒ Ⓓ
12. Ⓐ Ⓑ Ⓒ Ⓓ	24. Ⓐ Ⓑ Ⓒ Ⓓ	

Section 3: Reading Comprehension

1. Ⓐ Ⓑ Ⓒ Ⓓ	13. Ⓐ Ⓑ Ⓒ Ⓓ	25. Ⓐ Ⓑ Ⓒ Ⓓ
2. Ⓐ Ⓑ Ⓒ Ⓓ	14. Ⓐ Ⓑ Ⓒ Ⓓ	26. Ⓐ Ⓑ Ⓒ Ⓓ
3. Ⓐ Ⓑ Ⓒ Ⓓ	15. Ⓐ Ⓑ Ⓒ Ⓓ	27. Ⓐ Ⓑ Ⓒ Ⓓ
4. Ⓐ Ⓑ Ⓒ Ⓓ	16. Ⓐ Ⓑ Ⓒ Ⓓ	28. Ⓐ Ⓑ Ⓒ Ⓓ
5. Ⓐ Ⓑ Ⓒ Ⓓ	17. Ⓐ Ⓑ Ⓒ Ⓓ	29. Ⓐ Ⓑ Ⓒ Ⓓ
6. Ⓐ Ⓑ Ⓒ Ⓓ	18. Ⓐ Ⓑ Ⓒ Ⓓ	30. Ⓐ Ⓑ Ⓒ Ⓓ
7. Ⓐ Ⓑ Ⓒ Ⓓ	19. Ⓐ Ⓑ Ⓒ Ⓓ	31. Ⓐ Ⓑ Ⓒ Ⓓ
8. Ⓐ Ⓑ Ⓒ Ⓓ	20. Ⓐ Ⓑ Ⓒ Ⓓ	32. Ⓐ Ⓑ Ⓒ Ⓓ
9. Ⓐ Ⓑ Ⓒ Ⓓ	21. Ⓐ Ⓑ Ⓒ Ⓓ	33. Ⓐ Ⓑ Ⓒ Ⓓ
10. Ⓐ Ⓑ Ⓒ Ⓓ	22. Ⓐ Ⓑ Ⓒ Ⓓ	34. Ⓐ Ⓑ Ⓒ Ⓓ
11. Ⓐ Ⓑ Ⓒ Ⓓ	23. Ⓐ Ⓑ Ⓒ Ⓓ	35. Ⓐ Ⓑ Ⓒ Ⓓ
12. Ⓐ Ⓑ Ⓒ Ⓓ	24. Ⓐ Ⓑ Ⓒ Ⓓ	36. Ⓐ Ⓑ Ⓒ Ⓓ

Section 4: Mathematics Achievement

1. Ⓐ Ⓑ Ⓒ Ⓓ	13. Ⓐ Ⓑ Ⓒ Ⓓ	25. Ⓐ Ⓑ Ⓒ Ⓓ
2. Ⓐ Ⓑ Ⓒ Ⓓ	14. Ⓐ Ⓑ Ⓒ Ⓓ	26. Ⓐ Ⓑ Ⓒ Ⓓ
3. Ⓐ Ⓑ Ⓒ Ⓓ	15. Ⓐ Ⓑ Ⓒ Ⓓ	27. Ⓐ Ⓑ Ⓒ Ⓓ
4. Ⓐ Ⓑ Ⓒ Ⓓ	16. Ⓐ Ⓑ Ⓒ Ⓓ	28. Ⓐ Ⓑ Ⓒ Ⓓ
5. Ⓐ Ⓑ Ⓒ Ⓓ	17. Ⓐ Ⓑ Ⓒ Ⓓ	29. Ⓐ Ⓑ Ⓒ Ⓓ
6. Ⓐ Ⓑ Ⓒ Ⓓ	18. Ⓐ Ⓑ Ⓒ Ⓓ	30. Ⓐ Ⓑ Ⓒ Ⓓ
7. Ⓐ Ⓑ Ⓒ Ⓓ	19. Ⓐ Ⓑ Ⓒ Ⓓ	31. Ⓐ Ⓑ Ⓒ Ⓓ
8. Ⓐ Ⓑ Ⓒ Ⓓ	20. Ⓐ Ⓑ Ⓒ Ⓓ	32. Ⓐ Ⓑ Ⓒ Ⓓ
9. Ⓐ Ⓑ Ⓒ Ⓓ	21. Ⓐ Ⓑ Ⓒ Ⓓ	33. Ⓐ Ⓑ Ⓒ Ⓓ
10. Ⓐ Ⓑ Ⓒ Ⓓ	22. Ⓐ Ⓑ Ⓒ Ⓓ	34. Ⓐ Ⓑ Ⓒ Ⓓ
11. Ⓐ Ⓑ Ⓒ Ⓓ	23. Ⓐ Ⓑ Ⓒ Ⓓ	35. Ⓐ Ⓑ Ⓒ Ⓓ
12. Ⓐ Ⓑ Ⓒ Ⓓ	24. Ⓐ Ⓑ Ⓒ Ⓓ	

SECTION 1
Time: 25 Minutes
40 Questions

This section includes two different types of questions: synonyms and sentence completions. There are directions and a sample question for each question type.

Part One

Directions: Each of the following questions consists of a word in capital letters followed by four words or phrases labeled (A), (B), (C), and (D). Select the one word or phrase that means most nearly the same as the word in capital letters.

Sample Question:

ESSENTIAL:
(A) dire
(B) confusing
(C) vital
(D) expert

Correct Answer: C

---

1. NOVICE:
   (A) burden
   (B) beggar
   (C) beginner
   (D) expression

2. FABRICATE:
   (A) stitch
   (B) falsify
   (C) deter
   (D) decorate

3. FRIENDLY:
   (A) amiable
   (B) sanctimonious
   (C) ambivalent
   (D) responsive

4. GENRE:
   (A) proposal
   (B) category
   (C) purpose
   (D) generation

5. SUMMIT:
   (A) conference
   (B) valley
   (C) essence
   (D) outline

6. DEFTLY:
   (A) wilfully
   (B) closely
   (C) quickly
   (D) skillfully

7. PROSPER:
   (A) strive
   (B) affect
   (C) gather
   (D) thrive

8. SPURN:
   (A) cross
   (B) betray
   (C) reject
   (D) hinder

9. VISAGE:
   (A) encounter
   (B) face
   (C) bandage
   (D) wound

GO ON TO THE NEXT PAGE.

10. RESPITE:
    (A) pause
    (B) presumption
    (C) recluse
    (D) blockage

11. REGRETFUL:
    (A) credulous
    (B) desultory
    (C) contrite
    (D) dubious

12. INCITE:
    (A) insist
    (B) dispel
    (C) assert
    (D) provoke

13. FACET:
    (A) goal
    (B) endeavor
    (C) tactic
    (D) aspect

14. ABSOLVE:
    (A) admonish
    (B) accede
    (C) clear
    (D) affirm

15. APLOMB:
    (A) confidence
    (B) ascent
    (C) epitome
    (D) omen

16. CORROBORATION:
    (A) confirmation
    (B) announcement
    (C) bulletin
    (D) ordeal

17. ERRATIC:
    (A) mistaken
    (B) unpredictable
    (C) opportune
    (D) inadvertent

18. ABSCOND:
    (A) choose
    (B) leave
    (C) remove
    (D) steal

19. IRRITABLE:
    (A) voluble
    (B) transitory
    (C) turgid
    (D) petulant

20. TRAVESTY:
    (A) disaster
    (B) misfortune
    (C) mockery
    (D) adage

GO ON TO THE NEXT PAGE.

Part Two

Directions: Each sentence below has one or two blanks. Each blank indicates that something is missing. Following each sentence are five words or sets of words labeled (A), (B), (C), and (D). You are to select the word or set of words that, when inserted in the sentence, best fits the meaning of the sentence as a whole.

Sample Question:

Due to the fact that the stray kitten was so _____, Ethan's mother allowed him to keep it.
(A) tardy
(B) humid
(C) disobedient
(D) adorable

Correct Answer: D

---

21. Due to the strong odor of onions _____ through the kitchen, Jason suddenly found himself with tears in his eyes.
    (A) submitting
    (B) surpassing
    (C) wafting
    (D) impeding

22. Despite the donor's self-proclaimed _____, the museum's board of directors soon realized they would never _____ a dime from him.
    (A) benevolence ... receive
    (B) inhibition ... secure
    (C) generosity ... propose
    (D) stature ... redeem

23. Always _____ and outgoing, Maria could liven up any event just by walking through the door.
    (A) agile
    (B) uneasy
    (C) gregarious
    (D) subdued

24. Although her upbringing had been _____, Tonya now lived in the most _____ neighborhood in the county.
    (A) modest ... dilapidated
    (B) humble ... affluent
    (C) mundane ... oppressive
    (D) ordinary ... sullen

25. Clearly annoyed with their lack of progress, Mr. Ramirez _____ the members of the orchestra for their _____ approach to practicing outside of school.
    (A) reprimanded ... fervid
    (B) scolded ... belligerent
    (C) berated ... exemplary
    (D) admonished ... lackadaisical

26. Faced with the loss of his blistering fastball, the baseball team's owner finally _____ to the pitcher's demand for a guaranteed contract.
    (A) alluded
    (B) sequestered
    (C) reneged
    (D) acceded

27. Carlos knew his goals were not easily _____, but he also knew he had the determination to _____.
    (A) deplorable ... succeed
    (B) obtainable ... relinquish
    (C) attainable ... persevere
    (D) approachable ... expel

28. Perhaps the country's most _____ female artist, Georgia O'Keeffe's paintings _____ landscapes in the American West.
    (A) distinguished ... obscure
    (B) renowned ... depict
    (C) prominent ... conceal
    (D) reviled ... portray

29. An _____ test taker, Theo studied hard and seemed to have a knack for always selecting the correct answer.
    (A) ambivalent
    (B) egregious
    (C) impulsive
    (D) astute

30. An _____ chef, every meal Andre prepared for his friends left them begging for more.
    (A) adept
    (B) expedient
    (C) affable
    (D) acrid

31. Ultimately, the activists' efforts to _____ the historic building proved _____ and it was soon demolished.
    (A) preserve ... futile
    (B) save ... inextricable
    (C) restore ... flagrant
    (D) destroy ... abundant

GO ON TO THE NEXT PAGE.

32. Unwilling to compromise his _____, Mario quit the disreputable corporation and started his own consulting firm.
   (A) representation
   (B) integrity
   (C) volition
   (D) motivation

33. Praised as an _____ biographer, Ana's faithful _____ left her readers feeling as though they knew the historic figures she wrote of.
   (A) awkward ... descriptions
   (B) esteemed ... countenances
   (C) errant ... portrayals
   (D) eloquent ... characterizations

34. A devoted fan, Maria showed her _____ for the actor by leading the ovation during his curtain call.
   (A) ascension
   (B) reluctance
   (C) reverence
   (D) disparagement

35. At her going away party, Ms. Greeley was _____ for both her business _____ as well as her amiable manner.
   (A) insulted ... skills
   (B) honored ... omission
   (C) lauded ... acumen
   (D) emulated ... expertise

36. Always the _____, Martin realized that he would have to start studying soon in order to do well on the test next week.
   (A) pragmatist
   (B) connoisseur
   (C) rival
   (D) detractor

37. Many historians agree that the Civil Rights movement _____ in Montgomery, Alabama, in 1955 when Rosa Parks refused to give up her seat on a bus.
   (A) originated
   (B) immersed
   (C) adhered
   (D) preceded

38. Due to the _____ weather, the principal decided to postpone tonight's open house until next Tuesday.
   (A) serene
   (B) inclement
   (C) squalid
   (D) celestial

39. The scout troop was excited because the money generated by their fund-raiser had _____ even the most generous estimates.
   (A) compensated
   (B) suppressed
   (C) subsidized
   (D) exceeded

40. After several hours of negotiating the two sides finally reached an _____ and were able to move beyond their disagreement.
   (A) exception
   (B) accord
   (C) ambiguity
   (D) extension

STOP!
If you finish before time is up, check your work on this section only.

SECTION 2
Time: 35 Minutes
35 Questions

Directions: For each of the following questions, mark the letter of your choice on the answer sheet.

1. Which of the following is closest to 2?
   - (A) 2.4
   - (B) 1.8
   - (C) 1.0
   - (D) 0.3

2. $4 \times 3 \times 6 \times 2$ is equal to the product of 24 and
   - (A) 6
   - (B) 7
   - (C) 8
   - (D) 9

3. One-quarter of 10,000 =
   - (A) 2,500
   - (B) 2,000
   - (C) 1,500
   - (D) 1,000

4. $6\frac{3}{4}\% =$
   - (A) 67.5
   - (B) 6.75
   - (C) 0.675
   - (D) 0.0675

5. If $6 + 12 + \_\_ = 5 + 11 + 6$, then __ =
   - (A) 2
   - (B) 3
   - (C) 4
   - (D) 5

6. Which pair of fractions is equivalent?
   - (A) $\frac{2}{3}, \frac{5}{6}$
   - (B) $\frac{9}{12}, \frac{5}{6}$
   - (C) $\frac{3}{4}, \frac{7}{8}$
   - (D) $\frac{4}{10}, \frac{2}{5}$

7. What is the least common multiple of 3, 4, and 18?
   - (A) 18
   - (B) 24
   - (C) 36
   - (D) 54

8. Which of the following is NOT equal to a whole number?
   - (A) $\frac{16}{4}$
   - (B) $6 \times \frac{2}{3}$
   - (C) $4 \div \frac{1}{4}$
   - (D) $\frac{1}{3} \times 4$

9. $10 \times (0.38 + 3.5) + 5.2 =$
   - (A) 15.25
   - (B) 24.15
   - (C) 32.40
   - (D) 44

10. Order from least to greatest: $\frac{3}{5}, 1\frac{1}{2}, 0.8$
    - (A) $\frac{3}{5}, 0.8, 1\frac{1}{2}$
    - (B) $0.8, 1\frac{1}{2}, \frac{3}{5}$
    - (C) $1\frac{1}{2}, \frac{3}{5}, 0.8$
    - (D) $0.8, \frac{3}{5}, 1\frac{1}{2}$

11. A student buys a sandwich for 80 cents, milk for 20 cents, and pie for 30 cents. How much did the meal cost?
    - (A) $1.00
    - (B) $1.20
    - (C) $1.30
    - (D) $1.40

12. The temperature at midnight was –12°C. It rose 2°C each hour. What was the temperature at 11:00 A.M.?
    - (A) –2°C
    - (B) 4°C
    - (C) 8°C
    - (D) 10°C

13. Will has $12,444.12 in his checking account. He writes checks for $8,204.94 and $890.99. How much is left in Will's account?
    - (A) $3,348.19
    - (B) $2,945.60
    - (C) $2,867.30
    - (D) $2,259.30

14. Rachel flies 2,880 miles in 9 hours. What is the average speed of her airplane?
    - (A) 285 miles/hour
    - (B) 315 miles/hour
    - (C) 320 miles/hour
    - (D) 340 miles/hour

15. Jake spent one-fifth of his life in school. If he is now 55, how many years did he spend in school?
    - (A) 9
    - (B) 11
    - (C) 13
    - (D) 15

GO ON TO THE NEXT PAGE.

16. Which of the following is NOT equal to a whole number?

(A) $\frac{30}{5} = 6$

(B) $4 \times \frac{12}{16} = \frac{48}{16} = 3$

(C) $16 \div \frac{1}{16} = 16 \times 16 = 156$

(D) $\frac{5}{9} \times 8 \quad \frac{40}{9}$

17. What is the greatest common factor of 16, 24, 96, and 120?

(A) 2
(B) 4
(C) 8
(D) 12

18. Aaron has 256 cans of soup that he needs to pack into boxes that hold 30 cans each. How many cans of soup are left over after he fills as many boxes as he can?

(A) 4
(B) 16
(C) 18
(D) 22

19. $-10 - (-5 - 4) =$

(A) -4
(B) -3
(C) -1
(D) 1

20. Alex's car gets an average of 26 miles per gallon of gas on the highway. If he drives 858 miles, how many gallons of gas will he use?

(A) 33 gallons
(B) 57 gallons
(C) 78 gallons
(D) 84 gallons

21. $2 + \frac{4}{25} =$

(A) 2.225
(B) 2.16
(C) 2.24
(D) 2.45

22. $2 \times 3 \times 5 \times 6$ is equal to the product of 30 and

(A) 6
(B) 7

(C) 8
(D) 9

23. $12 + (-8) + (-9) + 6 =$

(A) -6
(B) -3
(C) 0
(D) 1

24. On a test with 75 questions, Cassidy answered 45 correctly. What percent did she answer correctly?

(A) 60%
(B) 72%
(C) 84%
(D) 89%

25. $11\frac{1}{2} - 9\frac{3}{4} =$

(A) $2\frac{1}{8}$
(B) 2
(C) $1\frac{7}{8}$
(D) $1\frac{3}{4}$

26. $\frac{3}{4} + \frac{1}{2} + \frac{2}{3} - \frac{5}{6} =$

(A) $1\frac{1}{12}$
(B) $1\frac{1}{3}$
(C) $1\frac{5}{6}$
(D) $2\frac{1}{6}$

27. $42 \div 7 \times 8 \times 5$ is equal to the product of 12 and

(A) 16
(B) 20
(C) 24
(D) 28

28. If $4 \times 3 \times \underline{\quad} = 5 \times 4 + 4$, then

$\underline{\quad} =$

(A) 2
(B) 3
(C) 4
(D) 5

29. A box of laundry soap contains 200 oz. If the cost for 5 ounces is 10 cents, how much does the box of soap cost?

(A) $3.10
(B) $3.60
(C) $3.80
(D) $4.00

30. Bob's i-Pod contains 800 songs. If 240 songs are either jazz or rap songs, what percent of his collection is jazz or rap?

(A) 15%
(B) 20%
(C) 25%
(D) 30%

31. Two numbers add to 1,500. One number is 4 times the size of the other. What are the two numbers?

(A) 300, 1,200
(B) 200, 1,300
(C) 500, 1,000
(D) 750, 750

32. $18 \div \frac{3}{4} =$

(A) 3
(B) 6
(C) 12
(D) 24

33. $71\frac{1}{5}\% =$

(A) 712
(B) 71.20
(C) 7.12
(D) 0.712

34. The number of sixth-grade students in the hill school is 8 more than $\frac{1}{6}$ of the whole student body. If there are 144 students in the school, how many are in sixth grade?

(A) 26
(B) 30
(C) 32
(D) 36

35. $62\frac{1}{2}\% =$

(A) 625
(B) 62.5
(C) 6.25
(D) 0.625

STOP!

If you finish before time is up, check your work on this section only.

Do I - 6

SECTION 3
Time: 40 Minutes
36 Questions

Directions: Each reading passage is followed by questions about it. Answer the questions that follow a passage on the basis of what is stated or implied in that passage. For each question, select the answer you think is best and record your choice by filling in the corresponding oval on the answer sheet.

Questions 1–6

Volcanoes are mountains, but they are very different from other mountains; they are not formed by folding and crumpling or by uplift and
5 erosion. Instead, volcanoes are built by the accumulation of their own eruptive products—lava, bombs (crusted over lava blobs), ashflows, and tephra (airborne ash and dust).
10 A *volcano* is most commonly a coni- cal hill or mountain built around a vent that connects with reservoirs of molten rock below the surface of the Earth. The term volcano also refers
15 to the opening or vent through which the molten rock and associated it is so hot that some rocks slowly melt and become a thick flowing substance called *magma*. Because it is lighter
20 than the solid rock around it, magma rises and collects in magma cham- bers. Eventually some of the magma pushes through vents and fissures in the Earth's surface and a volcanic
25 eruption occurs. Magma that has erupted is called *lava*.

Some volcanic eruptions are explosive and others are not. How explosive an eruption is depends on
30 how runny or sticky the magma is. If magma is thin and runny, gases can escape easily from it. When this type of magma erupts, it flows out of the volcano. Because they move
35 slowly enough for people to get out of their way, lava flows rarely kill people.

They can, however, cause consider- able destruction to buildings in their path. If magma is thick and sticky,
40 gases cannot escape easily. Pressure builds up until the gases escape violently and explode. In this type of eruption, the magma blasts into the air and breaks apart into pieces
45 called *tephra*. Tephra can range in size from tiny particles of ash to house-size boulders. Large-sized tephra typically falls back to the ground on or close to the volcano
50 and progressively smaller fragments are carried away from the vent by wind. Volcanic ash, the smallest tephra fragments, can travel hundreds to thousands of kilometers downwind
60 from a volcano.

1. A primary difference between volcanoes and other mountains is in
   (A) their height
   (B) their age
   (C) where they are located
   (D) how they are formed

2. A volcanic eruption is likely to be most explosive if magma
   (A) is thin and runny
   (B) is thick and sticky
   (C) rises and collects in magma chambers
   (D) pushes out through fissures in the Earth's surface

3. The author uses italic print primarily to
   (A) emphasize words that are used in an unusual way
   (B) indicate words that are difficult to pronounce
   (C) highlight important terms that are defined in the text
   (D) indicate words that are not necessary to understanding the passage

4. All of the following can be explicitly answered by the passage EXCEPT:
   (A) What factors contribute to hot temperatures deep inside the Earth?
   (B) Why are some volcanic eruptions explosive while others are not?
   (C) Why does magma rise and collect in chambers?
   (D) Why does pressure build up in magma that is thick and sticky?

5. This passage would most likely appear in
   (A) a newspaper
   (B) a science textbook
   (C) an adventure novel
   (D) a safety manual

GO ON TO THE NEXT PAGE.

6. Which of the following statements is NOT true of tephra?
   (A) It can range in size from tiny particles of ash to huge boulders.
   (B) It can travel thousands of kilometers from a volcano.
   (C) It can be found trapped in magma.
   (D) It is the term for rock fragments erupted into the air by volcanoes.

STOP DON'T DO ANY MORE !

Questions 7–10

The following speech was delivered by Frederick Douglass at a meeting of the Anti-Slavery Society in Pittsburgh in 1863.

I am one of those who believe that it is the mission of this war to free every slave in the United States. I am one of those who believe that
5 we should consent to no peace which shall not be an Abolition peace. I am, moreover, one of those who believe that the work of the American Anti-Slavery Society will not have been
10 completed until the black men of the South, and the black men of the North, shall have been admitted, fully and completely, into the body politic of America. I look upon slavery
15 as going the way of all the earth. It is the mission of the war to put it down. I know it will be said that I ask you to make the black man a voter in the South. It is said that the coloured
20 man is ignorant, and therefore he shall not vote. In saying this, you lay down a rule for the black man that you apply to no other class of your citizens. If he knows enough to be
25 hanged, he knows enough to vote. If he knows an honest man from a thief, he knows much more than some of our white voters. If he knows enough to take up arms in defence
30 of this Government and bare his breast to the storm of rebel artillery, he knows enough to vote.

All I ask, however, in regard to the blacks, is that whatever rule you
35 adopt, whether of intelligence or wealth, as the condition of voting for whites, you shall apply it equally to the black man. Do that, and I am satisfied, and eternal justice is satisfied;
40 liberty, fraternity, equality, are satisfied, and the country will move on harmoniously.

7. According to Douglass, the mission of the Civil War is to
   (A) destroy the Confederacy
   (B) punish the rebel soldiers
   (C) preserve the Union
   (D) end slavery

8. Douglass believes the work of the Anti-Slavery Society should not be considered complete until
   (A) slavery is abolished
   (B) blacks can move freely between the South and the North
   (C) black men of the North and South have the right to vote
   (D) all conditions for voting are ended

9. What does Douglass mean by calling for black men to be admitted "fully and completely into the body politic of America" (lines 13–14)?
   (A) They must have the same rights and privileges as all other citizens.
   (B) They must be able to vote.
   (C) They must be able to run for office.
   (D) They must take up arms to defend the Government.

10. The purpose of Douglass' speech was to
    (A) inform members of the society of the horrors of slavery
    (B) convince listeners to adopt fair and equal voting requirements
    (C) inform listeners of the progress of the war
    (D) convince members of the society that slavery should be ended

STOP

Questions 11–17

The great Pullman was whirling onward with such dignity of motion that a glance from the window seemed simply to prove that the
5 plains of Texas were pouring eastward. Vast flats of green grass, dull-hued spaces of mesquite and cactus, little groups of frame houses, woods of light and tender trees, all were
10 sweeping into the east, sweeping over the horizon, a precipice.

A newly married pair had boarded this coach at San Antonio. The man's face was reddened from many days
15 in the wind and sun, and a direct result of his new black clothes was that his brick-colored hands were constantly performing in a most conscious fashion. From time to time
20 he looked down respectfully at his attire. He sat with a hand on each knee, like a man waiting in a barber's shop. The glances he devoted to other passengers were furtive and shy.
25   The bride was not pretty, nor was she very young. She wore a dress of blue cashmere, with small reservations of velvet here and there and with steel buttons abounding.
30 She continually twisted her head to regard her puff sleeves, very stiff, straight, and high. They embarrassed her. It was quite apparent that she had cooked, and that she expected
35 to cook, dutifully. The blushes caused by the careless scrutiny of some passengers as she had entered the car were strange to see upon this plain, under-class countenance, which
40 was drawn in placid, almost emotionless lines. They were evidently very happy. "Ever been in a parlor-car before?" he asked, smiling with delight.
45   "No," she answered, "I never was. It's fine, ain't it?"

"Great! And then after a while we'll go forward to the diner and get a big layout. Finest meal in the
50 world. Charge a dollar."

"Oh, do they?" cried the bride. "Charge a dollar? Why, that's too much—for us—ain't it, Jack?"

GO ON TO THE NEXT PAGE.

"Not this trip, anyhow," he
55 answered bravely. "We're going to go the whole thing."

Stephen Crane from "The Bride Comes to Yellow Sky"

11. The tone of the passage suggests that the author regards the newly married couple with
    (A) embarrassment
    (B) disrespect
    (C) sympathy
    (D) scorn

12. Which word best describes the newly wed couple?
    (A) well-to-do
    (B) sad
    (C) unpleasant
    (D) unsophisticated

13. When this passage takes place, the bride and groom were most probably
    (A) in a hotel
    (B) on a stagecoach
    (C) in a diner
    (D) on a train

14. As it is used in line 24 the word "furtive" most nearly means
    (A) stealthy
    (B) steady
    (C) focused
    (D) unabashed

15. The narrator of this story is
    (A) the groom
    (B) the bride
    (C) an outside observer
    (D) an adult looking back on his life

16. The main purpose of this passage is to
    (A) express an opinion
    (B) introduce characters and setting
    (C) resolve a crisis
    (D) set up a conflict between two characters

17. By saying, "It was quite apparent that she had cooked, and that she expected to cook, dutifully," the author is suggesting that the bride
    (A) expects to eat out regularly
    (B) has led a life of hard work
    (C) has never eaten in a restaurant before
    (D) wants to learn more about cooking

Questions 18–22

Over two decades ago, scientists in the Agricultural Research Service Vegetable Crops Research Unit at Madison, Wisconsin, began a quest
5 to breed carrots packed with beta-carotene—an orange pigment used by the body to create vitamin A. Thanks largely to their work, today's carrots provide consumers with
10 75 percent more beta-carotene than those available 25 years ago.

The researchers, led by plant geneticist Philipp Simon, haven't limited themselves to the color orange.
15 They've selectively bred a rainbow of carrots—purple, red, yellow, even white. Scientists are learning that these plant pigments perform a range of protective duties in the
20 human body.

Red carrots derive their color mainly from lycopene, a type of carotene believed to guard against heart disease and some cancers.
25 Yellow carrots accumulate xantho-phylls, pigments similar to beta-carotene that support good eye health. Purple carrots possess an entirely different class of pigments—
30 anthocyanins—which act as powerful antioxidants. While colored carrots are unusual, they're not exactly new. "Purple and yellow carrots were eaten more than 1,000 years ago in
35 Afghanistan and 700 years ago in western Europe," says Simon. "But the carrot-breeding process has gone on intensively for just 50 years."

In nature, different strains of
40 carrots contain varying types and amounts of carotenoids—the pigments responsible for orange, yellow, and red colors. To assist seed companies and growers who wish to
45 produce nutrient-rich carrots, Simon and his lab are working to map all the genes that play a part in synthesizing carotenoids in major carrot lines. Simon now knows of 20 genes
50 that are involved. But determining a particular gene's role in generating carotenoids is not that straightforward. Aside from enhancing the nutritional value of carrots—as well
55 as onions, garlic, and cucumbers—researchers at Simon's laboratory also work to improve the vegetable's culinary quality and appeal.

With their compelling health ben-
60 efits and a thumbs-up from taste testers, Simon's colorful carrots will be a great addition to supermarket produce aisles once consumers create a demand for them.

18. The main purpose of this passage is to
    (A) report on enhancements to the nutritional value of carrots
    (B) point out the health benefits of carotenoids
    (C) explain why carrots can be various colors
    (D) encourage people to buy carrots of various colors

19. The author's tone can best be described as
    (A) emotional
    (B) sentimental
    (C) optimistic
    (D) informative

20. According to the passage, carrots have been bred in all of the following colors EXCEPT:
    (A) yellow
    (B) green
    (C) red
    (D) purple

21. The type of carotene that gives carrots a red color is
    (A) lycopene
    (B) xanthophyll
    (C) anthocyanin
    (D) beta-carotene

GO ON TO THE NEXT PAGE.

22. This passage can best be described as
    (A) a biography
    (B) a research report
    (C) propaganda
    (D) an editorial

Questions 23–26

From the outskirts of the town,
Where of old the mile-stone stood,
Now a stranger, looking down
I behold the shadowy crown
5 Of the dark and haunted wood

Is it changed, or am I changed?
Ah! the oaks are fresh and green,
But the friends with whom I ranged
10 Through their thickets are estranged
By the years that intervene.

Bright as ever flows the sea,
Bright as ever shines the sun,
15 But alas! they seem to me
Not the sun that used to be,
Not the tides that used to run.
　　　—Henry Wadsworth Longfellow
　　　　　　"Changed"

23. The author's tone is best described as
    (A) lighthearted
    (B) optimistic
    (C) nostalgic
    (D) humorous

24. This poem is written from the point of view of
    (A) a frightened child
    (B) a disinterested adult
    (C) a sympathetic outside observer
    (D) a sad observer of a transformation

25. In line 5, the author most probably refers to the woods as "haunted" in order to
    (A) make the narrator seem foolish and superstitious
    (B) hint at the narrator's acceptance of death
    (C) reveal the narrator's belief in spirits
    (D) indicate the woods were filled with memories

26. Which of the following best expresses the theme of this poem?
    (A) the power of the sun
    (B) the passage of time
    (C) the fluctuation of the tide
    (D) nature's renewal

Questions 27–32

The Statue of Liberty was a gift to the people of the United States from the people of France in recognition of the friendship established 5 between the two nations during the American Revolution. Over the years, the Statue of Liberty has come to symbolize freedom and democracy as well as this international friendship. 10 Sculptor Frederic Auguste Bartholdi was commissioned to design a sculpture with the year 1876 in mind for completion, to commemorate the centennial of the 15 American Declaration of Independence. Alexandre Gustave Eiffel (designer of the Eiffel Tower) was called in to address the structural issues of Bartholdi's colossal sculp- 20 ture. The Statue was a joint effort between America and France and it was agreed upon that the American people would build the pedestal, and the French people would be respon- 25 sible for the Statue and its assembly here in the United States. Lack of funds was a problem on both sides of the Atlantic Ocean. In France, public fees, various forms of enter- 30 tainment, and a lottery were among the methods used to raise funds. In the United States, benefit theatrical events, art exhibitions, auctions and prize fights helped to provide 35 the needed funds. When fundraising for the pedestal lagged, Joseph Pulitzer (noted for the Pulitzer Prize) used the editorial pages of his newspaper *The World* to aid in the 40 fundraising effort. Pulitzer's campaign of harsh criticism against both the rich, who had failed to finance the pedestal construction, and the middle class, who were content to 45 rely upon the wealthy to provide the funds, was successful in motivating the people of America to donate.

Financing for the pedestal was completed in August 1885, and pedestal 50 construction was finished in April of 1886. The Statue was completed in France in July, 1884 and arrived in New York Harbor in June of 1885 on board the French frigate *Isere*. 55 In transit, the Statue was reduced to 350 individual pieces and packed in 214 crates. The Statue was re-assembled on her new pedestal in four months time. On October 60 28th 1886, in front of thousands of spectators, President Grover Cleveland accepted the Statue on behalf of the United States. She was a centennial gift ten years late.

27. According to the passage, the Statue of Liberty was intended to celebrate the
    (A) centennial of the Declaration of Independence
    (B) end of the Civil War
    (C) end of hostilities between France and the United States
    (D) start of the Twentieth Century

28. In line 18, which word can be substituted for "address" without changing the meaning of the sentence?
    (A) speak to
    (B) focus on
    (C) lecture
    (D) label

29. According to the passage, the Statue of Liberty symbolizes
    I. democracy
    II. freedom
    III. international friendship
    IV. a treaty between the United States and France
    (A) I only
    (B) II only
    (C) I and III only
    (D) I, II, and III only

GO ON TO THE NEXT PAGE.

30. According to the passage, all of the following are true EXCEPT:
    (A) The United States agreed to finance and build the pedestal.
    (B) Bartholdi needed help with structural issues of the statue.
    (C) Joseph Pulitzer was instrumental in raising money for the pedestal.
    (D) The designer of the Eiffel Tower was called in to help raise funds for the project.

31. The main purpose of the passage is to
    (A) inform the reader about the history of the Statue of Liberty
    (B) describe how Bartholdi designed the Statue of Liberty
    (C) compare fundraising efforts in the United States and France
    (D) explain how the Statue was assembled on her pedestal

32. This passage would most likely appear in a
    (A) short story
    (B) textbook
    (C) engineering journal
    (D) newspaper

Questions 33–36

At the end of what seemed a tedious while, I had managed to pack my head full of islands, towns, bars, "points," and bends; and a curi-
5 ously inanimate mass of lumber it was, too. However, inasmuch as I could shut my eyes and reel off a good long string of these names without leaving out more than ten
10 miles of river in every fifty, I began to feel that I could take a boat down to New Orleans if I could make her skip those little gaps. But of course my complacency could hardly get start
15 enough to lift my nose a trifle into the air, before Mr. Bixby would think of something to fetch it down again. One day he turned on me suddenly with this settler: — "What is the shape
20 of Walnut Bend?"
    He might as well have asked me my grandmother's opinion of proto-plasm. I reflected respectfully, and then said I didn't know it had any
25 particular shape. My gunpowdery chief went off with a bang, of course, and then went on loading and firing until he was out of adjectives.
    I had learned long ago that he
30 only carried just so many rounds of ammunition, and was sure to subside into a very placable and even remorseful old smooth-bore as soon as they were all gone. That word
35 "old" is merely affectionate; he was not more than thirty-four. I waited. By and by he said, —
    "My boy, you've got to know the shape of the river perfectly. It is all
40 there is left to steer by on a very dark night. Everything else is blotted out and gone. But mind you, it hasn't the same shape in the night that it has in the day-time."
45 "How on earth am I ever going to learn it, then?"
    "How do you follow a hall at home in the dark? Because you know the shape of it. You can't see it."
50 "Do you mean to say that I've got to know all the million trifling varia-tions of shape in the banks of this interminable river as well as I know the shape of the front hall at home?"
55 "On my honor you've got to know them better than any man ever did know the shapes of the halls in his own house."
    "I wish I was dead!"
    Mark Twain from Life on the Mississippi

33. What is the meaning of "gunpowdery" in line 25?
    (A) explosive
    (B) smoky
    (C) strong
    (D) loud

34. Which of the following best describes the narrator's reaction to the information that he will need to know the shape of the river perfectly even at night?
    (A) anger
    (B) regret
    (C) amazement
    (D) despair

35. The tone of this passage can best be described as
    (A) humorous
    (B) serious
    (C) analytical
    (D) tense

36. This passage can best be described as
    (A) propaganda
    (B) an autobiography
    (C) a research report
    (D) a textbook excerpt

STOP!
If you finish before time is up, check your work on this section only.

Handwritten at top right:
12.98
47.23
22.97
14.77
15.00
112.95

Handwritten: WAIT FOR DAN

SECTION 4
Time: 40 Minutes
35 Questions

Directions: For each of the following questions, mark the letter of your choice on the answer sheet.

1. $\dfrac{2}{3} \div \dfrac{5}{6} =$ *(handwritten:* $\frac{4}{6} \div \frac{5}{6}$ *)*
    (A) $\dfrac{4}{5}$
    (B) $\dfrac{5}{18}$
    (C) $\dfrac{15}{6}$
    (D) $2\dfrac{1}{2}$

2. If $9 + 3 + \underline{\ 6\ } = 8 + 6 + 4$, then *(handwritten: 18)*
    ___ =
    (A) 3
    (B) 4
    (C) 5
    (D) 6

3. $12 + -6 \times 3 =$ *(handwritten: STOP)*
    (A) 21
    (B) 6
    (C) −6
    (D) −12

4. Ashley buys 48 apples. There are 12 Red Delicious applies and 16 Granny Smith apples. What fraction of the apples are not Red Delicious or Granny Smith?
    (A) $\dfrac{1}{5}$
    (B) $\dfrac{1}{4}$
    (C) $\dfrac{1}{3}$
    (D) $\dfrac{5}{12}$

Handwritten near 4: 20-16; 48; $\frac{12}{48}$ RD; $\frac{16}{48}$ GS; $\frac{5}{12}$

5. $12 \div 3\,3/4 =$
    (A) $2\dfrac{2}{3}$

Handwritten: 12 ÷ 3

6. Andre had a birthday party and spent $12.98 on balloons, $47.23 on party favors, $22.97 on a cake, $14.77 on ice cream, and $15.00 on invitations. How much did Andre spend on the party?
    (A) $87.25
    (B) $112.95 ✓
    (C) $125.20
    (D) $127.30

7. Christine spends 2 days a week painting houses and 3 days a week doing carpentry. If she earns $300 a day for painting and $240 a day for carpentry, how much does she earn in a week?
    (A) $1,280
    (B) $1,320
    (C) $1,360
    (D) $1,440

Handwritten: 600; 240; 240; 240; 1320

8. $102\,3/4\% =$
    (A) 102.75
    (B) 10.275
    (C) 1.0275
    (D) 0.10275

9. If $16 \div 4 \times \underline{\ 6\ } = 5 \times 8 - 16$, then ___ = *(handwritten: 4, 6)*
    (A) 6
    (B) 5

Handwritten: 40 − 16 = 24

(B) $2\dfrac{7}{16}$
(C) $3\dfrac{5}{8}$
(D) $3\dfrac{9}{13}$

(C) 4
(D) 3

10. $23.4 \div 6 =$
    (A) 39
    (B) 3.9   *(handwritten: guess)*
    (C) 0.39
    (D) 0.039

11. A teacher has assigned 315 pages of reading. If Jessica starts reading on Monday and reads 65 pages each day, on what day will she complete the assignment?
    (A) Wednesday
    (B) Thursday
    (C) Friday
    (D) Saturday

Handwritten: M 65; T 65; 130; W 65; 195; T 65; 260; F 65; 325

12. What is 2% of 5,000?
    (A) 10
    (B) 80
    (C) 100
    (D) 105

13. Louisa went to the grocery store and bought a package of hamburger patties for $6.16, a package of buns for $2.10, a container of mustard for $1.78, a jar of relish for $2.16, and a bag of charcoal for $5.35. What was her total bill?
    (A) $12.64
    (B) $14.74
    (C) $16.15
    (D) $17.55

Handwritten: 6.16; 2.10; 1.78; 2.16; 5.35; 17.55

GO ON TO THE NEXT PAGE

14. A $400 television is on sale for 15% off. What is the sale price?
    - (A) $340
    - (B) $350
    - (C) $375
    - (D) $385

15. Riverside School has 150 fewer students than twice the number of students at Hillside School. If Riverside School has 500 students, how many students attend Hillside School?
    - (A) 325
    - (B) 300
    - (C) 250
    - (D) 150

16. If $12a + 4a - 7a = 27$, $a =$
    - (A) 1
    - (B) 2
    - (C) 3
    - (D) 4

17. $4\frac{3}{10}\% =$
    - (A) 43
    - (B) 4.3
    - (C) 0.43
    - (D) 0.043

18. $^{18}/_{25} =$
    - (A) 0.72
    - (B) 0.68
    - (C) 0.66
    - (D) 0.63

19. Kyle can ride his bike 30 km in 2 hours. At the same rate, how far can he ride in 7 hours?
    - (A) 90 km
    - (B) 105 km
    - (C) 125 km
    - (D) 130 km

20. A rectangular garden is 40 yards long and 15 yards wide. Darryl runs once around the edge of the garden. How far does Darryl run?
    - (A) 55 yards
    - (B) 80 yards
    - (C) 100 yards
    - (D) 110 yards

21. $25\frac{3}{5} \times 1\frac{1}{2} =$
    - (A) $38\frac{2}{5}$
    - (B) $35\frac{1}{3}$
    - (C) $32\frac{2}{3}$
    - (D) $30\frac{5}{3}$

22. $18 \div {}^{3}/_{4} =$
    - (A) 3
    - (B) 6
    - (C) 12
    - (D) 24

23. $46\frac{3}{4}\% =$
    - (A) 467.5
    - (B) 46.75
    - (C) 4.675
    - (D) 0.4675

24. What is the greatest common factor of 75, 90, and 120?
    - (A) 5
    - (B) 10
    - (C) 15
    - (D) 20

25. In the Northshore Swimming Club, 6 of 48 members are females. What is the ratio of females to males?
    - (A) $\frac{3}{16}$
    - (B) $\frac{1}{15}$
    - (C) $\frac{1}{4}$
    - (D) $\frac{1}{8}$

26. Karen is driving to a town 175 miles away. If she drives at a steady speed of 50 miles per hour, how long will the trip take?
    - (A) 2 hours 50 minutes
    - (B) 3 hours
    - (C) 3 hours 10 minutes
    - (D) 3 hours 30 minutes

27. If $3.4a + 8.7a = 38.72$, $a =$
    - (A) 2.9
    - (B) 3.2

    - (C) 3.5
    - (D) 3.9

28. What is the perimeter of the following rectangle?

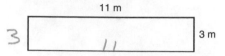

    11 m

    3 m

    - (A) 12 m
    - (B) 18 m
    - (C) 24 m
    - (D) 28 m

29. $^{1}/_{2} + {}^{1}/_{4} + {}^{3}/_{16} =$
    - (A) $\frac{3}{5}$
    - (B) $\frac{5}{6}$
    - (C) $\frac{7}{8}$
    - (D) $\frac{15}{16}$

30. 60 is approximately what percent of 90?
    - (A) 30%
    - (B) 33%
    - (C) 45%
    - (D) 67%

31. What is the least common multiple of 13, 26, and 2?
    - (A) 26
    - (B) 13
    - (C) 7
    - (D) 6

32. $3.5 \times 0.93 =$
    - (A) 2.886
    - (B) 2.965
    - (C) 3.255
    - (D) 3.311

33. Rosa buys a blouse for $23.95. The sales tax is 6.5%. What is the total cost of the blouse, including the sales tax?
    - (A) $24.35
    - (B) $24.78
    - (C) $25.20
    - (D) $25.51

GO ON TO THE NEXT PAGE.

34. The number of students who won awards at the science fair this year was 2 more than 3 times as many as last year. If 20 students won awards this year, how many won awards last year?

(A) 6
(B) 8
(C) 12
(D) 15 —

35. A clock shows 2:05. What time is it when 4 hours 58 minutes have passed?

— (A) 7:03
(B) 6:54
(C) 6:46
(D) 6:38

STOP!
If you finish before time is up, check your work on this section only.

ISEE Exam I: Section 4   **357**

$$\frac{1}{3} + \frac{1}{2}$$

$$\frac{1}{3} \times \frac{2}{2} = \frac{2}{6}$$

$$\frac{1}{2} + \frac{1}{2} = \frac{2}{2} = 1$$

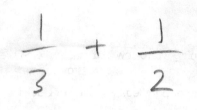

$$= \frac{2}{6} + \frac{3}{6} = \frac{5}{6}$$

SECTION 5
Time: 30 Minutes

Directions: You will have 30 minutes to plan and write an essay on the topic given below. You must write on the assigned topic only. An essay on another topic will not be acceptable. You may make notes in the space provided for that purpose.

Write your final essay on the two lined pages of your answer sheet. Write or print legibly in blue or black ink. A copy of your essay will be sent to each school that will be receiving your test results.

> What scientific advance do you think has most changed people's lives? Explain why you have chosen this advance.

USE THIS SPACE FOR NOTES

Lasers

(how) security

surgery
eye surgery (how)

each gets
its own
sentence

Fbi
(how)

Jewelry store (how)

House guns
laser scopes

1) Describe your choice
2.) what are the uses?
3.) why did I choose this one at most important
4.) Closing; Restate your selection/choice + one
   Key

Lasers

I think lasers have been the scientific advance that has changed peoples lives the most.

In security for the F.B.I. they need to put on their alarm which is lasers that are hooked up to the alarm. In jewelry stores its basically the same thing, laser hooked up to an alarm.

In guns the scope has lasers in it which helps in aiming.

In eye surgery the laser cuts the lens which corrects the eye vision.

So you see lasers have helped us in many different ways.

I think lasers are more impotant because lasers

help us
have kept us safe, aim with
guns, and help people see better

ISEE Practice Exam I

Answer Key

Section 1 Verbal Reasoning

1.	C	15.	A	29.	D
2.	B	16.	A	30.	A
3.	A	17.	B	31.	A
4.	B	18.	B	32.	B
5.	A	19.	D	33.	D
6.	D	20.	C	34.	C
7.	D	21.	C	35.	C
8.	C	22.	A	36.	A
9.	B	23.	C	37.	A
10.	A	24.	B	38.	B
11.	C	25.	D	39.	D
12.	D	26.	D	40.	B
13.	D	27.	C		
14.	C	28.	B		

Section 2 Quantitative Reasoning

1.	B	13.	A	25.	D
2.	A	14.	C	26.	A
3.	A	15.	B	27.	B
4.	D	16.	D	28.	A
5.	C	17.	C	29.	D
6.	D	18.	B	30.	D
7.	C	19.	C	31.	A
8.	D	20.	A	32.	D
9.	D	21.	B	33.	D
10.	A	22.	A	34.	C
11.	C	23.	D	35.	D
12.	D	24.	A		

Section 3 Reading Comprehension

1.	D	13.	D	25.	D
2.	B	14.	A	26.	B
3.	C	15.	C	27.	A
4.	A	16.	B	28.	B
5.	B	17.	B	29.	D
6.	C	18.	A	30.	D
7.	D	19.	D	31.	A
8.	C	20.	B	32.	B
9.	A	21.	A	33.	A
10.	B	22.	B	34.	D
11.	C	23.	C	35.	A
12.	D	24.	D	36.	B

Section 4 Mathematics Achievement

1.	A	13.	D	25.	D
2.	D	14.	A	26.	D
3.	C	15.	A	27.	B
4.	D	16.	C	28.	D
5.	D	17.	D	29.	D
6.	B	18.	A	30.	D
7.	B	19.	B	31.	A
8.	C	20.	D	32.	C
9.	A	21.	A	33.	D
10.	B	22.	D	34.	A
11.	C	23.	D	35.	A
12.	C	24.	C		

Answers and Explanations

Section 1 Verbal Reasoning

1. **C is correct.** A *novice* is a person new to a field or activity—a *beginner.*

2. **B is correct.** To *fabricate* is to concoct in order to deceive—in other words, to *falsify.*

3. **A is correct.** *Friendly* means agreeable in disposition, good-natured and likeable, or *amiable.*

4. **B is correct.** A *genre* is a type or class. The choice that best fits this definition is *category.*

5. **A is correct.** A *summit* is a conference or meeting of high-level officials, typically called to shape a course of action.

6. **D is correct.** To do something *deftly* is to do it quickly and *skillfully.*

7. **D is correct.** To *prosper* is to be fortunate or successful, especially in terms of one's health or finances—in other words, to *thrive.*

8. **C is correct.** To *spurn* is to reject disdainfully or contemptuously; *scorn.*

9. **B is correct.** *Visage* is the *face* or facial expression of a person; *countenance.*

10. **A is correct.** A *respite* is a usually short interval of rest or relief—in other words, a *pause.*

11. **C is correct.** *Regretful* means feeling troubled, remorseful or *contrite* for one's sins or offenses.

12. **D is correct.** To *incite* is to *provoke* or *urge on.*

13. **D is correct.** A *facet* is one of numerous *aspects*, as of a subject.

14. **C is correct.** To *absolve* is to *clear* someone of guilt or blame.

15. **A is correct.** *Aplomb* is self-assurance or *confidence.*

16. **A is correct.** *Corroboration* is ratification or *confirmation* that some statement or fact is true.

17. **B is correct.** Behavior that is *erratic* lacks consistency, regularity, or uniformity; in other words it is *unpredictable.*

18. **B is correct.** To *abscond* is to *leave* quickly and secretly and hide oneself, often to avoid arrest or prosecution.

19. **D is correct.** *Irritable* means easily provoked, impatient, ill-tempered, or *petulant.*

20. **C is correct.** A *travesty* is a debased or grotesque likeness or a *mockery.*

21. **C is correct.** The clue to this sentence is the phrase "the air." Try thinking of a word on your own. Maybe you came up with *hanging* or *floating*. Don't be fooled by *surpassing* (choice B), as that means "going beyond the limit." The correct answer is *wafting*, meaning "to send floating through the air or over water."

22. **A is correct.** "Despite" is a clue that indicates contrast, and the phrase "self-professed" lets you know that this man might see himself in a way that others do not. So, in spite of the man's self-professed benevolence (meaning an "inclination to perform kind, charitable acts"), the museum's board of directors soon realized they would never receive a dime from him.

23. **C is correct.** In this sentence you are looking for a word that works well alongside of someone described as *outgoing*. *Gregarious*, meaning "sociable or seeking and enjoying the company of others," is the only possible correct choice.

24. **B is correct.** "Although" is another one of the words you may see on the test that signals a contrast within a two-blank sentence. When you come across words or phrases such as "despite," "although" or "even though," keep in mind that the pair of words you are looking for are likely to have opposite meanings. Of the choices available, only *humble . . . affluent* (choice B), offers sufficient contrast.

25. **D is correct.** Since all of the first blank answers are synonymous with each other, turn your attention to the second blank. Of the choices available, only a *lackadaisical* approach (meaning "lacking spirit, liveliness, or interest") to practicing outside of school is likely to lead their instructor to have admonished them.

26. **D is correct.** The logic of this sentence implies that the owner agreed to the pitcher's demands for a guaranteed contract. *Acceded*, meaning "to give one's consent often at the insistence of another; concede," is the correct answer.

27. **C is correct.** Often when you encounter a two-blank question, a good strategy is to try and fill in one of the blanks first so that you can eliminate some of the incorrect answer choices. If you begin with the second blank of this question, you will see that you are able to eliminate choices B and D almost immediately. Now, ask yourself: which sounds better, the fact that Carlos knew his goals were not easily *attainable* or easily *deplorable*? Choice C is correct.

28. **B is correct.** Since choices A, B, and C all have similar meanings, you can discount choice D and focus on the second-blank choices. Of the three, *depict* (meaning to "represent in a picture or a sculpture") is clearly the best choice and fits the context of the sentence.

29. **D is correct.** *Astute* (meaning "having or showing shrewdness or discernment") is the best word of the choices to describe someone who studies hard and seems to have a knack for doing well on tests.

30. **A is correct.** Another way of describing a person who is highly skilled or an expert at something is to say that he is *adept* at it. *Expedient* means "fast," *affable* means "friendly," and *acrid* means "unusually sharp, unpleasant, or bitter to the taste or smell."

31. **A is correct.** Because it's unlikely that activists would try to destroy a building that was ultimately torn down, you can eliminate choice D. *Inextricable* means "so entangled as to make escape impossible," and *flagrant* means "conspicuously bad, offensive, or reprehensible." *Futile* "means having no useful result" and best fits the context of the sentence.

32. **B is correct.** "Disreputable" is a key word in this sentence, and you should look for a word that does not fit well with it. *Integrity* means "a strict adherence to a moral or ethical code," and because Mario felt his integrity was being compromised by working for a disreputable corporation, he decided to quit.

33. **D is correct.** Since it is unlikely that an *awkward* or *errant* biographer would be praised, you can eliminate choices A and C. *Countenance* means "appearance, especially the expression of the face," and does not fit the context of the sentence. Choice D is correct.

34. **C is correct.** *Reverence* (meaning "a feeling of profound awe and respect and often love") is the only word that fits the context here. Since Maria is a devoted fan, she would probably not show her *reluctance* or *disparagement* when the actor came out for his curtain call. *Ascension*, meaning "the act or process of rising" is incorrect as well.

35. **C is correct.** A person is not likely to be *insulted* or *emulated* (meaning "to strive to equal or excel, especially through imitation") at her going-away party. As well, *omission* does not make sense in the sentence. Choice C is correct.

36. **A is correct.** A *pragmatist* is a person who takes a practical approach to problems and is concerned primarily with the success or failure of her actions. This is the best answer to the question.

37. **A is correct.** After reading the sentence, you can probably figure out the word you are looking for means "started or began." *Originated*, meaning "to bring into being or to create," is the only appropriate answer.

38. **B is correct.** This sentence seems to be saying that the open house was rescheduled due to bad weather. *Inclement*, meaning "stormy," is the correct answer.

39. **D is correct.** If results go beyond your expectations, you might say that they *exceeded* your expectations. This is the only answer that fits the context of the scouts' fund-raising efforts.

40. **B is correct.** An *accord* is an agreement, or a settlement or compromise of conflicting opinions. Choice B is the correct answer.

Section 2 Quantitative Reasoning

1. **B is correct.** $2.4 - 2 = 0.4$; $2 - 1.8 = 0.2$; $2 - 1.0 = 1.0$; $2 - 0.3 = 1.7$. Of the choices, the closest to 2 is 1.8.

2. **A is correct.** $4 \times 3 \times 6 \times 2 = 144$; $144 \div 24 = 6$.

3. **A is correct.** $1/4 \times 10,000 = {}^{10,000}/4 = 2,500$.

4. **D is correct.** $6^{3}/4\% = 0.0675$.

5. **C is correct.** $5 + 11 + 6 = 22$; $6 + 12 = 18$; and $22 - 18 = 4$.

6. **D is correct.** $4/10$ can be simplified to $2/5$.

7. **C is correct.** The least common multiple of a group of numbers is the least whole number (greater than 0) that is a multiple of all of the numbers. The least common multiple of 3, 4, and 18 is 36 (3×12, 4×9, 2×18).

8. **D is correct.** $16/4 = 4$; $6 \times 2/3 = 12/3 = 4$; $4 \div 1/4 = 4 \times 4/1 = 16$. However, $1/3 \times 4 = 4/3$, which is not a whole number.

9. **D is correct.**
   $10 \times (0.38 + 3.5) + 5.2$
   $= (10 \times 0.38) + (10 \times 3.5) + 5.2$
   $= 3.8 + 35 + 5.2$
   $= 44$

10. **A is correct.** Convert to equivalent expressions. $3/5 = 6/10$; $0.8 = 8/10$; $1 1/2 = 1 5/10 = 15/10$. $6/10 < 8/10 < 15/10$.

11. **C is correct.** $\$0.80 + \$0.20 + \$0.30 = \$1.30$.

12. **D is correct.** From midnight to 11:00 A.M. there are 11 hours. If the temperature rose 2°C each hour, then it rose 22°C.
    $(-12) + 22 = 10°C$

13. **A is correct.** Add the amount of the checks and subtract the total from the current amount in the checking account.
    $\$12,444.12 - (\$8,204.94 + \$890.99) = \$3,348.19$

14. **C is correct.** $2,880 \div 9 = 320$ miles per hour.

15. **B is correct.** In this problem you need to find $1/5$ of 55; $55 \div 5 = 11$.

16. **D is correct.** $30/5 = 6$; $4 \times 12/16 = 48/16 = 3$; $16 \div 1/16 = 16 \times 16/1 = 256$. However, $5/9 \times 8 = 40/9 = 4 4/9$, which is not a whole number.

17. **C is correct.** The greatest common factor of a group of numbers is the largest whole number that is a factor of all the numbers. The greatest common factor of 16, 24, 96, and 120 is 8.

18. **B is correct.** If Aaron has 256 cans of soup to pack into boxes of 30, he can fill $256 \div 30 = 8$ boxes with 16 cans of soup left over.

19. **C is correct.**
$-10 - (-5 - 4)$
$= -10 - (-9)$
$= -10 + 9 = -1$

20. **A is correct.** In this problem you need to calculate the number of 26-mpg units there are in 858. Do this by dividing 858 by 26.
$858 \div 26 = 33$ gallons

21. **B is correct.** $2 + \frac{4}{25} = 2.16$.

22. **A is correct.** $2 \times 3 \times 5 \times 6 = 180$. $\frac{180}{30} = 6$.

23. **D is correct.** $12 + (-8) + (-9) + 6 = 4 + (-9) + 6 = -5 + 6 = 1$.

24. **A is correct.** To calculate the percent, divide the number of items answered correctly by the total number of items. $45 \div 75 = 0.60$. To change that to a percent, move the decimal point two places to the right and add the percent sign to get 60%.

25. **D is correct.**
$11\frac{1}{2} - 9\frac{3}{4} = 11\frac{2}{4} - 9\frac{3}{4}$
$= 10\frac{6}{4} - 9\frac{3}{4}$
$= 1\frac{3}{4}$

26. **A is correct.**
$\frac{3}{4} + \frac{1}{2} + \frac{2}{3} - \frac{5}{6}$
$= \frac{9}{12} + \frac{6}{12} + \frac{8}{12} - \frac{10}{12}$
$= \frac{23}{12} - \frac{10}{12}$
$= \frac{13}{12}$
$= 1\frac{1}{12}$

27. **B is correct.** $42 \div 7 \times 8 \times 5 = 240$; $240 \div 12 = 20$.

28. **A is correct.** $5 \times 4 + 4 = 24$; $4 \times 3 = 12$; and $24 \div 12 = 2$.

29. **D is correct.** To calculate the answer, divide 200 by 5.
$200 \div 5 = 40$

30. **D is correct.** To calculate the percent, divide the number of jazz and rap songs by the total number of songs. $240 \div 800 = 0.30$ To change that to a percent, move the decimal point two places to the right and add the percent sign to get the correct answer of 30%.

31. **A is correct.** You are told that two numbers add to 1,500 and that one of the two is 4 times the size of other. Create an equation:
$x + 4x = 1,500$
Solve for x.
$5x = 1,500$
$x = 300$
$4x = 1,200$
So the two numbers are 300 and 1,200.

32. **D is correct.** $18 \div \frac{3}{4} = \frac{18}{1} \div \frac{3}{4} = \frac{18}{1} \times \frac{4}{3} = \frac{72}{3} = 24$.

33. **D is correct.** $71\frac{1}{5}\% = 0.712$.

34. **C is correct**. Set up an equation. If x = number of students in sixth grade,

$$x = {}^{144}\!/_6 + 8$$
$$x = 24 + 8$$
$$x = 32$$

35. **D is correct**. $62\tfrac{1}{2}\% = 0.625$.

Section 3 Reading Comprehension

1. **D is correct**. As stated in the first two sentences, "Volcanoes are mountains, but they are very different from other mountains; they are not formed by folding and crumpling or by uplift and erosion. Instead, volcanoes are built by the accumulation of their own eruptive products — lava, bombs (crusted over lava blobs), ashflows, and tephra (airborne ash and dust)."

2. **B is correct**. As stated in the second paragraph, "How explosive an eruption is depends on how runny or sticky the magma is. ... If magma is thick and sticky, gases cannot escape easily. Pressure builds up until the gases escape violently and explode." Choice A is wrong because if magma is thin and runny, "gases can escape easily from it," and when this type of magma erupts, "it flows out of the volcano." Choices C and D are both true of magma, but neither indicates how explosive an eruption will be.

3. **C is correct**. The words in italics are scientific terms for which the author provides definitions within the text. ("A *volcano* is most commonly a conical hill or mountain built around a vent that connects with reservoirs of molten rock below the surface of the Earth." "Magma that has erupted is called *lava*.")

4. **A is correct**. The passage states that "Deep within the Earth it is so hot that some rocks slowly melt and become a thick flowing substance called *magma*." However, the passage does not mention the factors that contribute to hot temperatures deep inside the Earth. Choice B is answered in lines 27–30. Choice C is answered in lines 19–22. Choice D is answered in lines 39–42.

5. **B is correct**. This passage explains how volcanoes are formed and the nature of volcanic eruptions using the scientific terminology and strictly factual presentation typical of information presented in a science textbook. There is nothing timely about the information, so it is not likely to be from a newspaper article as in choice A. There is no evidence of a plot or characters, so you can easily eliminate choice C. There is no mention of safety, so choice D cannot be correct.

6. **C is correct**. During a volcanic eruption, magma blasts into the air and breaks apart into pieces called tephra; thus choice D is true. As explained in the last paragraph, tephra can vary greatly in size (choice A), and it can travel hundreds to thousands of kilometers downwind from a volcano (choice B). Gases, not tephra, may be trapped in magma; therefore choice C is the only choice that is NOT true of tephra.

7. **D is correct**. Douglass makes this point in the very first sentence when he says, "I am one of those who believe that it is the mission of this war to free every slave in the United States." Choices A, B, and C might all be consequences of the Civil War, but in this speech Douglass mentions only freeing every slave in the United States as the mission of the war.

8. **C is correct**. Douglass believed that "the work of the American Anti-Slavery Society will not have been completed until the black men of the South, and the black men of the North, shall have been admitted, fully and completely, into the body politic of America." He specifically mentions that voting rights should be extended equally to all black men. He does not mention that voting rights should be extended to everyone (choice D). Douglass advocates the abolition of slavery as the "mission of the war," but he believes that the work of the Anti-Slavery Society should go beyond this goal to the greater goal of setting the same conditions for voting for black men and white men.

9. **A is correct**. The *body politic* means "the people of a politically organized nation or state." To be fully and completely admitted to the body politic means to have all the rights accorded to any other citizen of the nation or state. Choices B, C, and D are rights and duties that are included in choice A.

10. **B is correct.** The passage is written in the first person and offers the views of the author on the subject of slavery and voting rights. The last paragraph makes it clear that the author is trying to convince members of the society that "whatever rule you adopt, whether of intelligence or wealth, as the condition of voting for whites, you shall apply it equally to the black man." He goes on to say that if they do that "I am satisfied, and eternal justice is satisfied; liberty, fraternity, equality, are satisfied, and the country will move on harmoniously." As stated in the italic text at the start of the article, this speech was given at a meeting of the Anti-Slavery Society. It is unlikely that members of an Anti-Slavery Society would need to be convinced that slavery should be so ended so choice D can be eliminated. Choices A and C can also be eliminated because the passage is a statement of the author's opinions on the subject, not just an objective presentation of information about the horrors of slavery (choice A) or the progress of the war (choice C).

11. **C is correct.** The author describes the newly married pair as uncomfortable in their new clothes, unused to taking trips in a "fine" parlor-car, and embarrassed by the scrutiny of other passengers. He seems to like the unsophisticated couple and to be sympathetic toward their situation. The bride and groom may be embarrassed, but the author is not, so choice A is incorrect. Choices B and D are incorrect because nothing in the passage supports the idea that the author regards the couple with *disrespect* (meaning "discourtesy" or "rudeness") or *scorn* (meaning "contempt" or "disdain").

12. **D is correct.** Both the bride and the groom were unaccustomed to wearing new clothes. The groom's face was "reddened from many days in the wind and sun." The bride had never traveled in a parlor car and she was clearly more used to cooking than to eating in a dining car. All of these clues point to the fact that the newlyweds were *unsophisticated* (meaning "innocent") country people. The fact that the bride thinks that a dollar is too much for them to spend on a meal indicates that the couple is not wealthy or well-to-do, so choice A is wrong. The passage mentions that the couple "were evidently very happy," so choice B is wrong. Although the couple is described as being shy and embarrassed by the attention of other passengers, there is nothing to support the idea that they were unpleasant (choice C).

13. **D is correct.** The story takes place on a train crossing the plains of Texas. You can tell this from the fact that the groom asks his bride, "Have you ever been in a parlor-car before?" and then mentions that they will "go forward to the diner and get a big layout." Parlor-cars and dining cars are found on trains. Although the passage states that the newly married pair "had boarded this coach at San Antonio," the coach that is referred to is a car on a train, not a stage coach, so choice B is wrong. The groom mentions that "after a while we'll go forward to the diner," but at the time this passage takes place, they have not yet gone to the diner to eat, so choice C is wrong. The couple has already boarded the train, so they cannot be in a hotel (choice A).

14. **A is correct.** Lines 23–24 states that "The glances he devoted to other passengers were furtive and shy." From this sentence you can tell that *furtive* must be something that goes with *shy*. *Unabashed* (meaning "unembarrassed" or "not shy") is the opposite of shy, so you can eliminate choice D. Similarly, you can eliminate choice C because *focused* means "clear and sharp," which is not commonly associated with *shy*. That leaves choice A, which is correct. A *furtive* glance is a secret or stealthy glance.

15. **C is correct.** The story is told in the third person by someone who is not a participant in the story. Therefore you can eliminate choices A and B. A story told by someone looking back on his life, the story would most likely be told in the first person (using "I" and "me" throughout). Because this story is told by someone who can see everything that is happening in the tale, but is not himself participating in the tale, it is most likely the work of an outside observer.

16. **B is correct.** This passage is actually the beginning of a short story. Its purpose is to introduce the characters and setting of the story to come. The passage is purely descriptive. There is no attempt to express an opinion (choice A) or resolve a crisis (choice C). At this point in the story there is no conflict between the major characters. In fact, the bride and groom are described as "evidently very happy."

17. **B is correct.** If you can tell by simply looking at the bride that "she had cooked, and that she expected to cook, dutifully," then the bride most probably has the red, rough hands indicative of a life of hard work. Just looking at a person is unlikely to reveal whether that person expects to eat out regularly or has ever eaten in a restaurant before, so choices A and C are incorrect. Similarly, it is impossible to tell what a person wants to or might expect to learn about cooking by observation alone, so choice D is also incorrect.

18. **A is correct.** The purpose of this passage is to report on the work done by scientists to breed carrots with enhanced nutritional value. The researchers have selectively bred carrots in a rainbow of colors and studied the effects of the various plant pigments on the human body.

19. **D is correct.** The passage is intended to inform readers of developments in carrot breeding. The passage does not contain any emotionally charged language; thus choice A can be eliminated. Nothing about the passage could be termed sentimental and, although the last sentence offers the opinion that colorful carrots will be a good addition to supermarket produce aisles, this is not enough to describe the entire passage as optimistic.

20. **B is correct.** As stated in lines 15–17, researchers have "selectively bred a rainbow of carrots—purple, red, yellow, even white." The only choice not mentioned is green.

21. **A is correct.** As stated in lines 21–24, "Red carrots derive their color mainly from lycopene, a type of carotene believed to guard against heart disease and some cancers." Xanthophyll (choice B) is found in yellow carrots. Anthocyanin (choice C) is the pigment found in purple carrots. Beta-carotene (choice D) is the pigment found in orange carrots.

22. **B is correct.** The passage reports on the work of agricultural research scientists as they attempt to breed nutrient-rich carrots. It is not the story of someone's life, so it cannot be a biography. It is not written for the purpose of promoting some doctrine or cause, so it does not fall into the category of propaganda. It is not primarily an expression of the opinion of the author, so it is not an editorial.

23. **C is correct.** Tone is the author's attitude toward a topic. It is created through details and language. The sense of this poem is that the narrator has returned to a place he once knew and finds himself "now a stranger" and laments the fact that nothing is as it used to be: "Not the sun that used to be, Not the tides that used to run." The best description of this tone is nostalgic, meaning "sentimental" or "evidencing bittersweet longing for things of the past." Words such as "shadowy crown," "dark and haunted wood," and "alas" are not consistent with a lighthearted, optimistic, or humorous tone, so you can rule out choices A, B, and D.

24. **D is correct.** The narrator of this poem is clearly an adult returning to a scene of his youth and feeling a sense of sadness at the transformation he observes. Old friends are "estranged," the sun is "not the sun that used to be," and the tides are "not the tides that used to run." Choice A is incorrect because the narrator is an adult, not a child. Choice B is incorrect because the narrator is not indifferent to what he sees. Choice C is incorrect because the narrator is not an outside observer, as evidenced by the use of the pronoun "I" throughout.

25. **D is correct.** The author's choice of the word *haunted*, which means "inhabited by the spirit of people and times gone by," serves to underscore the idea of memories of friendships past. Choices A and B do not fit the poem at all. Choice C reflects one meaning of the word *haunted*, but misses the point that the poem is about memories, not spirits.

26. **B is correct.** The theme of the poem is the main idea the poem conveys. In this case, the theme is the passage of time. The poem mentions both the sun (choice A) and the tide (choice C), but each shows only that time has passed. The poem is not about renewal (choice D), but rather about the changes brought about by the passage of time.

27. **A is correct.** As stated in the second paragraph, the sculpture was commissioned to be completed in 1876, "to commemorate the centennial of the American Declaration of Independence." Choice B is incorrect because the Statue commemorated the friendship between the United States and France during the Revolutionary War, not the Civil War. Choice C is incorrect because the passage mentions only friendship between France and the United States; there is no mention of hostility between the two nations. Choice D is incorrect because the Statue was supposed to have been completed in 1876, which is 24 years before the start of the twentieth century.

28. **B is correct.** Eiffel was called in to *attend to* or *focus on* the structural issues of the sculpture. All of the choices are synonyms for the word *address*, but only choice B fits the context of this sentence.

29. **D is correct.** As stated in the first paragraph, the Statue was a gift to the people of the United States "in recognition of the friendship established between the two nations during the American Revolution." Over the years, however, "the Statue of Liberty has come to symbolize freedom and democracy as well as this international friendship." There is no mention in the passage of a treaty between the United States and France.

30. **D is correct.** Alexandre Gustave Eiffel, who designed the Eiffel Tower, was called in "to address the structural issues of Bartholdi's colossal sculpture," not to help raise money for the project. Choice A is mentioned in lines 22–23. Choice B is mentioned in lines 16–19. Choice C is mentioned in lines 35–40.

31. **A is correct.** This passage is entirely devoted to telling the history of the Statue of Liberty from design to financing to completion. It does not describe how Bartholdi designed the Statue (choice B), but only tells that he did so with the help of Eiffel. It mentions fund-raising in the United States and France (choice C), but it is not devoted to comparing them. Only one sentence in the entire passage is devoted to assembling the Statue on her pedestal (choice D).

32. **B is correct.** This informational article is most likely to be found in a textbook. Choice A is easily eliminated because the passage is fact, not fiction. Choice D is incorrect because the passage tells of events that happened long ago, not timely current events as would be reported in a newspaper article. The passage does not describe the engineering aspects of the Statue, so choice C is not a likely answer.

33. **A is correct.** In describing Bixby's response to the narrator's not knowing the shape of Walnut Bend, the author says, "My gunpowdery chief went off with a bang, of course, and then went on loading and firing until he was out of adjectives." The word that best describes something that goes off with a bang and keeps on firing until the ammunition runs out is *explosive*.

34. **D is correct.** Upon learning that he must know all the variations of shape in the banks of the river as well as he knows "the shape of the front hall at home," the narrator replies, "I wish I was dead!" This reaction can best be described as "hopelessness" or "despair."

35. **A is correct.** Tone is the writer's attitude toward a topic. It is revealed through the writer's word choice. Statements such as "a curiously inanimate mass of lumber it was" and "He might as well have asked me my grandmother's opinion of protoplasm" help to reveal the humor with which the author regards the situation.

36. **B is correct.** The passage is written in the first person and appears to describe events that occurred in the life of the author. These are characteristic of autobiographical writing.

Section 4 Mathematics Achievement

1. **A is correct.** When dividing fractions, invert and multiply. See if you can simplify the fractions.
$$\frac{2}{3} \div \frac{5}{6} = \frac{2}{3} \times \frac{6}{5} \text{ Multiply}$$
$$= \frac{12}{15} \text{ Simplify}$$
$$= \frac{4}{5}$$

2. **D is correct.** $8 + 6 + 4 = 18$; $9 + 3 = 12$; and $18 - 12 = 6$.

3. **C is correct.**
$12 + -6 \times 3$
$= 12 + (-18)$
$= -6$

4. **D is correct.** 12 Red Delicious apples + 16 Granny Smith apples = 28 apples. $48 - 28 = 20$ apples that are not Red Delicious or Granny Smith. $^{20}/_{48} = {}^5/_{12}$.

5. **D is correct.**
$12 \div 3^3/_4 = {}^{12}/_1 \div {}^{13}/_4$
$= {}^{12}/_1 \times {}^4/_{13}$
$= {}^{48}/_{13} = 3^9/_{13}$

6. **B is correct.** This is a simple addition problem. Add the amounts of $12.98, $47.23, $22.97, $14.77, $15.00 to get the total of $112.95.

7. **B is correct.** $(2 \times \$300) + (3 \times \$240) = \$600 + \$720 = \$1,320$.

8. **C is correct.** $102\frac{3}{4}\% = 1.0275$.

9. **A is correct.** $5 \times 8 - 16 = 24$; $16 \div 4 = 4$; and $24 \div 4 = 6$.

10. **B is correct.**
    $23.4 \div 6 = 3.9$

11. **C is correct.** If Jessica has 315 pages of reading and reads 65 pages each day, on Monday she has read 65 pages, on Tuesday she has read 2(65) or 130 pages, on Wednesday she has read 3(65) or 195 pages, and on Thursday she has read 4(65) or 260 pages. On Friday, Jessica would need to read only 55 pages to complete the assignment. Another way to do this is to divide 315 by 65 to get 4.85. If Monday is 1, Tuesday is 2, Wednesday is 3, and Thursday is 4, then Friday would be 5. On Friday Jessica would complete the assignment.

12. **C is correct.** 2% is the equivalent of 0.02. $0.02 \times 5,000 = 100$.

13. **D is correct.** This is a simple addition problem. Add the amounts to get the total of $17.55.

14. **A is correct.** 15% of $400 = $0.15 \times 400 = \$60$; $400 - \$60 = \$340$.

15. **A is correct.** Create an equation:
    Riverside = 2 × Hillside −150
    $500 = 2x - 150$
    $750 = 2x$
    $325 = x$

16. **C is correct.** Solve the equation.
    $12a + 4a - 7a = 27$
    $16a - 7a = 27$
    $9a = 27$
    $a = 3$

17. **D is correct.** $4\frac{3}{10}\% = 0.043$.

18. **A is correct.** $\frac{18}{25} = \frac{72}{100} = 0.72$.

19. **B is correct.** Set up a proportion:
    $30/2 = n/7$
    $n = 105$

20. **D is correct.** The edge of the garden is its perimeter. To find the perimeter of a rectangle, add the lengths of the sides: $40 + 15 + 40 + 15 = 110$ yards.

21. **A is correct.**
    $25\frac{3}{5} \times 1\frac{1}{2}$
    $= \frac{128}{5} \times \frac{3}{2}$
    $= \frac{384}{10} = 38\frac{4}{10} = 38\frac{2}{5}$

22. **D is correct.** $18 \div \frac{3}{4} = \frac{18}{1} \div \frac{3}{4} = \frac{18}{1} \times \frac{4}{3} = \frac{72}{3} = 24$.

23. **D is correct.** $46\frac{3}{4}\% = 0.4675$.

24. **C is correct.** The greatest common factor of a group of numbers is the greatest whole number that is a factor of all the numbers. The greatest common factor of 75, 90, and 120 is 15.

25. **D is correct.** To find the ratio of one number to another, create a fraction to show the relationship. In this problem there are 6 female club members in a total of 48 club members. The fraction that shows the relationship is $^6/_{48}$. This fraction can be simplified to $^1/_8$, the correct answer.

26. **D is correct.** Use the formula $d = r \times t$ where d = distance, r = rate, and t = time.
$d = r \times t$
$175 = 50 \times t$
$t = ^{175}/_{50}$
$t = 3.5$ hours = 3 hours 30 minutes

27. **B is correct.**
$3.4a + 8.7a = 38.72$
$12.1a = 38.72$
$a = 3.2$

28. **D is correct.** To find the perimeter of a quadrilateral, add the lengths of the four sides. In this instance, 11 meters + 11 meters + 3 meters + 3 meters = 28 meters, the correct answer.

29. **D is correct.** Convert to equivalent expressions: $^1/_2 = ^8/_{16}$; $^1/_4 = ^4/_{16}$.
$^8/_{16} + ^4/_{16} + ^3/_{16} = ^{15}/_{16}$

30. **D is correct.** $60 = x$ % of 90
$60 = 90x$ Solve for x.
$x = \dfrac{60}{90} =$
$x = \dfrac{6}{9}$
$x = \dfrac{2}{3}$ Divide 2 by 3 to get 0.6666 or 67%

31. **A is correct.** The least common multiple of a group of numbers is the least whole number, greater than 0, that is a multiple of all of the numbers. The least common multiple of 13, 26, and 2 is 26.

32. **C is correct.**
$$\begin{array}{r} 3.5 \\ \times\, 0.93 \\ \hline 1\ 05 \\ 31\ 5 \\ \hline 3.255 \end{array}$$

33. **D is correct.** $23.95 \times 0.065 = \$1.56$; $\$23.95 + \$1.56 = \$25.51$.

34. **A is correct.** Let n be the number of students who won awards last year. Set up an equation:
$3n + 2 = 20$
$3n = 18$
$n = 6$

35. **A is correct.** When 4 hours have passed, the time is 6:05. After another 58 minutes the time is 7:03.

ISEE Practice Test II

(Middle Level: For Candidates for Grades 7 and 8)

The following practice test is designed to be just like the real ISEE that you will take if you are applying for admission to grades 7 or 8. It matches the actual test in content coverage and level of difficulty. The test is in five sections: Verbal Reasoning, Quantitative Reasoning, Reading Comprehension, Mathematics Achievement, and the Essay.

This practice test will be an accurate reflection of how you'll do on test day if you treat it as the real examination. Here are some hints on how to take the test under conditions similar to those of the actual exam:

- Find a quiet place to work and set aside a period of approximately 3 hours when you will not be disturbed.

- Work on only one section at a time, and use your watch or a timer to keep track of the time limits for each test part.

- Tear out your answer sheet and mark your answers by filling in the ovals for each question.

- Write your essay on the pages provided.

- Become familiar with the directions for each part of the test. You'll save time on the actual test day by already being familiar with this information.

At the end of the test you'll find Answer Keys for each section and explanations for every question. Check your answers against the keys to find out how you did on each section of the test and what test topics you might need to study more. Then review the explanations, paying particular attention to the ones for the questions that you answered incorrectly.

ISEE Practice Test II

ANSWER SHEET

Note: If there are more answer lines than there are questions in a section, leave the extra answer lines blank.

Section 1: Verbal Reasoning

1. Ⓐ Ⓑ Ⓒ Ⓓ	17. Ⓐ Ⓑ Ⓒ Ⓓ	33. Ⓐ Ⓑ Ⓒ Ⓓ
2. Ⓐ Ⓑ Ⓒ Ⓓ	18. Ⓐ Ⓑ Ⓒ Ⓓ	34. Ⓐ Ⓑ Ⓒ Ⓓ
3. Ⓐ Ⓑ Ⓒ Ⓓ	19. Ⓐ Ⓑ Ⓒ Ⓓ	35. Ⓐ Ⓑ Ⓒ Ⓓ
4. Ⓐ Ⓑ Ⓒ Ⓓ	20. Ⓐ Ⓑ Ⓒ Ⓓ	36. Ⓐ Ⓑ Ⓒ Ⓓ
5. Ⓐ Ⓑ Ⓒ Ⓓ	21. Ⓐ Ⓑ Ⓒ Ⓓ	37. Ⓐ Ⓑ Ⓒ Ⓓ
6. Ⓐ Ⓑ Ⓒ Ⓓ	22. Ⓐ Ⓑ Ⓒ Ⓓ	38. Ⓐ Ⓑ Ⓒ Ⓓ
7. Ⓐ Ⓑ Ⓒ Ⓓ	23. Ⓐ Ⓑ Ⓒ Ⓓ	39. Ⓐ Ⓑ Ⓒ Ⓓ
8. Ⓐ Ⓑ Ⓒ Ⓓ	24. Ⓐ Ⓑ Ⓒ Ⓓ	40. Ⓐ Ⓑ Ⓒ Ⓓ
9. Ⓐ Ⓑ Ⓒ Ⓓ	25. Ⓐ Ⓑ Ⓒ Ⓓ	
10. Ⓐ Ⓑ Ⓒ Ⓓ	26. Ⓐ Ⓑ Ⓒ Ⓓ	
11. Ⓐ Ⓑ Ⓒ Ⓓ	27. Ⓐ Ⓑ Ⓒ Ⓓ	
12. Ⓐ Ⓑ Ⓒ Ⓓ	28. Ⓐ Ⓑ Ⓒ Ⓓ	
13. Ⓐ Ⓑ Ⓒ Ⓓ	29. Ⓐ Ⓑ Ⓒ Ⓓ	
14. Ⓐ Ⓑ Ⓒ Ⓓ	30. Ⓐ Ⓑ Ⓒ Ⓓ	
15. Ⓐ Ⓑ Ⓒ Ⓓ	31. Ⓐ Ⓑ Ⓒ Ⓓ	
16. Ⓐ Ⓑ Ⓒ Ⓓ	32. Ⓐ Ⓑ Ⓒ Ⓓ	

Section 2: Quantitative Reasoning

1. Ⓐ Ⓑ Ⓒ Ⓓ	13. Ⓐ Ⓑ Ⓒ Ⓓ	25. Ⓐ Ⓑ Ⓒ Ⓓ
2. Ⓐ Ⓑ Ⓒ Ⓓ	14. Ⓐ Ⓑ Ⓒ Ⓓ	26. Ⓐ Ⓑ Ⓒ Ⓓ
3. Ⓐ Ⓑ Ⓒ Ⓓ	15. Ⓐ Ⓑ Ⓒ Ⓓ	27. Ⓐ Ⓑ Ⓒ Ⓓ
4. Ⓐ Ⓑ Ⓒ Ⓓ	16. Ⓐ Ⓑ Ⓒ Ⓓ	28. Ⓐ Ⓑ Ⓒ Ⓓ
5. Ⓐ Ⓑ Ⓒ Ⓓ	17. Ⓐ Ⓑ Ⓒ Ⓓ	29. Ⓐ Ⓑ Ⓒ Ⓓ
6. Ⓐ Ⓑ Ⓒ Ⓓ	18. Ⓐ Ⓑ Ⓒ Ⓓ	30. Ⓐ Ⓑ Ⓒ Ⓓ
7. Ⓐ Ⓑ Ⓒ Ⓓ	19. Ⓐ Ⓑ Ⓒ Ⓓ	31. Ⓐ Ⓑ Ⓒ Ⓓ
8. Ⓐ Ⓑ Ⓒ Ⓓ	20. Ⓐ Ⓑ Ⓒ Ⓓ	32. Ⓐ Ⓑ Ⓒ Ⓓ
9. Ⓐ Ⓑ Ⓒ Ⓓ	21. Ⓐ Ⓑ Ⓒ Ⓓ	33. Ⓐ Ⓑ Ⓒ Ⓓ
10. Ⓐ Ⓑ Ⓒ Ⓓ	22. Ⓐ Ⓑ Ⓒ Ⓓ	34. Ⓐ Ⓑ Ⓒ Ⓓ
11. Ⓐ Ⓑ Ⓒ Ⓓ	23. Ⓐ Ⓑ Ⓒ Ⓓ	35. Ⓐ Ⓑ Ⓒ Ⓓ
12. Ⓐ Ⓑ Ⓒ Ⓓ	24. Ⓐ Ⓑ Ⓒ Ⓓ	

Section 3: Reading Comprehension

1. Ⓐ Ⓑ Ⓒ Ⓓ   17. Ⓐ Ⓑ Ⓒ Ⓓ   33. Ⓐ Ⓑ Ⓒ Ⓓ
2. Ⓐ Ⓑ Ⓒ Ⓓ   18. Ⓐ Ⓑ Ⓒ Ⓓ   34. Ⓐ Ⓑ Ⓒ Ⓓ
3. Ⓐ Ⓑ Ⓒ Ⓓ   19. Ⓐ Ⓑ Ⓒ Ⓓ   35. Ⓐ Ⓑ Ⓒ Ⓓ
4. Ⓐ Ⓑ Ⓒ Ⓓ   20. Ⓐ Ⓑ Ⓒ Ⓓ   36. Ⓐ Ⓑ Ⓒ Ⓓ
5. Ⓐ Ⓑ Ⓒ Ⓓ   21. Ⓐ Ⓑ Ⓒ Ⓓ   37. Ⓐ Ⓑ Ⓒ Ⓓ
6. Ⓐ Ⓑ Ⓒ Ⓓ   22. Ⓐ Ⓑ Ⓒ Ⓓ   38. Ⓐ Ⓑ Ⓒ Ⓓ
7. Ⓐ Ⓑ Ⓒ Ⓓ   23. Ⓐ Ⓑ Ⓒ Ⓓ   39. Ⓐ Ⓑ Ⓒ Ⓓ
8. Ⓐ Ⓑ Ⓒ Ⓓ   24. Ⓐ Ⓑ Ⓒ Ⓓ   40. Ⓐ Ⓑ Ⓒ Ⓓ
9. Ⓐ Ⓑ Ⓒ Ⓓ   25. Ⓐ Ⓑ Ⓒ Ⓓ
10. Ⓐ Ⓑ Ⓒ Ⓓ   26. Ⓐ Ⓑ Ⓒ Ⓓ
11. Ⓐ Ⓑ Ⓒ Ⓓ   27. Ⓐ Ⓑ Ⓒ Ⓓ
12. Ⓐ Ⓑ Ⓒ Ⓓ   28. Ⓐ Ⓑ Ⓒ Ⓓ
13. Ⓐ Ⓑ Ⓒ Ⓓ   29. Ⓐ Ⓑ Ⓒ Ⓓ
14. Ⓐ Ⓑ Ⓒ Ⓓ   30. Ⓐ Ⓑ Ⓒ Ⓓ
15. Ⓐ Ⓑ Ⓒ Ⓓ   31. Ⓐ Ⓑ Ⓒ Ⓓ
16. Ⓐ Ⓑ Ⓒ Ⓓ   32. Ⓐ Ⓑ Ⓒ Ⓓ

Section 4: Mathematics Achievement

1. Ⓐ Ⓑ Ⓒ Ⓓ   17. Ⓐ Ⓑ Ⓒ Ⓓ   33. Ⓐ Ⓑ Ⓒ Ⓓ
2. Ⓐ Ⓑ Ⓒ Ⓓ   18. Ⓐ Ⓑ Ⓒ Ⓓ   34. Ⓐ Ⓑ Ⓒ Ⓓ
3. Ⓐ Ⓑ Ⓒ Ⓓ   19. Ⓐ Ⓑ Ⓒ Ⓓ   35. Ⓐ Ⓑ Ⓒ Ⓓ
4. Ⓐ Ⓑ Ⓒ Ⓓ   20. Ⓐ Ⓑ Ⓒ Ⓓ   36. Ⓐ Ⓑ Ⓒ Ⓓ
5. Ⓐ Ⓑ Ⓒ Ⓓ   21. Ⓐ Ⓑ Ⓒ Ⓓ   37. Ⓐ Ⓑ Ⓒ Ⓓ
6. Ⓐ Ⓑ Ⓒ Ⓓ   22. Ⓐ Ⓑ Ⓒ Ⓓ   38. Ⓐ Ⓑ Ⓒ Ⓓ
7. Ⓐ Ⓑ Ⓒ Ⓓ   23. Ⓐ Ⓑ Ⓒ Ⓓ   39. Ⓐ Ⓑ Ⓒ Ⓓ
8. Ⓐ Ⓑ Ⓒ Ⓓ   24. Ⓐ Ⓑ Ⓒ Ⓓ   40. Ⓐ Ⓑ Ⓒ Ⓓ
9. Ⓐ Ⓑ Ⓒ Ⓓ   25. Ⓐ Ⓑ Ⓒ Ⓓ   41. Ⓐ Ⓑ Ⓒ Ⓓ
10. Ⓐ Ⓑ Ⓒ Ⓓ   26. Ⓐ Ⓑ Ⓒ Ⓓ   42. Ⓐ Ⓑ Ⓒ Ⓓ
11. Ⓐ Ⓑ Ⓒ Ⓓ   27. Ⓐ Ⓑ Ⓒ Ⓓ   43. Ⓐ Ⓑ Ⓒ Ⓓ
12. Ⓐ Ⓑ Ⓒ Ⓓ   28. Ⓐ Ⓑ Ⓒ Ⓓ   44. Ⓐ Ⓑ Ⓒ Ⓓ
13. Ⓐ Ⓑ Ⓒ Ⓓ   29. Ⓐ Ⓑ Ⓒ Ⓓ   45. Ⓐ Ⓑ Ⓒ Ⓓ
14. Ⓐ Ⓑ Ⓒ Ⓓ   30. Ⓐ Ⓑ Ⓒ Ⓓ
15. Ⓐ Ⓑ Ⓒ Ⓓ   31. Ⓐ Ⓑ Ⓒ Ⓓ
16. Ⓐ Ⓑ Ⓒ Ⓓ   32. Ⓐ Ⓑ Ⓒ Ⓓ

SECTION 1
Time: 20 Minutes
40 Questions

This section includes two different types of questions: synonyms and sentence completions. There are directions and a sample question for each question type.

Part One

Directions: Each of the following questions consists of a word in capital letters followed by four words or phrases labeled (A), (B), (C), and (D). Select the one word or phrase that means most nearly the same as the word in capital letters.

Sample Question:

ESSENTIAL:
(A) dire
(B) confusing
(C) vital
(D) expert

Correct Answer: C

1. SHAME:
   (A) grief
   (B) anguish
   (C) remorse
   (D) humiliation

2. TELL:
   (A) censure
   (B) preclude
   (C) dissuade
   (D) divulge

3. CONCISE:
   (A) clever
   (B) brief
   (C) small
   (D) subdued

4. INQUIRY:
   (A) testimony
   (B) subpoena
   (C) investigation
   (D) verification

5. ATTITUDE:
   (A) disposition
   (B) dissension
   (C) charisma
   (D) dispensation

6. TEDIOUSLY:
   (A) delicately
   (B) relentlessly
   (C) fearlessly
   (D) tiresomely

7. DEPLETE:
   (A) deride
   (B) reduce
   (C) deprecate
   (D) discredit

8. CAUTIOUS:
   (A) discreet
   (B) anxious
   (C) scared
   (D) stricken

9. SPARSE:
   (A) spatial
   (B) thin
   (C) vivid
   (D) lifeless

10. AVERSION:
    (A) model
    (B) portrayal
    (C) dislike
    (D) arrangement

11. DORMANT:
    (A) inactive
    (B) restful
    (C) covert
    (D) arbitrary

12. MALCONTENT:
    (A) sickly
    (B) troublesome
    (C) dissatisfied
    (D) malicious

GO ON TO THE NEXT PAGE.

13. MERIT:
   (A) deserve
   (B) require
   (C) necessitate
   (D) pardon

14. PROMINENT:
   (A) excellent
   (B) accomplished
   (C) admirable
   (D) conspicuous

15. OBJECTIVE:
   (A) interest
   (B) observation
   (C) intention
   (D) concern

16. PERMANENT:
   (A) historical
   (B) indelible
   (C) permissive
   (D) conspicuous

17. SHREWD:
   (A) poignant
   (B) astute
   (C) copious
   (D) tactile

18. CLANDESTINE:
   (A) secret
   (B) criminal
   (C) apprehensive
   (D) disgraceful

19. COERCE:
   (A) twist
   (B) mislead
   (C) perceive
   (D) compel

20. PLETHORA:
   (A) quandary
   (B) resonance
   (C) excess
   (D) veneer

GO ON TO THE NEXT PAGE.

Part Two

Directions: Each sentence below has one or two blanks. Each blank indicates that something is missing. Following each sentence are four words or sets of words labeled (A), (B), (C), and (D). You are to select the word or set of words that, when inserted in the sentence, best fits the meaning of the sentence as a whole.

Sample Question:

Due to the fact that the stray kitten was so _____, Ethan's mother allowed him to keep it.
(A) tardy
(B) humid
(C) disobedient
(D) adorable

Correct Answer: D

---

21. History has shown that two of the most _____ patriots of the Revolutionary War were Samuel Adams and John Hancock.
(A) destitute
(B) covert
(C) spontaneous
(D) eminent

22. Knowing that the bonuses being offered were not easily _____, the union decided not to _____ the new contract.
(A) attainable . . . ratify
(B) reachable . . . nullify
(C) restricted . . . validate
(D) obtainable . . . repudiate

23. For _____ results with the product, the manufacturer advised customers to carefully read the manual or download the _____ tutorial from its Web site.
(A) superior . . . abbreviated
(B) unparalleled . . . selective
(C) optimum . . . comprehensive
(D) conventional . . . extensive

24. Although the effects of the tornado were destructive, it brought the town together through a sense of _____.
(A) aversion
(B) camaraderie
(C) virulence
(D) animosity

25. After staying up all night and working interminably to finish the project, Gerard finally let himself _____ to sleep.
(A) posture
(B) succumb
(C) dissent
(D) regress

26. Despite her _____ temper, the actress typically displayed a _____ demeanor.
(A) modest...humble
(B) caustic...maniacal
(C) explosive...timid
(D) manageable...courteous

27. The ending of the play was so _____ that many questions the audience had were left unanswered.
(A) derivative
(B) lucid
(C) explicit
(D) equivocal

28. The supervisor forced his workers to indulge his every whim, lest they find themselves _____ from his good graces.
(A) garnered
(B) exiled
(C) abetted
(D) incited

29. Citing overwhelming evidence, many believed the judge would _____ justice by not reversing her earlier decision.
(A) impel
(B) hasten
(C) impede
(D) gratify

30. Much of Langston's Hughes' poetry tries to _____ the rhythms of blues music, the music he _____ to be the true expression of his spirit.
(A) emulate . . . believed
(B) capture . . . doubted
(C) forgo . . . considered
(D) mollify . . . maintained

GO ON TO THE NEXT PAGE.

31. Perhaps the best known constellation in the sky, Orion is occasionally visible throughout the Northern Hemisphere and _____ with the naked eye.
    (A) imperceptible
    (B) audible
    (C) discernible
    (D) diminished

32. Initially standing by his _____ alibi, the main suspect in the scandal later retracted it and agreed to cooperate with the prosecution.
    (A) feasible
    (B) incontrovertible
    (C) tenuous
    (D) furtive

33. The mayor's suggestion to raise property taxes in order to subsidize a new stadium was met with an _____ response from homeowners.
    (A) exuberant
    (B) affable
    (C) illustrious
    (D) ambivalent

34. The girls were often _____ at camp for their _____ behavior and willingness to comfort the younger children, many of whom were away from home for the first time.
    (A) praised . . . commendable
    (B) unnerved . . . exemplary
    (C) reviled . . . meritorious
    (D) recognized . . . contemptible

35. Due to the fact that she could often be seen carting away boxfuls of books from rummage sales, one could say that Ms. Tompkins had a _____ for accumulation.
    (A) consortium
    (B) propensity
    (C) chagrin
    (D) prospect

36. Having suffered numerous injuries over the course of her career, the gymnast demonstrated her _____ by overcoming adversity and winning the gold medal.
    (A) consternation
    (B) viscosity
    (C) dexterity
    (D) resilience

37. One would think that the _____ bear, fresh from months of hibernation would eat everything in sight, but he is surprisingly picky.
    (A) hirsute
    (B) ravenous
    (C) fastidious
    (D) lethargic

38. At the hotel, the angry couple behaved rather _____ after being informed by the manager that their reservation had been _____ once the payment did not clear.
    (A) bellicosely . . . rescinded
    (B) morosely . . . everted
    (C) extraneously . . . canceled
    (D) lavishly . . . confirmed

39. Even though the architect's designs were _____ to the surrounding buildings, she had to _____ them because of the impending deadline.
    (A) disproportionate . . . submit
    (B) comparable . . . deliver
    (C) excessive . . . affirm
    (D) consistent . . . present

40. By noon, the newspaper staff had been _____ with phone calls about the power outage, and by evening, it seemed as though the _____ would continue.
    (A) deplete . . . barrage
    (B) overwhelmed . . . dearth
    (C) harassed . . . spate
    (D) inundated . . . deluge

STOP!
If you finish before time is up, check your work on this section only.

This section includes two different types of questions: multiple-choice math questions and quantitative comparisons, there are directions for each question type.

Part One

Directions: For each of the following questions, mark the letter of your choice on the answer sheet.

---

1. $48 \div 6 \times 8 \times 8$ is equal to the product of 16 and
   - (A) 16
   - (B) 32
   - (C) 24
   - (D) 28

2. Paula is 3 years older than Lindsey, who is 2 years younger than Dave. If Paula is 17, how old is Dave?
   - (A) 16
   - (B) 17
   - (C) 19
   - (D) 21

3. $3/4 - 5/12 =$
   - (A) $\dfrac{1}{12}$
   - (B) $\dfrac{3}{12}$
   - (C) $\dfrac{1}{3}$
   - (D) $\dfrac{2}{3}$

4. 20 is approximately what percent of 80?
   - (A) 20%
   - (B) 25%
   - (C) 30%
   - (D) 60%

5. A fence along a road is divided into sections that are each 5 meters long. If the fence is 0.5 kilometers long, how many sections are there?
   - (A) 10
   - (B) 50
   - (C) 100
   - (D) 250

6. Which pair of fractions are equivalent?
   - (A) $\dfrac{6}{12}, \dfrac{3}{12}$
   - (B) $\dfrac{2}{8}, \dfrac{1}{4}$
   - (C) $\dfrac{4}{8}, \dfrac{2}{16}$
   - (D) $\dfrac{3}{9}, \dfrac{5}{9}$

7. What is the least common multiple of 9, 2, and 5?
   - (A) 45
   - (B) 60
   - (C) 90
   - (D) 180

8. Bobby's test scores for social studies are 93, 76, 91, 83, and 72. What is his average score?
   - (A) 83
   - (B) 87
   - (C) 91
   - (D) 93

9. At the amusement park, Karen uses $1/3$ of her tickets for rides and $1/6$ of her tickets for food. What fraction of her tickets is left?
   - (A) $\dfrac{1}{6}$
   - (B) $\dfrac{1}{4}$
   - (C) $\dfrac{1}{2}$
   - (D) $\dfrac{2}{3}$

10. If $6 \times 8 \div \underline{\quad} = 5 \times 4 + 4$, then $\underline{\quad} =$
    - (A) 2
    - (B) 3
    - (C) 4
    - (D) 5

11. Which of the following is NOT equal to a whole number?
    - (A) $\dfrac{32}{4}$
    - (B) $4 \times \dfrac{8}{16}$
    - (C) $8 \div \dfrac{1}{8}$
    - (D) $\dfrac{5}{12} \times 8$

GO ON TO THE NEXT PAGE.

12. The distance around a rectangular park is 1 mile. If the width of the park is 880 feet, what is its length?
    (A) 1,760 ft
    (B) 1,510 ft
    (C) 1,250 ft
    (D) 840 ft

13. If $\frac{1}{4}$ of a number is 12, then $\frac{1}{6}$ of the same number is
    (A) 8
    (B) 9
    (C) 12
    (D) 15

14. A truck travels 126 miles in 3 hours. At that speed, in how many hours will the truck reach its destination, 924 miles away?
    (A) 22 hours
    (B) 24 hours
    (C) 25.5 hours
    (D) 28 hours

15. $5/6 - 2/3 - 1/2 =$
    (A) $\frac{1}{12}$
    (B) $\frac{1}{6}$
    (C) $\frac{1}{4}$
    (D) $\frac{1}{3}$

16. What is the mean of the following numbers?
    24, 34, 12, 16, 34, 104, 890
    (A) 48
    (B) 64
    (C) 148
    (D) 152

17. It costs $12.00 dollars to buy 24 cookies. At the same rate, how many dollars will it cost to buy 6 cookies?
    (A) $3.00
    (B) $2.00
    (C) $48.00
    (D) $72.00

18. In the product shown below, what digit does □ represent?
    $(4\square5)(3) = 1,275$
    (A) 1
    (B) 2
    (C) 3
    (D) 4

19. Which of the following is NOT equal to a whole number?
    (A) $\frac{20}{5}$
    (B) $5 \times \frac{3}{4}$
    (C) $6 \div \frac{1}{6}$
    (D) $\frac{3}{5} \times 10$

20. There are 15 black marbles and 10 white marbles in a bag. If you pick a marble from the bag without looking, what are your chances of picking a white marble?
    (A) $\frac{1}{25}$
    (B) $\frac{3}{25}$
    (C) $\frac{2}{5}$
    (D) $\frac{3}{5}$

Part Two

Directions: For each of the following questions, two quantities are given—one in column A, the other in column B. Compare the two quantities and mark your answer sheet as follows:

(A) if the quantity in Column A is greater
(B) if the quantity in Column B is greater
(C) if the quantities are equal
(D) if the relationship cannot be determined from the information given

Notes

- Information concerning one or both of the compared quantities will be centered above the two columns for some items.
- Symbols that appear in both columns represent the same thing in Column A as in Column B.
- Letters such as *x*, *n*, and *k* are symbols for real numbers.
- Figures are drawn to scale unless otherwise noted.

GO ON TO THE NEXT PAGE.

	Column A	**Column B**
21.	7,542 − 1,036	10,308 − 4,036
22.	75% of 120	50% of 160
23.	3(c + 2)	3c + (3 • 2)

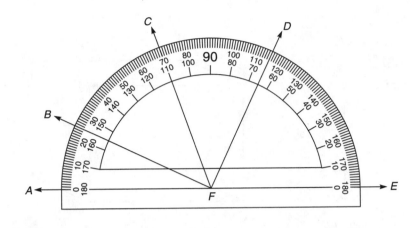

24.	m∠DFE	m∠AFC

Janet walks 125 yards in 3 minutes.
Victoria walks 206 yards in 5 minutes.

25.	The average number of yards Janet walks in minute.	The average number of yards Victoria walks in minute.
26.	$\sqrt{150}$	15

Jeff reaches without looking into this box filled with letter blocks,
and picks out one block.

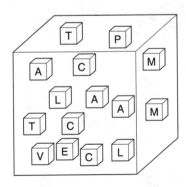

27.	The probability of picking a vowel	The probability of picking an L or a T

GO ON TO THE NEXT PAGE.

28. The perimeter of a square having an area of 64 ft².   The perimeter of a rectangle having an area of 48 ft².

29. $4\frac{2}{5} \div \frac{3}{10}$ $7\frac{1}{2} \div \frac{2}{3}$

30. $-|4|$ $|-4|$

$$x + 1 = 15$$
$$y - 7 = 7$$

31. x y

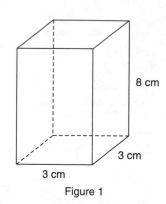

Figure 1   Figure 2

32. Surface Area of Figure 1   Surface Area of Figure 2

33. The greatest common factor of 56, 96, and 200.   The greatest common factor of 27, 81, and 189.

34. 2.76×2.57 21.4×0.53

35. 8 quarts 1 cup   264 fluid ounces

STOP!
If you finish before time is up, check your work on this section only.

SECTION 3

Time: 40 Minutes
40 Questions

Directions: Each reading passage is followed by questions about it. Answer the questions that follow a passage on the basis of what is stated or implied in that passage. For each question, select the answer you think is best and record your choice by filling in the corresponding oval on the answer sheet.

Questions 1–5

At the Thirteenth Annual Convention of the National Negro Business League in 1912, no women were included on the sched-
5 ule of speakers. Madam C. J. Walker, a highly successful inventor and distributor of hair care products for African-American women, shocked the participants when she walked up
10 and claimed the podium from moderator Booker T. Washington:

"Surely you are not going to shut the door in my face. I feel that I am in a business that is a credit to the wom-
15 anhood of our race. I am a woman who started in business seven years ago with only $1.50 . . . this year (up to the 19th day of this month . . .) I had taken in $18,000. (Prolonged
20 applause.) This makes a grand total of $63,049 made in my hair business in Indianapolis. (Applause.) I have been trying to get before you busi-ness people to tell you what I am
25 doing. I am a woman that came from the cotton fields of the South; I was promoted from there to the wash-tub (laughter); then I was promoted to the cook kitchen, and from there I
30 promoted myself into the business of manufacturing hair goods and preparations. . . . I am not ashamed of my past; I am not ashamed of my

humble beginning. Don't think that
35 because you have to go down in the wash-tub that you are any less a lady!" (prolonged applause.)

1. The purpose of Madam Walker's speech was to
   (A) demonstrate her hair products to the league
   (B) lash out at Booker T. Washington for ignoring her
   (C) make the members of the league take notice of her business success
   (D) influence the members of the league to admit more women

2. As reflected in her speech, Madam Walker's attitude is best described as
   (A) envious
   (B) proud
   (C) reverent
   (D) cautious

3. The reaction of the members of the league to Madam Walker's speech can be described as
   (A) indifferent
   (B) angry
   (C) favorable
   (D) critical

4. The reference to her promotion from the cotton fields to the wash-tub to the cook kitchen is used to
   (A) show how far she has come
   (B) establish a connection with her audience
   (C) debunk a myth about African-American women
   (D) make people feel sorry for her

5. What does Madam Walker mean when she says, "Don't think that because you have to go down in the wash-tub that you are any less a lady" (lines 34-37)?
   (A) Ladies should not have to scrub and cook.
   (B) Getting down on your knees to scrub is hard work for a lady.
   (C) It is not ladylike to work with your hands.
   (D) There is nothing demeaning about hard work.

GO ON TO THE NEXT PAGE.

Questions 6–11

On March 20, 1980, a series of small earthquakes signaled the awakening of Mount St. Helens from a 123-year slumber. Over the next
5 two months more than 10,000 earth-quakes followed as magma moved into the volcano, wedging the volcano apart at a rate of five feet per day. Heat from a rising plume of volcanic
10 ash melted glacial ice, creating cement-like slurries of rock and ash called mudflows. Superheated ava-lanches of hot gas, magma caused a visible swelling of the volcano's north
15 flank creating a feature that scientists called "the bulge."

Many geologists weren't surprised by Mount St. Helens' awakening. In the 1950's, geologists had begun
20 an extensive study of the deposits around Mount St. Helens. In 1975, they published a report predicting that Mount St. Helens was the volcano in the lower 48 states most
25 likely to erupt by the end of the century.

On the morning of May 18, 1980, a magnitude 5.1 earthquake triggered the collapse of the summit and north
30 flank of Mount St. Helens and formed the largest landslide in recorded history. Gas-rich magma and super-heated groundwater trapped inside the volcano were suddenly released
35 in a powerful lateral blast. In less than three minutes, 230 square miles of forest lay flattened. The hot gas and magma melted the snow and ice that covered the volcano. The result-
40 ing floodwater mixed with the rock and debris to create concrete-like mudflows that scoured river valleys surrounding the mountain.

A plume of volcanic ash and
45 pumice billowed out of the volcano reaching a height of 15 miles and transformed day into night across Eastern Washington. Avalanches of super-heated gas and pumice, called
50 pyroclastic flows, swept down the flanks of the volcano. While the land-slide and lateral blast were over within minutes, the eruption column, mudflows and pyroclastic flows
55 continued throughout the day and

following night. By the following morning major eruptive activity had ceased and the landscape appeared to be a gray wasteland.

6. The primary purpose of this passage is to
    (A) offer general information about volcanoes
    (B) describe a specific volcanic eruption
    (C) offer specific advice about what to do when a volcano erupts
    (D) provide historical background about volcanoes

7. The first sentence implies that
    (A) Mount St. Helens had never before erupted
    (B) Mount St. Helens erupts every 123 years
    (C) Mount St. Helens last erupted in 1857
    (D) no one suspected that Mount St. Helens could erupt

8. As used in line 9, "rising" most nearly means
    (A) ascending
    (B) approaching
    (C) maturing
    (D) advancing

9. The statement that "Many geologists weren't surprised by Mount St. Helens' awakening," (lines 17–18) primarily suggests that
    (A) geologists were able to predict when Mount St. Helens would erupt
    (B) the assumptions geologists had made about Mount St. Helens were being proven
    (C) the longer a volcano remains dormant, the more likely it is to become active
    (D) nothing is surprising to geologists

10. The author describes the events of May 18, 1980, mainly by means of
    (A) scientific analysis
    (B) detached and impartial observation
    (C) vivid language and dramatic images
    (D) presentation of facts in chronological order

11. By calling the landscape "a gray wasteland" (line 59), the author implies that
    (A) the landscape was covered with a blanket of dirty snow
    (B) the landscape was littered with garbage and other waste matter
    (C) the trees were all covered with gray ash
    (D) the landscape had been striped bare and covered in volcanic ash

Questions 12–18

It was Paul's afternoon to appear before the faculty of the Pittsburgh High School to account for his vari-ous misdemeanors. He had been
5 suspended a week ago, and his father had called at the Principal's office and confessed his perplexity about his son. Paul entered the fac-ulty room suave and smiling. His
10 clothes were a trifle outgrown, and the tan velvet on the collar of his open overcoat was frayed and worn; but for all that there was something of the dandy about him, and he wore
15 an opal pin in his neatly knotted black four-in-hand, and a red car-nation in his buttonhole. This latter adornment the faculty somehow felt was not properly significant of the
20 contrite spirit befitting a boy under the ban of suspension.

Paul was tall for his age and very thin, with high, cramped shoulders and a narrow chest. His eyes were
25 remarkable for a certain hysterical brilliancy, and he continually used them in a conscious, theatrical sort of way, peculiarly offensive in a boy.

GO ON TO THE NEXT PAGE.

The pupils were abnormally large,
30 as though he were addicted to
belladonna, but there was a glassy
glitter about them which that drug
does not produce.

When questioned by the Principal
35 as to why he was there Paul stated,
politely enough, that he wanted to
come back to school. This was a lie,
but Paul was quite accustomed to
lying; found it, indeed, indispensable
40 for overcoming friction. His teachers
were asked to state their respective
charges against him, which they did
with such a rancor and aggrievedness as evinced that this was not a
45 usual case. Disorder and impertinence were among the offenses
named, yet each of his instructors
felt that it was scarcely possible to
put into words the real cause of the
50 trouble, which lay in a sort of hysterically defiant manner of the boy's; in
the contempt which they all knew he
felt for them, and which he seemingly made not the least effort to
55 conceal. Once, when he had been
making a synopsis of a paragraph
at the blackboard, his English
teacher had stepped to his side and
attempted to guide his hand. Paul
60 had started back with a shudder and
thrust his hands violently behind
him. The astonished woman could
scarcely have been more hurt and
embarrassed had he struck at her.
65 The insult was so involuntary and
definitely personal as to be unforgettable. In one way and another he had
made all his teachers, men and
women alike, conscious of the same
70 feeling of physical aversion. In one
class he habitually sat with his hand
shading his eyes; in another he
always looked out of the window
during the recitation; in another he
75 made a running commentary on the
lecture, with humorous intention.

Willa Cather from "Paul's Case:
A Study in Temperament"

12. This passage can best be
characterized as
(A) an amusing story about
a high school escapade
(B) a fond remembrance of
the narrator's youth
(C) a polite appeal for
forgiveness
(D) a penetrating
examination of a young
man's character

13. In lines 13–14, the expression
"there was something of the
dandy about him" means that
Paul
(A) was afraid of appearing
before the faculty
(B) paid great attention to
his clothes
(C) did not care how he
looked
(D) was in need of new
clothes

14. The red carnation in Paul's
buttonhole in lines 16–17
made the faculty feel that Paul
(A) did not take his
suspension seriously
enough
(B) did not really want to
come back to school
(C) was trying to impress the
principal
(D) was sincere in his desire
to improve his behavior

15. In the eyes of the faculty, Paul's
most serious offense was his
(A) inability to control his
temper
(B) failure to complete his
assignments
(C) obvious contempt for his
teachers
(D) lack of attention in class

16. Which adjective best describes
Paul?
(A) contrite
(B) defiant
(C) violent
(D) embarrassed

17. As used in line 43, the word
"rancor" means
(A) turmoil
(B) bitterness
(C) remorse
(D) dismay

18. In lines 60–62, Paul shuddered
and threw his hands behind
him because
(A) his teacher had touched
his hand
(B) he could not answer the
teacher's question
(C) he was afraid of the
teacher
(D) he wanted to strike the
teacher

Questions 19–23

The Homestead Act of 1862 has
been called one the most important
pieces of legislation in the history of
the United States. Designed to spur
5 Western migration, the Homestead
Act culminated a twenty-year battle
to distribute public lands to citizens
willing to farm. Opposition to the Act
came from Northern businessmen,
10 who feared it would lower property
values and reduce the supply of
cheap labor, and from Southerners,
who feared homesteaders would
add to the voices calling for the abo-
15 lition of slavery. With Southerners
out of the picture in 1862, the legislation finally passed and was signed
into law by Abraham Lincoln. Under
this Act, 270 million acres, or 10% of
20 the area of the United States, was
claimed and settled.

A homesteader had only to be
the head of a household and at least
21 years of age to claim a 160-acre
25 parcel of land. Settlers from all walks
of life including newly arrived immigrants, farmers without land of their
own from the East, single women
and former slaves came to meet the
30 challenge of "proving up" and keeping this "free land." Homesteaders
were required to live on the land,
build a home, make improvements,
and farm for 5 years before they
35 were eligible to "prove up." A total
filing fee of $18 was the only money

GO ON TO THE NEXT PAGE.

required, but settlers paid a big price in sacrifice and hard work.

People interested in Home-
40 steading first had to file their intentions at the nearest Land Office where they paid a fee of $10 to claim the land temporarily, and a $2 commission to the land agent.
45 The homesteader then returned to the land to begin the process of building a home and farming the land, both requirements for "proving up." After five years of living on and
50 working the land, the homesteader had to find two neighbors or friends willing to vouch for the truth of his or her statements about the land's improvements and sign the "proof"
55 document. With the successful completion of this final form and payment of a $6 fee, the homesteader received the patent (or deed) for the land, signed with the name of the
60 current President of the United States.

19. The primary purpose of the passage is to
   (A) discuss the reasons for westward expansion in the United States
   (B) argue in favor of extending the Homestead Act
   (C) point out the difficulties of homesteading
   (D) explain the provisions of the Homestead Act

20. In line 40, "file" most nearly means
   (A) record
   (B) classify
   (C) sharpen
   (D) arrange in order

21. In order to acquire land under the Homestead Act, claimants had to meet all of the following conditions EXCEPT:
   (A) be at least 21 years of age
   (B) be a native-born U.S. citizen
   (C) farm the land for five years
   (D) build a house on the land

22. How much U.S. land was transferred to individuals under the terms of the Homestead Act?
   (A) 160 acres per person
   (B) 1.6 million acres
   (C) 270 million acres
   (D) 30% of all U.S. land

23. The author calls the Homestead Act one of the most important pieces of legislation in United States history because it
   (A) helped to settle the West
   (B) provided cheap labor
   (C) lowered land values
   (D) helped to end slavery

Questions 24–29

Manatees and dugongs, also known as sea cows, belong to the scientific order Sirenia. In ancient mythology, "siren" was a term used
5 for monsters or sea nymphs who lured sailors and their ships to treacherous rocks and shipwreck with mesmerizing songs. Throughout history, sailors sometimes thought
10 they were seeing mermaids when they were probably seeing manatees or dugongs. With a little imagination, manatees have an uncanny resemblance to human form that could only
15 increase after long months at sea. In fact, manatees and dugongs may have helped to perpetuate the myth of mermaids. Like the mythological creatures for which they were named,
20 all sirenians living on earth today are vulnerable to extinction

Manatees and dugongs are the only completely aquatic mammals that are herbivores. Unlike the other
25 marine mammals (dolphins, whales, seals, sea lions, sea otters, walruses, and polar bears) sirenians eat only seagrasses and other aquatic vegetation. Unlike other marine mammals,
30 sirenians have an extremely low metabolism and zero tolerance for cold water. Like dolphins and whales, manatees and dugongs are totally aquatic mammals that never leave
35 the water—not even to give birth. The combination of these factors

means that sirenians are restricted to warm shallow coastal waters, estuaries, and rivers, with healthy
40 ecosystems that support large amounts of seagrass and other vegetation.

The average adult manatee is about three meters (9.8 feet) long and
45 weighs between 362–544 kilograms (800–1,200 pounds). It is estimated that a manatee can eat about 10–15% of its body weight in vegetation daily. So, for example, a 453-kilogram
50 (1,000-pound) manatee would probably eat between 45–68 kilograms (100–150 pounds) of sea grass and water hyacinths a day!

24. Paragraph 1 is primarily concerned with
   (A) the origin of the scientific classification Sirenia
   (B) the similarities between manatees and mermaids
   (C) how manatees cause shipwrecks
   (D) a comparison between manatees and dugongs

25. As used in line 8, "mesmerizing" most nearly means
   (A) discordant
   (B) high pitched
   (C) hypnotic
   (D) mysterious

26. The passage supports which of the following conclusions?
   (A) Manatees are like other marine mammals in their diet.
   (B) Manatees leave the water only to give birth.
   (C) Because of their low metabolism manatees tolerate cold water well.
   (D) All sirenians are endangered.

GO ON TO THE NEXT PAGE.

27. The author develops paragraph 2 by presenting
    (A) two sides of an issue
    (B) a thesis followed by specific examples
    (C) a description of similarities and differences
    (D) an opinion and reasons why it is held

28. According to the passage, manatees prefer the shallow coastal waters of Florida because of which of the following?
    I. Availability of vegetation
    II. Favorable water temperatures
    III. Safety

    (A) I only
    (B) I and II only
    (C) II only
    (D) I, II, and III

29. Which of the following represents the number of pounds of food an average adult manatee consumes in a day?
    (A) 10–15
    (B) 100–150
    (C) 352–544
    (D) 800–1000

Questions 30–36

Day had broken cold and gray, exceedingly cold and gray, when the man turned aside from the main Yukon trail and climbed the high
5 earth-bank, where a dim and little-travelled trail led eastward through the fat spruce timberland. It was a steep bank, and he paused for breath at the top, excusing the act to
10 himself by looking at his watch. It was nine o'clock. There was no sun nor hint of sun, though there was not a cloud in the sky. It was a clear day, and yet there seemed an
15 intangible pall over the face of things, a subtle gloom that made the day dark, and that was due to the absence of sun. This fact did not worry the man.
20 As he turned to go on, he spat speculatively. There was a sharp, explosive crackle that startled him. He spat again. And again, in the air, before it could fall to the snow, the
25 spittle crackled. He knew that at fifty below spittle crackled on the snow, but this spittle had crackled in the air. Undoubtedly it was colder than fifty below — how much colder he did not
30 know. But the temperature did not matter. He was bound for the old claim on the left fork of Henderson Creek, where the boys were already. They had come over across the
35 divide from the Indian Creek country, while he had come the roundabout way to take a look at the possibilities of getting out logs in the spring from the islands in the Yukon.
40 At the man's heels trotted a dog, a big native husky, the proper wolf-dog, gray-coated and without any visible or temperamental difference from its brother, the wild wolf. The
45 animal was depressed by the tremendous cold. It knew that it was no time for traveling. Its instinct told it a truer tale than was told to the man by the man's judgment. . . It experienced a
50 vague but menacing apprehension that subdued it and made it slink along at the man's heels, and that made it question eagerly every unwonted movement of the man as
55 if expecting him to go into camp or to seek shelter somewhere and build a fire.

Jack London from "To Build a Fire"

30. In the first paragraph the author establishes a mood of
    (A) promise
    (B) serenity
    (C) hostility
    (D) foreboding

31. As used in line 1,"broken" most nearly means
    (A) dawned
    (B) separated
    (C) shattered
    (D) interrupted

32. The statement that "It was a steep bank, and he paused for breath at the top, excusing the act to himself by looking at his watch," (lines 7–10) suggests that the man
    (A) was worried about running late
    (B) was not accustomed to hiking in the Yukon
    (C) was disoriented by the extreme cold
    (D) had traveled farther than he thought

33. The discussion of spitting into the air (lines 20–27) serves primarily to suggest
    (A) the strangeness of the landscape
    (B) the gloom of the day
    (C) the frustration of the dog
    (D) the severity of the cold

34. In line 22, the author includes the detail that the sharp, explosive crackle "startled him" primarily to emphasize
    (A) the man's fragile state of mind
    (B) how eerily quiet it had become
    (C) that it was colder than the man thought
    (D) the danger the man was in

35. Which word best describes how the author regards the man in the story?
    (A) clever
    (B) cautious
    (C) ambitious
    (D) foolish

36. With which of the following statements is the author most likely to agree?
    (A) The dog is wiser than the man.
    (B) The dog is unfazed by the cold.
    (C) The man is jealous of the dog.
    (D) The man is right to press on.

GO ON TO THE NEXT PAGE.

I was asked not long ago to tell something about the sports and pastimes that I engaged in during my youth. Until that question was asked

5 it had never occurred to me that there was no period of my life that was devoted to play. From the time that I can remember anything, almost every day of my life has been

10 occupied in some kind of labor; though I think I would now be a more useful man if I had had time for sports. During the period that I spent in slavery I was not large enough to

15 be of much service, still I was occupied most of the time in cleaning the yards, carrying water to the men in the fields, or going to the mill, to which I used to take the corn, once a

20 week, to be ground. The mill was about three miles from the plantation. This work I always dreaded. The heavy bag of corn would be thrown across the back of the horse, and the

25 corn divided about evenly on each side; but in some way, almost without exception, on these trips, the corn would so shift as to become unbalanced and would fall off the horse,

30 and often I would fall with it. As I was not strong enough to reload the corn upon the horse, I would have to wait, sometimes for many hours, till a chance passer-by came along who

35 would help me out of my trouble. The hours while waiting for some one were usually spent in crying. The time consumed in this way made me late in reaching the mill, and by the

40 time I got my corn ground and reached home it would be far into the night. The road was a lonely one, and often led through dense forests. I was always frightened. The woods

45 were said to be full of soldiers who had deserted from the army, and I had been told that the first thing a deserter did to a Negro boy when he found him alone was to cut off his

50 ears. Besides, when I was late in getting home I knew I would always get a severe scolding or a flogging.

Booker T. Washington from
Up from Slavery: An Autobiography

37. In line 3, "engaged" means most nearly
(A) pledged
(B) occupied
(C) participated
(D) reserved

38. The author's "trouble" in line 35 is
(A) having to travel alone in the dark
(B) not being able to reload the corn that had fallen off the horse
(C) not knowing the way through the woods
(D) facing a flogging for being late

39. The author was always frightened on his way home from the mill for all of the following reasons EXCEPT:
(A) There were few people on the road at night.
(B) The woods were full of soldiers.
(C) He feared having his ears cut off.
(D) He thought he might be kidnapped.

40. The author's attitude toward his youth is best described as
(A) affectionate nostalgia
(B) analytical detachment
(C) open hostility
(D) deep sorrow

STOP!
If you finish before time is up, check your work on this section only.

Time: 45 Minutes
45 Questions

Directions: For each of the following questions, mark the letter of your choice on the answer sheet.

1. If 6 is added to the products of 9 and 5, the result is
   (A) 20
   (B) 25
   (C) 38
   (D) 51

2. It costs $48.00 dollars to buy 64 cans of soda. At the same rate, how many dollars will it cost to buy 48 cans?
   (A) $12.00
   (B) $9.00
   (C) $36.00
   (D) $64.00

3. $32 \div (2 + 6) - 4$
   (A) 0
   (B) 4
   (C) 8
   (D) 10

4. In a dresser drawer there are 3 pairs of white socks, 5 pairs of black socks, and 4 pairs of blue socks. If you pick a pair without looking, what are the chances that you will pick a blue pair?
   (A) $\dfrac{1}{12}$
   (B) $\dfrac{1}{6}$
   (C) $\dfrac{1}{4}$
   (D) $\dfrac{1}{3}$

5. $6 \div \frac{2}{3} =$
   (A) 3
   (B) 4
   (C) 6
   (D) 9

6. Maleka had a birthday party and spent $4.68 on balloons, $35.32 on party favors, $17.77 on a cake, $16.35 on ice cream, and $18.00 on invitations. How much did Maleka spend on the party?
   (A) $89.75
   (B) $92.12
   (C) $95.20
   (D) $103.10

7. 35% of 70 =
   (A) 65
   (B) 50
   (C) 35
   (D) 24.5

8. If Tino rides his bike at a steady speed of 9 miles per hour, how far will he ride in 3 hours 40 minutes?
   (A) 27 miles
   (B) 33 miles
   (C) 36 miles
   (D) 39 miles

9. Ashley practiced the piano for 1¾ hours on Monday and for 45 minutes on Tuesday. For how many hours did she practice on the two days together?
   (A) 2
   (B) $2\dfrac{1}{4}$
   (C) $2\dfrac{1}{2}$
   (D) $2\dfrac{3}{4}$

10. Donna is *d* years old. Frank is *f* years old. Frank is 4 years younger than Donna. Which equation represents the relationship between Donna's and Frank's age?
    (A) $d = \dfrac{f}{4}$
    (B) $d = 4 - f$
    (C) $f = d - 4$
    (D) $f = 4 - d$

11. Matt took a bike trip. On the first day he rode 15 miles. On the second day he rode 35 miles, and the third day he rested. On the fourth day he rode 57 miles, and on the fifth day he rode 43 miles. What is the average number of miles that he rode per day?
    (A) 25
    (B) 27
    (C) 30
    (D) 32

12. One kilometer is approximately equal to 0.6 mile. How many kilometers are in 8 miles?
    (A) about 6
    (B) about 7
    (C) about 11
    (D) about 13

GO ON TO THE NEXT PAGE.

13. A snowstorm started on Tuesday at 2:12 P.M. and ended on Wednesday at 5:46 A.M. How long did it snow in hours and minutes?
    (A) 15 hours, 24 minutes
    (B) 15 hours, 34 minutes
    (C) 16 hours, 14 minutes
    (D) 16 hours, 44 minutes

14. In a group of 9 hikers, each person carries $\frac{3}{4}$ of a pound of trail mix. How much trail mix do they carry all together?
    (A) $6\frac{3}{4}$ lb
    (B) 7 lb
    (C) $7\frac{1}{4}$ lb
    (C) $7\frac{1}{2}$ lb

15. $0.4 \times 0.5 =$
    (A) 0.02
    (B) 0.20
    (C) 2
    (D) 20

16. Which lists all the common factors of 27 and 45?
    (A) 3
    (B) 3, 5
    (C) 3, 5, 9
    (D) 1, 3, 9

17. $\frac{7}{21}$ is equivalent to the fractions in which list?
    (A) $\frac{2}{6}, \frac{3}{9}, \frac{9}{27}$
    (B) $\frac{6}{10}, \frac{15}{25}, \frac{30}{50}$
    (C) $\frac{2}{3}, \frac{14}{28}, \frac{24}{40}$
    (D) $\frac{3}{4}, \frac{9}{12}, \frac{24}{32}$

18. On Monday, x people took buses to work. There were 6 buses with an equal number in each bus. Which expression shows the number of people in each bus?
    (A) $6x$
    (B) $\frac{x}{6}$
    (C) $x + 6$
    (D) $x - 6$

19. Barbara is filling two pots with water. Each pot holds 4 liters. How many milliliters do the two pots hold?
    (A) 80
    (B) 800
    (C) 8,000
    (D) 80,000

20. Karen hiked 23.62 miles. Anthony hiked 19.8 miles. How much farther did Karen hike than Anthony?
    (A) 2.46 miles
    (B) 2.98 miles
    (C) 3.46 miles
    (D) 3.82 miles

21. At 4:00 A.M. on a winter morning the temperature was −11°F. Every hour after that the temperature rose by 3°F. What was the temperature at 11:00 A.M.?
    (A) −2°F
    (B) 9°F
    (C) 10°F
    (D) 13°F

22. $9\frac{3}{5} + 2\frac{1}{4} =$
    (A) $11\frac{17}{20}$
    (B) $11\frac{9}{10}$
    (C) $12\frac{3}{20}$
    (D) $12\frac{1}{10}$

23. $12 \div 3\frac{1}{4} =$
    (A) $2\frac{11}{12}$
    (B) $3\frac{1}{6}$
    (C) $3\frac{2}{3}$
    (D) $3\frac{9}{13}$

24. If $8y + 5 = 41$, $y =$
    (A) 4.2
    (B) 4.5
    (C) 5.1
    (D) 5.5

25. $(8 + 2)^2 - 2^3 \times (5 - 3) =$
    (A) 84
    (B) 86

    (C) 92
    (D) 104

26. What is the value of the expression $85.1 - a$ for $a = 26.3$?
    (A) 63.1
    (B) 61.4
    (C) 60.2
    (D) 58.8

27. The melting point of oxygen is −218°C. Its boiling point is only 35°C higher. What is the boiling point of oxygen?
    (A) −253°C
    (B) −183°C
    (C) 183°C
    (D) 253°C

28. $3° =$
    (A) −3
    (B) −1
    (C) 1
    (D) 3

29. Marlene bought a hat and a scarf. The hat cost $5.96 more than the scarf. The total for the two items, before tax, was $63.94. What was the cost of the hat?
    (A) $26.39
    (B) $26.99
    (C) $28.49
    (D) $28.99

30. Order from least to greatest: $-1\frac{2}{5}, -1\frac{3}{5}, -1\frac{1}{3}$
    (A) $-1\frac{2}{5}, -1\frac{1}{3}, -1\frac{3}{5}$
    (B) $-1\frac{3}{5}, -1\frac{2}{5}, -1\frac{1}{3}$
    (C) $-1\frac{3}{5}, -1\frac{1}{3}, -1\frac{2}{5}$
    (D) $-1\frac{1}{3}, -1\frac{2}{5}, -1\frac{3}{5}$

31. $\frac{1}{4} - \frac{2}{3} \times \frac{3}{4} =$
    (A) $1\frac{1}{6}$
    (B) $\frac{7}{12}$
    (C) $\frac{-1}{12}$
    (D) $\frac{-1}{4}$

GO ON TO THE NEXT PAGE.

32. Hideki drove the 81 miles from Glendale to Roseville in $1\frac{1}{2}$ hours. What was his average speed?
   (A)   54 mph
   (B)   56 mph
   (C)   57 mph
   (D)   58 mph

33. The half-life of a radioactive element is 1 second. If you start with 32 grams of it, how much will be left in 4 seconds?
   (A)   2 g
   (B)   4 g
   (C)   8 g
   (D)   16 g

34. Keisha rides an elevator up 2 floors and down 11 floors and gets off. She is on floor 3. Where did she get on?
   (A)   floor 4
   (B)   floor 7
   (C)   floor 10
   (D)   floor 12

35. The difference between 4 times a number and 16 is 4. What is the number?
   (A)   5
   (B)   6
   (C)   8
   (D)   9

36. The distance around a running track is 440 yards. How many times must you run around the track to run 3 miles?
   (A)   8
   (B)   9
   (C)   12
   (D)   14

37. A rectangular playground is 200 yd long and 120 yd wide. What is the length in yards of a fence all around the edge of the playground?
   (A)   620 yd
   (B)   640 yd
   (C)   660 yd
   (D)   680 yd

38. $x/4 = 45/36$. $x =$
   (A)   3
   (B)   4
   (C)   5
   (D)   6

39. Jorge hiked 45 miles in 3 days. If he hikes at the same rate, how many miles can he hike in 2 weeks?
   (A)   180 mi
   (B)   195 mi
   (C)   205 mi
   (D)   210 mi

40. Which shows $3/8$ written as a percent?
   (A)   37.5%
   (B)   40%
   (C)   44.5%
   (D)   45%

41. What percent of 144 is 108?
   (A)   65%
   (B)   68%
   (C)   72%
   (D)   75%

42. What is the total cost of a $450 television set, including an 8.5% sales tax?
   (A) $476.75
   (B) $488.25
   (C) $492.50
   (D) $494.75

43. $5\frac{1}{2}$ quarts is how many pints?
   (A)   9
   (B)   10
   (C)   11
   (D)   12

44. What is the value of the 8 in 54.986?
   (A)   8 thousandths
   (B)   8 hundredths
   (C)   8 tenths
   (D)   8 tens

45. $-5.2 \times 2.4 =$
   (A)   12.8
   (B)   10.6
   (C) -7.6
   (D) -12.48

STOP!
If you finish before time is up, check your work on this section only.

SECTION 5
Time: 30 Minutes

Directions: You will have 30 minutes to plan and write an essay on the topic given below. You must write on the assigned topic only. An essay on another topic will not be acceptable. You may make notes in the space provided for that purpose.

Write your final essay on the two lined pages of your answer sheet. Write or print legibly in blue or black ink. A copy of your essay will be sent to each school that will be receiving your test results.

If you could meet one famous person from the present or the past, who would it be? Explain why you have chosen this person.

USE THIS SPACE FOR NOTES

George washington

done great
things

General in revolutionarywar

Answer Key

Section 1 Verbal Reasoning

1.	D	15.	C	29.	C
2.	D	16.	B	30.	A
3.	B	17.	B	31.	C
4.	C	18.	A	32.	C
5.	A	19.	D	33.	D
6.	D	20.	C	34.	A
7.	B	21.	D	35.	B
8.	A	22.	A	36.	D
9.	B	23.	C	37.	B
10.	C	24.	B	38.	A
11.	A	25.	B	39.	A
12.	C	26.	C	40.	D
13.	A	27.	D		
14.	D	28.	B		

Section 2 Quantitative Reasoning

1.	B	13.	A	25.	A
2.	A	14.	A	26.	B
3.	C	15.	A	27.	C
4.	B	16.	C	28.	D
5.	C	17.	A	29.	A
6.	B	18.	B	30.	B
7.	C	19.	B	31.	C
8.	A	20.	C	32.	A
9.	C	21.	A	33.	B
10.	A	22.	A	34.	B
11.	D	23.	C	35.	C
12.	A	24.	B		

Section 3 Reading Comprehension

1.	C	15.	C	29.	B
2.	B	16.	B	30.	D
3.	C	17.	B	31.	A
4.	A	18.	A	32.	B
5.	D	19.	D	33.	D
6.	B	20.	A	34.	C
7.	C	21.	B	35.	D
8.	A	22.	C	36.	A
9.	B	23.	A	37.	C
10.	C	24.	A	38.	B
11.	D	25.	C	39.	D
12.	D	26.	D	40.	B
13.	B	27.	C		
14.	A	28.	B		

Section 4 Mathematics Achievement

1.	D	16.	D	31.	D
2.	C	17.	A	32.	A
3.	A	18.	B	33.	A
4.	D	19.	C	34.	D
5.	D	20.	D	35.	A
6.	B	21.	C	36.	C
7.	D	22.	A	37.	B
8.	B	23.	D	38.	C
9.	C	24.	B	39.	D
10.	C	25.	A	40.	A
11.	C	26.	D	41.	D
12.	D	27.	B	42.	B
13.	B	28.	C	43.	C
14.	A	29.	D	44.	B
15.	B	30.	B	45.	D

Answers and Explanations

Section 1 Verbal Reasoning

1. **D is correct.** *Shame* is a painful emotion caused by a strong sense of guilt, embarrassment, unworthiness, or disgrace. Another word for shame is *humiliation*.

2. **D is correct.** To *divulge* something is to make it known, especially something private or a secret—to *tell*.

3. **B is correct.** *Concise* is an adjective meaning expressing much in few words; clear and succinct—in other words, *brief*.

4. **C is correct.** An *inquiry* is a close examination of a matter in a search for information or truth. An *inquiry* is synonymous with an *investigation*.

5. **A is correct.** Like *disposition*, an *attitude* is a state of mind or feeling.

6. **D is correct.** To do something *tediously* is the same as doing it *tiresomely* by reason of length, slowness, dullness, or boredom.

7. **B is correct.** To *deplete* something is to decrease the fullness of it; use it up; or empty it out—in other words, to *reduce* it.

8. **A is correct.** *Cautious* describes someone who is careful, tentative, restrained, or guarded. Another way to describe such a person would be to say that she is *discreet*.

9. **B is correct.** *Sparse* is an adjective describing conditions that are not thick or dense. *Thin* is synonymous with sparse.

10. **C is correct.** An *aversion* is an avoidance of a thing, situation, or behavior because it has been associated with an unpleasant or painful stimulus. If you have an aversion to something you have a fixed, intense *dislike* for it.

11. **A is correct.** When something is *dormant* it is lying asleep, or as if asleep. That is, it is *inactive*.

12. **C is correct.** If someone is described as *malcontent*, he is *dissatisfied* with existing conditions.

13. **A is correct.** To *merit* means to earn or *deserve*.

14. **D is correct.** If something is *prominent*, it is immediately noticeable—in other words, *conspicuous*.

15. **C is correct.** An *objective* is something worked toward or striven for. *Intention* is synonymous with *objective*.

16. **B is correct.** Something that is *indelible* is impossible to remove, erase, or wash away. Therefore, it is *permanent*.

17. **B is correct.** A *shrewd* person is characterized by keen awareness, sharp intelligence, and often a sense of the practical. As well, a person described as *astute* has or shows discernment, awareness, and intelligence.

18. **A is correct.** *Clandestine* is an adjective meaning kept or done in *secret*, often to conceal an illicit or improper purpose.

19. **D is correct.** To *coerce* someone is to force that person to act or think in a certain way by use of pressure, threats or intimidation. *Compel* can be used synonymously with *coerce*.

20. **C is correct.** A *plethora* is an abundance or an *excess*.

21. **D is correct.** Ask yourself: Which choice best reflects a description of two famous (rather than infamous) historical figures? *Eminent* (choice D) denotes a person of prominence or high ranking. This is the only choice that fits the context of the sentence and thus it is the correct answer.

22. **A is correct.** Since choices A, B, and D all have similar first blank meanings, you can discount choice C and focus on the second-blank choices. Of the three, *ratify* (meaning "to approve or confirm") is the best choice and works well with the idea that the sentence is trying to convey.

23. **C is correct.** By focusing on the first blank, you can almost immediately discount choice D by logically inferring that a product manufacturer would likely want a consumer to achieve better than "conventional" results with its product. Now, you will find that one of the three remaining answer choices clearly makes more sense than the other two, because it is unlikely that a tutorial would be *abbreviated* or *selective*. *Optimum . . . comprehensive* is the correct answer.

24. **B is correct.** "Although" is one of the words you may see on the test that signals a contrast within a two-clause sentence. When you come across words or phrases such as "despite," "although" or "even though," keep in mind that the word you are looking for is likely to contrast with another point the sentence makes. Of the choices available, only *camaraderie* (meaning "goodwill among or between friends") offers sufficient contrast to a tornado that had ruinous effects.

25. **B is correct.** *Succumb*, meaning "to submit to an overpowering force or yield to an overwhelming desire; to give up or give in," is the correct answer.

26. **C is correct.** By noticing the "despite" construction, you are given a clue that the pair of words you are looking for will have a contrast in meaning. *Explosive . . . timid* is the only choice that offers the proper contrast.

27. **D is correct.** *Equivocal*, meaning "open to two or more interpretations and often intended to mislead," is the only possible correct answer. *Equivocal* can be used synonymously with *ambiguous*.

28. **B is correct.** *Exiled*, meaning "banished," is the correct answer. *Garnered* means "to have gathered or stored"; *abetted* means "to have approved, encouraged, or supported"; and *incited* means "to have provoked or urged on."

29. **C is correct.** The logic of this sentence suggests that many people do not agree with an earlier decision the judge made. *Impede*, meaning "to hinder or obstruct the process of," is the correct answer. Don't be fooled by the similar looking *impel*, which means "to urge to action through moral pressure," or "to drive."

30. **A is correct.** This question is made much easier if you are able to discount choices C and D because you know that *forgo* means "to abstain from," and *mollify* means "to calm in temper or soothe." Logic tells you that it is unlikely Langston Hughes doubted blues music to be the true expression of his soul. *Emulate . . . believed* is the correct answer (*emulate* meaning "to strive to equal or excel, especially through imitation").

31. **C is correct.** *Discernible*, meaning "perceptible as by the faculty of vision or intellect," is the correct answer. *Imperceptible* (choice A), is an antonym. Pay attention to prefixes and be aware how they alter the meaning of the words you may be looking for.

32. **C is correct.** "Initially" is a key word in this sentence as it conveys the logic that the main suspect later changed his mind and agreed to cooperate with the prosecution. Indeed, had his alibi been foolproof, solid, or *feasible* (choice A), he likely would have stuck to his original story. So, the word you are looking for is *tenuous*, meaning "flimsy or having little substance."

33. **D is correct.** Logically you can infer that property owners would not be *exuberant* (choice A) over the mayor's proposal to raise property taxes in order to fund a new stadium. As well, because *exuberant* has connotations similar to *illustrious* (choice C), you should be able to eliminate both answer choices. *Ambivalent* (choice D), meaning "characterized by a mixture of opposite meanings or attitudes," is correct.

34. **A is correct.** Because this sentence lacks words or phrases that signal contrast, you should be looking for a pair of words that will complement one another. From the choices you are given, you can see that only choice A, *praised . . . commendable,* fits this criteria. All of the other choices are word pairs that have conflicting meanings.

35. **B is correct.** Seemingly, Ms. Tompkins favors collecting books. Therefore, you could say that she has a *propensity* (meaning "an innate inclination or tendency") for accumulation.

36. **D is correct.** *Resilience* (choice D) is the ability to recover quickly from illness, change, or misfortune. *Dexterity* (choice C), meaning "skill and grace in physical movement," is an attractive distracter, but the focus of the sentence is that the gymnast was able to overcome injuries. Choice D is the best answer.

37. **B is correct.** *Fastidious* (choice C) is incorrect because its meaning is similar to *picky*, which is contradicted by the conjunction "but." *Ravenous* (choice B), meaning "extremely hungry," conveys the meaning of the sentence, which is that you would expect the bear to be extremely hungry when in fact he is rather picky. *Hirsute* means "covered in hair."

38. **A is correct.** If you are unsure of the correct word pair in a two-blank question, try focusing on one of the blanks first. Focusing on the first blank, it is unlikely that an angry couple would behave *morosely* (choice B) or *lavishly* (choice D), so you can eliminate these choices. Additionally, you should be able to recognize that words with the prefix "extra-" rarely have negative connotations. *Bellicosely* (meaning "warlike in manner or temperament") is the only correct first-blank choice. *Rescinded* means to "have made void; repealed or annulled."

39. **A is correct.** *Comparable* (choice B) and *consistent* (choice D) do not fit the "even though" construction of this sentence. *Excessive* fits the first blank, though *affirm* (meaning "to declare positively" or "maintain to be true") makes no sense in the second blank. *Disproportionate . . . submit* (choice A) is the correct answer.

40. **D is correct.** This sentence is another example of a two-blank question in which the correct choice of words will complement, rather than contrast, with one another. Because both choice A and choice B are pairs that offer contrasting meanings, you can eliminate them. Focusing on the two remaining pairs, you can conclude that the newspaper was unlikely to be responsible for the power outage, and therefore *harassed* is an inappropriate answer. *Inundated . . . deluge* (choice D) is correct.

Section 2 Quantitative Reasoning

1. **B is correct.** $48 \div 6 \times 8 \times 8 = 512$; $512 \div 16 = 32$.

2. **A is correct.** Create equations to solve this problem.
   Paula = Lindsey + 3
   Lindsey = Dave − 2
   You are told that Paula is 17. Substitute that information into the first equation.
   17 = Lindsey + 3
   Lindsey = 14
   Substitute that into the second equation.
   14 = Dave − 2
   Dave = 16

3. **C is correct.** $3/4 - 5/12 = 9/12 - 5/12 = 4/12 = 1/3$.

4. **B is correct.** $20 = x \%$ of 80.
   $20 = 80x$ Solve for x.
   $x = {}^{20}/_{80} =$
   $x = {}^{2}/_{8}$
   $x = 1/4$ Divide 1 by 4 to get 0.25 or 25%

5. **C is correct.** 0.5 km = 500 meters; $500 \div 5 = 100$.

6. **B is correct.** $2/8$ can be simplified to $1/4$

7. **C is correct.** The least common multiple of a group of numbers is the least whole number (greater than 0) that is a multiple of all of the numbers. The least common multiple of 9, 2 and 5 is 90 (9×10, 2×45, 5×18).

8. **A is correct.** To find the average, add the numbers and divide by the number of numbers. In this problem the numbers add to 415. Dividing that by 5 gives an average of 83.

9. **C is correct.** $1/3 + 1/6 = 2/6 + 1/6 = 3/6$.
   $3/6 = 1/2$, so if Karen has used $1/2$ of her tickets, $1/2$ are left.

10. **A is correct.** $5 \times 4 + 4 = 24$; $6 \times 8 = 48$; and $48 \div 34 = 2$.

11. **D is correct.** $32/4 = 8$; $4 \times 8/16 = 32/16 = 2$; $8 \div 1/8 = 8 \times 8/1 = 64$. However, $5/12 \times 8 = 40/12 = 3^1/_3$, which is not a whole number.

12. **A is correct.** 1 mile = 5,280 ft. If the width of the park is 880 ft, then two sides of the park measure 880 + 880 = 1,760 ft. 5,280 − 1,760 = 3,520. The other two sides of the park must each measure one-half of 3,520 ft. 3,520 ÷ 2 = 1,760 ft.

13. **A is correct.**
    $1/4 x = 12$
    $x = 48$
    $1/6 x = 8$

14. **A is correct.** Set up a proportion:
    $3/_{126} = x/_{924}$
    $3 \times 924 = 126x$
    $2,772 = 126x$
    $^{2,772}/_{126} = x$
    $22 = x$

15. **A is correct.**
    $5/6 - 2/3 - 1/_{12}$
    $= 10/_{12} - 8/_{12} - 1/_{12}$
    $= 2/_{12} - 1/_{12}$
    $= 1/_{12}$

16. **C is correct.** When calculating the average or mean, add the numbers and then divide by the number of numbers. The sum of 24, 36, 18, 30, 90, and 690 is 888, divided by 6 is 148

17. **A is correct.** It costs $12.00 dollars to buy 24 cookies. 6 cookies are 1/4 of 24, so the cost of 6 cookies will be $1/4 \times \$12.00 = \$3.00$ dollars.

18. **B is correct.** $3 \times 425 = 1,275$.

19. **B is correct.** $20/5 = 4$; $6 \div 1/6 = 6 \times 6/1 = 36$; $3/5 \times 10 = 30/5 = 6$; However, $5 \times 3/4 = 15/4 = 3 \ 3/4$, which is not a whole number.

20. **C is correct.** There are 10 + 15 = 25 marbles in the bag. If you pick one without looking, your chances of picking a white marble are $10/_{25}$ or $2/5$.

21. **A is correct.** This is a quantitative-comparison question in which you are asked to compare two whole number differences. Did you notice that the last 3 digits in the numbers being subtracted are the same? The last 3 digits in the number you are subtracting from is greater in Column A than in Column B.

22. **A is correct.**
    $75\% = 3/4$ and $25\% = 1/4$.
    Column A: 75% of 120 = $3/4 \times 120 = 90$
    Column B: 50% of 160 = $1/2 \times 160 = 80$

23. **C is correct.**
    The distributive property states that $a(b + c) = (a \bullet b) + (a \bullet c)$
    Use the distributive property to simplify the expression in Column A:
    $3(c + 2) = (3 \bullet c) + (3 \bullet 2)$

Simplify this quantity in Column A as follows: $(3 \cdot c) + (3 \cdot 2) = 3c + 6$
Simplify the quantity in Column B as follows: $3c + (3 \cdot 2) = 3c + 6$

24. **B is correct.**
   The vertex of both angles is at the center of the protractor.
   Ray *FE* of ∠*DFE* passes through the zero mark on the inner scale of the protractor.
   Ray FD of ∠*DFE* passes through 65 on the inner scale.
   m∠*DFE* = 65°
   Ray *AF* of ∠*AFC* passes through the zero mark on the outer scale of the protractor.
   Ray *FC* of ∠*AFC* passes through 70 on the outer scale.
   m ∠AFC = 70°

25. **A is correct.**
   To find the average number of yards per minute, divide the total number of yards walked by the number of minutes it took to walk them.
   Column A: Divide the total number of yards Janet walked (125) by the number of minutes it took her to walk this distance (3). $125 \div 3 = 41\frac{2}{3}$
   Column B: Divide the total number of yards Victoria walked (206) by the number of minutes it took her to walk this distance (5). $206 \div 5 = 41\frac{1}{5}$
   $41\frac{2}{3} > 41\frac{1}{5}$

26. **B is correct.**
   $\sqrt{150}$ is the number whose square is 150.
   $\sqrt{150}$ is a number between 12 and 13, since $12 \times 12 = 144$ and $13 \times 13 = 169$.

27. **C is correct.**
   The probability of an event is the ratio of favorable outcomes to possible outcomes. This ratio can be written as a fraction.
   The number of possible outcomes equals the number of letter blocks, which is 15.
   Column A: Find the number of favorable outcomes by counting all the blocks that contain vowels. This includes As (3) and Es (1), for a total of 4 favorable outcomes.
   Column B: Find the number of favorable outcomes by counting all the blocks that contain Ts (2) or Ls (2), for a total of 4 favorable outcomes.
   $\frac{4}{15} = \frac{4}{15}$

28. **D is correct.**
   The perimeter of a rectangle is $p = 2l + 2w$. The perimeter of a square is $p = 4s$.
   The area of a rectangle is $A = l \times w$. The area of a rectangle is $A = s^2$.
   Column A: Since you were given the area as 64 ft², find *s* by finding $\sqrt{64} = 8$, and then find *p*, the perimeter = $4 \times 8 = 32$ ft.
   Column B: If the area is 48 ft², there are many different whole number values *l* and *w* can equal. For example, $6 \times 8 = 48$, $3 \times 16 = 48$, $2 \times 24 = 48$, and $1 \times 48 = 48$.
   Use these various values for *l* and *w* to find the perimeter of the rectangle.
   Some values will result in perimeters less than 32 ft, such as *l* = 6 and *w* = 8, $p = 2(6) + 2(8) = 28$. Some values will result in perimeters greater than 32, such as *l* = 3, *w* = 16, $p = 2(3) + 2(16) = 38$. Thus the relationship between the two quantities cannot be determined from the information given.

29. **A is correct.**
   Column A: Rewrite $4\frac{2}{5}$ as $\frac{22}{5}$.
   Column B: Rewrite $7\frac{1}{2}$ as $\frac{15}{2}$.
   Rewrite the division as a multiplication by first finding the reciprocal of the divisor, and then multiplying the dividend by the reciprocal of the divisor.
   Column A: Rewrite $4\frac{2}{5} \div \frac{3}{10}$ as $\frac{22}{5} \times \frac{10}{3}$.
   $\frac{22}{5} \times \frac{10}{3} = \frac{220}{15} = 14\frac{10}{15} = 14\frac{2}{3}$
   Column B: Rewrite $7\frac{1}{2} \div \frac{2}{3}$ as $\frac{15}{2} \times \frac{3}{2}$.
   $\frac{15}{2} \times \frac{3}{2} = \frac{45}{4} = 11\frac{1}{4}$
   $14\frac{2}{3}$ is greater than $11\frac{1}{4}$.

30. **B is correct.**

The absolute value is the distance from a number line to zero.
The absolute value of any number is a positive number.
Column A: Since $|4| = 4$, then $-|4| = -4$
Column B: $|-4| = 4$

31. **C is correct.**

Column A: Solve the equation for x using the subtraction property:
$x + 1 = 15$; $x + 1 - 1 = 15 - 1$; $x = 14$
Column B: Solve the equation for y using the addition property:
$y - 7 = 7$; $y - 7 + 7 = 7 + 7$; $y = 14$

32. **A is correct.**

The figures are rectangular prisms. The formula for finding the surface area of a prism is $SA = 2lw + 2lh + 2wh$
Column A: $SA = 2(3 \times 3) + 2(3 \times 8) + 2(3 \times 8) = 18 + 48 + 48 = 114$ cm²
Column B: $SA = 2(6 \times 2) + 2(6 \times 4) + 2(2 \times 4) = 24 + 48 + 16 = 88$ cm²

33. **B is correct.**

Column A: List all the factors for 56, 96, and 200:
56: 1, 2, 4, 7, 8, 14, 28, 56
96: 1, 2, 3, 4, 6, 8, 12, 16, 24, 32, 48, 96
200: 1, 2, 4, 5, 8, 10, 20, 25, 50, 100, 200
The factors that are common to all three numbers are 1, 2, 4, and 8, and 8 is the largest of these factors.
Column B: List all the factors for 27, 81, and 189:
27: 1, 3, 9, 27
81: 1, 3, 9, 27, 81
189: 1, 3, 7, 9, 21, 27, 63, 189
The factors that are common to all three numbers are 1, 3, 9, and 27, and 27 is the largest of these factors.

34. **B is correct.**

Column A: Estimate by rounding each decimal factor to its leading digit: $2.76 \times 2.57 \rightarrow 3 \times 3 = 9$
The actual product is *less than 9*, since your estimate used numbers greater than the actual factors.
Column B: Estimate by rounding each decimal factor to its leading digit: $21.4 \times 0.53 \rightarrow 20 \times 0.5 = 10$
The actual product is *greater than 10*, since your estimate used numbers less than the actual factors.

35. **C is correct.**

1 qt = 32 fl oz., and 1 c = 8 fl oz
Column A: 8 qt 1 c = $(8 \times 32) + (1 \times 8) = 256 + 8 = 264$ fl oz.
The quantity in Column A is equal to the quantity in Column B.

Section 3 Reading Comprehension

1. **C is correct.** As she says in lines 22–25, "I have been trying to get before you business people to tell you what I am doing." Choice A can be eliminated because Madam Walker was not trying to demonstrate her products to the members of the league, but merely to make them aware of what she was doing and how well she was doing. Choice B is wrong because Madam Walker was addressing her remarks to the entire league, not just to Booker T. Washington. Choice D is wrong because there is no support in the passage for this choice.

2. **B is correct.** Madam Walker came to the podium uninvited and boasted of her business success. She tells how she came from "the cotton fields" to the "wash-tub" to the "cook kitchen" and finally to head of a thriving business. She says "I am not ashamed of my past; I am not ashamed of my humble beginning." Clearly, she is proud of her accomplishments.

3. **C is correct.** The reactions of the audience are indicated in parentheses throughout the speech. The fact that the audience reacted with applause, laughter, and prolonged applause indicates that their reaction was favorable. It is unlikely that the audience would applaud and laugh if they were indifferent (choice A), angry (choice B), or critical (choice D) of the speech.

4. **A is correct**. Walker uses the reference to her promotions from farm laborer, to laundress, to cook to show just how far she has come to get to her current position as head of a company that has made more than $63,000 (a great deal of money in 1912) in only seven years.

5. **D is correct.** Madam Walker says, "I am not ashamed of my past; I am not ashamed of my humble beginning. Don't think that because you have to go down in the wash-tub that you are any less a lady!" By this she means that hard work, like washing and scrubbing, is nothing to be ashamed of. Nor does it diminish a woman's status as a lady who is entitled to be treated with respect.

6. **B is correct**. The entire passage discusses the 1980 eruption of Mount St. Helens. The information provided is specific to a particular volcano, so choices A and D are incorrect. The passage does not tell readers what to do when a volcano erupts, so choice C is wrong.

7. **C is correct**. A 123-year slumber means that Mount St. Helens had no eruptions going back 123 years from 1980. That puts the last eruption at 1857. Choice A is wrong because if Mount St. Helens had been "sleeping" for 123 years, it must have been active 123 years ago. Choice B is wrong because there is nothing to support the idea that Mount St. Helens erupts every 123 years. Choice D is wrong because if Mount St. Helens erupted 123 years ago, it could always erupt again.

8. **A is correct**. *Rising* is used in the following sentence: "Heat from a rising plume of volcanic ash melted glacial ice creating cement-like slurries of rock and ash called mudflows." Each of the answer choices is a possible meaning for *rising*. However, in context, the best meaning is *ascending*.

9. **B is correct**. The passage states that the geologists were not surprised by Mount St. Helens' awakening because they had been studying Mount St. Helens for many years and in 1975 they "published a report predicting Mount St. Helens was the volcano in the lower 48 states most likely to erupt by the end of the century." Thus, the assumptions they had made about Mount St. Helens based on extensive studies of deposits found around the volcano were proving to be correct. Choice A is wrong because the geologists predicted only that Mount St. Helens was the volcano "most likely to erupt by the end of the century." They did not predict when it would erupt, but only that it was most likely to erupt. The passage provides no information to support either choice C or choice D.

10. **C is correct**. The author's use of vivid language is illustrated by such words as "triggered," "blast," "flattened," "scoured," "billowed," and "swept." Examples of dramatic images include these: "In less than three minutes, 230 square miles of forest lay flattened," " . . . concrete-like mudflows that scoured river valleys," "A plume of volcanic ash and pumice billowed out of the volcano reaching a height of 15 miles and transformed day into night."

11. **D is correct**. A wasteland is barren land with no vegetation. The author mentions in lines 31–43 that the landslides flattened the forest and concrete-like mudflows scoured river valleys surrounding the mountain. Choice A is wrong because the landscape was covered in volcanic ash, not snow. Choice B is wrong because a wasteland is barren, not covered in waste matter. Choice C is wrong because the trees had been flattened and swept away.

12. **D is correct**. The entire passage focuses on Paul's attitude and his demeanor. The red carnation in his buttonhole, the fact that he "was quite accustomed to lying," the contempt he shows for his teachers, all are evidence of the author's penetrating look at the character of the young man in question.

13. **B is correct**. A dandy is a man who is very concerned about his appearance and so pays great attention to his clothes. This description fits Paul who, even though his clothes were a trifle outgrown and the collar of his overcoat was frayed, still wore an opal pin in his necktie and a red carnation in his buttonhole.

14. **A is correct**. The faculty felt that the red carnation "was not properly significant of the contrite spirit befitting a boy under the ban of suspension." His jaunty dress made them feel that Paul was not sufficiently humbled by his suspension or sorry about his actions.

15. **C is correct**. As stated in lines 50–51, the real cause of the trouble "lay in a sort of hysterically defiant manner of the boy's; in the contempt which they all knew he felt for them, and which he seemingly made not the least effort to conceal." There is no mention of Paul's inability to control his temper or failure to complete assignments, so choices A and B are wrong. The passage mentions that Paul looked out the window during recitation, which

indicates that he was inattentive in class (choice D), but this offense is minor in comparison to the obvious contempt he displayed toward his teachers.

16. **B is correct**. Paul is described as having a "defiant manner," which means he is impertinent, insolent, or boldly resistant to authority. There is no evidence in the passage that Paul is either *contrite* (remorseful) or *embarrassed* (ashamed), so choices A and D are wrong. He moves his hands violently behind him when the English teacher attempts to guide his hand, but his actions in general cannot be described as *violent*, so choice C is wrong.

17. **B is correct**. As stated in lines 43–44, the teachers stated the charges against Paul with "rancor and aggrievedness." *Rancor* means "bitterness" or "malice." *Turmoil*, which means "confusion," does not make sense in relation to stating a case, so choice A is wrong. *Remorse* (choice C), which means "regret" and *dismay* (choice D), which means "discouragement" or "despair," do not fit the context of the passage.

18. **A is correct**. This story is presented as an example of the contempt which all the teachers knew Paul felt for them and which he seemed to make no effort to conceal. Paul shuddered and thrust his hands violently behind him when the English teacher attempted to guide his hand as he worked at the blackboard. "The insult was so involuntary and definitely personal as to be unforgettable. In one way and another he had made all his teachers, men and women alike, conscious of the same feeling of physical aversion." Paul's reaction had nothing to do with not being able to answer the question, so choice B is incorrect. Likewise, there is no indication that he was afraid of the teacher (choice C) or that he wanted to strike the teacher (choice D). The passage says only that the teacher "could scarcely have been more hurt and embarrassed had he struck at her."

19. **D is correct**. This informative passage tells about the Homestead Act of 1862, including the provisions of the Act and the part it played in the settling of the American West. Choice A is wrong because the passage focuses on the Homestead Act, not on the settling of the West. Choice B is wrong because the passage says nothing about extending the Act. Choice C is wrong because although the passage briefly mentions the hard work and sacrifices of homesteaders, this is not the primary purpose of the entire passage.

20. **A is correct**. *File* is used in the following sentence: "People interested in Homesteading first had to file their intentions at the nearest Land Office where they paid a fee of $10 to claim the land . . . " Although each of the choices is a possible meaning for the word *file*, the one that makes sense in the context of this sentence is *record* (choice A).

21. **B is correct**. As stated in paragraph 2, "A homesteader had only to be the head of a household and at least 21 years of age to claim a 160-acre parcel of land," Also, homesteaders were required "to live on the land, build a home, make improvements, and farm for 5 years before they were eligible to 'prove up'." There is no mention of settlers' having to be native-born citizens. In fact, the passage specifically mentions "newly arrived immigrants" as would-be homesteaders.

22. **C is correct**. As stated in paragraph 1, "Under this Act 270 million acres, or 10% of the area of the United States, was claimed and settled." Choice A is wrong because each homesteader could claim a 160-acre parcel of land, but that does not means that every person was entitled to 160 acres of land. Choice D is wrong because the passage states that 10 percent, not 30 percent, of all U.S. lands passed into the hands of individuals.

23. **A is correct**. The Homestead Act was designed "to spur Western migration." As a result of this Act, "270 million acres, or 10% of the area of the United States, was claimed and settled." Thus the Act served its purpose of helping settle the West.

24. **A is correct.** The first paragraph tells how manatees and dugongs came to be called sirenians because of their resemblance to the sirens, or sea nymphs, of Greek mythology. Choice B is wrong because although the passage mentions that sailors—particularly those who have spent many months at sea—may have mistaken a manatee for a mermaid, it does not provide specific similarities between manatees and mermaids. Choice C is wrong because it was the sirens of mythology who are said to have caused shipwrecks. Choice D is wrong because the passage does not compare manatees and dugongs, except to say that both are sirenians.

25. **C is correct**. The second sentence of the passage tells how the sirens "lured sailors and their ships to treacherous rocks and shipwreck with mesmerizing songs." *Mesmerizing* means "captivating," spellbinding," or "hypnotic."

26. **D is correct**. The last sentence of paragraph 1 ("Like the mythological creatures for which they were named, all sirenians living on earth today are vulnerable to extinction.") supports the idea that all sirenians are endangered. Information in the passage contradicts each of the other answer choices.

27. **C is correct**. Lines 29–35 ("Unlike . . . birth.") of the passage are devoted to listing the ways in which sirenians are different from and similar to other marine mammals.

28. **B is correct**. As stated in the passage, "sirenians eat only seagrasses and other aquatic vegetation." These grasses grow best in shallow waters where sunlight can penetrate. Additionally, "sirenians have an extremely low metabolism and zero tolerance for cold water"; therefore, they need the warmer temperatures of Florida's coastal waters. There is no mention of safety in the passage, and in fact, these very waters are also attractive to people in speedy powerboats, who pose the biggest danger to slow-moving manatees.

29. **B is correct**. The average adult manatee "weighs between 362–544 kilograms (800–1,200 pounds)" and eats "between 45–68 kilograms (100–150 pounds) of sea grass and water hyacinths a day!"

30. **D is correct**. Mood is the pervading spirit or feeling of a passage as transmitted by the author's choice of words. In this passage the day is described as "exceedingly cold and gray" with "no sun nor hint of sun, though there was not a cloud in the sky." There was "an intangible pall over the face of things, a subtle gloom that made the day dark." And yet, despite these warning signs, the man was not worried. Taken together this information imparts a sense of impending misfortune or foreboding.

31. **A is correct**. All of the choices are definitions of the word *broken*, but only choice A makes sense in context. The day was cold and gray, when it came into being or dawned.

32. **B is correct**. Clearly, the facts that the man is traveling a little-used trail, is unconcerned about the extremely cold temperature, and does not notice that the dog seems almost hesitant to follow, indicate that the man is not accustomed to such activity. Choices A and D are wrong because the passage makes no mention of when the man is expected to meet the others, so it cannot be inferred that he is either behind or ahead of schedule. Choice C is wrong because even though it is extremely cold out, there is no evidence, at this point, that the man is disoriented.

33. **D is correct**. The man knew that "at fifty below spittle crackled on the snow." Obviously he wanted to test the temperature of the air. When he found that this spittle "had crackled in the air," he realized that the temperature was even lower than fifty below, which indicates very severe cold.

34. **C is correct**. The man was startled because he was not expecting to hear his spittle crackle before it fell to the snow. The passage goes on to say that the man knew "that at fifty below spittle crackled on the snow, but this spittle had crackled in the air. Undoubtedly it was colder than fifty below."

35. **D is correct**. The day is described as "exceedingly cold and gray." The man determines that "it was colder than fifty below," and yet he continues to travel on. Even the dog "was depressed by the tremendous cold. It knew that it was no time for traveling." Under these circumstances, the best description of the man's actions is foolish.

36. **A is correct**. As stated in lines 45–46, "The animal was depressed by the tremendous cold. It knew that it was no time for travelling. Its instinct told it a truer tale than was told to the man by the man's judgment." These statements clearly support choice A.

37. **C is correct**. Each of the answer choices is a meaning of the word *engaged*. However, only *participated* makes sense in place of the word *engaged* in this sentence: "I was asked not long ago to tell something about the sports and pastimes that I engaged in during my youth."

38. **B is correct.** The author's "trouble" was not being strong enough to get the corn back up on the horse once it had fallen off. Thus he was forced to wait until someone older and stronger came along to help before he could continue on his way to the mill. Choice A is wrong because although the author mentions being afraid to travel at night, this is not the trouble referred to in line 15. Choice C is wrong because the author seems to know his way, and choice D is wrong because the mention of flogging comes much later in the passage.

39. **D is correct.** There is no mention of kidnapping in the passage. Choice A is wrong because the passage states "the road was a lonely one" and this contributed to the author's fear. Choice B is wrong because the passage says "the woods were said to be full of soldiers who had deserted from the army," another reason for his fear. Choice C is wrong because the author had been told that "the first thing a deserter did to a Negro boy when he found him alone was to cut off his ears."

40. **B is correct.** The author recounts the events of his youth analytically, He tells that "there was no period of my life that was devoted to play," and mentions that "From the time that I can remember anything, almost every day of my life has been occupied in some kind of labor." He relates his experience in taking the corn to the mill to be ground, and although he says he dreaded it and mentions crying as he waited for help, he relates the experience in a detached and matter-of-fact way. Certainly the author shows no longing to return to the days of his youth, so choice A cannot be correct. The language of the passage is too straightforward to be described as hostile; thus eliminating choice C. And while his story may seem sad to readers, the author does not appear to be consumed by sorrow over the days of his youth (choice D).

Section 4 Mathematics Achievement

1. **D is correct.** $9 \times 5 = 45$; $45 + 6 = 51$.

2. **C is correct.** It costs $48.00 to buy 64 cans of soda. 48 cans are $3/4$ of 64, so the cost of 40 cans of soda will be $3/4 \times \$48.00 = \$36.00$.

3. **A is correct.** $6 + 2 = 8$; $32 \div 8 = 4$; $4 - 4 = 0$.

4. **D is correct.** The total number of pairs in the drawer is $3 + 5 + 4 = 12$. If there are 4 pairs of blue socks, then the chances of picking a blue pair are $4/12$ or $1/3$.

5. **D is correct.** $6 \div 2/3 = 6/1 \div 2/3 = 6/1 \times 3/2 = 18/2 = 9$.

6. **B is correct.** This is a simple addition problem. Add the amounts of $4.68, $35.32, $17.77, $16.35, and $18.00 to get the total of $92.12.

7. **D is correct.** 35% can be rewritten as 0.35; $0.35 \times 70 = 24.5$.

8. **B is correct.** Use the formula $r \times t = d$ where $r =$ rate, $t =$ time, and $d =$ distance.
   3 hours 40 minutes = $3^2/3$ hours.
   $r \times t = d$
   $9 \times 3^2/3 = 33$ miles

9. **C is correct.** 45 minutes = $3/4$ hour; $1^3/4 + 3/4 = 1^6/4 = 2^2/4 = 2^1/2$.

10. **C is correct.** If Frank is 4 years younger than Donna, then the relationship between their two ages can be expressed by the equation $f = d - 4$.

11. **C is correct.** To find the average, add up the numbers and divide by the number of numbers. In this instance the number of miles Matt rode adds to 150. The number of days is 5, so the average number of miles per day he rode is $150 \div 5 = 30$. Don't make the mistake of dividing by 4 because on one day Matt's number of miles was 0. That number needs to be used in calculating the average.

12. **D is correct.** $8 \div 0.6 = 13.33$, so there are about 13 kilometers in 8 miles.

13. **B is correct.** The storm started at 2:12 P.M. on Tuesday and ended at 5:46 A.M. on Wednesday. From 2:12 P.M. to 5:12 A.M. the next day is 15 hours. From 5:12 to 5:46 is 34 minutes. The storm lasted 15 hours, 34 minutes.

14. **A is correct.** $3/4 \times 9 = 27/4 = 6 3/4$.

15. **B is correct.** $0.4 \times 0.5 = 0.20$.

16. **D is correct.** The common factors of 27 and 45 are 1, 3, and 9.

17. **A is correct.** $17/21 = 1/3$; $2/6$, $3/9$, and $9/27$ all also equal $1/3$.

18. **B is correct.** There were x people, divided evenly among 6 buses. So the number of people in each bus was $x/6$.

19. **C is correct.** 1 liter = 1,000 milliliters. The two pots together hold 8 liters. 8 liters = 8,000 milliliters.

20. **D is correct.** 23.62 miles − 19.8 miles = 3.82 miles.

21. **C is correct.** The length of time from 4:00 A.M. to 11:00 A.M. is 7 hours. $7 \times 3 = 21$, so during that time the temperature rose by 21 °F. The starting point was −11 °F, so: −11 + 21 = 10 °F.

22. **A is correct.** $9 3/5 + 2 1/4 = 9 12/20 + 2 5/20 = 11 17/20$.

23. **D is correct.** $12 \div 3 1/4 = 12/1 \div 13/4$
    $= 12/1 \times 4/13 = 48/13 = 3 9/13$.

24. **B is correct.** $8y + 5 = 41$, so $8y = 41 − 5 = 36$.
    $y = 36/8 = 4 4/8 = 4 1/2 = 4.5$

25. **A is correct.** Follow the order of operations:
    $(8 + 2)^2 − 2^3 \times (5 − 3) = (10)^2 − 2^3 \times (2)$
    $= 100 − 8 \times 2$
    $= 100 − 16 = 84$

26. **D is correct.** If $a = 26.3$, then $85.1 − a = 85.1 − 26.3$
    $= 58.8$.

27. **B is correct.** −218 °C + 35 °C = −183 °C.

28. **C is correct.** Any number with 0 as an exponent equals 1.

29. **D is correct.** hat + scarf = $63.94; scarf = hat + $5.96;
    hat + (hat + $5.96) = $63.94.
    2(hat) = $57.98.
    hat = $28.99

30. **B is correct.** $−1 2/5, −1 3/5, −1 1/3 = −1 12/30, −1 15/30, −1 10/30$
    Ordering from least to greatest: $−1 15/30, −1 12/30, −1 10/30$
    $= −1 3/5, −1 2/5, −1 1/3$.

31. **D is correct.** $1/4 − 2/3 \times 3/4 = 1/4 − 6/12$
    $= 1/4 − 1/2$
    $= −1/4$

32. **A is correct.** $81 \div 1.5 = 54$ mph.

33. **A is correct.** If the element has a half-life of 1 second, one-half of its mass decays each second. If you start with 32 g, after 1 second, $32/2 = 16$ g are left. After 2 seconds, $16/2 = 8$ g are left. After 3 seconds, $8/2 = 4$ g are left. After 4 seconds, $4/2 = 2$ g are left.

34. **D is correct.** $x + 2 - 11 = 3$.
$$x - 9 = 3$$
$$x = 12$$

35. **A is correct.** Let x be the unknown number.
$$4x - 4 = 16$$
$$4x = 20$$
$$x = 5$$

36. **C is correct.** 1 mile = 1,760 yards; 3 miles = $1,760 \times 3 = 5,280$ yd;
$5280 \div 440 = 12$.

37. **B is correct.** The playground measures 200 yd × 120 yd. A fence around the perimeter would measure
$200 + 120 + 200 + 120 = 640$ yd.

38. **C is correct.** $x/4 = {}^{45}/_{36}$.
$$x = 4(45/36)$$
$$x = 1(45/9)$$
$$x = 5$$

39. **D is correct.** Jorge hiked 45 miles in 3 days. ${}^{45}/_3 = 15$ mi per day. 2 weeks = 14 days. $14 \times 15 = 210$ mi.

40. **A is correct.** ${}^3/_8 = 0.375 = 37.5\%$.

41. **D is correct.** ${}^x/_{100} \times 144 = 108$.
$${}^{144x}/_{100} = 108$$
$$1.44x = 108$$
$$x = {}^{108}/_{1.44}$$
$$= 75\%$$

42. **B is correct.** On a $450 television set, the 8.5% sales tax = 450×0.085
= $38.25; $450 + $38.25 = $488.25.

43. **C is correct.** 1 qt = 2 pt; $5\frac{1}{2}$ qt = $5\frac{1}{2}(2)$ pt
= 11 pt.

44. **B is correct.** In the number 54.986, the 8 is two places to the right of the decimal point, so it indicates 8 hundredths.

45. **D is correct.** $-5.2 \times 2.4 = -12.48$. Remember that the product of a positive number and a negative number is a negative number.

ISEE Practice Test III

(Upper Level: For Candidates for Grades 9–12)

The following practice test is designed to be just like the real ISEE that you will take if you are applying for admission to grades 5 or 6. It matches the actual test in content coverage and level of difficulty. The test is in five sections: Verbal Reasoning, Quantitative Reasoning, Reading Comprehension, Mathematics Achievement, and the Essay.

This practice test will be an accurate reflection of how you'll do on test day if you treat it as the real examination. Here are some hints on how to take the test under conditions similar to those of the actual exam:

- Find a quiet place to work and set aside a period of approximately 3 hours when you will not be disturbed.

- Work on only one section at a time, and use your watch or a timer to keep track of the time limits for each test part.

- Tear out your answer sheet and mark your answers by filling in the ovals for each question.

- Write your essay on the pages provided.

- Become familiar with the directions for each part of the test. You'll save time on the actual test day by already being familiar with this information.

At the end of the test you'll find Answer Keys for each section and explanations for every question. Check your answers against the keys to find out how you did on each section of the test and what test topics you might need to study more. Then review the explanations, paying particular attention to the ones for the questions that you answered incorrectly.

ISEE Practice Test III

ANSWER SHEET

Note: If there are more answer lines than there are questions in a section, leave the extra answer lines blank.

Section 1: Verbal Reasoning

1. Ⓐ Ⓑ Ⓒ Ⓓ	17. Ⓐ Ⓑ Ⓒ Ⓓ	33. Ⓐ Ⓑ Ⓒ Ⓓ
2. Ⓐ Ⓑ Ⓒ Ⓓ	18. Ⓐ Ⓑ Ⓒ Ⓓ	34. Ⓐ Ⓑ Ⓒ Ⓓ
3. Ⓐ Ⓑ Ⓒ Ⓓ	19. Ⓐ Ⓑ Ⓒ Ⓓ	35. Ⓐ Ⓑ Ⓒ Ⓓ
4. Ⓐ Ⓑ Ⓒ Ⓓ	20. Ⓐ Ⓑ Ⓒ Ⓓ	36. Ⓐ Ⓑ Ⓒ Ⓓ
5. Ⓐ Ⓑ Ⓒ Ⓓ	21. Ⓐ Ⓑ Ⓒ Ⓓ	37. Ⓐ Ⓑ Ⓒ Ⓓ
6. Ⓐ Ⓑ Ⓒ Ⓓ	22. Ⓐ Ⓑ Ⓒ Ⓓ	38. Ⓐ Ⓑ Ⓒ Ⓓ
7. Ⓐ Ⓑ Ⓒ Ⓓ	23. Ⓐ Ⓑ Ⓒ Ⓓ	39. Ⓐ Ⓑ Ⓒ Ⓓ
8. Ⓐ Ⓑ Ⓒ Ⓓ	24. Ⓐ Ⓑ Ⓒ Ⓓ	40. Ⓐ Ⓑ Ⓒ Ⓓ
9. Ⓐ Ⓑ Ⓒ Ⓓ	25. Ⓐ Ⓑ Ⓒ Ⓓ	
10. Ⓐ Ⓑ Ⓒ Ⓓ	26. Ⓐ Ⓑ Ⓒ Ⓓ	
11. Ⓐ Ⓑ Ⓒ Ⓓ	27. Ⓐ Ⓑ Ⓒ Ⓓ	
12. Ⓐ Ⓑ Ⓒ Ⓓ	28. Ⓐ Ⓑ Ⓒ Ⓓ	
13. Ⓐ Ⓑ Ⓒ Ⓓ	29. Ⓐ Ⓑ Ⓒ Ⓓ	
14. Ⓐ Ⓑ Ⓒ Ⓓ	30. Ⓐ Ⓑ Ⓒ Ⓓ	
15. Ⓐ Ⓑ Ⓒ Ⓓ	31. Ⓐ Ⓑ Ⓒ Ⓓ	
16. Ⓐ Ⓑ Ⓒ Ⓓ	32. Ⓐ Ⓑ Ⓒ Ⓓ	

Section 2: Quantitative Reasoning

1. Ⓐ Ⓑ Ⓒ Ⓓ	13. Ⓐ Ⓑ Ⓒ Ⓓ	25. Ⓐ Ⓑ Ⓒ Ⓓ
2. Ⓐ Ⓑ Ⓒ Ⓓ	14. Ⓐ Ⓑ Ⓒ Ⓓ	26. Ⓐ Ⓑ Ⓒ Ⓓ
3. Ⓐ Ⓑ Ⓒ Ⓓ	15. Ⓐ Ⓑ Ⓒ Ⓓ	27. Ⓐ Ⓑ Ⓒ Ⓓ
4. Ⓐ Ⓑ Ⓒ Ⓓ	16. Ⓐ Ⓑ Ⓒ Ⓓ	28. Ⓐ Ⓑ Ⓒ Ⓓ
5. Ⓐ Ⓑ Ⓒ Ⓓ	17. Ⓐ Ⓑ Ⓒ Ⓓ	29. Ⓐ Ⓑ Ⓒ Ⓓ
6. Ⓐ Ⓑ Ⓒ Ⓓ	18. Ⓐ Ⓑ Ⓒ Ⓓ	30. Ⓐ Ⓑ Ⓒ Ⓓ
7. Ⓐ Ⓑ Ⓒ Ⓓ	19. Ⓐ Ⓑ Ⓒ Ⓓ	31. Ⓐ Ⓑ Ⓒ Ⓓ
8. Ⓐ Ⓑ Ⓒ Ⓓ	20. Ⓐ Ⓑ Ⓒ Ⓓ	32. Ⓐ Ⓑ Ⓒ Ⓓ
9. Ⓐ Ⓑ Ⓒ Ⓓ	21. Ⓐ Ⓑ Ⓒ Ⓓ	33. Ⓐ Ⓑ Ⓒ Ⓓ
10. Ⓐ Ⓑ Ⓒ Ⓓ	22. Ⓐ Ⓑ Ⓒ Ⓓ	34. Ⓐ Ⓑ Ⓒ Ⓓ
11. Ⓐ Ⓑ Ⓒ Ⓓ	23. Ⓐ Ⓑ Ⓒ Ⓓ	35. Ⓐ Ⓑ Ⓒ Ⓓ
12. Ⓐ Ⓑ Ⓒ Ⓓ	24. Ⓐ Ⓑ Ⓒ Ⓓ	

Section 3: Reading Comprehension

1. (A) (B) (C) (D)
2. (A) (B) (C) (D)
3. (A) (B) (C) (D)
4. (A) (B) (C) (D)
5. (A) (B) (C) (D)
6. (A) (B) (C) (D)
7. (A) (B) (C) (D)
8. (A) (B) (C) (D)
9. (A) (B) (C) (D)
10. (A) (B) (C) (D)
11. (A) (B) (C) (D)
12. (A) (B) (C) (D)
13. (A) (B) (C) (D)
14. (A) (B) (C) (D)
15. (A) (B) (C) (D)
16. (A) (B) (C) (D)

17. (A) (B) (C) (D)
18. (A) (B) (C) (D)
19. (A) (B) (C) (D)
20. (A) (B) (C) (D)
21. (A) (B) (C) (D)
22. (A) (B) (C) (D)
23. (A) (B) (C) (D)
24. (A) (B) (C) (D)
25. (A) (B) (C) (D)
26. (A) (B) (C) (D)
27. (A) (B) (C) (D)
28. (A) (B) (C) (D)
29. (A) (B) (C) (D)
30. (A) (B) (C) (D)
31. (A) (B) (C) (D)
32. (A) (B) (C) (D)

33. (A) (B) (C) (D)
34. (A) (B) (C) (D)
35. (A) (B) (C) (D)
36. (A) (B) (C) (D)
37. (A) (B) (C) (D)
38. (A) (B) (C) (D)
39. (A) (B) (C) (D)
40. (A) (B) (C) (D)

Section 4: Mathematics Achievement

1. (A) (B) (C) (D)
2. (A) (B) (C) (D)
3. (A) (B) (C) (D)
4. (A) (B) (C) (D)
5. (A) (B) (C) (D)
6. (A) (B) (C) (D)
7. (A) (B) (C) (D)
8. (A) (B) (C) (D)
9. (A) (B) (C) (D)
10. (A) (B) (C) (D)
11. (A) (B) (C) (D)
12. (A) (B) (C) (D)
13. (A) (B) (C) (D)
14. (A) (B) (C) (D)
15. (A) (B) (C) (D)
16. (A) (B) (C) (D)

17. (A) (B) (C) (D)
18. (A) (B) (C) (D)
19. (A) (B) (C) (D)
20. (A) (B) (C) (D)
21. (A) (B) (C) (D)
22. (A) (B) (C) (D)
23. (A) (B) (C) (D)
24. (A) (B) (C) (D)
25. (A) (B) (C) (D)
26. (A) (B) (C) (D)
27. (A) (B) (C) (D)
28. (A) (B) (C) (D)
29. (A) (B) (C) (D)
30. (A) (B) (C) (D)
31. (A) (B) (C) (D)
32. (A) (B) (C) (D)

33. (A) (B) (C) (D)
34. (A) (B) (C) (D)
35. (A) (B) (C) (D)
36. (A) (B) (C) (D)
37. (A) (B) (C) (D)
38. (A) (B) (C) (D)
39. (A) (B) (C) (D)
40. (A) (B) (C) (D)
41. (A) (B) (C) (D)
42. (A) (B) (C) (D)
43. (A) (B) (C) (D)
44. (A) (B) (C) (D)
45. (A) (B) (C) (D)

SECTION 1
Time: 20 Minutes
40 Questions

This section includes two different types of questions: synonyms and sentence completions. There are directions and a sample question for each question type.

Part One

Directions: Each of the following questions consists of a word in capital letters followed by four words or phrases labeled (A), (B), (C), and (D). Select the one word or phrase that means most nearly the same as the word in capital letters.

Sample Question:

> ESSENTIAL:
> (A) dire
> (B) confusing
> (C) vital
> (D) expert
>
> Correct Answer: C

---

1. BIAS:
   - (A) preference
   - (B) conversion
   - (C) resolution
   - (D) conclusion

2. INHABIT:
   - (A) confine
   - (B) surround
   - (C) dwell
   - (D) exhibit

3. GENEROUS:
   - (A) radiant
   - (B) precocious
   - (C) sociable
   - (D) benevolent

4. AGGREGATE:
   - (A) median
   - (B) organization
   - (C) total
   - (D) equipment

5. IMPLEMENT:
   - (A) idea
   - (B) detail
   - (C) instrument
   - (D) component

6. GRACIOUSLY:
   - (A) gratefully
   - (B) kindly
   - (C) easily
   - (D) comfortably

7. MEANDER:
   - (A) manage
   - (B) exercise
   - (C) review
   - (D) wander

8. CONCUR:
   - (A) alleviate
   - (B) agree
   - (C) conspire
   - (D) contribute

9. AGILE:
   - (A) able
   - (B) listless
   - (C) willful
   - (D) nimble

10. ADDITION:
    - (A) inclusion
    - (B) origin
    - (C) antecedent
    - (D) inception

11. PERSISTENT:
    - (A) perceptible
    - (B) considerable
    - (C) pretentious
    - (D) determined

12. ENCOURAGE:
    - (A) foster
    - (B) conduct
    - (C) develop
    - (D) cope

GO ON TO THE NEXT PAGE.

13. SCOLD:
    (A) scream
    (B) incense
    (C) berate
    (D) infuriate

14. COMMENCEMENT:
    (A) justification
    (B) beginning
    (C) announcement
    (D) conclusion

15. CRITICIZE:
    (A) abuse
    (B) disparage
    (C) avenge
    (D) hinder

16. OBVIOUSLY:
    (A) substantially
    (B) momentously
    (C) allegedly
    (D) apparently

17. INCESSANT:
    (A) annoyed
    (B) disturbed
    (C) constant
    (D) irrevocable

18. ACQUIRE:
    (A) abstain
    (B) prefer
    (C) produce
    (D) procure

19. VENERABLE:
    (A) respected
    (B) bright
    (C) varied
    (D) measured

20. PROCLIVITY:
    (A) inclination
    (B) finesse
    (C) resurgence
    (D) weakness

GO ON TO THE NEXT PAGE.

Part Two

Directions: Each sentence below has one or two blanks. Each blank indicates that something is missing. Following each sentence are four words or sets of words labeled (A), (B), (C), and (D). You are to select the word or set of words that, when inserted in the sentence, best fits the meaning of the sentence as a whole.

Sample Question:

> Due to the fact that the stray kitten was so _____, Ethan's mother allowed him to keep it.
> (A) tardy
> (B) humid
> (C) disobedient
> (D) adorable
>
> Correct Answer: D

21. Wary of defeat, the rebel factions _____ into a single army to fight the approaching invaders.
    (A) consolidated
    (B) diffused
    (C) fragmented
    (D) appealed

22. According to the editorial, the most _____ error the governor made was _____ the public's trust in him by trying to cover up the scandal.
    (A) grievous . . . appeasing
    (B) defenceless . . . gleaning
    (C) abhorrent . . . placating
    (D) egregious . . . breaching

23. Lacking any interesting qualities, the _____ movie featured cheap special effects, an unlikely plot, and ridiculously bad acting.
    (A) insipid
    (B) hilarious
    (C) optimistic
    (D) uproarious

24. Despite the player's occasionally _____ play, he recently signed a _____ contract.
    (A) stellar . . . covert
    (B) negligent . . . reticent
    (C) sloppy . . . nebulous
    (D) shaky . . . lucrative

25. The company's hope was to _____ short-term sales expectations in order to reward investors and properly _____ the staff.
    (A) suspend . . . compensate
    (B) exceed . . . remunerate
    (C) surpass . . . determine
    (D) attest . . . compromise

26. On the last weekend of summer break at the seashore, the roads were jammed with traffic as the beach _____ with vacationers.
    (A) dispersed
    (B) maintained
    (C) deprecated
    (D) teemed

27. Reports of the senator's _____ displays of wealth have done little to _____ her standing among working-class families or help her bid for reelection.
    (A) flagrant . . . undermine
    (B) reserved . . . solidify
    (C) grandiose . . . propel
    (D) flamboyant . . . curtail

28. Although the tone of the play was _____, the subject matter was rather _____.
    (A) sobering . . . farcical
    (B) ominous . . . morbid
    (C) grave . . . pensive
    (D) solemn . . . bleak

29. Because she had recorded the fastest official time, Cheryl was given _____ from the qualifying races and automatically entered in the state finals.
    (A) an occurrence
    (B) an emulsion
    (C) a quandary
    (D) an exemption

30. Faced with the _____ of babysitting Friday night or going to the movies, Angela decided she would rather earn money than spend money.
    (A) endeavor
    (B) predicament
    (C) dismay
    (D) principle

31. After the band failed to _____ the audience or sell many tickets, the offer for an extended engagement was _____.
    (A) overcome . . . negated
    (B) impress . . . revoked
    (C) accept . . . approved
    (D) inspire . . . established

GO ON TO THE NEXT PAGE.

32. After a series of argumentative negotiations, both sides seemed ready for _____ so they could get back to the task at hand.
    - (A) an admonition
    - (B) an abatement
    - (C) a reconciliation
    - (D) a validation

33. _____ even from a distance, Mount Everest is the highest mountain in the world, and certainly one of nature's wonders.
    - (A) Monumental
    - (B) Glacial
    - (C) Gilded
    - (D) Speculative

34. The fact that the developer's plans for the land no longer included space for a public park was a _____ of his earlier proposal.
    - (A) presumption
    - (B) progression
    - (C) detriment
    - (D) contradiction

35. Despite being mistakenly _____ for leaving the gate open, Derrick was _____ once the puppy crawled out from underneath the couch.
    - (A) lectured . . . responsible
    - (B) punished . . . amended
    - (C) chastised . . . exonerated
    - (D) criticized . . . atoned

36. The benching of the star midfielder was largely seen as an act of _____ after she skipped the team meeting.
    - (A) probation
    - (B) annihilation
    - (C) peculiarity
    - (D) retribution

37. When the owner provided a _____ certificate of authenticity, the art historian declared the painting a forgery.
    - (A) legitimate
    - (B) spurious
    - (C) turgid
    - (D) precocious

38. _____ by his _____ lifestyle, King Henry I habitually indulged his every whim until he died of food poisoning in 1135.
    - (A) Strengthened . . . gratuitous
    - (B) Undeterred . . . gluttonous
    - (C) Fortified . . . permissive
    - (D) Befallen . . . durable

39. After losing for the sixth time in a row, the basketball team hoped they had reached the _____ of their season.
    - (A) nadir
    - (B) malady
    - (C) pinnacle
    - (D) conclusion

40. Largely due to the prolonged drought, there has been a _____ of fresh produce available at the farmer's market this summer.
    - (A) beacon
    - (B) sustenance
    - (C) dearth
    - (D) confluence

STOP!
If you finish before time is up, check your work on this section only.

SECTION 2

Time: 35 Minutes
35 Questions

This section includes two different types of questions: multiple-choice math questions and quantitative comparisons. There are directions for each question type.

Part One

Directions: For each of the following questions, mark the letter of your choice on the answer sheet.

---

1. What is the next number in the sequence 5, 8, 11, 14, 17...
    (A) 18
    (B) 20
    (C) 21
    (D) 23

2. On a hike, Kurt saw 3 times as many sparrows as finches. He saw 12 birds of these two species in all. If s is the number of sparrows Kurt saw, which number sentence can be used to find out how many birds of each species he saw?

    (A) $s + \dfrac{s}{3} = 12$

    (B) $s - 3s = 12$

    (C) $\dfrac{3s}{12} = s$

    (D) $s + 3s = 12$

3. Gary scored a total of 27 points in two games. He scored twice as many points in the second game as in the first. What were his scores in each game?
    (A) game 1: 5; game 2: 22
    (B) game 1: 6; game 2: 21
    (C) game 1: 7; game 2: 20
    (D) game 1: 9; game 2: 18

4. Jen bought 10 apples at $1.20 per pound. The apples weighed a total of 5.75 lb. What did she pay for all 10 apples?
    (A) $6.90
    (B) $7.20
    (C) $8.14
    (D) $9.55

5. Maria earns $9 per hour on weekdays and $12 per hour on weekends. This week she worked 8 hours on Tuesday, 6 hours on Thursday, 7 hours on Friday, and 9 hours on Saturday. How much did she earn?
    (A) $214
    (B) $279
    (C) $297
    (D) $312

6. Which of the following is greater than 1.2 but less than 1.3?
    (A) 1.196
    (B) 1.268
    (C) 1.302
    (D) 1.375

7. Smoke alarms in a house require 27 batteries. Batteries come in packs of 4. How many packs should you buy if you want 2 complete packs left over?
    (A) 6
    (B) 7
    (C) 8
    (D) 9

8. Jamal has $1.85 in quarters and dimes only. He has a total of 11 coins. How many of each coin does he have?
    (A) 5 quarters, 6 dimes
    (B) 4 quarters, 7 dimes
    (C) 3 quarters, 8 dimes
    (D) 2 quarters, 9 dimes

9. The mean of Mark's, Linda's, and Karen's ages is 18. Mark is 20 years old. Linda is 18 years old. How old is Karen?
    (A) 16
    (B) 17
    (C) 18
    (D) 19

GO ON TO THE NEXT PAGE.

10. A prescribed diet makes a dog lose 0.33 lb each month. After 4 months, the dog weighs 37.18 lb. What was its original weight?
    (A) 38.5 lb
    (B) 38.33 lb
    (C) 38.12 lb
    (D) 37.67 lb

11. In a survey of 950 people, 46% of them said they listened to jazz. How many people in the group did not say they listened to jazz?
    (A) 437
    (B) 478
    (C) 502
    (D) 513

12. A television set is on sale at a 25% discount. Its original price was $650. the sales tax is 12%. What will Beth pay, including tax, for the television set?
    (A) $524
    (B) $546
    (C) $589
    (D) $610

13. In a group of friends, 17 people are on the chess team, 13 people are in the band, and 8 people are both in the band and on the chess team. How many people are in the group of friends?
    (A) 18
    (B) 19
    (C) 22
    (D) 24

14. A clock is showing 6:00. What is the measure of the angle formed by the hour and minute hands?
    (A) 180°
    (B) 120°
    (C) 100°
    (D) 90°

15. A rectangular play area measures 20 yards by 15 yards. What would be the perimeter if the length and width were doubled?
    (A) 70 yd
    (B) 140 yd
    (C) 300 yd
    (D) 1,200 yd

16. A poster measures 2 feet 4 inches by 3 feet 8 inches. What length of framing is needed to frame it?
    (A) 10 ft
    (B) 10 ft 8 in
    (C) 11 ft 6 in
    (D) 12 ft

17. How many 4-in^2 squares fit inside a rectangle that measures 4 by 6 inches?
    (A) 4
    (B) 6
    (C) 8
    (D) 10

18. In 28 mi^2 there are 560 houses. What is the average number of houses per square mile?
    (A) 20
    (B) 24
    (C) 28
    (D) 32

19. A canoe trip costs $60 for 4 hours. At that rate, what would 6 hours cost?
    (A) $70
    (B) $80
    (C) $90
    (D) $100

20. A cube has edges that each measure 4 in. What is the surface area?
    (A) 44 in^2
    (B) 48 in^2
    (C) 64 in^2
    (D) 96 in^2

GO ON TO THE NEXT PAGE.

Part Two

Directions: For each of the following questions, two quantities are given—one in column A, the other in column B. Compare the two quantities and mark your answer sheet as follows:

(A) if the quantity in column A is greater
(B) if the quantity in column B is greater
(C) if the quantities are equal
(D) if the relationship cannot be determined from the information given

Notes

• Information concerning one or both of the compared quantities will be centered above the two columns for some items.
• Symbols that appear in both columns represent the same thing in column A as in column B.
• Letters such as *x*, *n*, and *k* are symbols for real numbers.
• Figures are drawn to scale unless otherwise noted.

Column A		**Column B**

21.   The original price of a shirt was $40.
                              During a sale, the price was reduced
                              by 25% and then the reduced price
                              was reduced by another 20%.

The price of the shirt $23
after the two reductions.

22. $(4 \times 10^3) + (6 \times 10^2) + (2 \times 10^0)$ 4,620

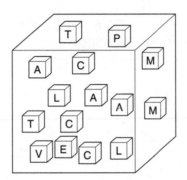

23.

The probability of picking a vowel.   The probability of picking a C or a T.

24.   The radius of a circle.   A chord in the same circle.

25.   The median of 40, 50, 60, 70.   The mean of 40, 50, 60, 70.

26. $\sqrt{64} + \sqrt{36}$ $\sqrt{100}$

GO ON TO THE NEXT PAGE.

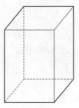

27.

    Number of vertices + 2.   Number of edges − 2.

28.   City A is 30 miles due east of City B and City C is 40 miles due south of City B.

     The shortest distance between City A and City C.   45 miles

29. g is an integer

   g −g

30.   Frank's weight is $1\frac{1}{4}$ of Bill's weight.

                            Jason weight is $\frac{4}{5}$ of Frank's weight.

   Jason's weight   Bill 's weight

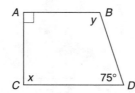

31.

                     The figure shown above is a trapezoid.

   $m\angle x$ $m\angle y$

32.   0.02 $1\frac{3}{4}\%$

33. $3 < x < 9$
                               $2 \le y \le 8$

   x y

GO ON TO THE NEXT PAGE.

34.

The navigator of a submarine kept track of the submarine's depth during a dive. The graph below tracks the depth over time during the entire dive.

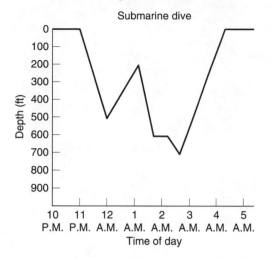

Submarine dive

Depth change from 10 P.M. to 12 A.M.	Depth change from 1 A.M. to 2:30 A.M.

35.

$$\frac{m}{6} = \frac{32}{48}$$

$$\frac{100}{50} = \frac{70}{n}$$

$8m$

$n - 1$

STOP!
If you finish before time is up, check your work on this section only.

SECTION 3
Time: 40 Minutes
40 Questions

Directions: Each reading passage is followed by questions about it. Answer the questions that follow a passage on the basis of what is stated or implied in that passage. For each question, select the answer you think is best and record your choice by filling in the corresponding oval on the answer sheet.

Questions 1–6

"The President shall from time to time give to Congress information of the State of the Union and recom-mend to their Consideration such
5 *measures as he shall judge neces-sary and expedient."* Article II, Sec. 3, U.S. Constitution

On a cold January morning in 1790, George Washington person-
10 ally delivered the first State of the Union address to a joint meeting of the two bodies of Congress at Federal Hall in New York City, which was then the provisional capital of
15 the United States. Since Washing-ton's first speech to Congress, U.S. Presidents have "from time to time" given Congress an assessment of the condition of the union. Presidents
20 have used the opportunity to present their goals and agenda through broad ideas or specific details. The annual message or "State of the Union" message's length, frequency,
25 and method of delivery have varied from President to President and era to era.

In 1801, Thomas Jefferson dis-continued the practice of delivering
30 the address in person, regarding it as too monarchial for the new repub-lic. Instead, Jefferson wrote out his address and sent it to Congress to be read by a clerk. This practice con-
35 tinued for the next 112 years. The first president to revive Washington's spoken precedent was Woodrow Wilson in 1913.

For many years, the speech was
40 referred to as "the President's Annual Message to Congress." The term "State of the Union" did not become widely used until after 1935 when Franklin Delano Roosevelt began
45 using the phrase.

With the advent of radio and television, the President's annual message has become not only a conversation between the President
50 and Congress but also an opportunity for the President to communicate with the American people at the same time. Calvin Coolidge's 1923 speech was the first to be broadcast on
55 radio. Harry S. Truman's 1947 address was the first to be broadcast on tele-vision. Lyndon Johnson's address in 1965 was the first delivered in the evening, and George W. Bush's 2002
60 address was the first to be broadcast live on the World Wide Web.

1. The author most likely included the quotation from the U.S. Constitution in lines 1–6 in order to
   - (A) illustrate the wording used in the Constitution
   - (B) explain the reason for the State of the Union address
   - (C) demonstrate how different Presidents have interpreted the same provision
   - (D) point out the difference between a constitutional duty and a custom

2. The phrase "from time to time" in lines 1–2 has been interpreted to mean
   - (A) once in a while
   - (B) in a timely manner
   - (C) annually
   - (D) when time allows

3. U.S. Presidents deliver State of the Union messages primarily because they
   - (A) are following a tradition started by George Washington
   - (B) are required to do so by the U.S. Constitution
   - (C) need to fulfill campaign promises
   - (D) are trying to unify opposing factions

4. Thomas Jefferson's State of the Union address differed from Washington's address in that Jefferson
   - (A) spoke first to the Senate and then to the House of Representatives
   - (B) broadcast his message on radio
   - (C) did not deliver his address in person
   - (D) had his speech printed in the newspaper

GO ON TO THE NEXT PAGE.

5. In the first half of the twentieth century, the State of the Union address was forever changed by
   (A) the advent of radio and television
   (B) Thomas Jefferson
   (C) Lyndon Johnson
   (D) newspaper coverage of the speech

6. Which of the following questions is answered by the information in the passage?
   (A) How many presidents have delivered spoken State of the Union messages?
   (B) When is the State of the Union message delivered?
   (C) Why did Woodrow Wilson revive the spoken State of the Union message?
   (D) Which president delivered the first televised State of the Union message?

Questions 7–13

While they cannot be seen from the air, or felt aboard an ocean-going ship, tsunamis can cause as great a loss of life and property as their other
5 natural disaster cousins—tornadoes and hurricanes. The tsunami that occurred on December 26, 2004 was the worst tsunami ever recorded in terms of lives lost. Triggered by a
10 powerful earthquake in the Indian Ocean, it ravaged the shores of Indonesia, Sri Lanka, India, and Thailand, and even hit the east coast of Africa more than 2,300 miles away.
15 A tsunami is a series of ocean waves generated by any rapid large-scale disturbance of the sea water. Most tsunamis are generated by earthquakes, but they may also be
20 caused by volcanic eruptions, land-slides, undersea slumps or meteor impacts. In 1963 the term "tsunami" was adopted internationally to describe this natural phenomenon.
25 A Japanese word, it is the combination of the characters *tsu* (harbor) and *nami* (wave). Tsunamis are often mistakenly called "tidal waves." However, the tides have nothing to
30 do with the formation of tsunamis.

The waves radiate outward in all directions from the disturbance and can propagate across entire ocean basins. For example, in 1960, an
35 earthquake in Chile caused a tsunami that swept across the Pacific to Japan. Tsunami waves are distinguished from ordinary ocean waves by their great length between peaks, often
40 exceeding 100 miles in the deep ocean, and by the long amount of time between these peaks, ranging from five minutes to an hour.

In the deep ocean, a tsunami is
45 barely noticeable, causing only a small rising and falling of the sea surface as it passes. Only as it approaches land does a tsunami become a hazard. As the tsunami
50 approaches land and shallow water, the waves slow down and become compressed, causing them to grow in height. In the best of cases, the tsunami comes onshore like a
55 quickly rising tide and causes a gentle flooding of low-lying coastal areas.

In the worst of cases, a bore will form. A bore is a wall of turbulent
60 water that can be several meters high and can rush onshore with great destructive power. Behind the bore is a deep and fast-moving flood that can pick up and sweep away
65 almost anything in its path. Minutes later, the water will drain away as the trough of the tsunami wave arrives, sometimes exposing great patches of the sea floor. But then the water
70 will rush in again as before, causing additional damage.

This destructive cycle may repeat many times before the hazard finally passes. Persons caught in the path
75 of a tsunami have little chance to survive. They can be easily crushed by debris or they may simply drown. Children and the elderly are particu-larly at risk, as they have less mobility,
80 strength and endurance.

7. The main purpose of this passage is to
   (A) describe the tsunami of 2004
   (B) point out the differences between tsunamis and tidal waves
   (C) explain the origin of the term "tsunami"
   (D) provide general information about tsunamis

8. The passage names all of the following as possible causes of a tsunami EXCEPT:
   (A) tornadoes
   (B) landslides
   (C) meteor impacts
   (D) earthquakes

9. The author cites the 1960 tsunami in Japan to show
   (A) how devastating a tsunami can be
   (B) how far a tsunami can reach
   (C) the importance of detecting a tsunami early
   (D) how quickly a tsunami can travel

GO ON TO THE NEXT PAGE.

10. Which of the following best describes the difference between a tsunami wave and a regular ocean wave?
   (A) Tsunami waves are more than 100 miles apart in the deep ocean, while regular ocean waves follow closely one after the other.
   (B) The length between peaks and the amount of time between peaks is greater in tsunami waves than it is in regular ocean waves.
   (C) Regular ocean waves are more harmful to young children, while tsunami waves are more likely to endanger the elderly.
   (D) Tsunami waves are more likely to affect boats in deep water than are regular ocean waves.

11. The style of the passage is most like that found in
   (A) an adventure novel
   (B) a weather report
   (C) a science textbook
   (D) a news article

12. A tsunami becomes a hazard as it approaches land because
   (A) the waves compress and grow higher in shallow water
   (B) the waves speed up as they approach the shore
   (C) the water drains away, exposing the sea floor
   (D) people get too close to the shore

13. As used in paragraph 5, the word "bore" means
   (A) hollow, cylindrical chamber
   (B) gauge
   (C) hole made by a drill
   (D) dangerous wave

Questions 14–18

To An Athlete Dying Young

The time you won your town the race
We chaired you through the market-place;
Man and boy stood cheering by,
5 And home we brought you shoulder-high.

Today, the road all runners come,
Shoulder-high we bring you home,
And set you at your threshold down,
10 Townsman of a stiller town.

Smart lad, to slip betimes away
From fields where glory does not stay,
And early though the laurel grows
15 It withers quicker than the rose.

Eyes the shady night has shut
Cannot see the record cut,
And silence sounds no worse than cheers
20 After earth has stopped the ears.

Now you will not swell the rout
Of lads that wore their honors out
Runners whom renown outran
And the name died before the man.

25 So set, before its echoes fade,
The fleet foot on the sill of shade,
And hold to the low lintel up
The still-defended challenge-cup.

And round that early-laurelled head
30 Will flock to gaze the strength less dead,
And find unwithered on its curls
The garland briefer than a girl's.
                                    —A. E. Housman

14. The athlete described in this poem is most likely a
   (A) tennis player
   (B) swimmer
   (C) runner
   (D) football player

15. The setting for this poem is a
   (A) victory celebration
   (B) funeral
   (C) field of laurels
   (D) rose garden

16. The "stiller town" referred to in line 10 means
   (A) a country village
   (B) home
   (C) death
   (D) a quiet town

17. The author admires the athlete for
   (A) winning his race
   (B) setting a new record
   (C) returning to his hometown
   (D) dying young

18. The author is likely to agree with which of the following statements?
   I. Glory is a fleeting thing.
   II. It is best to die at the peak of one's fame.
   III. An athlete's fame lives on even after retirement.

   (A) I only
   (B) II only
   (C) III only
   (D) I and II only

Questions 19–24

   The earthquake shook down in San Francisco hundreds of thousands of dollars worth of walls and chimneys. But the conflagration that
5 followed burned up hundreds of millions of dollars' worth of property. There is no estimating within hundreds of millions the actual damage wrought. Not in history has a modern
10 imperial city been so completely destroyed. San Francisco is gone. Nothing remains of it but memories and a fringe of dwelling-houses on its outskirts. Its industrial section is
15 wiped out. Its business section is wiped out. Its social and residential section is wiped out. The factories and warehouses, the great stores and newspaper buildings, the hotels and
20 the palaces of the nabobs, are all gone. Remains only the fringe of dwelling houses on the outskirts of what was once San Francisco.

   Within an hour after the earth-
25 quake shock the smoke of San Francisco's burning was a lurid tower visible a hundred miles away. And for three days and nights this

GO ON TO THE NEXT PAGE.

lurid tower swayed in the sky, red-
30 dening the sun, darkening the day,
and filling the land with smoke.

On Wednesday morning at a
quarter past five came the earthquake. A minute later the flames
35 were leaping upward. In a dozen
different quarters south of Market
Street, in the working-class ghetto,
and in the factories, fires started.
There was no opposing the flames.
40 There was no organization, no communication. All the cunning adjustments of a twentieth century city had
been smashed by the earthquake.
The streets were humped into ridges
45 and depressions, and piled with the
debris of fallen walls. The steel rails
were twisted into perpendicular and
horizontal angles. The telephone and
telegraph systems were disrupted.
50 And the great water-mains had
burst. All the shrewd contrivances
and safeguards of man had been
thrown out of gear by thirty seconds'
twitching of the earth-crust.
55 By Wednesday afternoon, inside
of twelve hours, half the heart of the
city was gone. At that time I watched
the vast conflagration from out on
the bay. It was dead calm. Not a
60 flicker of wind stirred. Yet from every
side wind was pouring in upon the
city. East, west, north, and south,
strong winds were blowing upon the
doomed city. The heated air rising
65 made an enormous suck. Thus did
the fire of itself build its own colossal
chimney through the atmosphere.
Day and night this dead calm continued, and yet, near to the flames, the
70 wind was often half a gale, so mighty
was the suck.

Wednesday night saw the
destruction of the very heart of the
city. Dynamite was lavishly used,
75 and many of San Francisco's proudest
structures were crumbled by man
himself into ruins, but there was no
withstanding the onrush of the flames.
Time and again successful stands
80 were made by the fire-fighters, and
every time the flames flanked around
on either side or came up from
the rear, and turned to defeat the
hard-won victory.

Jack London from "The Story of
an Eyewitness"

19. The first paragraph of the
passage establishes a mood of
(A) awe and disbelief
(B) desperate longing
(C) cautious optimism
(D) heartfelt pity

20. The author describes the
effects of the earthquake by
relying on
(A) scientific knowledge
(B) comparisons to similar
events in history
(C) vivid images appealing
primarily to the sense of
sight
(D) confirmed statistical data

21. In line 20, "nabob" most nearly
means
(A) elected official
(B) wealthy person
(C) native son
(D) descendant of royalty

22. The statement that "All the
cunning adjustments of a
twentieth century city had
been smashed by the
earthquake" (lines 41–43)
suggests primarily that
(A) the city had been
reduced to a primitive
existence
(B) the earthquake
destroyed many of the
city's newest buildings
(C) numerous irreplaceable
mechanisms were lost
during the earthquake
(D) only necessities such as
plumbing and electricity
remained intact

23. Which best describes the
overall organization of the
passage?
(A) a description of events in
spatial order
(B) a description of events in
chronological order
(C) an enumeration of facts
supported by statistical
data
(D) a statement of opinion
backed up by reasons

24. The primary purpose of the
passage is to
(A) present a scientific
explanation of the San
Francisco earthquake
(B) convey the despair of
San Francisco residents
as they watched the
destruction of their city
(C) provide an eyewitness
report of the San
Francisco earthquake
(D) describe the conditions
that allowed the fires to
spread

Questions 25–29

Over 200 years ago, English
physician Edward Jenner observed
that milkmaids stricken with a viral
disease called cowpox were rarely
5 victims of a similar disease, smallpox. This observation led to the
development of the first vaccine.
In an experiment that was to prove a
revelation, Jenner took a few drops
10 of fluid from a pustule of a woman
who had cowpox and injected the
fluid into a healthy young boy who
had never had cowpox or smallpox.
Six weeks later, Jenner injected the
15 boy with fluid from a smallpox pustule. Miraculously, the boy remained
free of the dreaded smallpox.

In those days, a million people
died from smallpox each year in
20 Europe alone, most of them children.
Those who survived were often left
with grim reminders of their ordeals:
blindness, deep scars, and deformities. When Jenner laid the foundation
25 for modern vaccines in 1796, he
started on a course that would ease
the suffering of people around the
world for centuries to come. By the
beginning of the 20th century, vac-
30 cines for rabies, diphtheria, typhoid
fever, and plague were in use, in
addition to the vaccine for smallpox.
By 1980, an updated version of
Jenner's vaccine led to the total
35 eradication of smallpox.

Since Jenner's time, vaccines
have been developed against more
than 20 infectious diseases such
as influenza, pneumonia, whooping

GO ON TO THE NEXT PAGE.

40 cough, rubella, meningitis, and hepatitis B. Due to tremendous advances
in molecular biology, scientists are
using novel approaches to develop
vaccines against deadly diseases
45 that still plague humankind.

Scientists use vaccines to "trick"
the human immune system into
producing antibodies or immune
cells that protect against the real dis-
50 ease-causing organism. Weakened
microbes, killed microbes, inactivated toxins, and purified proteins
or polysaccharides derived from
microbes are the most common
55 components used in vaccine development strategies. As science
advances, researchers are developing even better vaccines.

25. Which of the following best
describes smallpox in the
years before 1796?
(A) It struck a million people
a year in Europe alone.
(B) It was common among
milkmaids.
(C) It was spread by cows.
(D) It killed more than a
million Europeans a year.

26. According to the passage
vaccines have been developed
for all of the following diseases
EXCEPT:
(A) pneumonia
(B) scarlet fever
(C) typhoid fever
(D) rubella

27. According to the passage,
which of the following are
components used in vaccine
development?
I. inactivated toxins
II. weakened microbes
III. purified proteins

(A) I only
(B) II only
(C) I and II only
(D) I, II, and III

28. The vaccine produced by
Jenner in 1796
(A) completely eradicated
smallpox
(B) was effective only
against cowpox
(C) served as the basis for
modern vaccines
(D) wiped out typhoid fever

29. Which of the following best
describes how vaccines work?
(A) They directly attack the
disease-causing
organism.
(B) They fool the body into
producing antibodies
that protect against the
real disease-causing
organism.
(C) They contain deadly
disease-producing
organisms that are
injected directly into the
blood stream.
(D) They contain antibodies
that protect the body
from deadly diseases.

Questions 30–35

The crimson hand, which at first
had been strongly visible upon the
marble paleness of Georgiana's
cheek, now grew more faintly out-
5 lined. She remained not less pale
than ever; but the birthmark, with
every breath that came and went,
lost somewhat of its former distinctness. Its presence had been awful;
10 its departure was more awful still.
Watch the stain of the rainbow
fading out of the sky, and you will
know how the mysterious symbol
passed away.
15 "By Heaven! It is well-nigh gone!"
said Aylmer to himself, in almost
irrepressible ecstasy. "I can scarcely
trace it now. Success! Success! And
now it is like the faintest rose color.
20 The lightest flush of blood across her
cheek would overcome it. But she is
so pale!"
He drew aside the window curtain and suffered the light of natural
25 day to fall into the room and rest
upon her cheek. At the same time he

heard a gross, hoarse chuckle, which
he had long known as his servant
Aminadab's expression of delight.
30 "Ah, clod! ah, earthly mass!" cried
Aylmer, laughing in a sort of frenzy.
"You have served me well! Matter
and spirit—earth and heaven—have
both done their part in this! Laugh,
35 thing of the senses! You have earned
the right to laugh."
These exclamations broke
Georgiana's sleep. She slowly
unclosed her eyes and gazed into
40 the mirror which her husband had
arranged for that purpose. A faint
smile flitted over her lips when she
recognized how barely perceptible
was now that crimson hand which
45 had once blazed with such disastrous brilliancy as to scare away all
their happiness. But then her eyes
sought Aylmer's face with a trouble
and anxiety that he could by no
50 means account for.
"My poor Aylmer!" murmured she.
"Poor? Nay, richest, happiest,
most favored!" exclaimed he. "My
peerless bride, it is successful! You
55 are perfect!"
"My poor Aylmer," she repeated
with a more than human tenderness,
"you have aimed loftily; you have
done nobly. Do not repent that with
60 so high and pure a feeling, you have
rejected the best the earth could
offer. Aylmer, dearest Aylmer, I am
dying!"

Nathaniel Hawthorne from
"The Birthmark"

30. The birthmark on Georgiana's
face had the shape of a
(A) rainbow
(B) rose
(C) hand
(D) butterfly

31. It can be reasonably inferred
from the story that Aylmer
(A) is a poor man
(B) does not love his wife
(C) is trying to kill his wife
(D) has performed an
operation on his wife

GO ON TO THE NEXT PAGE.

32. Which of the following best describes what happens to the mark on Georgiana's cheek?
    (A) It takes a new shape.
    (B) It becomes very faint.
    (C) It grows larger.
    (D) It turns a deep red color.

33. Which word best describes how Aylmer regards Georgiana at the end of the passage?
    (A) flawless
    (B) amusing
    (C) tiresome
    (D) brilliant

34. Georgiana's feelings toward Aylmer could best be described as
    (A) bitter
    (B) angry
    (C) happy
    (D) tender

35. Which is the best expression of the main idea of this passage?
    (A) Love is blind.
    (B) Birthmarks should be removed.
    (C) Perfection cannot be achieved on earth.
    (D) Beauty is in the eye of the beholder.

Questions 36–40

The summers we spent in the country, now at one place, now at another. We children, of course, loved the country beyond anything. We dis-
5 liked the city. We were always wildly eager to get to the country when spring came, and very sad when in the late fall the family moved back to town. In the country we of course had
10 all kinds of pets—cats, dogs, rabbits, a coon, and a sorrel Shetland pony named General Grant. When my younger sister first heard of the real General Grant, by the way, she was
15 much struck by the coincidence that some one should have given him the same name as the pony. (Thirty years later my own children had *their* pony Grant.) In the country we children
20 ran barefoot much of the time, and the seasons went by in a round of uninterrupted and enthralling pleasures—supervising the haying and harvesting, picking apples,
25 hunting frogs successfully and woodchucks unsuccessfully, gathering hickory-nuts and chestnuts for sale to patient parents, building wigwams in the woods, and sometimes
30 playing Indians in too realistic manner by staining ourselves (and incidentally our clothes) in liberal fashion with poke-cherry juice. Thanksgiving was an appreciated festival, but it in
35 no way came up to Christmas. Christmas was an occasion of literally delirious joy. In the evening we hung up our stockings—or rather the biggest stockings we could borrow
40 from the grown-ups—and before dawn we trooped in to open them while sitting on father's and mother's bed; and the bigger presents were arranged, those for each child on its
45 own table, in the drawing-room, the doors to which were thrown open after breakfast. I never knew any one else have what seemed to me such attractive Christmases, and in the
50 next generation I tried to reproduce them exactly for my own children.
    Theodore Roosevelt from
    An Autobiography

36. This passage serves mainly to
    (A) recount the author's experience working on a farm in summer
    (B) provide a description of the author's summer home
    (C) describe the joys of being in the country
    (D) convey the author's love of family celebrations

37. In lines 9–12, the author includes the story of the pony's name primarily to
    (A) show his love for animals
    (B) poke good-hearted fun at his sister
    (C) show his love for his own children.
    (D) emphasize the friendship between the Roosevelt and Grant families

38. All of the following can be explicitly answered by information in the passage EXCEPT:
    (A) Where did the author and his siblings prefer to spend their childhood summers?
    (B) How did the author and his siblings spend their time in the country?
    (C) Where did the author and his siblings stay while in the country?
    (D) How did the author feel about Thanksgiving?

39. The statement that "I never knew any one else have what seemed to me such attractive Christmases, and in the next generation I tried to reproduce them exactly for my own children" (lines 47–51) primarily suggests that the author
    (A) wanted his children to follow his example
    (B) missed the Christmases from his childhood
    (C) went to great lengths trying to recreate his childhood
    (D) carried on certain traditions because he thought his children would enjoy them, too

40. The passage is told from the point of view of
    (A) an adult looking back fondly on his own life
    (B) a child describing his life
    (C) a child describing events that happened to someone else
    (D) an adult filled with regret over the passing of time

STOP!
If you finish before time is up, check your work on this section only.

Directions: For each of the following questions, mark the letter of your choice on the answer sheet.

1. What value of x will make the expression $(x+8)/4x$ equal to zero?
   (A)   0
   (B)   2
   (C)   3
   (D)   4

2. If $4/a = b/6$, which of the following must be true?
   (A) $\dfrac{4}{b} = \dfrac{6}{a}$
   (B) $4a = 6b$
   (C) $\dfrac{a}{b} = \dfrac{6}{4}$
   (D) $ab = 24$

3. $39.9 + 57.3 = (39.9 + 0.1) + (57.3 - x)$
   $x =$
   (A)   0.01
   (B)   0.1
   (C)   1.0
   (D)   1.1

4. $3,000 \times 0.002 =$
   (A)   0.6
   (B)   6
   (C)   60
   (D)   600

5. In the equilateral triangle shown, what is the measure of each angle?

   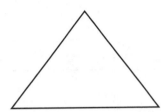

   (A)   60°
   (B)   90°
   (C)   120°
   (D)   140°

6. $y \div 72 = 21.4$
   $y -$
   (A)   1,260.1
   (B)   1,384.6
   (C)   1,460.25
   (D)   1,540.8

7. It costs n dollars to buy 10 boxes of crackers. At the same rate, how many dollars will it cost to buy 25 boxes of crackers?
   (A) $2.5n$
   (B) $25n$
   (C) $\dfrac{2n}{5}$
   (D) $\dfrac{5n}{2}$

8. In the figure below, if $\angle 1$ is 33°, what is the measure of $\angle 2$?

   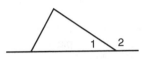

   (A)   56°
   (B)   110°
   (C)   130°
   (D)   147°

9. Large ice cream cones cost twice as much as small ones. Linda bought 3 large cones and 3 small cones for $13.50. How much does a small cone cost?
   (A) $0.75
   (B) $1.00
   (C) $1.25
   (D) $1.50

10. $7.426 \div 1,000 =$
   (A)   0.0007426
   (B)   0.007426
   (C)   0.07426
   (D)   0.7426

11. Paul has a garden that is 4 meters by 7 meters. If he uses 2 ounces of fertilizer per square meter, how many ounces must he use?
   (A)   42 oz
   (B)   44 oz
   (C)   50 oz
   (D)   56 oz

GO ON TO THE NEXT PAGE.

12. Steve is measuring the growth of a tomato plant. The chart below indicates his measurements for the past five weeks. Based on the information in the chart, what should he predict will be the height of the plant at week 6?

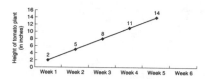

(A) 15 inches
(B) 17 inches
(C) 18 inches
(D) 21 inches

13. What digit is in the thousandths place in 5,624.03917?
(A) 5
(B) 3
(C) 9
(D) 1

14. A ladder is placed against a building. If the ladder makes a 55° angle with the ground, what is the measure of the angle that the ladder makes with the building?
(A) 25°
(B) 30°
(C) 35°
(D) 40°

15. If $\frac{2}{25} = \frac{n}{500}$, what is n?
(A) 20
(B) 40
(C) 60
(D) 8

16. Each edge of a cube measures 5 in. What is the volume?
(A) 10 in³
(B) 25 in ³
(C) 100 in ³
(D) 125 in ³

17. Renee deposits $4,000 in a saving account that earns 2% simple interest per year. How much interest will she earn after 2 years?
(A) $100
(B) $160
(C) $165
(D) $180

18. In the figure shown, the two outer rays form a right angle. If angle 1 measures 65°, what is the measure of angle 2?

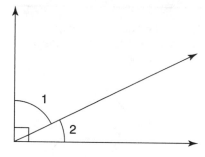

(A) 90°
(B) 60°
(C) 35°
(D) 25°

19. Which of the following numbers is evenly divisible by 4?
(A) 8,376,014
(B) 3,027,690
(C) 7,616,550
(D) 5,921,728

20. In the figure shown, if angle 2 measures 45°, what is the measure of angle 4?

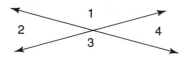

(A) 135°
(B) 75°
(C) 45°
(D) 35°

21. Which if the following is divisible only by itself and 1?
(A) 61
(B) 81
(C) 171
(D) 207

22. Figure WXYZ is a parallelogram. Which of the following is NOT necessarily true?

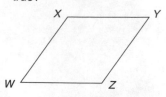

(A) Side WX is parallel to side ZY.
(B) Side XY is parallel to side WZ.
(C) ∠W has the same measure as ∠Y.
(D) Side WX is the same length as side XY.

23. Renee wants to carpet her living room. The rectangular room measures 15 feet × 18 feet. How many square yards of carpet must Renee purchase?
(A) 20 yd²
(B) 30 yd²
(C) 32 yd²
(D) 35 yd²

24. Last month, the librarian at a certain library kept track of all books checked out. The graph below shows the results by category of book. In the two most popular categories, how many books were checked out last month?

(A) 520
(B) 750
(C) 970
(D) 1,300

GO ON TO THE NEXT PAGE.

25. In the triangle shown, ∠ACB measures 55° and ∠CAB measures 65°. What is the measure of ∠CBA?

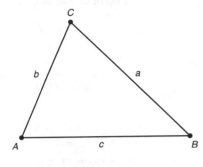

(A) 50°
(B) 60°
(C) 80°
(D) 90°

26. What are all the common factors of 24 and 36?
(A) 1, 2, 3, 12, 18
(B) 1, 2, 4, 12, 18, 24
(C) 1, 2, 12, 18, 24, 36
(D) 1, 2, 3, 4, 6, 12

27. Which fraction is in simplest form?
(A) $\frac{15}{18}$

(B) $\frac{99}{100}$

(C) $\frac{56}{133}$

(D) $\frac{45}{72}$

28. In the following figure, if ∠6 measures 90°, what is the measure of ∠1?

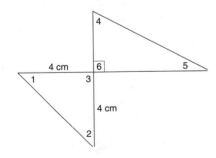

(A) 25°
(B) 35°
(C) 45°
(D) 55°

29. High school students were asked to pick their favorite kind of birthday party. The results are shown in the chart below. What percent of students chose either ice skating or sleepover?

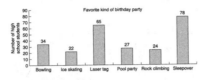

(A) 40%
(B) 45%
(C) 50%
(D) 60%

30. If Joanne tosses a 1–6 number cube, what is the probability that the cube number facing up will be even?
(A) $\frac{1}{2}$

(B) $\frac{1}{3}$

(C) $\frac{1}{4}$

(D) $\frac{1}{5}$

31. In the triangle shown, side a is 4 ft long, side b is 6 ft long, and side c is 8 ft long. What is the area of the triangle?

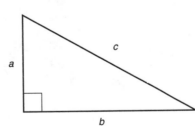

(A) 12 ft²
(B) 18 ft²
(C) 24 ft²
(D) 36 ft²

32. Donna is d years old. Frank is f years old. Frank is 4 years younger than Donna. Which equation represents the relationship between Donna's and Frank's age?

(A) $d = f/4$
(B) $d = 4 - f$
(C) $f = d - 4$
(D) $f = 4 - d$

33. The drama club is spending $224 to put on a play. They plan to sell tickets at $3.00 each. If they sell n tickets, which of the following represents their profit after expenses?
(A) $3n - 224$
(B) $224 + n/3$
(C) $3n + 224$
(D) $224(n + 3)$

34. A circle has a radius of 1.35 meters. Wire costs 2¢ per centimeter. How much will it cost to stretch a wire between two points on the circle if it passes through the center?
(A) $5.40
(B) $5.56
(C) $5.64
(D) $5.72

35. Order from least to greatest: $\frac{2}{8}$, $\frac{2}{3}$, $\frac{2}{9}$
(A) $\frac{2}{8}, \frac{2}{9}, \frac{2}{3}$

(B) $\frac{2}{9}, \frac{2}{8}, \frac{2}{3}$

(C) $\frac{2}{9}, \frac{2}{3}, \frac{2}{8}$

(D) $\frac{2}{3}, \frac{2}{8}, \frac{2}{9}$

36. 2.004 =
(A) $2\frac{4}{100}$

(B) $2\frac{2}{1,000}$

(C) $2\frac{1}{250}$

(D) $2\frac{1}{200}$

37. Order from least to greatest: $2\frac{4}{5}$, 2.4, $\frac{10}{4}$
(A) $2.4, \frac{10}{4}, 2\frac{4}{5}$

(B) $2\frac{4}{5}, \frac{10}{4}, 2.4$

(C) $\frac{10}{4}, 2.4, 2\frac{4}{5}$

(D) $\frac{10}{4}, 2\frac{4}{5}, \frac{10}{4}$

GO ON TO THE NEXT PAGE.

38. Adrinda is 8 years older than Marsha. Daryl is 3 years older than Marsha. Which equation correctly relates Adrinda's age (*a*) and Daryl's age (*d*)?
(A) $d = a - 5$
(B) $d = a + 5$
(C) $d = a - 3$
(D) $d = a + 3$

39. $5\tfrac{5}{8} \times 2\tfrac{2}{5} =$
(A) $10\dfrac{3}{4}$
(B) $13\dfrac{1}{2}$
(C) $15\dfrac{17}{20}$
(D) $18\dfrac{4}{5}$

40. $5 \times 6 \div (2 + 1) =$
(A) 15
(B) 14
(C) 11
(D) 10

41. A rule is used to generate the following sequence: 12, 17, ___, ___, 32, 37. Which are the missing numbers?
(A) 19, 28
(B) 21, 31
(C) 22, 27
(D) 24, 28

42. $\tfrac{1}{2} = 3x + \tfrac{1}{3}$. $x =$
(A) $\dfrac{1}{18}$
(B) $\dfrac{1}{6}$
(C) $\dfrac{2}{3}$
(D) $\dfrac{5}{6}$

43. $24 \div -4\tfrac{2}{3} =$
(A) $-4\dfrac{1}{6}$
(B) $4\dfrac{1}{3}$
(C) $5\dfrac{5}{6}$
(D) $-5\dfrac{1}{7}$

44. Cara spins a spinner divided into equal spaces numbered 1 through 12. What is the probability that the spinner will land on a number that is less than 5?
(A) $\dfrac{1}{6}$
(B) $\dfrac{1}{4}$
(C) $\dfrac{1}{3}$
(D) $\dfrac{1}{2}$

45. A map scale reads "1 in = 40 km." $6\tfrac{7}{8}$ inches on the map equals how many kilometers?
(A) 275 km
(B) 278 km
(C) 280 km
(D) 286 km

STOP!
If you finish before time is up, check your work on this section only.

SECTION 5
Time: 30 Minutes

Directions: You will have 30 minutes to plan and write an essay on the topic given below. You must write on the assigned topic only. An essay on another topic will not be acceptable. You may make notes in the space provided for that purpose.

Write your final essay on the two lined pages of your answer sheet. Write or print legibly in blue or black ink. A copy of your essay will be sent to each school that will be receiving your test results.

If you could change one thing about your school, what would you change and why?

USE THIS SPACE FOR NOTES

Answer Key

Section 1 Verbal Reasoning

1.	A	15.	B	29.	D
2.	C	16.	D	30.	B
3.	D	17.	C	31.	B
4.	C	18.	D	32.	C
5.	C	19.	A	33.	A
6.	B	20.	A	34.	D
7.	D	21.	A	35.	C
8.	B	22.	D	36.	D
9.	D	23.	A	37.	B
10.	A	24.	D	38.	B
11.	D	25.	B	39.	A
12.	A	26.	D	40.	C
13.	C	27.	C		
14.	B	28.	A		

Section 2 Quantitative Reasoning

1.	B	13.	C	25.	C
2.	D	14.	A	26.	A
3.	D	15.	B	27.	C
4.	A	16.	D	28.	A
5.	C	17.	B	29.	D
6.	B	18.	A	30.	C
7.	D	19.	C	31.	B
8.	A	20.	D	32.	A
9.	A	21.	A	33.	D
10.	A	22.	B	34.	C
11.	D	23.	B	35.	B
12.	B	24.	D		

Section 3 Reading Comprehension

1.	B	15.	B	29.	B
2.	C	16.	C	30.	C
3.	B	17.	D	31.	D
4.	C	18.	D	32.	B
5.	A	19.	A	33.	A
6.	D	20.	C	34.	D
7.	D	21.	B	35.	C
8.	A	22.	A	36.	C
9.	B	23.	B	37.	B
10.	B	24.	C	38.	C
11.	C	25.	D	39.	D
12.	A	26.	B	40.	A
13.	D	27.	D		
14.	C	28.	C		

Section 4 Mathematics Achievement

1.	A	16.	D	31.	A
2.	D	17.	B	32.	C
3.	B	18.	D	33.	A
4.	B	19.	D	34.	A
5.	A	20.	C	35.	B
6.	D	21.	A	36.	C
7.	A	22.	D	37.	A
8.	D	23.	B	38.	A
9.	D	24.	C	39.	B
10.	B	25.	B	40.	D
11.	D	26.	D	41.	C
12.	B	27.	B	42.	A
13.	C	28.	C	43.	D
14.	C	29.	A	44.	C
15.	B	30.	A	45.	A

Answers and Explanations

Section 1 Verbal Reasoning

1. **A is correct.** A *bias* is a *preference* or an inclination, especially one that inhibits impartial judgment.

2. **C is correct.** To *inhabit* is to live in or reside in—in other words, to *dwell*.

3. **D is correct.** *Generous* is an adjective meaning liberal in giving or sharing. Similarly, *benevolent* is an adjective meaning characterized by or suggestive of doing good, often in regard to charity.

4. **C is correct.** *Aggregate* is a *total*, constituting or amounting to a whole.

5. **C is correct.** An *implement*, used here as a noun, is a tool or *instrument* used in doing work—for instance, a gardening implement.

6. **B is correct.** To behave *graciously* is to behave in a *kindly* or warm manner.

7. **D is correct.** To *meander* is to move aimlessly and idly without a fixed direction—in other words, to *wander*.

8. **B is correct.** To *concur* is to be of the same opinion—to *agree*.

9. **D is correct.** *Agile* is an adjective used to describe someone or something that is quick, light, and moves with ease. The choice that best fits this definition is *nimble*.

10. **A is correct.** *Addition* is the act or process of adding something extra to a thing; something added. Similarly, *inclusion* is the act or state of being included; something included.

11. **D is correct.** When someone is *persistent*, she refuses to give up or let go—in other words, she is *determined*.

12. **A is correct.** To *encourage* is to give support to or to cultivate. Similarly, to *foster* is to promote the development and growth of.

13. **C is correct.** To *scold* is to reprimand or to criticize harshly and usually angrily—in other words, to *berate*.

14. **B is correct.** A *commencement* is a *beginning* or a start.

15. **B is correct.** To *criticize* is to find fault with. Similarly, to *disparage* is to speak of in a slighting or disrespectful way.

16. **D is correct.** *Obviously* is defined as easily perceived or understood. *Apparently*, its synonym, is defined as readily understood.

17. **C is correct.** *Incessant* describes something that continues without interruption—something that is *constant*.

18. **D is correct.** To *acquire* is to gain possession of. *Procure*, which means "to obtain," is its synonym.

19. **A is correct.** *Venerable* is an adjective, usually used to describe a person who commands respect by virtue of age, character, dignity, or position. A person who is described as venerable could similarly be described as *respected*.

20. **A is correct.** *Proclivity* is a noun meaning a natural *inclination*, predisposition, or propensity.

21. **A is correct.** *Consolidated*, meaning "to have united into one system or whole; to have combined," is the only choice that effectively conveys the meaning of the sentence.

22. **D is correct.** Since all of the first-blank choices seem to fit, you might do better by focusing on the second blank. Because choices A and C are so similar in meaning, you can discount both of them. *Gleaning* (choice B)

means "gathering or collecting bit by bit" and makes no sense in the context of the sentence. *Breaching* (choice D) means "breaking or violating, especially an agreement," and is clearly the best answer.

23. **A is correct.** The key to this question is the phrase "lacking any interesting qualities." Of the four choices, only *insipid* has enough of a negative connotation to set it apart from the other choices. In fact, the key phrase in the sentence is essentially the definition of *insipid*, which means "lacking qualities that excite, stimulate, or interest."

24. **D is correct.** "Despite" is one of the words you may see on the test that signals a contrast within a two-clause sentence. When you come across words or phrases such as "despite," "although" or "even though," keep in mind that the words you are looking for are likely to contrast with each other. Of the choices available, only *shaky . . . lucrative* (choice D) offers the sufficient contrast needed to properly convey the logic of the "despite" construction.

25. **B is correct.** Logically, you can assume that a company would not hope to suspend short-term sales expectations, thus, you can eliminate choice A. Choice D can be eliminated as well, as *attest* makes no sense in the context of the sentence. Of the remaining choices, both choice B and choice C offer appropriate first-blank options; however it is unlikely that the company had to "properly determine the staff." *Remunerate* (choice B) meaning "to pay a person a suitable equivalent in return for goods provided, services rendered, or losses incurred," is the correct answer.

26. **D is correct.** Knowing the definitions of the words you have to choose from will help you select the correct answer to this question. Neither *dispersed* (choice A) nor *maintained* (choice B) fits the context of the sentence, and both can be eliminated. *Deprecated* (choice C), meaning "to have expressed disapproval," is incorrect as well. *Teemed* (choice D), meaning "to have been full of things, abounded, or swarmed," is the only possible correct answer.

27. **C is correct.** *Reserved* (choice B) is easily eliminated as a first-blank choice, and you should notice that the second-blank options for choices A and D are too alike to be distinguishable from each other. That leaves choice C, *grandiose . . . curtail*; the only pair of words that properly conveys the meaning of the sentence.

28. **A is correct.** By now you should be able to recognize that words such as "although" and "despite" (along with the phrase "even though") signal that a two-clause sentence is likely to contain a contrast from one clause to the next. Notice that choices B, C, and D all contain pairs of words that lack the proper contrast to correctly convey the meaning of the "although" construction. Choice A, however, pairs *sobering* (meaning "marked by seriousness, gravity, or solemnity of conduct or character") with *farcical* (meaning "ludicrous or ridiculously funny").

29. **D is correct.** An *exemption* is a release from an obligation granted by or as if by an authority. Therefore, choice D is the correct answer and the only choice that fits the context of the sentence. An *emulsion* (choice B) is "a suspension of one liquid in a second liquid with which the first will not mix" (oil and water for instance), and a *quandary* (choice C) is "a state of uncertainty or perplexity; a predicament."

30. **B is correct.** Initially, you may believe that *endeavor* (choice A), which means "a purposeful or industrious activity," is the correct answer. However, keep in mind that the problem Angela faces is whether she should babysit or go to the movies on Friday night. Knowing she can only do one or the other, you can logically conclude that Angela needs to make a choice. *Predicament* (choice B), meaning a "situation that requires a choice between two options that are or seem equally unfavorable or mutually exclusive," is the correct answer.

31. **B is correct.** The easiest way to solve a two-blank question is by eliminating choices from one of the blanks based on the fact that one answer in the word pair is obviously wrong. Neither *overcome* (choice A) nor *accept* (choice C) seems appropriate for the first blank, and thus, they can be discounted. Focusing on the second blank, you can conclude that the band's offer for an extended engagement would likely not be *established* (choice D) by their failure to inspire the audience. That leaves *impress . . . revoked* (choice B) as the only remaining choice, and this is the correct answer.

32. **C is correct.** The key to this question is the phrase "after a series of argumentative negotiations." Logically, you can conclude that the two sides are ready to move past their differences "so they could get back to the task at hand." A *resolution* (choice C) is a "solution to a problem," and this is the correct answer. An *admonition* (choice A) is "a warning or cautionary advice," and an *abatement* (choice B) is "a reduction."

33. **A is correct.** The answer to this question is actually revealed by the phrase "the highest mountain in the world." *Monumental* (choice A), meaning "impressively large, sturdy, or enduring," is correct.

34. **D is correct.** The logic of this question indicates that the developer's plan for the land originally included space for a public park but no longer does. Therefore, he has first said one thing and then changed his mind to say another. *Contradiction* (choice D), meaning "an inconsistency or a discrepancy," is the correct answer choice.

35. **C is correct.** This sentence contains another example of the "despite" construction. Keep in mind that, when you encounter a sentence such as this one, the correct answer will likely be a pair of words with meanings that contrast with one another. *Chastised . . . exonerated* (choice C) offers the best choice of words with contrasting meanings, and this is the correct answer. *Chastised* means "punished or criticized severely," and *exonerated* means "freed from blame."

36. **D is correct.** It may seem an act of *peculiarity* (choice C) for the star midfielder to be benched, but a better answer is that it was an act of *retribution* (choice D), meaning "something given or demanded in repayment, especially punishment."

37. **B is correct.** Likely, you can conclude that if the owner had provided a *legitimate* (choice A) certificate of authenticity, the art historian would not have declared the painting a forgery. As well, *turgid* (choice C) means "swollen," or "excessively ornate or complex in style or language," and does not fit the context of the sentence. *Precocious* (choice D) means "characterized by unusually early development or maturity" and is also wrong. *Spurious* (choice B), meaning "not genuine" or "lacking authenticity or validity," is correct.

38. **B is correct.** If you are unsure of the correct word pair in a two-blank question, try focusing on one of the blanks first. Focusing on the first blank, it is unlikely that a person who died of food poisoning would be described as "strengthened" or "fortified" by a lifestyle that "indulged his every whim." *Befallen* (choice D) is a good first-blank match, however *durable* does not fit well in the second blank. *Undeterred . . . gluttonous* (meaning "indulging in something to excess") is correct.

39. **A is correct.** Chances are that a team would not consider a six-game losing streak to be the *pinnacle* (meaning "the highest point") of their season. As well, *conclusion* (choice D) can be eliminated as the team would likely know when their season was over. *Nadir* (choice A), meaning "the lowest point" or "the time of greatest depression or adversity" is the correct answer.

40. **C is correct.** Knowing the definitions of the answer choices will help you solve this question. A *beacon* (choice A) is "a signaling or guiding device, such a light"; *sustenance* (choice B) is "something, usually food, which sustains life or health"; a *dearth* (choice C) is "a scarce supply or a lack"; and a *confluence* is "a gathering, meeting, or flowing together at one juncture or point." *Dearth* (choice C) is correct.

Section 2 Quantitative Reasoning

1. **B is correct.** Each number in the sequence is 3 more than the preceding number. $17 + 3 = 20$.

2. **D is correct.** If Kurt saw s sparrows, 3 times as many finches, and 12 birds of both species in all, you can find out how many birds of each species he saw by using the number sentence $s + 3s = 12$.

3. **D is correct.** Gary scored 27 points in the two games, and he scored twice as many in game 2 as in game 1. Let p = number of points Gary scored in game 1. Write an equation:
$p + 2p = 27$
$3p = 27$
$p = 9$
So in game 1, Gary scored 9 points, and in game 2 he scored $2(9) = 18$ points.

4. **A is correct.** $5.75 \text{ lb} \times \$1.20/\text{lb} = \$6.90$.

5. **C is correct.** Maria earns $9 per hour on weekdays and $12 per hour on weekends. For 8 hours of work on Tuesday she earned $8 \times \$9 = \$72$. For 6 hours of work on Thursday she earned $6 \times \$9 = \$54$. For 7 hours of work on Friday she earned $7 \times \$9 = \$63$. For 9 hours of work on Saturday she earned $9 \times \$12 = \$108$. $\$72 + \$54 + \$63 + \$108 = \$297$.

6. **B is correct.** 1.268 is greater than 1.2 but less than 1.3.

7. **D is correct.** 27 batteries $= {}^{27}/_4 = 7$ packs with 1 battery left over. If you want 2 complete packs left over, you must buy 9 packs.

8. **A is correct.** 5 quarters $= \$1.25$; 6 dimes $= \$0.60$; $\$1.25 + \$0.60 = \$1.85$.

9. **A is correct.** Let $x =$ Karen's age. $\dfrac{(20 + 18 + x)}{3} = 18$.

$$\dfrac{(38 + x)}{3} = 18$$
$$(38 + x) = 54$$
$$x = 16$$

10. **A is correct.** In 4 months the dog loses $4 \times 0.33 = 1.32$ lb; $37.18 + 1.32 = 38.5$ lb.

11. **D is correct.** If 46% of 950 people said that they listened to jazz, 54% did not say they listened to jazz. 54% of $950 = 0.54 \times 950 = 513$.

12. **B is correct.** 25% of $\$650 = 0.25 \times 650 = \$162.50$, so the sale price of the television set is $\$650.00 - \$162.50 = \$487.50$. The tax is 12%, so Beth will pay $\$487.50 + (\$487.50 \times 0.12) = \$487.50 + \$58.50 = \$546$.

13. **C is correct.** 8 people are both on the chess team and in the band. That means that there are $17 - 8 = 9$ additional chess players and $13 - 8 = 5$ additional band members. $8 + 9 + 5 = 22$ people in the group.

14. **A is correct.** At 6:00 the hour and minute hands on a clock form a straight angle, which measures 180°.

15. **B is correct.** If the length and width were doubled, the new dimensions would be 40 yards by 30 yards. Perimeter $= 40 + 30 + 40 + 30 = 140$ yd.

16. **D is correct.** The poster measures 2 feet 4 inches by 3 feet 8 inches. Convert to inches: 2 feet 4 inches $= 28$ inches; 3 feet 8 inches $= 44$ inches. Perimeter $= 28 + 44 + 28 + 44 = 144$ inches $= 12$ feet

17. **B is correct.** The rectangle has an area of $4 \times 6 = 24$ in²; $24 \div 4 = 6$.

18. **A is correct.** $560 \div 28 = 20$.

19. **C is correct.** Let x be the cost for 6 hours. Set up a proportion:

$$\dfrac{60}{4} = \dfrac{x}{6}$$
$$(60 \times 6) = 4x$$
$$360 = 4x$$
$$x = \$90$$

20. **D is correct.** The edges of the cube each measure 4 in, so the area of each face of the cube is $4 \text{ in}^2 \times 4 \text{ in}^2 = 16$ in². There are six faces, so the total surface area is 6×16 in² $= 96$ in².

21. **A is correct.**
25% of $\$40 = \$10$; $\$40 - \$10 = \$30$;
20% of $\$30 = \$6$; $\$30 - \$6 = \$24$

22. **B is correct.**
$(4 \times 10^3) + (6 \times 10^2) + (2 \times 10^0) =$
$(4 \times 1{,}000) + (6 \times 100) + (2 \times 1) =$
$4{,}602$

23. **B is correct.**
    There are 3As and 1 E, so P (vowel) = $^4/_{15}$.
    There are 3 Cs and 2 Ls, so P (C or T) = $^5/_{15}$.

24. **D is correct.**
    The radius could be less than, equal to, or greater than the chord.

25. **C is correct.**
    Mean = (40 + 50 + 60 + 70) ÷ 4 =
    220 ÷ 4 = 55
    Median = mean of two middle numbers
    = (50 + 60) ÷ 2 = 110 ÷ 2 = 55

26. **A is correct.**
    $\sqrt{64} + \sqrt{36} = 8 + 6 = 14$

    $\sqrt{100} = 10$

27. **C is correct.**
    A rectangular prism has 8 vertices and 12 edges.
    8 + 2 = 10; 12 − 2 = 10

28. **A is correct.**
    Cities A, B, and C form a right triangle. Using the Pythagorean Theorem, the distance
    between City A and City $C = \sqrt{(30^2 + 40^2)} = \sqrt{(900 + 1,600)} = \sqrt{2,500} = 50$.

29. **D is correct.**
    If $g > 0$, then g is greater.
    If $g < 0$, then $-g$ is greater.
    If $g = 0$, then g and $-g$ are equal.

30. **C is correct.**
    Let w = Frank's weight
    Jason's weight = $^5/_4 w$
    Bill's weight = $^4/_5(^5/_4)w = w$

31. **B is correct.**
    Since $ABDC$ is a trapezoid, $\overline{AB} \parallel \overline{CD}$.
    Since $\angle A$ is a right angle, $\angle C$ is a right
    angle. So, $m\angle x = 90°$.

    The sum of the angles in a quadrilateral is equal to 360°.
    $90° + 90° + 75° + m\angle y = 360°$
    $255° + m\angle y = 360°$
    $m\angle y = 105°$

32. **A is correct.**
    $1^3/_4\% = 1.75 \% = 0.0175$

33. **D is correct.**
    x and y can take on values to make either one greater, or to make them equal.

34. **C is correct.**
    At 10 P.M. ship is a sea level, 0 depth.
    At 12 A.M. ship is 500 ft below sea level, −500 depth.
    Depth change: 0 − (−500) = 500.

    At 1A.M. ship is 200 ft below sea level, −200 depth.
    At 2:30 A.M. ship is 700 feet below sea level, −700 depth.
    Depth change: −200 − (−700) = 500

35. B is correct.

$$\frac{m}{6} = \frac{32}{48}$$

$$48m = 6(32)$$

$$48m = 192$$

$$m = 4$$

$$8m = 32$$

$$\frac{100}{50} = \frac{70}{n}$$

$$100n = 70(50)$$

$$100n = 3,500$$

$$n = 35$$

$$n - 1 = 34$$

Section 3 Reading Comprehension

1. **B is correct**. The quotation shows that the President has a duty to report to Congress on the State of the Union and to recommend necessary and expedient measures. This annual message to Congress came to be known as the State of the Union. Choice A is wrong because although the quotation does illustrate the actual wording of this section of the Constitution, it is not intended to illustrate the wording of the entire Constitution. Choice C is wrong because there is no demonstration of different interpretations of this provision. The differences cited are in the form, content, and delivery method of the message, not in the need to report to Congress. Choice D is wrong because the passage does not distinguish between constitutional duty and custom. The report on the State of the Union is mandated by the Constitution.

2. **C is correct.** The Constitution required the president to give Congress information on the state of the union "from time to time." Throughout the passage, the State of the Union message is referred to as the president's "annual message." Clearly, the phrase "time to time" has come to mean "annually."

3. **B is correct**. This information is found in the opening quote from the U.S. Constitution, which says that presidents have a constitutional duty to "give to Congress information of the State of the Union."

4. **C is correct.** Thomas Jefferson thought Washington's oral presentation was "too monarchial for the new republic." So Jefferson "wrote out his address and sent it to Congress to be read by a clerk."

5. **A is correct.** As stated in the last paragraph, "With the advent of radio and television, the President's annual message has become not only a conversation between the President and Congress but also an opportunity for the President to communicate with the American people at the same time." Choices B and C are wrong because Thomas Jefferson was president in the nineteenth century and Lyndon Johnson in the second half of the twentieth century. Choice D is wrong because newspaper coverage of the State of the Union message began long before the start of the twentieth century.

6. **D is correct**. As stated in the last paragraph, "Harry S. Truman's 1947 address was the first to be broadcast on television." None of the other questions is answered by information in the passage.

7. **D is correct**. Although the passage touches upon the tsunami of 2004 (Choice A), the difference between a tsunami and a tidal wave (choice B), and the origin of the word "tsunami" (choice C), each of these choices is too narrow to cover the overall purpose of the passage, which is to provide information about tsunamis in general.

8. **A is correct**. As stated in the second paragraph, "Most tsunamis are generated by earthquakes, but they may also be caused by volcanic eruptions, landslides, undersea slumps or meteor impacts." Tornadoes are mentioned along with hurricanes, not as a cause of tsunamis, but rather as another kind of natural disaster

9. **B is correct**. The author mentions the 1960 tsunami in Japan in the third paragraph: "The waves radiate outward in all directions from the disturbance and can propagate across entire ocean basins. For example, in 1960, an earthquake in Chile caused a tsunami that swept across the Pacific to Japan." The words "for example" indicate that the reference to Japan is intended to show how far the waves radiated from the earthquake in Chile.

10. **B is correct**. The answer to this question is found in paragraph 3 which says, "Tsunami waves are distinguished from ordinary ocean waves by their great length between peaks, often exceeding 100 miles in the deep ocean, and by the long amount of time between these peaks, ranging from five minutes to an hour." Choice A is wrong because the passage does not mention that regular waves follow closely one after the other. Choice C is wrong because it has no support in the passage. Choice D is wrong because the passage states that in deep water "a tsunami is barely noticeable, causing only a small rising and falling of the sea surface as it passes."

11. **C is correct.** This passage is full of the kind of strictly factual scientific information most likely to be found in a science textbook. Choice A cannot be correct because the passage is clearly fact, not fiction. Choice D is wrong because the passage merely mentions the tsunami of 2004, but does not go on to provide the details of that particular event as a news article would.

12. **A is correct.** The answer to this question can be found in paragraph 4: "As the tsunami approaches land and shallow water, the waves slow down and become compressed, causing them to grow in height." In the best of cases the tsunami comes ashore like a rising tide causing flooding of coastal areas. In the worst of cases, a wall of turbulent water several meters high rushes ashore with great destructive power.

13. **D is correct.** All of the choices are meanings of the word "bore." However, only choice (D) is correct in context. As stated in the second sentence of paragraph 5, "A bore is a wall of turbulent water that can be several meters high and can rush onshore with great destructive power."

14. **C is correct.** Line 1 mentions that the athlete "won your town the race." "Runners" are also mentioned in lines 7 and 23, and line 26 mentions "the fleet of foot." All of these references make it obvious that the athlete in this poem is a runner.

15. **B is correct.** The setting is revealed in lines 7–10: "Today, the road all runners come, Shoulder-high we bring you home, And set you at your threshold down, Townsman of a stiller town." These words describe a funeral procession for a young champion being carried to his grave. Lines 1–6 describe a victory celebration that happened at some earlier point in time. The word "today" in line 7 indicates that the poem takes place at the funeral for a young athlete.

16. **C is correct.** The second stanza describes a funeral. The athlete is carried to his gravesite and in death becomes a "townsman of a stiller town."

17. **D is correct.** The author calls the athlete a "smart lad" to die before his glory fades (line 11). Lines 21 to 24 praise the athlete for not becoming one of those "lads that wore their honors out," meaning an athlete who continues to compete even though he can no longer keep up.

18. **D is correct.** Lines 14–15 ("And early though the laurel grows/It withers quicker than the rose") express the poet's belief that although the athlete's glory came early, it will not last. In other words, glory withers and dies as quickly as a rose, and statement I is correct. Statement II is confirmed by lines 11–13 ("Smart lad, to slip betimes away/From fields where glory does not stay") as well as lines 21–24 ("Now you will not swell the rout/Of lads that wore their honors out/Runners whom renown outran/And the name died before the man."). Nothing in the poem supports statement III.

19. **A is correct.** The constant repetition of "gone" and "wiped out" in lines 11–21 serves to emphasize the author's inability to believe that such devastation could possibly occur. "San Francisco is *gone*. . . . Its industrial section is *wiped out*. Its business section is *wiped out*. Its social and residential section is *wiped out*. The factories and warehouses, the great stores and newspaper buildings, the hotels and the palaces of the nabobs, are all *gone*." Choices B, C, and D are wrong because there are no words in the paragraph that support a mood of desperate longing, cautious optimism, or heartfelt pity.

20. **C is correct.** Here are just a few examples of the vivid images provided by the author: ". . . the smoke of San Francisco's burning was a lurid tower visible a hundred miles away . . . " "The streets were humped into ridges and depressions, and piled with the debris of fallen walls." "The steel rails were twisted into perpendicular and horizontal angles."

21. **B is correct.** A *nabob* is "a rich and important person." Choice D is wrong because although the passage mentions "the palaces of nabobs," a nabob does not have to be of royal blood. Choices A and C have nothing to do with the word "nabob."

22. **A is correct.** The passage tells mainly of the massive destruction the San Francisco earthquake caused; roads and rail systems were destroyed, telephone and telegraph systems were "disrupted," and the "water-mains had burst." Thus, the statement conveys the idea that all modern conveniences had been lost, and the city had been reduced to living without twentieth-century amenities.

23. **B is correct**. The passage is arranged in chronological order. This is evident in the first few words of paragraphs 3, 4, and 5. Paragraph 3 starts with the words "On Wednesday morning," paragraph 4 starts with "By Wednesday afternoon," and paragraph 5 starts with "Wednesday night."

24. **C is correct**. As evidenced by lines 57–59 ("At that time I watched the vast conflagration from out on the bay."), the author was an eyewitness to the earthquake. His primary purpose for writing this passage was to report what he saw during that terrible time. Choice A is wrong because the passage provides no scientific explanation telling how earthquakes occur. Choice B is wrong because the passage describes the events of the earthquake, but does not go into the feelings of the residents. Choice D is wrong because only one paragraph of the account is devoted to the winds that helped the fire spread.

25. **D is correct**. As stated in the second paragraph, "In those days, a million people died from smallpox each year in Europe alone . . . " Choice A is wrong because the passage states that a million people died from smallpox. Since some people did survive smallpox, it can be assumed that the disease struck many more than a million people each year. Choices B and C are wrong because milkmaids contracted cowpox, not smallpox, from the cows.

26. **B is correct**. Choices A and D are both mentioned in paragraph 3: "Since Jenner's time, vaccines have been developed against more than 20 infectious diseases such as influenza, pneumonia, whooping cough, rubella, rabies, meningitis, and hepatitis B." Choice C is mentioned in paragraph 2, "By the beginning of the 20th century, vaccines for rabies, diphtheria, typhoid fever, and plague were in use, in addition to the vaccine for smallpox." The only answer choice not mentioned is choice B, scarlet fever.

27. **D is correct**. As stated in the last paragraph, "Weakened microbes, killed microbes, inactivated toxins, and purified proteins or polysaccharides derived from microbes are the most common components used in vaccine development strategies."

28. **C is correct**. The answer to this question is found in the second paragraph, which states that "Jenner laid the foundation for modern vaccines" and "started on a course that would ease the suffering of people around the world for centuries to come." Choice A is wrong because it was not until 1980 that "an updated version of Jenner's vaccine led to the total eradication of smallpox." Choice B is wrong because Jenner used cowpox-producing organisms to make the vaccine that protected people from the more deadly smallpox. Choice D is wrong because although Jenner's work was the basis for the development of a vaccine for typhoid fever, the vaccine Jenner produced in 1796 was for smallpox only.

29. **B is correct**. According to the last paragraph, "Scientists use vaccines to 'trick' the human immune system into producing antibodies or immune cells that protect against the real disease-causing organism." Choice A is wrong because the vaccine does not directly attack the disease-causing organism, instead it causes the body to produce antibodies against the disease-causing organism. Choice C is wrong because vaccines contain "weakened microbes, killed microbes, inactivated toxins, and purified proteins or polysaccharides derived from microbes," not deadly disease-producing organisms. Choice D is wrong because the vaccine does not contain antibodies, rather it triggers the body to produce antibodies.

30. **C is correct**. The first sentence describes the birthmark as a "crimson hand, which at first had been strongly visible upon the marble paleness of Georgiana's cheek." The birthmark fades like "the stain of the rainbow fading out of the sky," but it is not shaped like a rainbow, so choice A is incorrect. The birthmark fades to "the faintest rose color," but is not described as having the shape of a rose, so choice B is incorrect. There is nothing in the passage to suggest that the birthmark is shaped like a butterfly, so choice D is incorrect.

31. **D is correct**. The first paragraph tells that the birthmark is fading. In the second paragraph Aylmer says, "Success! Success!" indicating that he is responsible for making the birthmark fade. Thus the most reasonable assumption is that Alymer had performed some kind of operation on his wife to remove her birthmark. The presence of a servant indicates that Aylmer is not a poor man, making choice A incorrect. Choices B and C can be eliminated because all the evidence indicates that Aylmer is striving to help his wife by removing the birthmark that "had once blazed with such disastrous brilliancy as to scare away all their happiness."

32. **B is correct.** Georgiana gazes into the mirror and sees "how barely perceptible was now that crimson hand which had once blazed with such disastrous brilliancy as to scare away all their happiness." A mark that is barely perceptible is very faint.

33. **A is correct.** When Georgiana awakens, Alymer calls her his "peerless bride" and proclaims, "You are perfect!" The best synonym for "perfect" is "flawless."

34. **D is correct.** Even though Georgiana knows she is dying as a result of Aylmer's attempt to remove her birthmark, she speaks to Alymer "with more than human tenderness," calling him "My poor Aylmer" and "dearest Aylmer." Her words do not indicate that she is bitter (choice A) or angry (choice B). She may be happy to see that the birthmark is gone, but that does not describe her feelings toward Aylmer, so choice C is wrong.

35. **C is correct.** Aylmer's attempt to make his wife perfect resulted in destroying her, thus illustrating the fact that perfection cannot be achieved on earth. Choice A is wrong because if love were blind Aylmer would not have attempted to remove the birthmark. Choice B is wrong because the passage proves the opposite to be true. Choice D is wrong because the effect of the birthmark was "to scare away all their happiness."

36. **C is correct.** Most of the passage is devoted to a description of the "enthralling pleasures" of life in the country. Choices A and B are wrong because neither one is covered in the passage. Choice D is wrong because it is covered by only one small part of the passage and is not the focus of the passage as a whole.

37. **B is correct.** The tone of the passage is one of carefree joy and happiness. Making fun of his sister for not knowing that General Grant was a real person is just one example of the light-heartedness of the entire passage.

38. **C is correct.** Although the author states that "summers we spent in the country" and we children "loved the country beyond anything," he never specifically mentions where the family stays while in the country. The only reference to where they stayed is the very vague "now at one place, now at another." Choice A is answered in lines 5–9: "We were always wildly eager to get to the country when spring came, and very sad when in the late fall the family moved back to town." Choice B is answered in lines 23–33 where the author states that they spent their time in the country "supervising haying and harvesting, picking apples, hunting frogs successfully and woodchucks unsuccessfully . . ." Choice D is answered in lines 33–35 where the author states that "Thanksgiving was an appreciated festival, but it in no way came up to Christmas."

39. **D is correct.** The statement primarily suggests that the author recreated the Christmases of his youth primarily because he wanted his own children to feel the same joy that he had experienced as a child. Choice A is wrong because there is no mention made that the author was setting an example that he wanted his children to follow. Choice B is wrong because the author never states that he misses the Christmases of his youth. Rather, he is reminiscing about some of his favorite childhood memories. Choice C is wrong because the passage does not imply that the author is trying to reproduce his entire childhood, but merely the Christmases of his past.

40. **A is correct.** The passage is narrated by an adult looking back with obvious fondness on his own happy childhood. The author tells of wonderful summers spent in the country. He also mentions something that happens "thirty years later" when he has children of his own. These clues are enough to determine that the passage was written by an adult and that it concerns his own life. Choices B and C are wrong because the passage is written from the point of view of an adult, not a child. Choice D is wrong because the author recalls his childhood with fondness, not regret.

Section 4 Mathematics Achievement

1. **A is correct.** If $x = 0$, the denominator of the fraction = $4(0) = 0$. If the denominator is 0, the whole expression = 0.

2. **D is correct.**
$$\frac{4}{a} = \frac{b}{6}$$
$$(6)(4/a) = (6)(b/6)$$
$$\frac{24}{a} = b$$
$$24 = ab$$

3. **B is correct.**
   $$39.9 + 57.3 = (39.9 + 0.1) + (57.3 - x)$$
   $$39.9 + 57.3 = (40) + (57.3 - x)$$
   $$97.2 = 40 + (57.3 - x)$$
   $$57.2 = 57.3 - x$$
   $$x = 0.1$$

4. **B is correct.** $3,000 \times 0.002 = 6$.

5. **A is correct.** In an equilateral triangle, all three angles are equal. Since the sum of the angles in a triangle is 180°, each angle must be $180 \div 3 = 60°$.

6. **D is correct.**
   $$y \div 72 = 21.4$$
   $$y = 21.4 \times 72$$
   $$y = 1,540.8$$

7. **A is correct.** It costs n dollars to buy 10 boxes. Since $25 = 2.5 \times 10$, it will cost $2.5n$ dollars to buy 25 boxes.

8. **D is correct.** A straight angle measures 180°. So if 1 is 33°, the other angle must measure $180° - 33° = 147°$.

9. **D is correct.** Let $x =$ cost of small cone. $2x =$ cost of large cone.
   3 small cones + 3 large cones = $13.50
   $$3x + 3(2x) = \$13.50$$
   $$3x + 6x = \$13.50$$
   $$9x = \$13.50$$
   $$x = \$1.50$$

10. **B is correct.** Count the zeros in the divisor and move the decimal point to the left that many places.
    $$7.426 \div 1,000 = 0.007426$$

11. **D is correct.** Calculate the number of square meters in the garden and then determine how many ounces of fertilizer are needed. The area of a rectangle is calculated by multiplying the length × the width. So the area of the garden is $4 \times 7 = 28$ m². Paul needs 2 oz of fertilizer for every square meter, so $2 \times 28 = 56$ oz.

12. **B is correct.** According to the chart, the plant is growing 3 inches taller each week. So in week 6, it should be $14 + 3 = 17$ inches tall.

13. **C is correct.** The thousandths place is three places to the right of the decimal point.

14. **C is correct.** In this problem you know two of the three angles, one measuring 55° and the other measuring 90° since the building forms a 90° angle with the ground. Together those two angles measure 145°. Since a triangle has a total of 180°, the third angle must measure $180° - 145° = 35°$.

15. **B is correct.** This item is set up as a proportion. To solve for n, cross-multiply so that the problem becomes $25n = 1000$. $n = 1000 \div 25 = 40$.

16. **D is correct.** Find the volume by multiplying length × width × height. Since all of these dimensions on a cube are the same, multiply:
    $$5 \times 5 \times 5 = 125 \text{ in}^3$$

17. **B is correct.** Simple interest problems use the formula $I = prt$ where I is the amount of interest, p is the principle or the amount saved or invested, r is the rate of interest, and t is the amount of time that the interest is accruing. In this problem, you are asked to find the interest, given that the principle is $4,000, the rate of interest is 2%, and the amount of time is 2 years. Substituting this information into the formula, you get
    $$I = 4,000(0.02)(2) = \$160 \text{ in interest.}$$

18. **D is correct.** A right angle measures 90°. If angle 1 measures 65°, then angle 2 must measure 90° − 65° = 25°.

19. **D is correct.** A number is evenly divisible by 4 if the number formed by the last two digits is divisible by 4.

20. **C is correct.** When two straight lines intersect as shown, they form opposite vertical angles. Those angles have the same measure, so if angle 2 measures 45°, then angle 4 must also measure 45°.

21. **A is correct.** 61 is divisible only by itself and 1. 81 ÷ 9 = 9; 171 ÷ 9 = 19; 207 ÷ 9 = 23.

22. **D is correct.** In a parallelogram, opposite sides are parallel and opposite angles are equal. However, adjacent sides are not necessarily the same length.

23. **B is correct.** The area of the room is 15 × 18 = 270 ft². One square yard = 9 square feet, so 270 ft² ÷ 9 = 30 yd².

24. **C is correct.** According to the graph, the two most popular categories were mysteries and nonfiction. The number of books in those categories checked out last month was 520 + 450 = 970.

25. **B is correct.** The angles in a triangle total 180°. The two given angles measure 55° + 65° = 120°. Thus the remaining angle must measure 180° − 120° = 60°.

26. **D is correct.** A common factor of two numbers is a whole number that is a factor of both numbers. The common factors of 24 and 36 are 1, 2, 3, 4, 6, and 12.

27. **B is correct.** Only $^{99}/_{100}$ is in simplest form. $^{15}/_{18} = ^{5}/_{6}$; $^{56}/_{133} = ^{8}/_{19}$; $^{45}/_{72} = ^{5}/_{8}$.

28. **C is correct.** In this problem ∠6 measures 90°. Thus 3 also measures 90° Because the two sides of the triangle are equal, it is an isosceles triangle. That makes 1 and ∠2 equal. Since ∠3 = 90°, that leaves 90° to be split equally between 1 and ∠2. So each angle measures 45°.

29. **A is correct.** The number of students polled was 34 + 22 + 65 + 27 + 24 + 78 = 250. The number who preferred ice skating or sleepover was 22 + 78 = 100. 100 ÷ 250 = 40%.

30. **A is correct.** Of the 6 numbers on the cube, 3 are even. So the probability that the number facing up will be even is $^{3}/_{6}$ or $^{1}/_{2}$.

31. **A is correct.** To find the area of a triangle, use the formula $A = (^{1}/_{2})bh$ where b is the base of the triangle and h is the height. Because the triangle shown is a right triangle, side a is the height. Substituting into the formula: $A = (^{1}/_{2})(6)(4) = 12$ ft².

32. **C is correct.** If Frank is 4 years younger than Donna, than the relationship between their two ages can be expressed by the equation $f = d − 4$.

33. **A is correct.** If the club sells n tickets at $3.00 each, the amount they will earn is $3n$. Their profit after paying $224 in expenses is $3n − 224$.

34. **A is correct.** A wire stretched between two points on a circle and passing through the center will form a diameter of the circle. Diameter = radius × 2. If the radius is 1.35 m, the diameter = 2(1.35) = 2.7 m = 270 cm. If wire costs 2¢/cm, the cost of the wire stretching across the circle will be 270 × 2¢ = 540¢ = $5.40.

35. **B is correct.** Convert to equivalent fractions using the lowest common denominator: $^{2}/_{9} = ^{16}/_{72}$, $^{2}/_{8} = ^{18}/_{72}$, $^{2}/_{3} = ^{48}/_{72}$.

36. **C is correct.** $2.004 = 2^{4}/_{1,000} = 2^{1}/_{250}$.

37. **A is correct.** $2.4 = 2^{4}/_{10} = 2^{8}/_{20}$; $^{10}/_{4} = ^{50}/_{20} = 2^{10}/_{20}$; $2^{4}/_{5} = 2^{16}/_{20}$.

38. **A is correct.** If Adrinda is 8 years older than Marsha and Daryl is 3 years older than Marsha , then Daryl must be 5 years younger than Adrinda. So $d = a - 5$.

39. **B is correct.**
$5\frac{5}{8} = \frac{45}{8} = \frac{225}{40}$
$2\frac{2}{5} = \frac{12}{5} = \frac{96}{40}$
$\frac{225}{40} \times \frac{96}{40} = \frac{21,600}{1600} = \frac{216}{16} = 13\frac{8}{16} = 13\frac{1}{2}$

40. **D is correct.** Follow the order of operations:
$5 \times 6 \div (2 + 1)$
$= 5 \times 6 \div 3$
$= 30 \div 3 = 10$

41. **C is correct.** The rule of the sequence is that each number is 5 more than the one before. So the missing numbers are $17 + 5 = 22$ and $22 + 5 = 27$.

42. **A is correct.**
$\frac{1}{2} = 3x + \frac{1}{3}$
$3x = \frac{1}{2} - \frac{1}{3}$
$3x = \frac{3}{6} - \frac{2}{6} = \frac{1}{6}$
$x = \frac{1}{6} \div 3 = \frac{1}{18}$

43. **D is correct.**
$24 \div -4\frac{2}{3}$
$= 24 \div \frac{-14}{3}$
$= 24 \times \frac{-3}{14}$
$= \frac{-72}{14} = -5\frac{2}{14} = -5\frac{1}{7}$

44. **C is correct.** There are four numbers less than 5: 1, 2, 3, and 4. The probability that the spinner will land on one of these four numbers is 4 in 12 or $\frac{4}{12} = \frac{1}{3}$.

45. **A is correct.** If 1 in = 40 km, 6 in = 240 km, and $\frac{7}{8}$ in = $\frac{7}{8} \times 40 = 35$ km; $240 + 35 = 275$ km.